The Forgotten Presidents

The Forgotten Presidents: Their Untold Constitutional Legacy

MICHAEL J. GERHARDT

OXFORD
UNIVERSITY PRESS

OXFORD
UNIVERSITY PRESS

Oxford University Press is a department of the University of Oxford.
It furthers the University's objective of excellence in research,
scholarship, and education by publishing worldwide.

Oxford   New York
Auckland   Cape Town   Dar es Salaam   Hong Kong   Karachi
Kuala Lumpur   Madrid   Melbourne   Mexico City   Nairobi
New Delhi   Shanghai   Taipei   Toronto

With offices in
Argentina   Austria   Brazil   Chile   Czech Republic   France   Greece
Guatemala   Hungary   Italy   Japan   Poland   Portugal   Singapore
South Korea   Switzerland   Thailand   Turkey   Ukraine   Vietnam

Oxford is a registered trademark of Oxford University Press
in the UK and certain other countries.

Published in the United States of America by
Oxford University Press
198 Madison Avenue, New York, NY 10016

Library of Congress Cataloging-in-Publication Data
Gerhardt, Michael J., 1956–
The forgotten presidents: their untold constitutional legacy / Michael J. Gerhardt.
p.   cm.
Includes bibliographical references and index.
ISBN 978-0-19-996779-7
1. Presidents—Legal status, laws, etc.—United States—History. 2. Executive power—United
States—History. 3. Constitutional law—United States—History. 4. United States—Politics
and government. I. Title.
KF5051.G47   2013
342.73—dc23   2012032612

9 8 7 6 5 4 3

Printed in the United States of America
on acid-free paper

Contents

Acknowledgments

I HAVE NEVER had more fun writing a book than I did writing this one. The idea for this book came in part from the work I had done on my last book, which was on precedent in constitutional law. I figured presidents should be the topic of my next book, since "president" sounds almost like "precedent." More seriously, a great deal of the focus of my last book, *The Power of Precedent*, was on nonjudicial precedent, and a great deal of the work I have been doing for years on nonjudicial precedent involved presidents. Indeed, the more work I did on presidents the more I realized I was discovering a lot of material on presidents that many scholars did not talk about or seem to know. Robby George and Brad Wilson at Princeton gave me the opportunities to refine my thinking about forgotten presidents by inviting me twice to deliver the Alpheus T. Mason Lecture in Constitutional Law at Princeton University. On each occasion, the fellows in the Madison Program in American Ideals and Institutions, particularly Patrick Deneen of Georgetown and Matthew Franck of Radford, as well as my friend Keith Whittington, pressed me to clarify my thinking about forgotten presidents in American constitutional law. I was especially gratified to have the opportunity to sit down after one of my Mason Lectures with one of the nation's finest presidential scholars, Fred Greenstein, whose validation of my thesis and thoughts about the project helped me a great deal. I am grateful as well for the similar opportunity given to me by Ken Kersch at Boston College to speak over the course of two days with faculty and students about the book. The other institution without whose support I could not have finished the book is where I teach, the University of North Carolina at Chapel Hill Law School. For four years, the constant expressions of support and curiosity from my dean Jack Boger and his wife, Jennifer, helped to convince me this was a project worth doing. I cannot thank my colleagues at UNC–Chapel Hill enough, including the Department of Politics, my friends in the law school, and my fellow fellows at the Institute for the Arts and Humanities, for the wonderful, constructive feedback I received at three workshops and numerous conversations about the book. I test-drove various chapters of the book and received helpful comments at workshops at the law schools at Cleveland State, Cornell, Duke, Fordham, Indiana University–Bloomington, Ohio State, Seton Hall, and the University of California–Irvine. At all of these places, I received encouragement and encountered some skepticism. It was enjoyable to expand my knowledge about constitutional history and sometimes to uncover information that many of my fellow law professors did not know or had forgotten. I was particularly gratified when skeptics became enthusiastic about the project, which happened, thankfully, much more often than not.

Several readers and colleagues went well out of their way to help. One of the greatest joys of being in this profession is interacting with great scholars who are willing to share their time and expertise. A number of them did so with me, and I am grateful. I owe special thanks to Josh Chafetz for his thoughtful feedback on more than one draft of the book. I always learn so much from my friend Akhil Amar, who, among the many ways he helped me, waited literally for hours for the skies to clear so my son and I could catch a flight out of New Haven. I appreciate Stuart Benjamin's repeated expressions of enthusiasm for this project. Mike Dorf helped put me and the book through our paces with his and Josh Chafetz's class at Cornell Law School; and my neighbor Kevin McGuire, his mentor Greg Caldeira at Ohio State, and my friends Marty Flaherty and Mac McCorkle enriched my understanding of the presidency. Thanks as well to my assistant Ashley Arthur and to Doug DeBaugh for printing, organizing, formatting, and preserving the book. Thanks also for the patience and support of my brother Jim and my two moms, Shivia Gerhardt and Sally Schwartz.

One of the other great joys of teaching has been my terrific students, including those who were willing to do research for this book—Alica Kerr, James Tristan Routh, John Noor, Ashley Holmes, Miriam Mirtenbaum, Evan Bolick, Alex May, Norah Warren, Mark Vaughn, Tina Eagle, Trevor Pressler, Andrew Salek-Raham, Joana Spruill, Cara Richards, Emily Evans, Joey Polonsky, and Ed Roche. Another student, Greg Day, deserves special commendation. Greg, who received his Ph.D. in political science from the University of Mississippi shortly after beginning law school in Chapel Hill, provided invaluable assistance in conceiving and constructing the appendix.

My editor, David McBride, deserves special thanks for support above and beyond the call of duty. There would be no book without David's quiet confidence. Thank you.

I reserve my most heartfelt gratitude to my family—my wife, Deborah, and our wonderful, delightful children, Ben, Daniel, and Noah—for their unwavering support, devotion, and love. Throughout the writing of this book, Deborah was my sounding board, my editor, and more. For this book, as well as for everything else I have done, she has been my inspiration. Her incomparable judgment and her unbounded confidence in me mean the world to me. My family's enthusiasm for the book, day in and day out, kept me going. Who knew that forgotten presidents could be so much fun? When I think of this book, I think of all the loving, shining, smiling faces of my family, sitting around the dinner table, as we discussed, one day to the next, the progress of this book from its beginning until this moment. So, it is to you, my beautiful family, that I dedicate this book, forever and always.

Introduction

FACED WITH ONE of the worst economic downturns in American history, the nation turned to the new president for leadership. As a senator, he had left little mark and seemed to have studiously avoided controversy, but hopes were high. The president's fellow Democrats quickly rallied to his side, while opposition leaders vowed to do everything they could to ensure that he was a one-term president. To the surprise of many, he promised bold, radical reform. His plan divided Americans and encountered stiff resistance in Congress. But, by a largely party-line vote, Congress eventually approved it. Furor over the plan intensified, as its fate became a major issue in the midterm elections. The president's critics denounced him as elitist and arrogant and his plan as extreme, unprecedented, dangerous, despotic, un-American, and plainly unconstitutional. While one might have expected the conservative Supreme Court to strike the plan down, it did not. Throughout his bid for reelection, his opponents railed against the radicalness of his plan, which they vowed to repeal.

Someone reading this description might think that the new president was Barack Obama, though it best fits Martin Van Buren. As the second Democrat elected president, Van Buren entered office in the midst of the nation's first great depression. His bold plan required reorganizing federal depositories and opposing the production of paper money. He based the plan on his conviction that the federal government had very limited authority to address a national economic crisis and had the power to coin money only in the form of gold or silver. But his plan did little to ease the nation's economic woes, and Van Buren became the first president to lose reelection because of the economy. Subsequently, every president, including the next four Democratic presidents who entered office in the midst of economic crises—Grover Cleveland, Franklin Roosevelt, Bill Clinton, and Barack Obama—understood that, as an adviser to Clinton famously said, "It's the economy, stupid." Each avoided Van Buren's example and read the Constitution as investing the national government with sufficient flexibility to address economic—and other national—crises.

In the more than a century after Van Buren's death, Americans have often forgotten that the Supreme Court is not the only institution that routinely grapples with constitutional questions and that the crises the nation confronts are rarely unprecedented. Harry Truman's observation that "the only surprises are the history we do not know" applies to a wide swath of constitutional activity, including the constitutional impact of Van Buren and many other presidents whom we have largely forgotten.

This book tells the stories of Van Buren and these other presidents. Their stories enrich our understanding of the relationship between the presidency and the Constitution. Most importantly, they show that the Constitution really matters. While many social scientists do not believe that the Constitution constrains courts or elected officials, forgotten presidents' stories illustrate how, by constitutional design, the office of the presidency draws its occupants into performing the role of president and asserting presidential prerogatives, often at the expense of the political support needed to maintain power. For instance, all four Whig presidents, who had pledged as candidates to weaken the presidency and secure congressional supremacy over domestic policymaking, actually fortified presidential prerogatives and buried their party's governance principles—and ultimately their party.

The stories of forgotten presidents illustrate how presidential power expands over time because the presidency's unique capacity for flexibility, determination, efficiency, and energy works to its advantages in protracted contests with other branches and the states. Forgotten presidents' tales dispel the popular myth that nineteenth-century presidents except for Jackson and Lincoln were weak or ineffective. The opposite is true: In the nineteenth century, forgotten presidents' strong assertions of their prerogatives provoked bold, often overwhelming political opposition. Forgotten nineteenth-century presidents lost power partly because their strong constitutional commitments alienated critical constituencies they needed to maintain power, often cost them reelection, placed them frequently on the losing side of history, and branded them as failures unworthy of study in constitutional law.

The stories of forgotten presidencies expand upon the insights of a group of social scientists known as historical institutionalists, including Stephen Skowronek, who analyzed how presidents have shaped and been shaped by the presidency.[1] In "assess[ing] presidents as agents of change," Skowronek examined "the different premises which presidents bring to the challenge of orchestrating political change, [the] capacity of the American presidency to deliver on these different premises, and [the] systemic political effects of presidential efforts to do so."[2] Skowronek developed a typology for understanding presidential leadership in light of "political time" or "the historical range of political possibilities for presidential leadership."[3] My focus is on the constitutional impact of certain presidents, who can best be understood in light of how they adapted (or did not adapt well enough) to the Constitution's demands, their office, and the peculiar legal, historical, cultural, and economic challenges of their times.

Forgotten presidents' stories dispel another popular misconception that constitutional change primarily results from the actions of the Supreme Court or a few great leaders. Constitutional scholar Bruce Ackerman constructed one such theory positing that constitutional law developed at special times called "constitutional moments," during which the leaders of the federal government's three branches interacted with each other and the American people to alter constitutional law in enduring ways.[4] Ackerman identified three such moments—the founding, Reconstruction, and the New Deal. He told the story of American constitutional law from the vantage point of its vistas, but the forgotten presidents' stories show that what is happening on the ground is essential for connecting the terrain and ensuring constitutional understandings and practices gain traction. They endure because of the commitments of national leaders working in conjunction with the American people over time, including forgotten presidents. Constitutional construction develops incrementally through collective, coordinated action, including national leaders interacting with each other and the public, to reinforce, revise, or extend constitutional judgments. Constitutional law develops through a series of commitments over time—not in a day.

This development is similar to common law made by courts. Like common law, the powers of the presidency have developed incrementally, one decision at a time, and depend on precedent made by presidents, not courts. Yet not everything presidents do counts as precedent. To be precedents, constitutional judgments must be discoverable, that is, they are past actions or judgments that subsequent authorities have invested with special normative force or power. The development of presidential power differs, however, from judge-made common law in that presidents do not issue judgments as courts do in the form of elaborate, self-identified opinions. Presidential judgments take many forms (often difficult to find); and because presidents are elected and subject to political reprisals, they are not bound by the evidentiary and procedural rules required by courts. Their judgments may be expressed informally and sometimes with little thought or input from others.

Obviously, this book relies on the premise that some presidents are forgotten. It focuses primarily not on why some presidents are forgotten but rather why forgotten presidents are worth studying in constitutional law. There are many ways to measure which presidents are "forgotten," such as the numbers of schools or streets named in their honor, their papers' economic value, the sales of presidential biographies and memoirs, or how often their names appear in constitutional law textbooks. After finding many of these measures are unworkable because their relevance is dubious or cannot be precisely determined, I developed a quantitative analysis to inform my determination of the forgotten presidents in constitutional law. This analysis measured (1) how often presidents are mentioned in the most popular American history textbooks used in middle and high schools; (2) how long ago presidents served; (3) biographies and other books about particular presidencies in the nation's largest university libraries; (4) presidential personalities based on their creativity and charisma; (5) rhetorical impact; (6) experts' rankings; and (7) presidential libraries. In the appendix, I explain in detail each of these factors and my quantitative analysis.

These factors are all pertinent to public familiarity with presidents' constitutional legacies. For instance, popular history textbooks and books about presidents in major university libraries reflect priorities in academic and popular research and education that are likely to shape the attitudes and knowledge that educated people have about presidencies.

Besides the empirical analysis described in the appendix, I employed some qualitative measures. First, I recognized that while the objective assessments of presidential scholars indicate some presidents did not accomplish much along standard lines of interest (such as handling wars or crises), their actions teach lessons that still resonate today. Second, I analyzed presidential rhetoric beyond quantitative measures. I assessed the quality of presidents' constitutional discourse based on its clarity, coherence, appeal, and influence over time. Quality, not just quantity, counts. In his Gettysburg Address, President Lincoln ironically declared, "The world will little note, nor long remember what we say here."[5] As we know, he was wrong. In fact, the world remembers Lincoln more than most other presidents partly because of the extraordinary eloquence of this speech. Even though many forgotten presidents gave longer speeches than Lincoln did in his less-than-270-word masterpiece at Gettysburg, none of their speeches matched the forcefulness or lyricism of his rhetoric. Subsequent generations have found more to admire in Lincoln than in the rhetoric or actions of most other presidents.

Using my criteria, I identify thirteen presidents as largely forgotten in constitutional law. This figure is remarkable, since it suggests we may have forgotten, insofar as constitutional law is concerned, almost 25 percent of the forty-three different men who have been president. While it may seem odd that Americans have forgotten so many people who occupied the most powerful office in the world, the list could be longer. The thirteen presidents whose stories I tell are representative of forgotten presidents. I devote a chapter each to Martin Van Buren, William Henry Harrison, John Tyler, Zachary Taylor, Millard Fillmore, Franklin Pierce, Chester Arthur, Grover Cleveland (twice), Benjamin Harrison, William Howard Taft, Calvin Coolidge, and Jimmy Carter. Each chapter focuses on a forgotten president's most significant constitutional judgments and consequences.

The conclusion reviews the themes connecting forgotten presidents. One of the most important is that presidents cannot wage war on the presidency. It has shaped and been shaped by them. They have adapted their constitutional convictions to comport with the Constitution and their office, and they have battled with Congress to protect their prerogatives. But forgotten presidents demonstrate the risks of entering office with unrealistic or untested notions of executive power and without the flexibility and imagination to adapt creatively and constructively to unforeseen crises. Forgotten presidents may differ from memorable ones, at least in part, because of their overabundance of caution and lack of imagination in pushing the boundaries of executive powers. Generally, more inventive, daring exercises of power, particularly when they have produced positive, politically popular outcomes, have drawn attention away from less creative, anachronistic, unimaginative exercises of presidential authority.

Being forgotten does not turn merely on the range or number of a president's constitutional activities. Some presidents are forgotten in part because they lost control of their narratives and had them tossed aside or left to the dictates of indifferent or hostile storytellers. Moreover, public familiarity with their stories depends on other factors, some of which are beyond presidents' control: Forgotten presidents often seem to have been leaders who failed to complete their terms or to face or solve memorable crises, were overshadowed by more charismatic or colorful leaders or dramatic events before or after their presidencies (indeed, nineteenth-century forgotten presidents often appeared in the background or margins, rather than at the center, of the political cartoons lampooning them), had limited rhetorical skills, and failed to capture the public's imagination during and after their presidencies. Forgotten presidents have not cultivated or maintained enduring popular support or adulation, inspired the investment of subsequent leaders, or championed constitutional commitments consistent with the American people's evolving values.

A few remaining clarifications are in order. First, some readers may wonder why focus on forgotten presidents? Why not write about presidential power generally and discuss forgotten presidents to the extent of their relevance? The focus on forgotten presidents is useful for several reasons. To begin with, I tell the stories of forgotten presidents to preserve them. Otherwise, their stories are lost, because conventional narratives on the rise of presidential power overwhelmingly pay attention to the more successful, popular, charismatic, creative chief executives. Focusing on forgotten presidents underscores how presidential power develops and continues to expand even at unexpected times. The stories of these presidents also remind us, as I have suggested, of how the Constitution constrains, or channels, its occupants into performing various tasks. These presidents often sacrificed political support for the sake of doing what they believed their office or the Constitution demanded of them.

The second, important clarification is that the proliferation of news outlets and archives makes forgetting presidents increasingly difficult. The Internet, the twenty-four-hour news cycle, smart phones, Wikipedia, systematic archiving, and standardizing presidential libraries ensure posterity will have ample records for future presidents, though the challenge will be clarifying their constitutional legacies. It is conceivable the proliferation of information about presidents might actually make it more difficult for them to control their narratives.

Third, I employ throughout the book an expansive view of the Constitution. On my view, anything counts as constitutional if it has some constitutional impact or is informed by or reflects constitutional attitudes. Thus, I treat as constitutional a wide range of presidential decisions, including White House staffing and executive branch reorganization, pardons, vetoes, and support of, or opposition to, important pieces of legislation and suggested constitutional amendments, to the extent that they have had discernible constitutional consequences or reflect, reinforce, undermine, or are driven by particular constitutional outlooks, philosophies, or modes of interpretation.

Fourth, being forgotten is relative. The term "legacy" refers to presidential actions that meant something important to subsequent leaders and generations, while "significance" conveys the normative force that subsequent authorities have invested in some prior action(s).

My purpose is not, however, to rate presidents or analyze the vast academic literature on the presidency. Rather, I seek to illuminate interesting but underappreciated patterns in presidential decision-making that have shaped various constitutional developments, including the increase in federal power at the expense of states, the constant growth of presidential power, and the persistent efforts of Congress to maintain equilibrium of power with the presidency. Throughout, I pay attention to primary materials and the consequences of various decisions and occasional incompleteness of historical records.

Nevertheless, some readers may quarrel with my choices of which presidents I deem forgotten. I excluded other, arguably deserving presidents because constitutional scholars evidently pay more attention to them—James Monroe because he was the last of the Virginia dynasty of presidents and gave name to America's long-standing promise to regard any European interference with the independence of existing states in North or South America as an act of hostility against the United States; James Buchanan because he rates among the worst presidents—if not as *the* worst—and set the stage for Lincoln's presidency; Rutherford Hayes because he won the controversial 1876 presidential election and dismantled Reconstruction; James Garfield and William McKinley because of their tragic deaths and lost promise; John Quincy Adams because of his involvement with the controversial 1824 election and his having been the first son of a president to win the presidency in his own right; James Polk because of his leadership in realizing the nation's manifest destiny and winning the Mexican War that secured Texas and set a precedent for a preemptive war to protect American interests; Warren Harding because of the unprecedented extent of his administration's corruption; and Gerald Ford because the story of Watergate cannot be told without him. While there is much to learn from these presidents' constitutional activities, this book focuses on thirteen other presidents to demonstrate what can happen when we include them in the conversation over constitutional law.

I further appreciate that telling these presidents' stories chronologically is hardly the only way to illustrate their constitutional impact. At the end of this introduction, I have therefore assembled a table showing in which chapters and on which page(s) I discuss various recurring subjects.

Finally, some readers may believe that characterizing presidents as forgotten is impossible or makes no sense. They may dispute that some presidents are really forgotten or that we can learn anything useful or meaningful from them. If you think this, you should consider which presidents significantly influenced Lincoln's thinking about the scope of presidential powers to preserve the Union. If you know the answer, I commend you. If you do not, read on.

Table I.1 Table of Recurrent Themes

	Appointments	Congressional Powers	Constitutional Interpretation	Federalism, State Sovereignty	Foreign Affairs	Misconduct	Judicial Review	Presidential Administration, Powers	Rights	Slavery	Territories
Martin Van Buren	14, 19, 20	6, 7, 8, 9, 12, 15, 16, 18, 21	5, 6, 7, 8, 9, 10, 11, 12, 16, 17, 18	3, 4, 5, 6, 8, 9, 11, 12, 15	13, 14, 16, 17	19, 20	4, 7, 9, 14, 21, 22, 23	3, 4, 7, 10, 13, 14, 15, 16, 17, 18, 19	20,	3, 4, 11, 12, 13, 14, 15	23
William Henry Harrison	26, 28, 29, 31, 32, 33	26, 30	26,		25, 62			26, 30, 32, 34			
John Tyler	48, 49, 50, 58, 59, 60, 62	38, 44, 45, 46, 47, 50, 53, 55, 56, 57, 60	38, 44, 45, 46, 50, 52, 53, 57, 64, 65, 66	38, 44, 62	40, 61, 62, 63, 64	42, 53	39	38, 39, 41, 42, 43, 44, 45, 46, 47, 48, 49, 50, 51, 52, 53, 54, 55, 57, 61, 66		63	63, 64
Zachary Taylor	73, 74	68, 76, 77	72, 73, 74			74, 77		67, 69, 71, 72, 73	78	69, 70, 71, 78	69, 70, 71, 78
Millard Fillmore	89, 90	83, 84, 86, 88	82, 83, 84, 85, 86, 88, 89, 90	83, 85, 88, 92	92		90	82, 83, 84, 85, 86, 89, 90, 91, 92	85	82, 83, 84, 85, 86, 87, 88, 89, 91	82, 83

Franklin Pierce	99, 100, 110	99	96, 97, 98, 99, 104, 105, 106, 108	97, 98, 106	101, 102	99, 103, 109	96, 98, 99, 100, 102, 103, 104, 107, 110, 112	99	96, 97, 98, 103, 104, 105, 106, 107, 109, 110, 111, 112
Chester Arthur	116, 117, 118, 119, 120, 123	116, 117, 122, 123, 124, 125, 126	116, 120, 122, 123, 125, 126			113, 117, 118	113, 115, 116, 117, 118, 120, 122, 123, 124, 125	115, 116	124
Grover Cleveland	133, 134, 135, 136, 137, 138, 139, 140	128, 129, 130, 131, 132, 133, 135, 136, 137, 138	128, 129, 130, 132, 133, 135, 137	129	160	134, 139	127, 128, 129, 130, 131, 132, 133, 135, 136, 137, 138	140	
Benjamin Harrison	141, 142, 143, 144, 145, 149, 150, 151, 154	146, 147, 148, 151, 152	145, 152, 153, 154			147, 148, 149, 151, 152, 153, 154	141, 142, 143, 146, 152, 153, 154	152	

(continued)

Table I.1 (*continued*)

	Appointments	Congressional Powers	Constitutional Interpretation	Federalism, State Sovereignty	Foreign Affairs	Mis-conduct	Judicial Review	Presidential Administration, Powers	Rights	Slavery	Territories
Grover Cleveland	155, 156, 157, 167, 168, 169	155, 156, 157, 158, 160, 161, 163	155, 156, 157, 158, 163, 164, 165, 169, 170	163, 164, 165	155, 159, 160, 161, 162, 163		158, 164, 165, 166, 169, 170	155, 156, 157, 158, 160, 161, 163, 164, 165, 166, 167, 169, 170	170		160, 161, 16
William Howard Taft	171, 172, 176, 184, 185, 186, 189	171, 172, 173, 174, 175, 176, 177, 178, 179, 180, 182, 186, 187, 188, 189	171, 172, 173, 174, 177, 178, 179, 180, 182, 185, 186, 187, 188			187	186, 187, 188, 189	171, 172, 173, 174, 175, 176, 177, 178, 179, 180, 189	182, 185, 186		

Calvin Coolidge	191, 196, 198, 199, 205, 206	192, 193, 195, 199, 200, 201, 202, 203, 204, 206, 207, 208, 209, 210, 211, 212, 213, 214	191, 192, 193, 194, 195, 199, 200, 201, 202, 204, 208, 209, 210, 211, 212, 213, 214	193, 194	191, 212, 213, 214, 215	196, 197, 198, 199, 200, 201, 202, 203, 204	199, 201, 202, 203, 208	191, 192, 193, 195, 196, 197, 200, 201, 202, 206, 207, 208, 209, 210, 213, 214	192, 193
Jimmy Carter	217, 219, 220, 221, 223, 224, 225, 226	218, 221, 223, 231, 233, 234	218, 221, 231, 232, 233, 234, 235, 236	234	218, 220, 232, 233, 228, 229, 234, 230, 231	224, 229, 232	233, 235, 236, 237	218, 219, 220, 221, 222, 223, 224, 228, 230, 231, 232, 233, 234, 236, 237, 239	218, 235, 236, 237, 239

Note: This table lists major recurring themes in the book. A detailed index is at the back of the book.

The Forgotten Presidents

1

Martin Van Buren, 1837–1841

MARTIN VAN BUREN was once one of America's most famous politicians. Prior to his election as president in 1836, he had served as New York's governor, Andrew Jackson's first secretary of state, and Jackson's second vice president. He earned the vice presidency and Jackson's undying gratitude after he had masterfully managed Jackson's presidential campaigns and Jackson's first vice president, John Calhoun, had cast the tie-breaking vote in the Senate to defeat Van Buren's nomination as minister to Great Britain as part of Jackson's reshuffling of his cabinet in his first term.[1] Van Buren was the first New Yorker to be elected president and was, at fifty-four, the youngest president elected to date. He was the last sitting vice president elected president until George H. W. Bush in 1989.

But Van Buren has been eclipsed by the seven men who preceded him as president, all of whom had been notable founders, had enjoyed greater political success in office, or had come from political dynasties. As the eighth president, he did not work on a blank slate; prior presidents had addressed many of the issues he confronted, particularly the scope of the federal government's power over slavery and the president's power to unilaterally remove officials within his administration. As the second Democratic president, he was the handpicked successor of his enormously popular predecessor, Andrew Jackson, who had first championed the president as the only elected representative of the whole nation, the natural leader of his party, and the official best situated to protect states from an overreaching Congress. Like Jackson, he also had to manage, or overcome, ideological and geographic divisions within his own party and strident opposition from the Whig Party, which took its name to emulate American Whigs who opposed British tyranny and was dedicated to defeating Jackson and his policies.

Consequently, the era's dramatic conflicts and outsized personalities within Congress have obscured Van Buren's constitutional impact. In fact, he was the first president to fully consider the federal government's powers to tackle a national economic crisis. The first great depression happened on his watch, and his conviction that the federal government lacked the authority to do much in response to the crisis wrecked his presidency and became an example for subsequent presidents to avoid. Nonetheless, he significantly shaped the constitutional debate over slavery through his efforts to bar federal interference with it and to support the gag rule banning slavery as a subject for discussion in the House. In an important, early slavery dispute, he reinforced judicial review; and he lost his reelection contest despite having helped to secure the party system as a permanent fixture within the constitutional order and to extend Jackson's consolidation of several unilateral powers of the presidency.

Defining Federal Authority to Relieve a National Economic Crisis

One of Van Buren's first challenges as president was unprecedented—determining the scope of federal power to address a national economic crisis. As a candidate, he had pledged to maintain Jackson's economic policies, particularly his Specie Circular, which required that all payments for public land be paid for in specie or hard currency—gold or silver. Jackson and Van Buren viewed the Circular as a solution to the growing problem of buyers using paper money that was depreciating or losing its value because it came from state banks not backed by hard money. After his election, Van Buren faced mounting pressures to revise the Circular to address unexpected, sudden, sharp increases in inflation that had arisen in its aftermath. While Van Buren deliberated, the crisis worsened: On May 10, 1837, New York banks, unable to meet continuing demands for specie, refused to convert paper money into gold or silver. Soon thereafter, a convergence of factors produced panic nationwide: More than a third of the nation's banks folded, credit was unavailable to start new businesses, crops failed, cotton prices fell dramatically, and the trade balance with England deteriorated. As unemployment and the price of food rose in the Northeast, riots broke out.

Van Buren had three choices: First, he could acquiesce to the opposition Whig Party's demands to abandon Jackson's Specie Circular, support the creation of the Third Bank of the United States, approve direct federal control of state funds, and agree to establish a uniform, national currency—namely, paper money. Second, Van Buren could abandon the Circular and maintain the deposit system as it was then constructed (allowing federal money to be deposited in banks other than the National Bank that Congress had created and placed under the president's control).[2] Third, Van Buren could maintain the Specie Circular, oppose rechartering the National Bank, and separate the federal government's management of money and other fiscal affairs from states and the private sector. The third option was the trickiest since Whigs wanted Congress to take the lead, while Democrats opposed federal intervention or supported paper currency.

Based on his constitutional commitments and party allegiance, Van Buren chose the third option. Van Buren was the consummate Democrat who had helped to define and was determined to fight for his party's basic tenets. These were fully on display at the outset of his presidency. Echoing both Jefferson and Jackson in his inaugural address, Van Buren pledged, first and foremost, to protect the states from congressional overreaching. He declared that

> the principle that will govern me in the high duty to which my country calls me is a strict adherence to the letter and spirit of the Constitution as it was designed by those who framed it. Looking back to it as a sacred instrument carefully and not easily framed, remembering it was throughout a work of concession and compromise, viewing it as limited to national objects, regarding it as leaving to the people and the States all power not explicitly parted with, I shall endeavor to preserve, protect, and defend it by assiduously referring to its provision for direction in every action.[3]

He promised not to allow the federal government to exceed its constitutional "limits" and reiterated Jefferson's conviction that the federal government was not obliged to help states or people in distress. He emphasized that its only duty was to refrain from extending special favors, to prevent evil, and to ensure uniform, equal enforcement of federal laws. Everything else fell within the domain of state sovereignty.

Later the same year, Van Buren reaffirmed these principles. He declared, "All communities are apt to look to government for too much[.] If, therefore, I refrain from suggesting to Congress any specific plan for regulating the exchanges of the country, relieving mercantile embarrassments, or interfering with the ordinary operations of foreign or domestic commerce, it is from a conviction that such measures are not within the constitutional province of the General Government."[4] He explained, "The framers of our excellent Constitution and the people who approved it with calm and sagacious deliberation ... wisely judged that the less government intervenes with private pursuits the letter for the general prosperity[.] Its ... duty ... is to enact, and enforce a system of general laws commensurate with, but not exceeding, the objects of its establishment, and to leave every citizen and every interest to reap under its benign protection the rewards of virtue, industry, and prudence."[5]

Van Buren blamed the country's economic troubles on the public and the Whig Party's rejection of republican values. On his view, republicanism required commitment to civic virtue (ennobling oneself and inculcating proper values in society through public service); and renewed commitment to republicanism, which would have required more self-discipline and sacrifice, would be the antidote to the unchecked self-indulgence, speculation, and lending (and Whigs' paternalistic policies) that had produced the depression. Central to this restoration was the separation of the federal treasury from the states and the private sector. Van Buren believed the separation would restore the system of finance "as old as the Constitution itself."[6] He argued that the Constitution authorized the federal government only to issue or coin hard money, left to states wide discretion over most economic affairs, and did not authorize Congress to establish paper currency or a National Bank, which Whigs had long favored as the principal means to assist the federal government in handling its fiscal affairs.

Prominent Democratic senators expressed similar constitutional themes in defending Van Buren's plan. The chair of the Senate Finance Committee, Silas Wright, led the defense. First, he defended the constitutionality of Van Buren's plan to adopt hard money as the only federally authorized currency. He explained that "[it] was high time that a more permanent standard, and one in conformity with the Constitution, should be established. Congress alone could establish it; and Congress . . . could only establish it in connection with the receipts and disbursements."[7] The Constitution provided the federal government with the unique authority "to coin money," and the plain meaning of the word "coin" meant something hard like gold or silver, and Congress's mistake was to produce any other kind of coinage. Second, Wright argued that the plan did not, as Clay and fellow Whig Daniel Webster had maintained, allow the executive's unconstitutional usurpation of legislative power. He explained that, under Van Buren's plan, the executive officers tasked with collecting federal monies "are all appointed by the President and Senate, by the president alone, or by the heads of some one of the Executive departments. They are all public officers of the Government, responsible to it, and to the people, for their official acts. [The] bill does not propose to change the mode of their appointments or to increase their inability to [be] dismiss[ed] from office by the Executive."[8] Wright concluded that Van Buren's plan "would increase [the] Executive responsibilities, not the Executive power. If the system proposed be adopted, the people will hold the President responsible for his selection of the officers to be entrusted with the safe keeping of their treasure; and they will hold the head of the Treasury Department responsible for an incessant and sleepless vigilance over these depositories. [The bill] will throw upon the Executive officers a great increase of care and responsibility—not an increase of power or influence" at the expense of Congress or the states.[9] Senator Thomas Hart Benton, one of Jackson's closest allies, proclaimed, "I am for restoring to the Federal treasury the currency of the Constitution. I am for carrying back this government to the solidity projected by the founders."[10]

Opposing Van Buren at almost every turn, as it had opposed Jackson, was the Whig Party, led by Jackson's great nemesis, Henry Clay, in the Senate. After running unsuccessfully against Jackson in 1832, Clay had founded the Whig Party to oppose Jackson's expansions of executive power at Congress's expense and to support his presidential aspirations. Whigs derided Jackson's consolidation of presidential power as tyrannical and as usurping the legislative authority granted Congress in the Constitution. Whigs argued that the Constitution established Congress as the supreme authority in shaping domestic policy and the president as a minister charged with carrying out Congress's will. They believed that Van Buren, like Jackson, had subverted republican principles by expanding the president's power at the expense of Congress and the people of the United States. Both the symbol and embodiment of the Whigs' solution was the National Bank, which they believed was instrumental to stabilizing the nation's credit and improving the handling of the federal government's financial affairs. They believed that Congress had the authority to charter such a bank (and its branches around the country) pursuant to the Necessary and Proper Clause[11] and thus agreed with the Supreme Court decision in *McCulloch v. Maryland*[12] construing this clause as granting Congress the implicit authority to do whatever it viewed as convenient or useful to implement its taxing and spending powers through the creation of the National Bank. Like Jackson, Van Buren disapproved, did not feel bound by *McCulloch*, and believed that Congress was limited to exercising only its enumerated powers, which did not include authority to create a national bank. Further, Van Buren believed, like Jackson, that the president had independent authority to determine whether the National Bank was "necessary" and that it was not. While Jackson expressed his convictions in his veto of the Second National Bank, Van Buren never had the same opportunity since the House never passed a bill reestablishing the bank.

Yet Van Buren did not oppose *all possible* federal intervention in the depression. He believed the Constitution granted narrow powers to Congress, based on its powers to coin money, to remedy the evil of "depreciated paper currency,"[13] and to enact limited reforms of the banking system as long as they did not directly interfere with state sovereignty. His proposals to provide much-needed debtor relief reflected this outlook. Though Congress did not enact Van Buren's proposal to close suspended banks that could not resume specie payments within a certain period of time, this measure reflected Van Buren's view that "a salutary check may doubtless be imposed on the issues of paper money and an effective remedy given to the citizens in a way at once equal in all parts of the Union and fully authorized by the Constitution."[14] He believed that his independent treasury plan[15] was appropriately respectful of state sovereignty, because it did not directly regulate states' fiscal affairs. The act affected states indirectly through the withdrawal of federal deposits from state banks. At the same time, Van Buren planned for tight, narrowly constricted controls over federal funds—specifically, to collect, store, and disburse public revenue through treasury agents and postal employees rather than allow the unrestricted discretion of a national bank.

In response, Whigs maintained that the coinage and commerce clauses empowered Congress to create a uniform national currency. Clay told the Senate that such currency was the answer to Jacksonian policies that had produced two classes of Americans—aristocratic, federal officeholders who were paid in specie and all others who were paid in less valuable, soft money. Daniel Webster, then serving as one of Massachusetts's two senators, expanded the Whig critique of Van Buren's plan. Webster believed that the Constitution imposed a duty on the federal government to help people in trouble: "Government must do for individuals [what] individuals cannot do for themselves."[16] This included rechartering the National Bank to check executive usurpation of legislative authority. Webster further explained that Congress had the authority to establish a uniform, national currency pursuant to its constitutional powers to enact uniform bankruptcy laws, to coin money, and to regulate interstate commerce. He agreed with Clay that such a currency would be more democratic than the hard money favored by Van Buren because it would be available to all Americans.

Senator James Buchanan (D.-Pa.) delivered a detailed response to Clay and Webster. First, he acknowledged, "I should treat with great deference and respect the former acts of Congress and the opinion of the Supreme Court; but [if] they should fail to convince me, I would consider myself guilty of moral perjury before heaven if I voted for such a bill. I have sworn to support the Constitution of the United States; and my own judgment must be convinced that a law is constitutional before, acting in a legislative capacity, I can give it my sanction."[17] Buchanan maintained that the Court sometimes upheld legislation that senators believed unconstitutional. He said that the Supreme Court's decision in *McCulloch* had been

> based upon the principle, that if Congress have determined such a bank to be an appropriate means to carry into execution this taxing power, the Judiciary could not interfere and declare that it was not. The degree and the urgency of this necessity must at last be left to the Legislature, unless in extreme cases. Upon an application for a new charter, the question appears thus to be referred by the Judiciary itself to the Legislative authority. Every member, should the case arise, must ask himself whether a [national bank] be a necessary and proper instrument to carry into execution the taxing power of the Government. If he decides in the negative, he cannot vote in favor of establishing such a bank, without personally violating the Constitution.[18]

Buchanan also disagreed that the federal government had the authority to issue paper currency. His view was that the framers

> have evinced their intention as clearly as human language can manifest it, that our currency should [be] gold and silver alone; and they have prohibited the States from making any thing else a legal tender. . . . The framers knew nothing of any paper currency, except that of the Revolution. This they would not touch; they did not name it. It was an example forever to be shunned, and never to be followed. And yet they have done their work with so little skill that they have authorized Congress to create a paper currency for the whole nation, which shall serve as the medium of our domestic and foreign exchanges! The Constitution has established gold and silver as the currency of the country and therefore it is contended that they have authorized the emission of a vast paper circulation![19]

Buchanan further explained that there were two ways to construe the Constitution: "The one favored a strict, the other a liberal construction of the [Constitution]. The one has been jealous of State rights, the other the advocate of federal power."[20] Buchanan favored a "strict" construction of the Constitution that indicated the federal government had "no power to regulate the state banks; but we can withhold from them our revenue, and thus protect them from using our means for the purpose of deranging the business of our society."[21] Buchanan, like Van Buren, Wright, and Benton, construed the Constitution's plain language in authorizing Congress to "coin" money, early historical practices, and the original meaning to indicate that the federal government lacked the authority to "coin" anything except gold and silver. The opposition to the issuance of paper money held, and it was not until after the Civil War that the Supreme Court[22] upheld and political authorities supported the constitutionality of paper currency.

The fight over the independence of federal treasury operations lasted three years.[23] In 1837 and 1838, Van Buren's proposal passed the Senate, in which Democrats had a decisive advantage, but it failed in the House, in which Democrats held only a one-seat margin over the Whigs. While this advantage enabled Democrats to elect the Speaker of the House (James Polk), they achieved little else. Although neither Whigs nor conservative Democrats had the votes to get their preferred legislative initiatives approved in either chamber, they persuaded Van Buren in 1838 to sign a bill into law repealing the Specie Circular. It proved to be the undoing of both their coalition and the economic recovery, for the Circular's repeal triggered widespread expansions of credit and borrowing that fueled inflation. By late 1839, several other events converged to cause widespread panic: Cotton prices declined, British capital stopped flowing into the United States, nearly half the nation's banks suspended specie payments, nine states defaulted on their debts, and the nation's largest bank closed. Van Buren argued that the panic discredited Whigs' economic policies and that his plan was the country's only hope. Democrats managed for the Senate to approve the plan a third time. It languished for months in the House, where it passed on June 30, 1840, by the margin of 124–107.

Democratic leaders praised its passage as restoring the Constitution. Van Buren waited to sign the bill until July 4, 1840, to underscore its historic importance. When he did, "Democrats hailed Van Buren as the new Thomas Jefferson and the sub-treasury law as 'the second declaration of independence.'"[24]

But opposition to the bill had several unintended effects. First, in pushing the president to address the economic crisis, Whigs had undermined the central, constitutional commitment of their party to a weak presidency bent on doing Congress's bidding. Van Buren called their bluff by calling for a special session of Congress. By taking the initiative, he strengthened the presidency's constitutional authority to initiate solutions to federal problems. Second, the delay produced by the opposition allowed Van Buren the opportunity to issue an executive order to federal collection officers to hold public funds rather than deposit them in state banks.[25] Consequently, four-fifths of the treasury expenditures in 1838 were made by drafts drawn on federal collection officers, thereby effectively creating the arrangement Van Buren wanted by fiat. Thus, Whigs inadvertently helped Van Buren to consolidate executive powers.[26]

Moreover, although Calhoun and Van Buren had not spoken in eight years, Calhoun had returned to the Senate, where he surprisingly announced that he supported Van Buren's plan. Van Buren accepted the support to facilitate the bill's passage, while Calhoun approved the plan as a "complete restoration of the Constitution" because it freed states from federal regulation of their fiscal affairs,[27] which included the production of cotton and maintenance of slavery. Thus, for Calhoun, the plan reinforced states' rights.

The enactment of the independent treasury plan produced several constitutional precedents. First, in taking the initiative to address the depression, Van Buren affirmed the president's capacity for leadership in domestic crises. Second, his plan was a precedent upholding the national government's intervening in a national economic crisis. Third, the plan's indirect regulation of states became a precedent on which states' rights advocates heavily relied for the next two decades to oppose any direct federal regulations of states.

Challenging Federal Authority to Regulate Slavery

The debate over the independent treasury plan was important not just for its own sake but also because it was intertwined with the greatest constitutional issue of the day—the extent to which the Constitution restricted federal power or guaranteed state sovereignty over slavery. This issue arose whenever Congress faced a question about the boundaries separating the federal and state governments. Relying partly on the Tenth Amendment, which "reserved" to the states or the people the powers not given to the federal government or prohibited to the states by the Constitution,[28] states' rights advocates construed all gaps, silences, and ambiguities in the Constitution in favor of state sovereignty, whereas most Whigs construed them in the opposite way—as accruing to the federal government's benefit. Like the Court in *McCulloch*, Whigs found it significant that the Tenth Amendment had dropped the word "expressly" (which had been used in the Articles of Confederation) before referencing federal "powers," implying that the federal government had powers beyond those expressly given to it. In interpreting the Constitution, states' rights advocates adopted the default rule of favoring state sovereignty, while Whigs' default rule was to favor federal authority. The differences between these approaches were manifest in virtually every congressional debate at the time, particularly one in February 1837 over several resolutions that Calhoun had proposed on slavery.

Calhoun called the debate over his resolutions "one of the greatest civil contests in modern times."[29] In the midst of the debates, he explained in a widely published letter that the fight over the resolutions would force both parties into "the old and natural division of state rights and national."[30] Calhoun placed himself on the side of the Constitution, which he believed guaranteed absolute state sovereignty over any matter over which it had not expressly vested regulatory authority in the federal government.

The debates gave Clay the chance to link Van Buren with Calhoun and to expose their radical constitutional views. Hence, he introduced, in the midst of the Senate debates over the independent treasury plan, a resolution recognizing federal authority to regulate slavery in the nation's capital. The resolution vexed Calhoun because it did not expressly recognize federal governmental power to restrict slaveholders' rights in the capital or elsewhere. He voted for the resolution after construing it as recognizing some, but not absolute, federal power over slavery. The resolution passed, in spite of Webster's warning, "Mr. Clay and Mr. Calhoun have attempted . . . *to make a new Constitution*."[31]

Van Buren was not an idle bystander in the debates. In fact, he had initiated them. In his inaugural address, he had challenged Congress by vowing opposition to any congressional attempt to abolish slavery in the District of Columbia.[32] Van Buren was careful not to become more involved in the debate or to publicly oppose the resolution since it was silent on whether Congress could restrict or abolish slavery. While Calhoun believed the resolution forced Clay to take a stand on the federal government's power to abolish slavery, Clay believed the resolution's passage vindicated Congress's broad powers over "interstate commerce," slavery, and the District of Columbia.

In every year of Van Buren's presidency, the Democratic majority in the House also affirmed a resolution allowing petitions pertaining to slavery to be introduced but then to be tabled without printing or referring them. In Van Buren's last year as president, House Democrats *and* the president went a step further. They supported a more extreme resolution expressly forbidding petitions pertaining to slavery to be introduced into the House and/or to be formally recognized in any way. With most southern members of the House supporting the resolution and most northern members opposing it, it barely passed the House 114–108 on January 28, 1840. The resolution, known as the gag rule, was largely attributed to Van Buren, since it was made possible only by the affirmative votes of twenty-six northern representatives who had supported it with the hope that its passage would help Van Buren win reelection. Whigs chastised Van Buren for sacrificing for his own benefit the First Amendment's guarantee that every House member could express his political views on any subject, while Democrats defended Van Buren as a man of principle who prioritized preserving the Union over the First Amendment.[33]

Slavery also took center stage when Van Buren became involved in the *Amistad* case, which tested the Supreme Court's authority to review presidential compliance with treaties. The story of the case is usually told from one of three perspectives. The first is the perspectives of the fifty-three Africans,[34] who had been captured in their homeland and shipped aboard the *Amistad* as slaves to Cuba. They mutinied and took control of the *Amistad*. But they kept alive two slave dealers to guide the ship to Africa who instead steered it toward Long Island. Once the ship entered American waters, an American Coast Guard vessel seized it and escorted the *Amistad* to New London, Connecticut, where American authorities arrested the surviving Africans for murder, mutiny, and piracy.

A second perspective is that of an international dispute pitting the Africans against the Spanish government, which claimed ownership of the ship and the Africans. In fact, the Spanish government had persuaded the Van Buren administration to release the ship and its occupants pursuant to the Treaty of 1795, "by which the United States had bound itself to extend good faith and credit to the official actions of the Spanish government," including Cuba.[35]

The third perspective is that of the Supreme Court, which rejected the claims of the Spanish government and ordered the Africans to be freed.[36] The Court's decision has received considerable attention from constitutional scholars because it was one of the few made against the interests of slaveholders in the antebellum era.

But the *Amistad* story is rarely told from Van Buren's perspective. He was not in Washington at the time of the mutiny or when the *Amistad* entered U.S. waters, and the initial decisions were made by three members of his cabinet who were in Washington when the ship arrived in Connecticut—Secretary of State John Forsyth, Postmaster General Amos Kendall, and Treasury Secretary Levi Woodbury, who decided on their own initiative to support the Spanish government's claims under the 1795 treaty.

Once Van Buren returned to Washington, he took charge. He consulted with Forsyth, Kendall, and Woodbury and directed Attorney General Felix Grundy to prepare an official opinion supporting their construction of the treaty and the federal government's obligations under it. Grundy did so.[37] Van Buren instructed Secretary of State Forsyth to direct the U.S. district attorney in Connecticut, William Holabird, to keep the dispute out of the courts and under executive control. Meanwhile, several prominent abolitionists contacted the Africans in prison and secured the permission of the nominal leader of the Africans, Cinque, to file a lawsuit contesting the Spanish government's claims and the criminal charges made against him and the other Africans in prison. In response, Van Buren directed Holabird to persuade the court that the Treaty of 1795 required returning the ship and the Africans to Cuba. Because he had appointed the judge presiding in the case, Van Buren expected a favorable judicial ruling and issued a confidential executive order directing the navy to be prepared to take the Africans to Cuba. Van Buren directed Holabird to give legal counsel to the two slave dealers whose lives the mutinying Africans had spared.[38] (Van Buren was embarrassed politically when his secret order came to light.) When the judge surprisingly rejected the administration's arguments, Van Buren directed Holabird to appeal the decision and seek its reversal on the grounds that the trial judge had no authority to inquire into the documentation on which the Spanish government was relying to describe the Africans as "illegal immigrants" when the Treaty of 1795 required accepting that the Spanish government was acting in good faith on commercial matters. When the circuit court upheld the lower-court order, Van Buren authorized an appeal to the Supreme Court. He asked his attorney general, who was then Henry Gilpin, to tell the Court that the Treaty of 1795 governed the matter, that the Court lacked the authority to inquire into the documentation filed by the Spanish government, and that it should presume the latter was acting in good faith.

On behalf of Cinque and the other Africans, John Quincy Adams and Roger Baldwin (for whom the cofounder of the American Civil Liberties Union was later named) presented their arguments to the Court three days before the end of Van Buren's term. Baldwin and Adams argued that the treaty was inapplicable since the Spanish government's claims were not made in good faith—in fact, they were based on fraudulent documents drafted to obscure the fact that the Africans were being sold into slavery. Emphasizing that this fraud undermined the integrity of judicial process, the Supreme Court upheld the circuit court's ruling six to one.[39] Thus, Van Buren lost at every stage of the judicial process.[40]

The outcome upheld several principles. First, it reaffirmed the president's authority to direct his cabinet and federal prosecutors in performing their job, a principle that remains intact. Second, it demonstrated the futility of a president's attempting to intimidate a judge to get a favorable ruling. The lower-court judgment is an important precedent upholding judicial independence from federal intimidation. Third, the case is an early instance of a president's using litigation for political cover.[41] Indeed, the treasury secretary had advised that "nothing is lost in point of public policy by letting the judiciary take all the responsibility . . . which they may choose to exercise."[42] Fourth, Van Buren did not follow the example of Jackson, who supposedly once declared in response to an unfavorable ruling that "John Marshall had made the decision now let him enforce it."[43] Though the Spanish minister pressed Van Buren throughout the litigation to take direct charge of the matter, the secretary of state responded that "the Constitution secured the judicial power against all interference on the part of the executive authority."[44]

While the *Amistad* case was pending, Van Buren took a surprising stance in another case involving the rights of African-Americans. In a court-martial in North Carolina, a naval officer had been convicted of flogging his sailors, but some eyewitnesses were African-Americans, whom North Carolina law barred from testifying in legal proceedings. The secretary of the navy requested an official opinion from Attorney General Gilpin, who advised that "an inquiry" into the right of the African-Americans to testify was "unnecessary" because their testimony was "in no respect material" to the conviction since there was corroborating evidence and "the verdict [was] substantially right."[45] The secretary of the navy accepted the attorney general's advice, and Van Buren backed them both. Calhoun and other southern leaders were "furious."[46] They believed that the court-martial and the president were bound to follow the North Carolina law. By rejecting Calhoun's position and upholding the decision of the court-martial in full, Van Buren was aligning himself with the principle associated with Jackson that the states should defer to the federal government when their laws conflicted. By doing this in the year in which he stood for reelection, he had exposed the constitutional divide separating him from Calhoun and other southern nullifiers when it hurt him the most.

Using Military Power

Van Buren strengthened the president's control over military and foreign affairs. He continued Jackson's controversial policy of Indian removals—forcibly relocating Indian tribes to open their land for white settlers, to protect Indians from each other, and to guarantee white settlers' security. The policy raised many issues, prompting eleven opinions from his attorney general and seven presidential messages on the subject.

One of the most pressing constitutional questions involved determining the requirements for his authorizing the use of military force. Neither Congress nor Van Buren maintained that a formal declaration of war was needed to authorize military action or that the forced removals were authorized by Congress's Article I power to regulate commerce with the Indian tribes.

Van Buren's answer came in the form of an official opinion from his attorney general. Attorney General Benjamin Butler, in response to an inquiry from the secretary of war about whether there was a war between the United States and the Seminoles, opined that there had been "since the 14th of January, 1836, a public war with the tribe of Indians, within the meaning of the rules and articles of war and the constitution of the United States."[47] Butler noted that "Congress, by a law approved on that day, recognized the commencement of these hostilities, and appropriated money to suppress them. Several appropriations for the same object have been made by law; so, although no formal declaration of war has been made (and probably because deemed unnecessary), the war, on our part, has been waged by the authority of the legislative department, to whom the power of making war has been given by the constitution."[48] He explained that "cases in which a war between the United States and a public enemy may exist without the sanction of Congress—as where an unexpected war is commenced against the United States and waged before Congress acts upon the subject."[49] Van Buren (and subsequent presidents) relied on this opinion for recognizing that Congress need not approve a president's use of military force in an emergency and for authorizing military force by means other than formal declarations of war, including appropriations measures.[50]

Van Buren was forced to further consider the conditions for using military force when, in response to some Americans' joining southern Canadians in rebelling against British rule, the British sank an American steamer, *Caroline*, which had transported supplies to the insurgents but was docked in Schlosser, New York. Van Buren issued a neutrality proclamation calling for strict adherence to the law and warning that "no aid or countenance" would be given by the government to any citizen arrested in Canada.[51] Aware that no specific law authorized his proclamation, Van Buren formally asked Congress to revise existing legislation and to empower him to prevent neutrality violations and punish those who did so.[52] On March 10, 1838, Congress enacted a neutrality law along the lines suggested by Van Buren, who quickly signed it into law.[53] Van Buren's actions gave Congress time to act, and the law, which lasted for two years, effectively ratified what Van Buren had done.[54]

Violence was threatening to break out on the United States' southern border as well. Prior to Van Buren's inauguration, Texas had assembled its own government, revolted against Mexican rule, and applied for statehood during Jackson's last days in office. On December 21, 1836, Jackson issued a special message advising Congress to recognize the sovereignty of Texas. Three days before Van Buren's inauguration, the Senate approved a resolution recognizing Texas as an independent nation. But the Senate left the question of annexation to Van Buren to decide. After his inauguration, Texas authorities demanded that he approve their request and threatened that if he failed they would sign treaties with other nations. Though he had called a special session of Congress on the issue to begin on September 4, 1837, Van Buren consulted with his cabinet and announced his opposition to the annexation on August 25. That same day, Secretary of State Forsyth delivered a statement in which he explained that there was no constitutional basis for annexing a sovereign state and suggested that such action might be construed as an act of war against Mexico. After negotiations with Mexico broke down, Van Buren asked Congress "to decide upon the time, the mode, and the measure of redress."[55] Nothing happened for the next several months until the Mexican government proposed on April 7, 1838, and Van Buren agreed soon thereafter, to submit injury claims of American citizens against the Mexican government to a special arbitration commission.[56] While this episode allowed Van Buren to reinforce the president's unilateral authority to take the initiative to determine the appropriate mode of settling international disputes, it angered southern leaders who were eager to admit Texas into the Union as a slave state.

The Indian removals, as well as the violence erupting over the United States' northern[57] and southern boundaries, prompted the war secretary, Joel Poinsett, to propose a standing army. For years, Congress had opposed authorizing a standing army because it was undemocratic and antithetical to the republican view that every citizen should have the requisite civic virtue to serve his country and that a standing army would undermine the American people's civic virtue since they would rely on the professionals to fight their battles. Nonetheless, Poinsett persuaded Van Buren to sign a bill enlarging the regular armed forces to over 12,000 troops.[58] When it did not appear that the bill's provisions would be enough to keep peace on the northern border, Van Buren considered a bill organizing state militias into providing additional support.[59]

This time, Van Buren balked. Whigs warned that, with the president in charge of an army of over 12,000 troops, he would be able to use military force to expand his powers and tenure. In response, Van Buren issued a lengthy public letter in which he withdrew support from Poinsett's militia plan. He explained that, had he read the proposal more thoroughly, he would have voiced his constitutional objections—that Congress did not have the power to "organize, arm, and discipline" the militia as Poinsett had suggested and that militia "training" was a power the Tenth Amendment reserved exclusively to the states.[60] Stopping the plan kept the president and Congress from directly interfering with state militias.

Shaping Presidential Administration

One of the most significant dimensions of Van Buren's presidency was his influence on presidential administration—the president's control over the personnel, organization, and entities functioning within the executive branch. First, he followed President Jackson's lead in endorsing rotation of office, the principle that the president had the authority unilaterally to remove all executive branch officials whenever and however he preferred. Based on this principle, Jackson had removed record numbers of executive branch personnel to create jobs for loyal Democrats. When Van Buren became president, he had little reason to remove people from office, since most were loyal Democrats. But, as one scholar noted, "Van Buren's removals, in 1839 and 1840 when he was looking forward to a second term, suggested . . . that a new rule of party allegiance, as well as party membership, was to be required of officeholders."[61]

While Van Buren's removals upset many senators who believed he should have consulted with them before removing officers whom the Senate had confirmed, his commitment to rotation in office was instrumental to establishing what has become known as the party system. In fact, Jackson and Van Buren introduced the notion of party government. Party government depended on national political parties, and Jackson, with Van Buren as his chief strategist, had won the presidency twice as the Democratic nominee with the assistance of a national campaign organization. A central component of party government was the spoils system that they helped to establish as a fixture of American politics. Their achievement is of constitutional importance, not only because of its implications for a president's control over his administration, but also as a rejection of the hopes of many framers (and former presidents such as John Quincy Adams) that the ravages of party could be avoided in favor of leadership by a disinterested class of elites who were committed to an apolitical "common good." Opponents of the party system claimed that it allowed leaders to subvert the public welfare to partisan interests. However,

Van Buren and Jackson disagreed. They believed that rotation in office ensured more democratic government, brought the government closer to the people, and made it more accountable while increasing a president's ability to put people into office that would be loyal to him and his constitutional and programmatic priorities.

The party system did not, however, always produce good outcomes. Sometimes party leaders pressured presidents to risk the public welfare for the sake of poor, even bad, appointments of political allies or friends. Van Buren's enemies were thus delighted when one of the beneficiaries of the party system he and Jackson had championed, Samuel Swartwout, proved to be historically awful. In fact, he was responsible for defrauding the federal government of more than one million dollars—the largest amount ever up to that time—while he was serving as the customs collector of New York City. Over Van Buren's objections, President Jackson had named Swartwout as the New York customs collector in January 1829 and reappointed him at the outset of his second term. When Swartwout's appointment expired on March 29, 1838, Van Buren refused to reappoint him to a third term in spite of strong pressure from Jackson and other loyal Jacksonians.

While his refusal to reappoint Swartwout underscored Van Buren's own commitment to rotation in office, he and congressional leaders from both parties realized that Swartwout's crimes had enormous consequences for the independent treasury plan then being debated in Congress. In fact, Whigs criticized the plan for loosening oversight of customs services, while Democrats believed it would tighten it. The Treasury Department and the House initiated formal investigations into Swartwout's misconduct in spite of the fact that he had left the country with the money he had stolen. With Whigs controlling the House investigation and the treasury secretary in charge of the department's inquiry, it was not surprising that their respective reports reflected the different viewpoints of Whigs and the Democrats on economic policy and the relative advantages or merits of the National Bank and an independent treasury.

Treasury Secretary Woodbury got the treasury report out first. It was the product of the president's conviction that he had the inherent authority to order such an investigation and that he was accountable for addressing the misconduct. The report was only a page long and documented that the fraud had largely occurred while the National Bank was the treasury's fiscal agent and was operating independently from the Treasury Department's control.[62] The report attributed the misconduct to the bank's lax oversight and corruption and included documentation of Swartwout's corrupt practices.

Six Whig House members who opposed the independent treasury plan wrote the majority report. Not surprisingly, it blamed the Van Buren administration for Swartwout's misconduct. It cited as the principal causes of the fraud Woodbury's lax oversight of the Treasury Department.[63] Democratic Senator William Rives from Virginia went further to charge Woodbury with corrupt or deceitful practices, including an undisclosed connection he had agreed to maintain with the National Bank, a connection that Woodbury vigorously denied and submitted documentation to disprove.[64]

The minority report primarily focused on the corruption within the customs house and possible reforms. It cited as a major reason for the fraud Swartwout's complete control over the appointments of the other officials in the New York customs house, who were thus loyal to him and not prone to question or monitor his conduct. The report suggested reforms for avoiding similar problems in the future, including empowering the president to appoint all responsible clerks and auditors (and therefore making them all accountable to him), requiring the clerks and auditors in the customs house to make regular reports to the Treasury Department, and arranging for frequent, unexpected inspections.[65]

The significance of the House committee report on Swartwout is that the president did not object to the constitutionality of the committee's investigation or censure of Swartwout and Woodbury. Whereas President Jackson had objected that his censure by the Senate was an unconstitutional bypass of the federal impeachment process, Van Buren left it to the minority on the investigating committee to respond to the majority report. Neither Van Buren nor the minority report questioned the constitutional authority of a House committee to censure—or criticize—a high-ranking executive branch official. Indeed, the committee's report, investigation, and censure became important precedents followed by the House for the remainder of the nineteenth century.

Van Buren's efforts to consolidate control over his administration included his issuing the first executive order on the maximum number of hours that federal employees could be required to work. He ordered "that all persons" who did physical labor on public works projects "be required to work the number of hours required by the ten-hour system" (which would have established a maximum ten-hour day for the workers covered).[66] This order was significant because it regulated activity that many members of Congress maintained was beyond the scope of federal power, much less the president's singular control. Nonetheless, they could not produce a law blocking Van Buren's initiative, which reinforced the president's unilateral authority to direct the activities and working conditions of executive branch personnel.

Last, Van Buren had mixed success in challenging congressional oversight and judicial review over executive action. The outcomes of his challenges had significant consequences for the independence of presidential control over his administration.

In his first year in office, Van Buren confronted a dilemma raising an issue similar to the one raised in the seminal case of *Marbury v. Madison*[67]—the extent of a cabinet officer's discretion *not* to follow a law or judicial order of which he disapproved. The officer involved was Amos Kendall, who served as postmaster general for both Jackson and Van Buren. While serving Jackson, Kendall rejected a contractor's claim against his department. Kendall asked Jackson to approve his decision, but Jackson referred the matter to Congress, which enacted a law authorizing the Treasury Department's solicitor to make a final settlement on the matter.[68] The solicitor authorized one, which Kendall refused to follow. The matter came back to Jackson, who both asked his attorney general to produce an official opinion and asked Congress to consider a possible legislative solution. The attorney general's opinion upheld the solicitor's authority and recognized the postmaster general's duty to comply with the solicitor's final settlement,[69] while the Senate determined no further legislation was required and adopted a report of its Post Office Committee directing Kendall to pay the disputed amount.[70] Kendall refused, and the contractor requested a writ of mandamus from the local circuit court. When the court issued the writ to Kendall,[71] he ignored it. By then, Van Buren was president, and he approved an appeal to the Supreme Court.

In *Kendall v. United States*,[72] the Court unanimously upheld the circuit court, one of the most important decisions on the obligations of executive officials to comply with judicial process. Justice Smith Thompson's opinion for the Court explained its three rulings: First, he found that although the president was "beyond the reach of any other department" (with the exception of the federal impeachment process),[73] other officers in the executive branch were not.[74] He rejected the Van Buren's administration contention that executive branch officials were not subject to any legal constraints (other than working for the president).[75] Justice Thompson explained that this position required "vesting in the President a dispensing power which has no countenance to its support in any part of the Constitution, and is asserting a principle which, if carried out in its results to all cases falling within it, would be clothing the President with a power to control the legislation of Congress, and paralyze the administration of justice. To contend that the obligation imposed on the President to see the laws faithfully executed implies a power to forbid their execution is a novel construction of the Constitution, and is entirely inadmissible."[76]

Second, the Court upheld Congress's power to assign "ministerial duties" to executive officials (other than the president). It had done so in its law requiring the postmaster general to comply with the findings of the Treasury Department solicitor. Such compulsion was, according to the Court, "a matter resting entirely in the discretion of Congress."[77]

Third, the Court upheld the circuit court's power to issue a writ of mandamus. Justice Thompson explained, "The power to issue a writ of mandamus in a proper case is a part of the common law, and it has been fully recognized as in practical operation in a case decided in the" highest court of a state or the District of Columbia.[78]

Van Buren's decision to fully litigate the matter proved disastrous for the unitary theory of the executive, which, in its strongest form, holds that the Constitution vests presidents with complete control over the exercise of all executive power.[79] Jackson had refused to allow the matter to be drawn into the courts and preferred to broker political compromises when disputes arose. In choosing to take the case to the Court, Van Buren risked losing not just Kendall's case but the opportunity for subsequent presidents to assert a similar theory of executive power. Moreover, Van Buren's compliance with the Court's orders validated the exercise of judicial review over an executive official's actions, and he reinforced this power when he failed to get the House to agree with the Senate to abolish the circuit court's mandamus power.[80]

Two years later, the Van Buren administration brought another case involving a similar issue. In this case, the widow of naval hero Commodore Stephen Decatur had requested naval secretary James Paulding to pay her pensions from both a general law authorizing pensions to widows of naval officers "who had died in the naval service"[81] and a separate law granting a special pension to Decatur's widow.[82] Based on an official opinion from the attorney general,[83] Paulding construed the two laws as allowing the widow to choose which pension she preferred but did not entitle her to both. Van Buren upheld Paulding's decision. In response to Paulding's refusal to pay, the widow asked for a writ of mandamus from the same circuit court that had issued one against Kendall. This time, it rejected the request, and the widow appealed the decision to the Supreme Court.

In *Paulding v. Decatur*,[84] the Supreme Court upheld the circuit court's ruling. In his opinion for the Court, Chief Justice Roger Taney explained that the controlling precedent was *Kendall*, particularly its recognition of the distinction between discretionary and ministerial acts. Taney found that neither the general pensions law nor the special one imposed a ministerial duty on Paulding. Instead, he found, Paulding had discretion under the laws to allow the widow a choice of which pension she preferred. Taney explained,

The duty required by the [special pension law] was to be performed by [the naval secretary] as the head of one of the executive departments in the ordinary discharge of his duties. In general, such duties, whether imposed by act of Congress or by resolution, are not merely ministerial duties. The head of an executive department of the government, in the administration of the various and important concerns of his office, is continually required to exercise judgment and discretion. He must exercise his judgment in expounding the laws and resolutions of Congress, under which he is from time to time required to act.[85]

He concluded that Paulding acted within his authority when he used his discretion to allow the widow a choice of which pension she preferred.

In *Kendall* and *Paulding*, both the legislative and executive branches secured important victories. In *Kendall*, the Court gave Congress the last word in imposing ministerial duties. But the ground arguably lost there by the Van Buren administration was regained in *Paulding*, and its victory in *Paulding* provided a useful precedent for subsequent executive officials to follow in seeking to oppose legislative direction or to insulate their acts from judicial review.

VAN BUREN'S CONSTITUTIONAL achievements laid the groundwork for the undoing of his presidency. First, the party system that he and Jackson had created provided a template for the Whigs to follow in the 1840 election. The Whigs improved on what Democrats had done in the previous two elections and assembled a more effective strategy and organization to secure their first victory in a presidential election. Second, Van Buren's restrictive view of federal power was disastrous. The independent treasury plan that it produced was a political calamity since it did not relieve the widespread hurt caused by the depression, and its failure underscored the futility and ineffectiveness of his unimaginative, narrow construction of federal power. Constitutionally and politically, Van Buren had become a pariah.

Van Buren left office a loser, a perception that he was unable to shake for the remainder of his life. The subsequent shifts in his political positions—and in the corresponding constitutional views to support them—reinforced the perception. His public opposition to the annexation of Texas to compete (unsuccessfully) for the Democratic nomination for president in 1844; his support in 1846 for the Wilmot Proviso, which banned slavery in territories; his third-party candidacy for the presidency in 1848 (the first by a former president), which cost the Democrats the election; and his rejoining the

Democrats in 1860 and supporting the Union and President Lincoln after the outbreak of the Civil War, made him look opportunistic rather than principled.

Van Buren's evolving constitutional convictions were costly to his political viability and reputation. Perhaps the best that could be said was that he was a constitutional work in progress. His understanding of executive power grew over time, and his defense of federal power intensified the more the states opposed it. As his principles developed, they increasingly alienated states' rights advocates, reinforced his enemies' perceptions of him as unremittingly self-serving, and sharpened the stakes of the constitutional debates throughout the remainder of the antebellum era.

2

William Henry Harrison, March–April 1841

BEING A FORGOTTEN president would be an improvement for William Henry Harrison. From 1948 through 2005, experts rated the presidents at least seven times, except for William Henry Harrison and James Garfield. They did not rank either Harrison or Garfield because each had served for less than a year as president. Garfield served for six and a half months, while Harrison died one month and a day after his inauguration. On March 4, 1841, Harrison, who had just turned sixty-eight, tried to demonstrate his physical stamina by delivering an inaugural address of more than 8,000 words. It was the longest inaugural address in American history. Unfortunately, he wore no hat or coat as he spoke in icy winds. He caught a severe cold, which lapsed into pneumonia and pleurisy, to which he succumbed. He was thus weak and ill throughout the thirty-one days of his presidency.

Yet Harrison's presidency is distinctive for many reasons. His father signed the Declaration of Independence, and he was the last president who was born a British subject.[1] At sixty-eight, he was the oldest man to be elected president until Ronald Reagan's inauguration in 1981. Harrison was the first Whig—the forerunner of the modern Republican Party—to be elected president and the first president to die in office. He holds the record for the shortest presidency in history. Moreover, the 1840 presidential campaign is the first to be waged between two well-organized national parties and the first in which women participated significantly.[2] Harrison was, like Washington and Jackson before him, elected president based on image—specifically, as an elder statesman and as the hero of the Battle of Tippecanoe, which had been fought against a confederacy of Native Americans. Harrison was the first president to promise to serve only for a single term, and he was the first of eight Ohioans elected president.[3] From 1828 to 1860, Harrison was the only president, besides Lincoln, who was not from the South or disposed to be reflexively sympathetic to slavery. Harrison was the third general elected president (after Washington and Jackson) and the first to pledge to reform the spoils system. He is the first of four presidents who made no Supreme Court appointments[4] and the only president whose grandson became president.[5]

While none of these distinctions is based on anything Harrison actually did as president, a closer look at Harrison's actions, particularly in the five months between his election in November 1840 and his death on April 4, 1841, indicates his growing resistance to the Whig Party's conception of the president as a weak figurehead who should defer to the will of Congress on domestic policymaking. Even during his brief presidency, Harrison began to show that Whigs' conception of the presidency was unworkable and that he was willing to sacrifice short-term political advantages to protect presidential prerogatives.

Confronting Clay and the Whigs

To understand Harrison's first blow against the Whig conception of presidency, we need to appreciate what Americans expected from him. His successful run for the presidency in 1840 was actually his second try. On both attempts, he ran as the newly formed Whig Party's nominee against Van Buren.

The Whig Party was primarily committed to two things: The first was opposition to Jackson's and Van Buren's usurpations of legislative authority. The second was commitment to legislative supremacy, particularly in domestic policymaking. The Whigs envisioned the president as a weak minister whose primary responsibilities were following Congress's lead and implementing the laws it enacted. In his inaugural address, Harrison was expressing Whig principles when he sharply distinguished himself from Jackson and Van Buren by emphasizing the limits of executive power and the broad scope of congressional authority. Harrison rejected any "fair construction" of the Constitution that "would be found to constitute the President a part of the legislative power."[6] He asserted, "It is preposterous to suppose that the President . . . could better understand the wants and wishes of the people than their own immediate representatives."[7] Thus, Harrison expressed the Whig Party line that the presidential veto should be used "only first, to protect the Constitution from violation; secondly, the people from the effects of hasty legislation where their will has probably been disregarded or not well understood and thirdly, to prevent the effects of combinations of the rights of minorities." These opinions were not just rejections of Jackson's and Van Buren's conceptions of presidential power. They should strike any reader as completely at odds with what we know about the modern presidency. For an important development in the American constitutional system was the ultimate repudiation of this "Whig" conception of the weak president in favor of the contemporary view of the president as a pivotal player in introducing legislation and then vetoing legislation he dislikes. The interesting question is to what extent Harrison believed or began to question his party's orthodoxy.

The first major surprise of Harrison's presidency involved his disastrous relationship with Henry Clay. As a founder of the Whig Party, Clay had run unsuccessfully as its presidential nominee against Jackson in 1832, and his desire to be president was as strong as ever in the run-up to the 1840 presidential election. Well before that election, Clay had known Harrison and been one of his most influential friends and sponsors. In the War of 1812, Clay helped Harrison to obtain a commission as a brigadier general in the regular army and later in full command of the Army of the Northwest. In 1828, Clay persuaded President John Quincy Adams to appoint Harrison, then one of Ohio's two U.S. senators, as minister to Colombia. By 1835, Harrison's fortunes turned, and the only job he found was clerk of the Cincinnati Court of Common Pleas. It thus came as a huge disappointment to Clay to lose the Whig presidential nomination to a man of Harrison's low stature in both 1836 and 1840. The 1840 defeat was particularly hard for Clay to take. He had hoped to erase the shame of losing to Jackson in 1832 by defeating Jackson's self-selected successor. By 1840, it was evident that, because of the economic depression, the Whig nominee for president was going to beat Van Buren in the general election.

But Harrison, not Clay, better understood how times had changed. In fact, the Whigs held the first national nominating convention in history that year, and Harrison's lieutenants—including New York's William Seward and his political mentor Thurlow Weed—were prepared. They arranged for the convention to count each state's votes for president as a whole, thereby nullifying the advantage Clay would have had if every delegate's vote counted. Counting all the delegates would have given Clay a winning margin, but counting each state as one worked to Harrison's advantage.

Though hurt and angered by his loss, Clay campaigned hard for Harrison in the 1840 general election. After Harrison won, Clay believed Harrison owed him—big time. He had helped Harrison win the popular vote in Kentucky and wanted nothing less than control over the new administration. To achieve this, he needed Harrison to put Clay's people in charge of the administration. Aware that other Whigs wanted appointments for themselves or their friends, Clay was determined to be the power driving the Harrison administration. When

Clay learned shortly after the election that Harrison was traveling to Frankfurt, Kentucky, to meet with Charles Wickliffe, an anti-Clay Whig who had not supported the National Bank that Clay had long championed, Clay went there immediately. Concerned about rumors that he was going to be Senator Clay's puppet, Harrison was wary of Clay. When he learned that Clay was on his way to intercept him, Harrison sent a letter telling Clay that he preferred to delay any meeting with him.[8] Clay ignored the message and tracked Harrison down. When the two finally met in person, Clay told Harrison what he wanted. Harrison knew he owed the senator and agreed to the first favor he asked—not to appoint Wickliffe to the cabinet. Clay went further and implored the president-elect to spend a week at his plantation nearby. Harrison reluctantly acquiesced. He appreciated the need to mollify Clay and accept the invitation; he had even joked in a speech on the way to meet Clay that, if the Constitution allowed it, he would have given the presidency to him.

During his ensuing stay with Clay, Harrison reputedly offered him any cabinet post he wanted, but Clay said he wished to remain in the Senate. Clay repeatedly pressed the incoming president to accept his recommendations of other cabinet appointments, including his political ally and fellow Kentucky senator, John J. Crittenden, as attorney general and John Clayton of Delaware as treasury secretary. Clay made other requests, urging Harrison to call a special session of Congress to address the ongoing fallout from the national depression that had proved to be Van Buren's undoing. Although Harrison's legendary eagerness to please was put to the test, it is significant that he managed to leave without committing himself on any matters, including appointments.

The next meeting between the two men went worse than the first. Shortly after Harrison arrived in Washington to prepare for his inauguration, Clay asked to meet with him to discuss cabinet appointments. By the time they met, the senator was upset because Harrison had decided not to appoint Clayton as treasury secretary but rather Thomas Ewing, who had been recommended by Clay's rival for leadership of the Whig Party in Congress, Massachusetts senator Daniel Webster. Clay told Harrison he was unhappy that Webster, whom Harrison had decided to appoint as secretary of state, was becoming the source of power in the new administration. Clay kept pressing Harrison to appoint Clayton to other posts. On the night before Harrison was going to announce that he was nominating George Badger of North Carolina as secretary of the navy, Clay called on Harrison to urge him to appoint Clayton instead. After Clay refused to take no for an answer, Harrison ended the meeting by declaring, "Mr. Clay, you forget that I am the President."[9] Clay angrily left the meeting, but he was not done.

While Clay did not press Harrison further on cabinet appointments because the cabinet turned out to be generally agreeable to him, including his friend Crittenden as attorney general, Clay was unhappy with Webster's expanding influence over administration appointments. After learning that Webster and three other cabinet members had approved Harrison's appointment of Edward Curtis to the collectorship of the port of New York City, Clay asked to meet again with Harrison. The collectorship controlled more patronage than any other governmental post except for postmaster general, and Clay resented Curtis because he had helped Harrison defeat Clay in the Whig primary in Pennsylvania. Clay urged Harrison to change his mind and appoint his preferred candidate. The president refused. The senator stormed out of the meeting after angrily chastising Harrison for not giving him his due in controlling patronage.

Clay's last encounter with Harrison ruptured their relationship for good. Just after the inauguration, Clay met the president, this time to continue pressing him to call a special session of Congress to deal with financial exigencies. Harrison and his advisers knew what the senator wanted, but they were distrustful because they knew the special session would allow him to address the nation and to assert control over the administration's agenda. Rather than decide himself, Harrison followed Webster's advice to put the question to his cabinet. It split three to three over the need to call a special session of Congress. Harrison broke the tie with a negative vote. When Clay heard the outcome, he quickly wrote a letter to Harrison saying that he hoped to dine with him that evening, urging him to reconsider the question, and suggesting any inaction on the matter would make the president look indecisive.[10] Clay enclosed with his letter a draft of the proclamation Harrison should sign to call the special session. The gesture pushed Harrison over the edge. Upon reading the letter, he angrily wrote back, "You use the privilege of a friend to lecture me and I will take the same liberty with you—you are too impetuous."[11] He said he would make no final decision before the beginning of the next week and concluded that he preferred "this mode of answering your note to a conversation in the presence of others."[12]

In another fit of anger, Clay responded in what turned out to be the final communication between the two men. Clay denied trying to dictate policy or appointments. He complained that his political enemies had poisoned Harrison's opinion of him. He suggested that if he could not express his opinions "as a citizen and as a Senator, in regard to public matters," he ought to retire from public life.[13] He expressed the "hope" that by remaining in the Senate he could be of service to his country. He closed the letter by writing, "I do not wish to trouble you with answering this note" and remarking that he trusted

Harrison would appreciate the purity of his motives, "whatever others may say or insinuate."[14] Clay then left Washington, though two days later financial exigencies—including the collapse of the national bank in Philadelphia, a depleted treasury, and the impending bankruptcy of several states—forced Harrison to call a special session of Congress to convene on May 31. Though it was only two weeks into Harrison's term, Clay never saw or spoke to Harrison again.

Clay's alienation of Harrison was remarkable because it meant that the nation's first Whig president was no longer speaking to the party's most powerful congressional leader. They were not speaking because Harrison had increasingly resisted becoming Clay's puppet. The breach was not just a clash in personalities; it derived in part from a fundamental disagreement over the Whigs' constitutional philosophy. By the time he died, Harrison had shown he had been recognizing the unworkability of the Whig notion of the president as a weak minister who should be subservient to the will of Congress. Given Clay's preeminence in the Senate, it would have been impossible to be subservient to the Senate while resisting Clay. Thus, it appears that Harrison understood that a president could be somewhat, perhaps even largely, deferential to Congress, but he could not always defer to congressional leaders' demands. More importantly, Harrison apparently realized that a president's reflexive deference to Congress undermined the Constitution's system of checks and balances, which required presidents to maintain their authority and to protect their prerogatives and the executive branch from congressional domination. Harrison had almost said as much at his inauguration—words that may have fallen on deaf ears: "the great danger to our institutions does not appear to me to be in a usurpation by the Government of power not granted by the people, but by the accumulation in one of the departments of that which was assigned to others. Limited as are the powers which have been granted, still enough which have been granted to constitute a despotism if concentrated in one of the departments."[15] By the time he died, Harrison had given signals that he understood that legislative supremacy posed the danger of allowing Congress to usurp presidential powers.

Harrison's resistance suggests he appreciated that the president had to be strong enough to protect its peculiar prerogatives from congressional encroachments. Moreover, Harrison's retorts to Clay reflect his apparent realization of the significance of the president's election itself, suggesting that he had some obligation to represent a different constituency than congressional leaders did. If checks and balances were to be genuinely meaningful, legislative supremacy could not be reconciled with presidential abdication of authority. Something had to give.

Of course, it is impossible to know what Harrison would have done had he completed his term. Even if Harrison and Clay made peace, it seems unlikely

FIGURE 2.1 A rare anti-Whig satire, giving a cynical view of the party's image-building and manipulation of candidate William Henry Harrison. Two influential Whigs, Senator Henry Clay (left) and Congressman Henry A. Wise, operate the strings of a "dancing-jack" toy figure of Harrison in military uniform.

Source: Library of Congress Prints and Photographs Division, Washington, D.C. 20540 USA http://hdl.loc.gov/loc.pnp/pp.print

that Harrison could forget the words he had spoken to Clay. Nor is it likely that Clay could forget them. Moreover, Harrison, who had pledged to serve a single term, was not likely inclined to weaken his defense of presidential prerogatives from further attacks by Clay. Harrison's resistance to Clay's domination was no secret. Nearly everyone understood why Clay had left town before the end of the legislative session, and its significance was not lost on two younger Whigs who revered Clay—Millard Fillmore and Abraham Lincoln, each of whom later resisted legislative supremacy even more than Harrison did.

Upholding Rotation in Office

As the ninth president of the United States, Harrison followed eight other chief executives, who had split over the practice known as rotation in office— replacing people appointed by their predecessors with their friends and allies. Four of Harrison's predecessors had opposed the practice—Washington (in his second term), John Adams, Madison, and John Quincy Adams, while Jefferson, Monroe, Jackson, and Van Buren had embraced it.[16] The presidents who opposed rotation in office maintained that federal appointees were entitled to remain in office as long as they were performing their jobs well. Monroe had signed the first Tenure in Office Act, which limited the tenure of certain federal appointees to four years but provided that they could be removed at the president's pleasure. John Quincy Adams consistently reappointed people who did not support him once their commissions expired.

With Van Buren's help, Jackson created a political firestorm when he implemented the spoils system, which was rotation in office by another name. The point of this system was to replace an outgoing president's appointees with allies of the incoming president. Jackson saw this system as a basic presidential privilege—one that was essential for ensuring that a president had in place people whom he could trust to carry out his preferred policies. He believed a president should have complete removal power over any executive branch officials to ensure that they implemented *his* preferred policies or could be replaced with people who would. While, as the last chapter showed, Van Buren supported rotation in office, he had little or no need to rotate Jackson's friends out of office, for they were also his political allies.[17]

As a candidate, Harrison followed the Whig orthodoxy of urging reform of the spoils system that Jackson and Van Buren had championed. In his inaugural address, Harrison had pledged, like a good Whig, not to replace Van Buren's appointees with Whigs or to coerce governmental employees to make contributions to the Whigs to retain their positions.

Harrison sought a middle ground between Jackson's and Van Buren's practice of rewarding their friends with appointments and John Quincy Adams's practice of allowing hostile, unsupportive political appointees to remain in office. Harrison's problem was that keeping Van Buren's people in place meant frustrating Whigs who had elected him. To many if not most Whigs, reforming the spoils system meant replacing Democrats with Whigs. Nevertheless, Harrison promised in his inaugural address that treasury officers should not be removed without cause and vowed he would not remove a treasury officer without explaining why to Congress.

After four weeks in office, Harrison had a mixed record in keeping his word not to replace political appointees for partisan reasons. Although Harrison had been the recipient of an unusually large number of political appointments, he repeatedly vowed to oppose the wholesale removal of Democrats without cause. The vow echoed sentiments he had written in a letter prior to the election of 1836 declaring that executive power was granted for the public good and "not to requite personal favors or gratify personal animosities."[18] Moreover, Harrison's cabinet included Webster and Thomas Ewing, both of whom had argued as senators against rotation of office.[19] Shortly after his inauguration, Harrison asked Webster to circulate to all department secretaries a message instructing them that the payment of contributions or assessments by governmental employees would be regarded as cause for dismissal. He issued a strict order to all public officers and agents against interference in popular elections and receipt of compensation for party services. He declared that federal employees "are not expected to take an active or officious part in attempts to influence the minds or votes of others, such conduct being deemed inconsistent with the spirit of the Constitution and the duties of public agents acting under it."[20] Harrison wanted efficiency and honesty in government and took the unusual step of visiting every department to observe its operations. He requested reports detailing the activities and responsibilities of every office, and he promised to protect officeholders who were performing their jobs well. Yet in spite of Harrison's protestations to the contrary, the pressure from other Whig leaders to remove Democrats to create jobs for their friends was enormous. (Their persistence was undoubtedly one of the pressures exacerbating Harrison's failing health.) Harrison's cabinet even voted to make an extensive purge of Democrats. Ironically, Ewing defended the purge to counter Van Buren's "policy . . . to retain in office none but their active political adherents, those who would go for them thorough in all things; and the performance of the official duty, was far less requisite to a tenure in office, than electioneering services. Hence the offices had become for the most part filled with brawling offensive political partisans, of a very low moral standard—their official duties performed by substitutes, nor not performed at all."[21] Postmaster General Francis Granger probably had the highest numbers of dismissals. As one historian found, Granger, during his six months in office, had removed "39 of the 133 presidential postmasters, and by September 1841 almost 2500 postmasters had been appointed in the lesser offices to vacancies [which were caused] by removals. Granger later boasted that that he had removed 1700 postmasters and had he remained in the cabinet two or three weeks longer he would have removed 3000 more."[22]

Although Harrison did not fulfill his pledge to reform civil service, his limited success reflected the powerful forces aligned against such reform. No other president did better than Harrison until the obstacles to genuine civil service reform were overcome in 1881.

Ordering the Cabinet

Harrison further deviated from Whig orthodoxy in using his cabinet. The Constitution provides that a president "may require the opinion, in writing, of the principal officer in each of the executive departments, upon any subject relating to the duties of their respective offices."[23] While Jefferson construed this text as allowing his cabinet to vote on the most important matters confronting the administration and vesting in him the power to overrule their decisions if he saw fit,[24] the eight other presidents who preceded Harrison did not believe that the cabinet had any authority to bind them and differed only to the extent to which they consulted their cabinets.[25] Nevertheless, the six members of Harrison's cabinet believed in the Whig principle that *they* should direct *all* presidential actions. This belief derived from the Whig conception that the presidency should be subservient to Congress and the cabinet, which occupied offices created by Congress, was appointed with Senate consent, and could check executive usurpation of legislative authority.[26] Harrison's cabinet allowed him to preside over their meetings, but they insisted decisions should be made by majority rule, with each cabinet member having a single vote and Harrison only having a tie-breaking vote if the cabinet was deadlocked.[27]

Harrison appears to have been ambivalent about being subservient to his cabinet. The most dramatic confrontation arose when Webster told Harrison that the cabinet had rejected his preferred candidate and instead appointed James Wilson as the governor of Iowa. After a prolonged silence, Harrison wrote a few words on a slip of paper, which he asked Webster to read to the cabinet. The message was succinct: "William Henry Harrison, President of the United States."[28] Rising to his feet, Harrison angrily told the cabinet, "And William Henry Harrison, President of the United States, tells you, gentlemen, that, by ——, John Chambers shall be Governor of Iowa."[29]

While Harrison deferred to his cabinet on other occasions, it is probably no coincidence that Harrison's declaration to his cabinet echoed his earlier remonstrance to Clay that he was the president. Clearly, it took some effort for Harrison to make these declarations. They went against his characteristic eagerness to please others and contradicted the fundamental philosophy of the party that had nominated him to be president and whose party leaders were insisting throughout his short presidency on compliance with their wishes on appointments and cabinet predominance. When Harrison's protestations are coupled together, they suggest that once in office (and freed from the need to run for reelection) Harrison was recognizing the need to protect the presidency's institutional prerogatives and needs. The second rebuke, like the first, reflected his growing awareness that the Whig conception of the presidency was impractical. He might have realized that Jackson was not wrong when he claimed that the president was entitled, even obliged, to assert constitutional views independently from Congress.

IN HARRISON'S SHORT time as president, he took stands on three constitutional issues—legislative supremacy, rotation in office, and the proper role of the cabinet—that were important, incremental steps in the development of modern presidential power. And he took these steps after having accepted the constitutional innovation of managing party government begun under Jackson and Van Buren. These steps were small, but neither Clay nor other Whig leaders forgot them as they attempted unsuccessfully to assert their dominance over the next two presidents, who were more determined than Harrison to protect presidential prerogatives from congressional encroachments.

3

John Tyler, 1841–1845

IF JOHN TYLER had done nothing more than take the oath of office as president, his place in constitutional history would be ensured: As the first vice president to succeed to the presidency upon the incumbent's death, he established an enduring constitutional precedent on presidential succession. At fifty-one, he was the youngest man to date to become president, and he was widely believed to be Clay's man in the Democratic Party, since as a senator he agreed Jackson had become tyrannical. Though he had supported Jackson's election in 1828, Tyler opposed Jackson's aggressive unilateral exercises of presidential power and was the only senator to vote against Jackson's 1833 request for congressional authorization to use military force to collect the federal tariff from the state of South Carolina.[1] A year later, Tyler supported Clay's controversial resolution censuring Jackson for refusing to share internal administration documents pertaining to his withdrawing federal funds from the National Bank for redeposit in state banks. In 1836, Tyler shocked the political world by resigning his Senate seat and membership in the Democratic Party to protest the Virginia legislature's instruction that he vote to expunge Jackson's censure.

In spite of this history, Tyler and Clay quickly became bitter political foes. Immediately after learning of Harrison's death, Clay, who had not yet returned to the capital, wrote to Tyler to extend his best wishes and to urge his support for rechartering the National Bank, which Jackson and Van Buren had blocked. Although Clay expected Tyler to be more pliable than Harrison had been, Clay was determined not to settle for mere declarations of loyalty—he wanted Tyler's unequivocal, clear expression of support for the Whig agenda. When Tyler's response did not contain the explicit reassurances that he had requested, Clay asked to meet with him in person. The meeting did not go well. Shortly after it began, Clay demanded that Tyler support the National Bank's rechartering, but the president demurred. He asked Clay to delay the bank's rechartering so other legislative initiatives could be considered first. Since Tyler had pledged to adhere to Harrison's priorities and Harrison had promised to back the Whig platform, Clay pressed Tyler harder to support the National Bank.

He again declined. The senator grew increasingly angry with Tyler's objections, and his mounting frustration angered Tyler more. Finally, Tyler, who was at least as stubborn as Clay, lost his temper, and the two men began shouting at each other. Tyler ended the meeting abruptly by saying, "Then, sir, I wish you to understand this—that you and I were born in the same district, that we have fed upon the same food, and have breathed the same natal air. Go you now, then, Mr. Clay, to your end of the avenue, where stands the Capitol, and there perform your duty to the country as you shall think proper. So help me God, I shall do mine at this end of it as I shall see proper."[2]

The conflicts reflected the two men's nearly diametrically opposite interpretations of the Constitution: Clay championed the Whig conception of legislative supremacy on almost every matter, a conception that included extensive federally sponsored internal improvements that were part of a program known as the American System, which included the National Bank. Tyler was a strict constructionist who considered state sovereignty the basic default rule of constitutional interpretation. He believed that all gaps and ambiguities in the Constitution should be construed in favor of state sovereignty. He consistently opposed as unconstitutional federal interference with slaveholder rights and the American System, including the protective tariff favored by Whigs. Consequently, Tyler's nearly four years as president featured some of the most heated congressional-presidential conflicts in American history: By the time he left office, he had become the first presidential incumbent to be denied the opportunity by a major party to run for another term, the first and only president to be expelled from his party, the first president to be investigated for impeachment by the House of Representatives, the second president to be censured by the House or Senate, and the first president to have a veto overridden by Congress. Of the five nineteenth-century vice presidents who became president because of the incumbent's death, Tyler served the longest as president and cast more vetoes than any other pre–Civil War president except for Jackson. He strongly defended the independence of the president's claims of executive privilege and exercises of his nominating and veto authorities, and he had the most cabinet *and* the most Supreme Court nominations rejected by the Senate, two records that remain important precedents supporting the independence of the Senate in the federal appointments process. Tyler helped to establish the single, most important precedent interpreting the Constitution's Republican Guarantee Clause, and Congress's repeated efforts to punish Tyler for perceived abuses of power established enduring precedents pertaining to impeachment, censure, and oversight. While Tyler was an unpopular president, he produced one of the richest constitutional legacies of any American president.

Fixing Presidential Succession

Tyler's resistance to Whig principles was apparent from the outset—indeed, with his first act in office: By declaring himself president rather than acting president, Tyler rejected the Whigs' understanding of presidential succession.

Immediately after Harrison's death, there was widespread uncertainty over Tyler's legal status. There was no precedent on point, and the pertinent constitutional provision was ambiguous:

> In case of the removal of the President from office, or of his death, resignation, or inability to discharge the powers and duties of the said office, the same shall devolve on the Vice-President, declaring what officer shall then act as President, and such officer shall act accordingly, and until the disability be removed, or a President shall be elected.[3]

The question was whether "the same" refers to the office or the president's powers and duties. Prominent authorities had divided over whether "the same" meant that a vice president automatically became president and maintained that status through the end of the term or that a vice president became merely an acting president, who had no entitlement to claim the office for himself since he had not been elected president.[4]

Since Tyler was not in Washington when Harrison died, the cabinet and congressional leaders had at least a day to ponder his status before he returned to the nation's capital.[5] In the Senate, Clay argued that the powers and duties of the office of the presidency, but not the office, devolved upon Tyler. Harrison's cabinet agreed with Clay and addressed Tyler as vice president in its first meeting with him. Just before the meeting, Secretary of State Daniel Webster had asked the clerk of the Supreme Court to relay a message requesting Chief Justice Roger Taney's counsel on the proper constitutional procedure. Taney declined.[6]

Tyler arrived in Washington on April 6, 1841, with a well-conceived strategy in mind.[7] His first order of business was to meet with Harrison's cabinet. After Webster began the meeting welcoming Tyler as the vice president, Tyler immediately objected. He told the cabinet that the office of the presidency and all of its powers and duties had fully devolved upon him, automatically and immediately, at the moment of Harrison's death.[8] While there are no records of all the discussion within the meeting about Tyler's status, the outcome was clear: By the meeting's end, the cabinet unanimously agreed to recognize Tyler as the duly authorized president.

Tyler's next step was to publicly take another oath to certify his claim to the presidency. Although Tyler believed his succession was automatic, he agreed, after persistent urging by Presiding Judge William Cranch of the District of Columbia Circuit Court, to take the oath of office with the entire cabinet present. Cranch believed the new oath was necessary to remove any doubts about Tyler's status,[9] and he filed a statement with his reasoning with the copy of the oath he administered over Tyler's objection. Three days later, Tyler delivered a short speech that substituted for an inaugural address. He acknowledged that "the Presidential office" had "devolved" on him, explained the "principles" governing his administration, and called himself "Chief Magistrate" and "President."[10] Immediately thereafter, he moved into the White House, called for a public day of prayer and fasting to honor Harrison, and met with several foreign ministers to allay international concerns about the legitimacy of the transfer of power.[11]

Some doubts persisted in Congress. Whigs distrusted Tyler because of his having been a Democrat, while Democrats disliked him for leaving their party. Not long after Tyler took the presidential oath, Congress convened a special session to address his status. On May 31, 1841, Representative Henry Wise of Virginia introduced a resolution referring to Tyler as the president. After heated debate, the resolution passed with no change in wording.[12] The next day, Ohio's two senators led a protest against Tyler's succession. After some debate, the Senate voted 38–8 to recognize him as president.[13] Congress's action settled the matter, though some people persisted in calling Tyler "Acting President"[14] or mocking him as "His Accidency"[15] or "Vice-President-Acting President."[16]

Tyler's succession to the presidency became an important precedent in constitutional law because of the concerted efforts of Tyler and other national leaders. After Tyler left office, seven vice presidents followed his example.[17] In 1967, the precedent was officially codified with the adoption of the Twenty-fifth Amendment.[18] In the only application of this amendment, Gerald Ford became president when Richard Nixon resigned from office in 1974.

Tyler's precedent on presidential succession was hardly his only significant constitutional achievement. Just after he secured his status, Clay intensified his efforts to test Tyler's fidelity to Whig principles of governance. The ensuing contest produced historic precedents on the scopes of various presidential powers and congressional authority to check presidential abuse of power.

Defending Presidential Prerogatives

Tyler struck several more blows against Whigs' conception of the presidency. They fortified presidential powers in ways we largely take for granted today.

The Veto

Tyler's most dramatic break with Whig orthodoxy was his use of the veto. He cast six vetoes, the most of any antebellum president. His four pocket vetoes (vetoing bills by taking no action on them before Congress adjourned) are the most of any antebellum president except for Jackson. Yet the constitutional significance of Tyler's vetoes primarily depends on their grounds *and* the congressional responses they provoked. Tyler's first two vetoes had the greatest impact and reflected most clearly his understanding of presidential authority.[19]

The Whig position on the veto was well known to Tyler and other national leaders at the time: Whigs had long objected to both vetoes and pocket vetoes; they claimed the former should be used only against bills that were plainly unconstitutional and the latter were plainly unconstitutional.[20]

Initially, Tyler was so careful in his public statements about his veto authority that he confused Whig leaders. On the one hand, Tyler had promised in his short address upon becoming president to approve "any constitutional measure, which originating in Congress, would have for its objective the restoration of a sound circulating medium, so essentially necessary to give confidence in all the transactions of life."[21] He further declared, "Those who are charged with . . . administration should carefully abstain from all attempts to enlarge the range of powers thus granted to the several departments of the Government other than by an appeal to the people for additional grants, lest by so doing they disturb that balance which the patriots and statesmen who framed the Constitution designed to establish between the Federal Government and the States comprising the Union."[22] Many Whigs construed these statements to mean that Tyler was prepared to accept incorporation of a national bank and a protective tariff. On the other hand, Tyler's omissions, ambiguities, and inferences upset Whig leaders. For instance, they were disturbed by his failures to expressly agree with two fundamental Whig principles—a president's promise not to run for reelection and a president's acknowledgment of legislative supremacy in domestic policymaking.

It had been the omissions and ambiguities in Tyler's April 9 address that prompted Clay to secure Tyler's express approval of the National Bank.[23]

After being banished to the Senate after his testy meeting with Tyler, Clay was determined to force the president to submit to his will or expose his infidelity to Whig principles of governance. Clay believed the opportunity was already on the calendar—the special session that Harrison had called for the end of May to address the continuing economic depression and the national government's impending bankruptcy. Clay was not moved, as were some Whigs, by Tyler's overtures to find common ground with Whig leaders or his declaration at the opening of the special session.[24] For Clay, actions spoke louder than words.

The first test came on August 6, 1841, when the House approved the bill that the Senate had previously approved establishing the Third National Bank.[25] Tyler warned Clay through his treasury secretary that the Supreme Court would likely find the provision establishing branch banks in the states to violate states' rights. Although Tyler tried to work out a solution to this problem with John Calhoun, Clay and his supporters rejected their suggestion and instead inserted into the final version of the provision a "compromise" enabling the states to disallow branches only immediately after the passage of the bank bill but allowing the National Bank to overrule these objections whenever it became "necessary and proper" to establish a branch office.[26]

Waiting the full ten days accorded to him by the Constitution before he acted, Tyler rejected the advice of his cabinet and vetoed the bill. In a special message, he explained his reasoning: First, he noted that the veto was completely consistent with the position he had taken on the constitutionality of the National Bank throughout his career. Second, he explained that signing the bill would have required him to violate his oath of office.[27] Third, Tyler pointed out two defective provisions—one that empowered the National Bank to discount notes and another that presumed conclusively state consent to the establishment of a bank in that state. The problem, in Tyler's opinion, was that the history of the discounting power demonstrated that it had "proved to be a fruitful source of favoritism and corruption, alike destructive to the public morals and the general weal." Since such a ground was not strictly constitutional, Tyler had, in proclaiming it a basis for his veto, demonstrated a veto did not have to be grounded only on constitutional bases. This was heresy insofar as Whigs were concerned, since Jackson had claimed the entitlement to base his vetoes on constitutional or policy grounds. Moreover, Tyler explained that the branching provision was constitutionally defective: "This iron rule is to give way to no circumstance—it is unbending and inflexible. It is the language of the master to the vassal—an unconditional answer is claimed forthwith; and delay, postponement or incapacity to answer, produces an implied assent, which is ever after irrevocable." The irrevocability of the implied assent of the states was "so violent, and, as they seem to me, so irrational, I cannot yield my consent. No court of justice would or could sanction them, without reversing all that is established in judicial proceeding, by introducing presumptions at variance with fact, and inferences at the expense of reason." Tyler concluded, "A State in a condition of duress would be presumed to speak, as an individual, manacled and in prison, might be presumed to be in enjoyment of freedom."

Tyler's veto exposed him to widespread ridicule and charges of "treason" by Whigs. Delighted that he had exposed Tyler's rejection of Whig principles, Clay began drafting a new bill before Tyler's message had been delivered to the Senate. Clay was determined that the new bill would end Tyler's presidency. Tyler asked Secretary of State Webster to broker a compromise that would be agreeable to both his administration and Whig leaders in Congress. He signaled to Clay and other Whigs in Congress that he was not opposed to a bill that created an institution in the District of Columbia that had agents in the states to handle the government's fiscal business, was not called a "bank," and lacked the power to discount notes. Tyler's efforts to broker a compromise was, however, a complete affront to the Whig conception of the presidency, since it showed that Tyler, like Jackson, wanted to take the lead in telling Congress what to do. Eager to call Tyler's bluff, Clay quickly pushed the Fiscal Corporation bill through the House and the Senate.

By the time the bill arrived on Tyler's desk, it was too late: He was no longer in the mood for compromise. Tyler had been pushed over the edge (or so he later claimed) by several intervening events. Among these were the flagrant disrespect that Clay had shown him by ridiculing Tyler's first veto on the Senate floor; a vicious letter in which Representative John Botts of Virginia, a Whig, accused Tyler of plotting treachery against the Whigs; and threats from the Whig Party to expel him and from his entire cabinet (except Webster) to resign if he vetoed the bill. After waiting six days, Tyler called everyone's bluff and vetoed the second bill. He concluded that the veto fulfilled his oath and enabled him to get rid of his cabinet.

The veto message of September 9, 1841, was a thorough, unambiguous rejection of Whig constitutional principles: First, the fact that it came to the House of Representatives in the form of a "Protest" conveyed the irreconcilable, widening political, constitutional, and ideological breaches between Tyler and the (Whig) leadership in Congress.[28] Indeed, this protest was the first of three that Tyler sent to the Congress.

At the outset of this first protest, Tyler explained that he had vetoed the bill "based upon the highest moral and religious obligations of conscience and the Constitution." Echoing Jackson again, the veto was not confined to constitutional grounds. Tyler went further to reject another basic tenet of the Whig Party, its conception of the constitutional order itself: "Mere regard to the will of the majority must not in a constitutional republic like ours control this sacred and solemn duty of a sworn officer." Tyler was advancing the notion, rejected by the Whigs, that the Constitution established a republic, not a democracy, in which the will of the popular majority should be strictly followed in adopting policies and exercising power. He next openly rejected the Whig conception of the veto, which had been linked to its conception of the polity as a democracy: "[T]o say that because a majority in Congress have passed a bill [the president] should therefore sanction it is to abrogate the power [of the veto] altogether and to render its insertion in the Constitution as a work of absolute supererogation." He explained that the "duty" of a president in deciding to sign a law or not "is to guard the fundamental will of the people themselves from (in this case, I admit, unintentional) change or infraction by a majority in Congress; and in that light alone do I regard the constitutional duty which I now most reluctantly discharge." The duty Tyler was describing was known as "the doctrine of presidential guardianship," which had been championed by Jackson himself. Tyler concluded with an expression of "regret[] that this department of the Government can not upon constitutional and other grounds concur with the legislative department in this last measure proposed to attain desirable objects." In short, the president was a separate constitutional authority who was not subservient to the will of the Congress.

The principal problem with the bill was, in Tyler's judgment, that it "assumes that Congress may invest a local institution with general or national powers." In Tyler's view, Congress's power to enact regulations for the District of Columbia was strictly akin to that of a state legislature in enacting laws for the state in which it operated, so that each was restricted to empowering an institution with strictly local authority within its respective jurisdiction. While the bill said it was doing nothing more than creating a local bank for the District of Columbia, it invested the fiscal corporation that it created with such extensive powers that "it can not be regarded as other than a national bank." It was bad enough that Congress was trying to do something different than it said, even worse that it had established the kind of institution that Tyler had repeatedly said was plainly bad policy and unconstitutional. In short, a national bank by any other name was a national bank, which was unconstitutional in Tyler's judgment.

The reaction to the veto was swift and dramatic: Within forty-eight hours, every member of the cabinet, with the exception of Webster, resigned in protest. (Although Webster publicly explained his reasons for remaining in the cabinet, he did not mention the most obvious one—resigning would have aligned him with Clay, his principal rival for leadership of the Whigs.) Within four days, a caucus of Whig members of Congress expelled Tyler from the Whig Party. Tyler had become, as Clay predicted, a man "without a party."

The friction between Tyler and the Whigs intensified in the next congressional session, even though Clay had resigned on March 31, 1842, to prepare for another presidential run. Indeed, it was the longest congressional session in history up until then and one of the most intense. For much of it, the Whigs persisted in calling for Tyler's resignation and refused to approve any legislation in order to deprive Tyler of another chance to exercise his veto.

But the failure to enact any legislation was a problem. The political pressure on Congress to raise tariffs was unbearable. The Compromise Tariff Act of 1833 had provided that the final reduction in duties to 20 percent or below was to be in place on July 1, 1842. If Congress made no change to the 1833 law, everyone recognized that a serious question was going to arise over whether any revenue could be lawfully collected after the first of July. It was already apparent at the outset of the summer of 1842 that the federal treasury was empty. Consequently, the House enacted the so-called Little Tariff Bill, which provided, in part, an extension until August 1, 1842, of all revenue laws in effect on June 1, 1842.[29] The purpose of the law was to continue rates above 20 percent and retain "the distribution of proceeds on the public lands." The bill posed an obvious challenge to Tyler by giving him the increase in tariffs he had long sought but at the price of a scheme—"distribution"—to which he had long objected as bad policy and unconstitutional.[30]

When Tyler vetoed the Little Tariff Bill, talk of impeachment intensified in the House. Though he had left Congress by then, Clay urged Congress to pass "just such another tariff as [Tyler] had vetoed. . . . Our friends ought to stand up firmly and resolutely for distribution. The more vetoes the better now!"[31] Clay wanted to stoke the movement to impeach Tyler by provoking him to veto something else. Congress obliged by passing another tariff-distribution bill. On August 9, 1842, Tyler delivered his Veto of Tariff and Land Distribution Bill to the House. Although he began his message by expressing his "regret" in vetoing the measure, he reaffirmed his rejection of the Whig conception of the presidency by reminding the House that the "exercise of some independence of judgment in regard to all acts of legislation is plainly implied in the responsibility of approving them."

He specified three principal grounds for the veto: First, he stressed that the "bill unites two subjects, which so far as having any affinity to one another, are incongruous in their character, it is both a revenue and appropriations bill. It thus imposes on the Executive, in the first place, the necessity of either approving that which he would reject or rejecting that which he might otherwise approve. This is a species of constraint to which the judgment of the Executive ought not . . . [be] subjected." Tyler warned that the "union of subjects wholly dissimilar in their character in the same bill, if it grew into a practice, would not fail to lead to consequences destructive of all wise and conscientious legislation."[32] In this passage, Tyler was rejecting the president's inherent authority to exercise a line-item veto authority while also foreseeing possible budget impasses similar to the one during the summer of 2011.

Second, Tyler objected to the scheme of distribution, which he characterized "as highly impolitic and unconstitutional." It was "impolitic" because it gave "away a fruitful source of revenue." It was unconstitutional for the same reason as the national bank and federally sponsored internal improvements— it exceeded the proper boundaries of congressional authority and encroached upon the sovereignty of the states. Moreover, Tyler explained, the bill made the monumental mistake of joining "the tariff question," on which the country was nearly united in supporting, and "distribution, as to which a serious conflict of opinion exist among the States and the people, and which enlists in its support a bare majority, indeed a bare majority of the two Houses of Congress."[33]

The next day, Representative John Quincy Adams moved that the House refer Tyler's veto to a select committee charged with investigating the propriety of impeaching Tyler.[34] Representative A. Lawrence Foster, a New York Whig, objected to the motion on the constitutional ground that the House "was not competent to make a motion to refer."[35] House Speaker John White, a close friend of Clay, "was understood to overrule the objection" and maintained that "the House alone had control of the matter, and the House could lay it on the table, or send it to either a select committee or a Committee of the Whole House." Representative John Underwood, a Kentucky Whig and another close friend of Clay, agreed with the Speaker and suggested that a veto message might refer to certain facts "of which Congress had no knowledge when a bill was passed," and the House had the authority to appoint a committee "to ascertain the truth of the statement, and to reexamine the facts." He said that if a committee had the authority to investigate matters of fact, it "could assuredly inquire into matters of opinion, and report on reasoning as well as facts."[36] The House adopted Adams's motion to refer the veto message to a select committee, and on August 13, 1842, it named the thirteen members of the special committee.[37] The committee report criticized Tyler harshly and proposed a constitutional amendment to enable Congress to override presidential vetoes by simple majorities.

Neither the House nor the Senate approved the suggested amendment. Although the Senate debated an identical proposal (introduced by Clay) for nearly three months, the Democrats uniformly aligned against it and succeeded in keeping the Senate from formally voting on it. While a majority of the House approved the committee report and the proposal 99–90, the vote on the proposed constitutional amendment fell short of the two-thirds needed. The amendment's failure reinforced the scope of the president's veto authority and, along with the report, the House response, and Tyler's protests had significant ramifications for several presidential and congressional authorities, including the veto.

The Cabinet's Constitutional Status

When nearly every member of his cabinet resigned in protest over Tyler's use of the veto, Tyler was no longer surrounded by "Clay men," and he intensified his rebellion against Whig principles of governance.[38] Among the other principles that Tyler interred was the Whig tenet on the proper relationship between a president and his cabinet. In spite of their rivalry, Clay and Daniel Webster agreed that the president should follow a majority of the cabinet on policy decisions and should only cast a vote if the cabinet were split. While Harrison needed a little time before questioning this principle, Tyler rejected it outright.

While Tyler devoted most of his first cabinet meeting to directing the cabinet to accept his view on presidential succession, this was not all that happened. Besides making clear to the cabinet that he had automatically become president upon the death of Harrison, Tyler took issue with Webster's suggestion that he should follow Harrison's practice of deciding policy on the basis of a majority vote of his cabinet. Tyler interjected that he rejected the practice because he did not believe cabinet members were coequal with the president. He declared, "I can never consent to being dictated to act as to what I shall or shall not do. I, as President, shall be responsible for my administration. I hope to have your hearty cooperation in carrying out these measures. So long as you see fit to do this, I shall be glad to have you with me. When you think otherwise, your resignations shall be accepted."[39] Thus, in the first meeting with his cabinet, Tyler twice refused to follow the Whigs' principle of deferring to his cabinet.

Subsequently, Tyler continued to act upon his conviction that he was not constitutionally obliged to consult with his cabinet before making decisions, much less to follow members' instructions. Without first consulting his cabinet, he vetoed legislation that would have created the Third National Bank, and then rejected the cabinet's advice that he sign the Fiscal Corporation bill. Thus, Tyler was determined to imprint upon the cabinet his view that the cabinet served him, not the other way around.

The ensuing cabinet's mass resignation was a political embarrassment to Tyler, but it did not force him to alter his constitutional convictions. To the contrary, he quickly accepted the resignations and suggested his own slate of nominees, again without consulting with the congressional or party leadership. Moreover, the suggestions themselves demonstrated his independence from Congress, since the common connection among the new nominees was that they were all anti-Clay men in the Whig Party. Although Clay hoped to stall the nominations, the Senate confirmed them all in record time. Despite the subsequent shifts in the cabinet's composition, Tyler never wavered on his conception of its proper role: He consulted it when he saw fit and only when it agreed with his views.

The Appointment Authority

Tyler vigorously defended and established significant precedents upholding the president's unilateral nominating and recess appointment authorities. His exercise of these authorities invigorated these powers and constituted further, direct assaults on the Whigs' conception of the presidency.

In exercising the president's nominating authority, Tyler never embraced the Whig principle that a president should defer to the dictates or preferences of congressional leaders on nominations to federal offices requiring Senate confirmation. From his presidency's outset, Tyler stressed to his entire cabinet and to Congress that the ultimate authority to nominate someone to confirmable office was his and his alone. Though he sometimes consulted with members of the cabinet and Congress, such consultation did not, in Tyler's view, constitute either a waiver of his prerogative or an obligation to follow the will of either the cabinet or Congress. In spite of provoking fierce, persistent opposition in the Senate, Tyler's actions bolstered the president's independent authority to make nominations to confirmable offices as he saw fit.

First, Tyler made the significant decision, after his expulsion from the Whig Party, to use patronage to ensure loyalty to his policies throughout his administration and to build support for a presidential run in 1844. Indeed,

Tyler remade his cabinet more than once, and his efforts to reconstruct a cabinet to meet his shifting political fortunes and needs were historic: twenty-one different people filled the six different posts during Tyler's presidency, the largest number of cabinet appointments made by a single president until Ulysses Grant (who made twenty-five cabinet appointments over the course of two full terms to fill seven cabinet offices). Including the cabinet secretaries that Tyler had inherited from Harrison, there were three secretaries of state (including Webster at the beginning and Calhoun at the end of his administration), four secretaries of war, four treasury secretaries, three attorneys general, two postmasters general, and five navy secretaries.[40] In making these and other appointments, Tyler embraced and extended the spoils system that the Whigs had been denouncing for years.

The Senate's persistent opposition to Tyler's nominations helped to push him to employ the president's recess appointment authority in response. As a senator, Tyler had objected to Jackson's using his recess appointment power to bypass submitting nominations to the Senate's advice and consent; and Tyler was the only president, besides William Henry Harrison, prior to the 1960s not to have made any recess appointments to fill judgeships. Yet Tyler, with the counsel of his second attorney general, Hugh Legare, construed this power to allow a president to fill any vacancy that either had not been filled by, or arose during, a recess in the legislative session. Legare's official opinion not only expressed agreement with the earlier, official opinion of Attorney General William Wirt[41] on the same subject[42] but also went further to ground its construction of the president's power to make recess appointments apparently *at any time* because of the "overruling necessity" of the president's constitutional responsibility to exercise "the whole executive power" "perpetually" and with "no interruption" by the Congress.[43] Thus, Tyler justified filling posts during a recess whenever he thought that Congress's obstruction had allowed it to go unfilled until then.

Tyler's rigorous defense of his unilateral, independent power to nominate without consulting or deferring to the Senate included his protests against House efforts to encroach upon his appointment power. On March 16, 1842, the House approved a resolution requesting that "the President of the United States and the heads of the several Departments [communicate] to the House of Representatives the names of such of the members (if any) of the 26th and 27th Congress who have been applicants for office, and for what offices, distinguishing between those who have applied in person, and those whose applications were made by friends, whether in person or in writing." A week later, Tyler submitted to the House a formal protest in which he explained that his refusal to comply with the resolution on the grounds that, among other things, "compliance with the resolution . . . would be a surrender of the duties and powers which the Constitution has conferred exclusively on the Executive."[44] He explained, "The appointing power, so far as it is bestowed on the President by the Constitution, is conferred without reserve or qualification. The reason for the appointment, and the responsibility of the appointment, rest with [the President] alone. I cannot perceive anywhere in the Constitution . . . any right conferred on the House . . . to hear the reasons which any applicant may urge for an appointment to office under the Executive department, or any duty resting upon the House . . . by which it may become responsible for any such appointment." He concluded that any "encroach[ment]" by the House "on the rights and duties of the Executive department [is] highly impolitic, if not unconstitutional." Tyler's defense of the president's authority to keep the House from encroaching upon (or even inquiring into) the domain of his appointment authority was no different than Jackson's before him or Polk's afterward.

The President's Removal Power

In his first address as president, Tyler vowed, consistently with Whig principles, "I will remove no incumbent from office who has faithfully and honestly acquitted himself of the duties of his office, except in cases where such officer has been guilty of an active partisanship by secret means—the less manly, and therefore the more objectionable—has given his official influence to the purposes of party, thereby bringing him the patronage of the Government in conflict with the freedom of elections." He added—tellingly—that while "[n]umerous removals may become necessary under this rule," his conduct, in removing officials, "will be regulated by a profound sense of what is due to the country and its institutions; nor shall I neglect to apply the same unbending rule to those of my own appointment. Freedom of opinion will be tolerated, the full enjoyment of the right of suffrage will be maintained as the birthright of every American citizen; but I say to the official corps, 'Thus far no farther.'"[45] It took, however, little time before Tyler's fundamental commitments were transparent, and his efforts to replace disloyal officials with those who were personally loyal to him intensified—rather than initiated— once he was expelled from the Whig Party. In 1841 alone, Tyler and Harrison removed over three hundred officials, the most in any single year in the antebellum era except for Jackson's first year in office.[46]

Bolstering Tyler's construction of his removal authority were several official opinions of Attorney General Legare that influenced subsequent thinking and practice pertaining to the president's removal power. In 1841, Attorney General Legare asserted, "If any authority were needed to enforce considerations which seem so obvious and conclusive in themselves, I think the celebrated debate on the removal power in the first Congress would furnish it. The whole country seems to have acquiesced in the argument of [then-Representative James] Madison, in favor of that power drawn from the character of the executive power and responsibility, and from the irresistible necessity of the case."[47] A year later, Legare commented further that "if the subject were res integra, it is now too late to dispute the settled construction of 1789. It is according to the construction, from the very nature of the executive power, absolute in the President, subject only to his responsibility to the country (his constituent) for a breach of such a vast and solemn trust."[48]

At the same time that the House was contemplating an amendment to alter the scope of the president's veto, it was considering an amendment constricting the president's nominating and removal authorities. The House ultimately failed to approve the proposed amendment, and Tyler (and others) construed the failure as vindicating the president's authority to remove officials within the executive branch.

The President's Term of Office

The House's failure to approve the proposed amendment to alter the president's veto authority coincided with its failure to approve a proposed constitutional amendment measure pushed by the Whigs to limit the president to a single term. The timing was not coincidental. By then, Tyler had not pledged to serve only a single term in office. This refusal, coupled with the fact that by 1842 Tyler was using his appointment and removal powers to support a run for the presidency in 1844, ended any doubt about his refusal to abide by the Whig commitment to a limited presidential term. In particular, from 1842 to 1844 Tyler deployed his nominating and removal authorities to assemble a core of officeholders who were dedicated to building a third party and making Tyler its nominee for president. His followers, who were an amalgam of anti-Clay Whigs in the North, conservative Democrats, and southern extremists, held their convention at the same time as the Democrats did and nominated him for the presidency. Tyler announced the end of his candidacy in late August after it had become clear that the Democrats, led by Polk, would welcome his followers into their fold. Though Tyler's bid to be elected to the presidency in his own right failed, he had struck a blow against the party's commitment to a limited presidential term.

Executive Privilege

Tyler refused to follow the Whig conception of the presidency in yet another way. Throughout his presidency, the House and the Senate peppered him with resolutions demanding that he turn over to one or the other particular information in either his or the executive branch's possession. More often than not, he complied with the resolutions,[49] but on three occasions he submitted for publication in the congressional record his reasons for refusing to comply with particular document requests from the House.

On February 21, 1842, the House approved a resolution asking Tyler to produce "all correspondence" relating to the negotiations between Tyler's administration and Great Britain over the boundaries of Maine. Tyler refused. On February 26, 1843, Tyler delivered to the House a brief message explaining that while he usually preferred "to lay before Congress and the public all information affecting the state of the country, to the fullest extent consistent with propriety and prudence," he declared that "no communication could be made by me at this time, on the subject of [the] resolution, without detriment or danger to the public interests."[50]

On March 23, 1842, Tyler delivered a special message to this House, this time in response to a resolution approved a week earlier that he produce the names of members of Congress who had asked (or who had others on their behalf ask for them) to be considered to be appointed to various federal offices. Tyler's protest claimed what he conceded was a less "effective and lofty" ground for noncompliance than the fact that the request constituted an impermissible interference with his nominating authority.[51] Tyler explained that

applications for office, or letters respecting appointments, or conversations held with individuals on such subjects, are not official proceedings, unless, after the nomination of such person so writing or conversing, the President shall think proper to lay such correspondence or such conversations before the Senate. Applications for office are, in their very nature, confidential; and if the reasons assigned for such applications, or the names of the applicants were communicated, not only would such implied confidence be wantonly violated but, in addition, it is quite obvious that a mass of vague, incoherent, and personal matter would be made public, at a vast consumption of time, money, and trouble, without accomplishing, or tending in any manner to accomplish . . . any useful object connected with a sound and constitutional administration of the Government, in any of its branches.[52]

It was, however, a dispute between Tyler and the House over information pertaining to possible fraud in land sales to Cherokee Indians that culminated in his most extensive defense of executive privilege. On May 18, 1842, the House approved a resolution requesting that Tyler's secretary of war, John Spencer, produce documents and information relating to the investigation that he had been overseeing into the possible frauds in land sales to Cherokee Indians. On June 1, 1842, Spencer responded that he could not comply with the resolution. He explained that the materials requested by the House contained information that he expected would become part of the negotiations between the War Department and the Cherokee Nation. He suggested that if the information were made public, the negotiations would be endangered. Moreover, he warned that an investigation was in progress, and people who had been charged with misconduct had not yet had the opportunity to respond to them. After a six-day debate, the House passed another resolution, this time specifically requesting Tyler give the House "all information communicated by him concerning the frauds that he was charged to investigate [and] all facts in the possession of the Executive relating to the subject."[53] Accompanying the resolution was a report of the Committee on Indian Affairs explaining that it was the right of the House to demand from the executive branch any information in the latter's possession relating to projects of interest to the House.

This time, Tyler did not respond immediately. He did not send a reply to the House until more than six months later in a special message dated January 31, 1843. After reminding the House of Spencer's reasons for not complying with the earlier resolution, Tyler directly challenged the House's authority to demand "information in its possession relating to any subject of the deliberation of the House, and within the sphere of its legitimate powers." He grounded the challenge in both his oath of office and his constitutional duty to "take care that the laws be faithfully executed," a duty that included, in his judgment, an obligation "to inquire into the manner in which all public agents perform the duties assigned to them by law." He explained further that, "[t]o be effective," his "inquiries" into the performance of the people conducting investigations in the executive branch "must often be confidential. . . . To maintain that the President can exercise no discretion as to the time in which the matters thus collected shall be promulgated or in respect to the character of the information obtained would deprive him at once of the means of performing one of the most salutary duties of his office." If the president were not able to use discretion in the dissemination of information collected in investigations, any inquiry could be stopped at its outset, and those under suspicion could evade detection. "To require from the Executive the transfer of this discretion to a coordinate branch of the Government is equivalent to the denial of its possession by him and would render him dependent upon that branch in the performance of a duty purely executive."[54]

Tyler next rejected the proposition that "all papers, documents, and information of every description which may happen by any means to come into the possession of the President or the heads of Departments, must necessarily be subject to the call of the House . . . merely because they relate to a subject of deliberations of the House, although that subject may be within the sphere of its legitimate powers." He suggested that the president was entitled to exercise his own discretion to avoid disclosures that would hurt innocent people. Moreover, he reminded the House that the "privilege" on which he was relying was not new to the courts or the legislature and that "the general authority to compel testimony must give way in certain cases to the paramount rights of individuals or of the Government."

Tyler then gave an elaborate, unprecedented explanation of executive privilege: First, he explained that the privilege on which he was relying was precisely the same as the one "claimed and exercised by [George] Washington in 1796," President James Monroe in 1825, and President Jackson in 1832. Moreover, he noted that the House's failure to challenge his refusal to comply with its resolution demanding "the names of the members of Congress who had applied for offices" seemed to raise the "fair inference that the House itself admitted that there were cases in which the president had a discretionary authority in respect to the transmission of information in the possession of any of the Executive departments."

Nevertheless, Tyler concluded that he had delivered to the House all papers that were either known or supposed to have relation to the army's investigation of alleged fraud. He explained that the reasons that he had declined earlier to send the requested information no longer had any force, because "of the death and removal out of those who would be called to testify."[55] Moreover, he said the delays were the House's fault because of a law enacted the previous year barring "the payment of any account or charge whatever growing out of or in any way connected with any commission or inquiry," except military and naval courts-martial or courts of inquiry, unless special appropriations had been made.

Subsequently, Tyler's refusals to comply with these resolutions have been construed as endorsing an absolute executive privilege. It is, however, not clear that Tyler understood it as such; his consistent position was that the president had an absolute right to make an initial judgment about the need to maintain confidentiality of materials or information in his or the executive branch's possession. Nonetheless, some scholars have gone further to construe these refusals as demonstrating Tyler's belief in the unitary theory of the executive. The difficulty with this characterization is that Tyler never claimed the president was entitled to an absolute privilege. An absolute privilege would have extended to maintaining the confidentiality of materials relating to whether a president had committed an impeachable offense or not, but, as we shall see in the next section, Tyler made no such claim when the opportunity arose.

Congressional Pushback

Congress did not stand idly by or simply acquiesce in Tyler's persistent efforts to assert presidential prerogatives. Congress repeatedly responded with equal, if not stronger, assertions of its own authority. The ensuing conflicts between Tyler and Congress provide some of the most extraordinary and dramatic illustrations of checks and balances at work. While some people might be inclined to believe that Tyler's strong defense of presidential prerogatives effectively endorsed the so-called unitary theory of the executive (the notion that the president controls, or should control, the exercise of all executive power or that all executive power is consolidated in the president), his presidency more precisely demonstrates how departmentalism operates and develops at the federal level. In short, the interaction between Tyler and Congress demonstrates that the powers of the different branches are dynamic and are shaped as much by the efforts to exercise and defend them as they have been by the efforts to resist or oppose them.

Impeachment and Censure

While Jackson had faced a serious movement within the Senate to censure him, there was never any serious possibility that he would be impeached, much less removed from office. The same cannot be said for Tyler. While we know that Tyler was never impeached, he came closer to being impeached than any president before Andrew Johnson. The fact that Tyler was ultimately censured but not impeached by the House established a significant precedent that shaped subsequent understandings and exercises of the House's authority to sanction or discipline the nation's chief executive.

In Congress, the most ardent proponent of Tyler's impeachment was fellow Virginian John Botts, his Whig nemesis who took the lead in urging the House to consider Tyler's removal. Botts's first proposal turned out to be the one that the House took the most seriously during Tyler's tenure. In the aftermath of Tyler's June 29, 1842, veto, Botts introduced a resolution on July 10, 1842, to appoint a special committee to investigate whether President Tyler had committed an impeachment offense. The resolution was significant, since it was the first request to initiate a presidential impeachment to be formally introduced in the House. While Botts figured the Whig majority in the House at the time would support his cause, Whig leaders in Congress, including Henry Clay, did not; they believed that the resolution was premature, and they preferred to embarrass Tyler further by provoking him into casting other vetoes. When Tyler did on August 9, 1842, the House referred his message to the special committee that Clay's close friend, the Speaker of the House, John White, appointed, and whose members included Botts as well as John Quincy Adams as chair.

A week later, the select committee issued a report harshly criticizing Tyler's actions, particularly his vetoes of the two bills attempting to recharter a national bank, for "gross abuse of constitutional power and bold assumptions of powers never vested in him by any law"; for having "deprived the people of self-government"; for having "assumed . . . the whole Legislative power to himself, and . . . levying millions of money upon the people, without any authority of law"; and for the "abusive exercise of the constitutional power of the President to arrest the actions of Congress upon measures vital to the welfare of the people." Significantly, the report found that, although Tyler's actions justified the invocation of the federal impeachment process, it did not recommend impeachment because "in the present state of public affairs, [it would] prove abortive." Significantly, the report was not unanimous: Representatives Charles Ingersoll of Pennsylvania and James Roosevelt of New York, both Democrats, issued a minority report defending Tyler, and Thomas Gilmer, a Virginia Whig, submitted a counterreport.[56] Ingersoll and Roosevelt defended the president's authority to veto bills on any ground he deemed appropriate, while Gilmer accused the House of violating tradition and the Constitution by referring Tyler's veto to a committee, instead of, as the Constitution specified, entering "the objections at large on their journal and proceed[ing] to reconsider the bill." Gilmer told the House that the Constitution did not make the president's veto absolute but specified that it could be overridden if there was adequate support in the House and Senate.[57] Meanwhile, Senator James Buchanan defended Tyler's actions on the Senate floor.

After virtually no discussion, the House approved and adopted the report by a vote of 100–80.[58] This vote marked the first time that the House had censured—or formally approved a resolution that was critical of—a president.

Nearly two weeks later, Tyler delivered a formal protest to the House.[59] Tyler began his protest by underscoring the unprecedented nature of both the House's referral of his veto to a special committee and the committee's actions in charging him with committing impeachable offenses but not going further to initiate actual impeachment proceedings against the president. Tyler suggested that if the charges could not be proved, the House, "which has the sole power of impeachment," had no discretion to do anything but to impeach him. If it were to do so, Tyler maintained, then he at least could confront his accusers in his Senate removal trial and demand a full and impartial inquiry. He acknowledged that the ordeal would be painful, but "as it is, I have been accused without evidence and condemned without a hearing . . . I am charged with violating pledges [to sign Whig bills] which I never gave, . . . with usurping powers not conferred upon the President by law, and above all, with using powers conferred by the Constitution from corrupt motives and for unwarrantable ends."

Tyler told the House that he was determined to uphold the constitutional authority of the president to the best of his ability and in defiance of all personal consequences. He refused to stand aside and witness the desecration of the Constitution, which he had sworn to preserve, protect, and defend. If, as the House report maintained, checks upon the will of Congress by the use of the veto would no longer be tolerated, an amendment to that effect would have to be submitted to the people of the several states. Until such time, Tyler intended to abide by the law "as it has been written by our predecessors."

Botts persuaded the Whig-dominated House to censure Tyler just as the Senate had censured Jackson. On his motion, the House refused to publish the protest, just as the Senate had refused to publish Jackson's protest. The House next adopted a resolution that Botts had proposed and modeled on the resolution approved by the Senate in 1834, which had specified its reasons for refusing to publish Jackson's protest against his censure by the Senate.[60] The irony was not lost on Tyler and Webster, who had both voted for the resolutions.

In the meantime, Tyler's and Botts's political fortunes shifted. In the midterm elections of 1842, Botts lost his House seat, and the Democrats took control of the House. Nevertheless, Botts kept pressing the House to consider his impeachment resolution. He persuaded his friends in the House to introduce the resolution for the full House's consideration on the floor on January 10, 1843. The resolution contained nine charges of impeachment. The next day, the House rejected the resolution 127–83,[61] the first time that the House voted on an impeachment resolution. While threats of impeachment persisted for the remainder of Tyler's presidency,[62] none came before the full House again.

Advice and Consent

The struggle between Tyler and the Senate for dominance of the appointments process was constant and historic: The Senate rejected seven of his twenty cabinet nominations—the largest number of cabinet nominations ever made by a single president to be rejected by the Senate. In Tyler's last two years in office, the Senate blocked a majority of his nominations (including four cabinet and two minister nominations), and the Senate rejected eight of his nine Supreme Court nominations—the largest number of unsuccessful Supreme Court nominations ever made by a single president.[63]

The first of these protracted contests involved Tyler's nomination of his political ally Caleb Cushing as his treasury secretary. By this time, almost all the Whigs in the Senate were aligned against Tyler, something that was bound to present a problem in getting his nominees confirmed since the Whigs controlled twenty-eight of the Senate's fifty-two seats. When Tyler's secretary of the treasury, Walter Forward, resigned, Tyler quickly nominated Cushing. It was a risky choice. Whigs hated Cushing for having left their party and the House but not before fiercely defending Tyler's assertions of power. Democrats distrusted Cushing as an opportunist. With the Twenty-seventh Congress winding down, the Senate rejected Cushing's nomination 27–19, but Tyler immediately resubmitted the nomination on the ground that it was his prerogative to choose his treasury secretary. This time, the Senate rejected the nomination by a larger margin 27–10 based in part on senators' defense of their independent prerogative to give their advice and consent to such nominations. Tyler refused to concede defeat and resubmitted the nomination a third time. This time, the Senate voted 29–2 to reject the nomination. Tyler then asked for the Senate's approval to move his secretary of war, John Spencer, to lead the Treasury Department, and the Senate agreed by a single vote.

Tyler mistakenly construed Spencer's confirmation as a sign that the Senate had reached the limits of its ability to obstruct his nominations. Just before the session's end, he submitted to the Senate his nomination of Henry Wise to replace Lewis Cass as minister to France. The nomination was doomed from the outset: Wise was unpopular with both parties, since he had left the Democrats to join the Whigs to protest Jackson's veto of the National Bank but then abandoned the Whigs to rejoin the Democrats to protest the Whigs' expulsion of Tyler. Wise was also an ally of John Calhoun, whom the Senate had begrudgingly confirmed as Tyler's last secretary of war but whom most senators were not otherwise disposed to do favors. The Senate stood its ground just as firmly as it had in rejecting Cushing's nomination and rejected Wise's nomination each of the three times that Tyler forced it on them.

At least as dramatic and significant as the Senate's rejections of the Cushing and Wise nominations were the Senate's response to Tyler's efforts to fill two vacancies on the Supreme Court in his last two years in office. Tyler's first opportunity arose when Associate Justice Smith Thompson died in mid-December 1843. On January 9, 1844, Tyler nominated John Spencer, whom the Senate had confirmed not long before as treasury secretary. Spencer seemed to satisfy the custom of replacing justices with nominees who came from the same state or circuit, since he, like Thompson, had come from the same state—New York. The problem was that this was a differently constituted Senate, which Whigs controlled. Though no longer in the Senate, Clay urged his Senate allies to reject Spencer—and several other people whose nominations were pending—because they were not "true or faithful or honest" Whigs. Accordingly, the Senate voted 26–21 to reject Spencer's nomination.

Subsequently, Tyler tried to break the impasse in filling Thompson's seat by nominating Reuben Walworth, who was then the well-respected chancellor of New York. But Walworth lacked the support of the Whigs who dominated New York state politics, including Thurlow Weed and his protégé, Governor William Seward. On June 17, 1844, the Senate voted 27–20 to postpone his nomination. That same day, Tyler renominated Walworth for the seat, but the Senate refused to take any action. On December 4, 1844, Tyler nominated Walworth a third time, but the Senate continued to refuse to act. Walworth finally withdrew his nomination from further consideration.

Meanwhile, Tyler was struggling to fill another vacancy that had arisen on the Court when Justice Henry Baldwin of Pennsylvania died on April 21, 1844. Initially, Tyler wanted to nominate Senator James Buchanan because he was from Pennsylvania and had defended Tyler vigorously from censure; however, Buchanan declined.[64] Consequently, Tyler nominated Judge Edward King from Philadelphia, on June 5, 1844; however, the Senate voted 29–18 on June 14, 1844, to postpone the nomination. At the beginning of the next congressional session, Tyler renominated King, but the Senate again voted to postpone the nomination. King withdrew his nomination in frustration on February 7, 1845. That same day, Tyler nominated John Read, a former U.S. attorney for Philadelphia who was admired by both Whigs and Democrats, but the Senate adjourned a week later without taking any action on the nomination. The seat was thus vacant when Polk came into office.

On the same day that Walworth withdrew his nomination, Tyler made one more attempt to fill the seat. Although he was a lame duck, Tyler broke the impasse with his nomination of the universally respected Samuel Nelson, the Democratic chief justice of the New York Supreme Court. Democrats in the Senate knew Polk could do no better, while Nelson was more agreeable to Whigs than any of the people whom they thought Polk was likely to nominate. On February 14, 1845, the Senate approved the nomination by voice vote.

The outcomes of these various contests established several enduring precedents: First, Tyler's persistence in nominating people to fill the cabinet, Supreme Court, and other offices, in spite of the obvious opposition they would meet in the Senate, reinforced the president's independence to make the final judgments, for better or worse, on his exercise of his nominating authority. Moreover, the Senate's persistent obstruction of Tyler's cabinet and ministerial appointments as well as eight of his nine nominations to the Court on political grounds reinforced the independence of the Senate's advice-and-consent authority. Indeed, the Senate's obstruction of Tyler's efforts to fill two vacancies on the Court establishes a record that is unlikely ever to be surpassed: To fill the two vacancies on the Court arising during his presidency, Tyler made a total of nine nominations, only one of which the Senate approved.[65] Third, the Senate's obstruction of Tyler's efforts to fill both seats during the lame-duck session of Congress in 1844–45 is one of the first, clearest instances of a practice, now well established, of stalling such nominations in election years. Last but not least, Tyler's successful nomination of Nelson to the Court is a reminder of the power that the Constitution vests even in a weak president, the power to forge compromises through the exercise of the nominating authority. The Constitution does not require presidents to avoid conflict, or to achieve consensus, through his exercise of his nominating authority. With his successful nomination of Nelson to the Court, Tyler became the first president to nominate someone from the opposing party as a Supreme Court justice. Both his success and earlier failures were not lost on later presidents.[66]

The Foreign Emoluments Clause

The Foreign Emoluments Clause of Article I provided Tyler with a rare basis for not battling with Congress and for following Van Buren's lead. The clause provides that "no person holding any Office of Profit or Trust under them shall, without the Consent of Congress, accept of any present, Emolument, Office, or Title, of any kind whatever, from any King, Prince, or Foreign State." Thinking that the clause applied to the president, Van Buren told the Imam of Muscat in 1840 that the Constitution forbade him from accepting several gifts that he had given to the president. At Van Buren's request, Congress issued a joint resolution authorizing him to dispose of the presents by giving some to the State Department and the proceeds from the sales of others to the treasury. When the imam gave two Arabian horses to Tyler, he followed Van Buren's precedent and submitted them to Congress, which authorized him to auction them off and give the proceeds to the treasury. Van Buren and Tyler thus set an example for other presidents.

Advancing the President's Independence in Foreign Affairs

In foreign affairs, Tyler made several constitutionally significant decisions. Among the most enduring of these are Tyler's initiatives in (1) formulating the Tyler Doctrine, (2) the opening of trade with China, (3) formulating the McLeod law, and (4) devising an alternative to the Senate's treaty power. With each of these, Tyler struck further blows against the Whig concept of the presidency and fortified presidential leadership in foreign affairs.

The Tyler Doctrine and the First Mission to China

Tyler set forth the Tyler Doctrine and initiative to open trade with China in the same special message. The Tyler Doctrine was a response to the intervention of France to stop American Protestants from persecuting Catholics in the Hawaiian Islands. The message acknowledged the special interests of the United States in preventing a foreign power from taking control of the Hawaiian Islands.[67] It declared that "it could not but create dissatisfaction on the part of the United States at any attempt by another power, should such attempt be threatened or feared, to take possession of the [Hawaiian] islands, colonize them, and subvert the native Government." The message declared that the United States rejected any claim to "the exclusive control over the Hawaiian government," but if there were "an opposite policy by any other power" to be adopted, the United States would be justified in "making a decided remonstrance."[68] Through this policy, Tyler extended the principles of the Monroe Doctrine to the Hawaiian Islands.[69]

In the same message, Tyler asked Congress to appropriate funds for a commissioner "to reside in China to exercise a watchful care over the concerns of American citizens and for the protection of their persons and property."[70] Since the British Empire had acquired Hong Kong, Tyler and Webster were determined to prevent the United States from being shut out altogether from the benefits of trading with China. Subsequently, Congress appropriated the funds, and Tyler named Caleb Cushing the first U.S. ambassador to China through a recess appointment.

It is significant that Tyler did not face the same opposition from Congress in formulating the nation's policies on trading with China and protecting the sovereignty of the Hawaiian Islands as he had routinely confronted on the domestic front. The Senate, which had opposed Cushing's nomination as treasury secretary, confirmed him as the ambassador to China. The same senators who condemned Tyler's assault on the Whig conception of the presidency ratified the treaty Cushing negotiated to open trade with China. These events showed that the Whig conception of the presidency stopped at the water's edge. Members of Congress, even Whigs, did not question Tyler's authority as president to take the initiative to set the nation's policies in foreign affairs.

The McLeod Affair

The McLeod affair produced challenges for both Harrison and Tyler. The affair is linked to the fate of a small steamer, the *Caroline*, which was owned by an American citizen and used to assist Canadian insurgents who were fighting to free Canada from British rule in 1837. In the midst of the conflict, Canadian troops, who were fighting for the British, seized the *Caroline* in a New York port and steered it into Canadian waters, where it was set on fire and sunk and a crewmember was killed. Subsequently, Alexander McLeod, a Canadian sheriff, made the mistake of boasting, while he happened to be in New York for other reasons, that he had participated in the killing of the *Caroline* crewmember. New York authorities arrested him and charged him with arson and murder. His arrest intensified frayed relations between the United States and Great Britain, which maintained that McLeod acted as a member of the British forces and threatened war if McLeod were executed. The American government sided with the British, but Harrison's attorney general, John Crittenden, had tried in vain to persuade the governor of New York, William Seward, to release McLeod to the British. After Harrison died, Tyler continued to press Seward to release McLeod, and thus the two men found themselves on the opposite sides of their usual constitutional stances: Seward maintained that the Constitution protected the sovereignty of New York's judicial process from being breached by the president or a foreign power. Tyler asserted that the problem between New York and the United States was the fault of the Constitution, which did not clearly provide for the federal jurisdiction that he maintained ought to prevail in these circumstances. Tyler told British authorities that he favored a federal law that would guarantee the national government's control in similar cases in the future. Ironically, Seward questioned the constitutionality of such a law and insisted that Tyler—and the federal government—did not have the authority to interfere in the internal affairs of the state of New York. In fact, the New York jury acquitted McLeod, who returned to Canada. Tyler kept his word to the British and approved the 1842 Remedial Justice Act,[71] which empowered federal judges to discharge any person who was in its custody but had proved to have acted pursuant to a foreign power's instructions.

Annexing Texas

One of Tyler's final acts as president was one of his most monumental. Whereas in 1842 the Senate had ratified the Webster-Ashburton Treaty, which settled many boundary disputes between Canada and the United States, senators split over the legality and ramifications of annexing Texas. By the time the annexation question reached the White House, the secretary of state was John Calhoun, who had returned to the position he had held under President Monroe. Calhoun believed Texas would become a proslavery state and thus tip the balance of power in the Senate in favor of the interests of slaveholders. He believed that a treaty between the United States and Texas, which saw itself as a small nation, was lawful; however, many Democrats and Whigs were concerned that Mexico would invade Texas if there were such a treaty. Many Democrats also wanted the next president to handle the matter. Whigs did not want war, but they opposed acquiring a territory that would become a slave state and happily opposed Tyler and Calhoun whenever possible.

In spite of the skepticism and threatened opposition, Calhoun and Tyler negotiated a treaty with Texas on April 12, 1844, which they sent to the Senate ten days later. Along with the treaty, they sent supporting documentation, including a letter from Tyler emphasizing that the treaty was in the best interests of everyone and that the federal government had the power to execute the treaty pursuant to its authority to acquire new territories and to admit new states. It was soon discovered that the documentation included two letters that Calhoun had written to Richard Pakenham, the British minister in Washington, D.C. In both letters, Calhoun explained that the treaty was needed to protect slavery in the United States.[72] Although the chances of ratification were uncertain before the two letters were released, they disposed all senators, except for those most committed to Calhoun, to reject the treaty's ratification.[73]

The Senate debated the treaty for nearly a month. Several prominent Democrats favored treaty ratification, while Whigs opposed it. Clay was pleased the Senate fell ten votes shy of the two-thirds required for treaty ratification.

Tyler did not quit. After consulting with Calhoun, he proposed an alternative to treaty ratification. He suggested that a simple majority in each chamber of Congress could approve the agreement with Texas. This was the same procedure required for acquiring territory or admitting a new state as provided by implication in Article IV.[74] Just two days after the Senate rejected the treaty, Tyler sent a copy of the agreement to the House with a message declaring that it had the authority to approve the agreement pursuant to the powers granted in Article IV to admit new states into the Union.

Construing Polk's victory in the 1844 presidential election as a mandate for annexation, Tyler pressed Congress to approve the agreement. Just a few days before Polk's inauguration, the House and Senate each approved a resolution giving the president the choice of annexing Texas according to the resolution that the House had approved *or* by opening new negotiations with Texas as specified in a resolution from Missouri senator Benton.[75] On March 1, Tyler signed the joint resolution. Shortly after his inauguration, President Polk chose not to challenge the authority of the joint resolution or Tyler's signature. Consequently, both Polk and Tyler approved an important alternative to the treaty power that became increasingly popular as an alternative means for codifying international agreements.

Enforcing the Republican Guarantee Clause

The Supreme Court's decision in *Luther v. Borden*[76] is familiar to students of constitutional law as the first, most significant ruling on the Republican Guarantee Clause.[77] Most students do not know, however, that the decision upheld the solution Tyler and Webster had designed to settle the Dorr Rebellion.

The Dorr Rebellion takes its name from Thomas Dorr, who led a group of people who objected to Rhode Island's charter restricting voting rights to white male adults who either owned property or paid annual rent in money. After failing to persuade the state government to alter the charter, Dorr and his followers—the Dorrites—organized a second state government to operate under a different charter that they called "the People's Constitution." The governor, Samuel King, objected and asked Tyler for assistance based on the Constitution's Article IV, which obliged the United States "to guarantee to every State in this Union, a Republican form of government" and to "protect each of them against invasion; and on application of the legislature, or of the executive (when the legislature cannot be convened) against domestic violence."

Initially, Tyler construed the Republican Guarantee Clause differently than King. He believed the Constitution did not invest the president with the authority to sanction the use of military force in anticipation of "domestic violence" within a state. Tyler claimed that federal force could only be used pursuant to this provision if there were an actual insurrection in Rhode Island, but there was none. Tyler told King that Congress had already recognized the existing government of the state as its lawful government and as having the requisite "Republican form of government" by seating its duly elected representatives and senators. Tyler suggested to King that it was up to the people of Rhode Island—not the federal government—to decide whether the existing government or the Dorrites were the lawful government of the state.[78]

Before the people of Rhode Island made a decision, the Dorrites attempted to seize control of state officers, and King declared martial law. Rather than intervene, Tyler advised King to ask the Rhode Island State Legislature to call a constitutional convention that would reorganize the state government "upon liberal principles." As King pondered the suggestion, the violence spread, and Tyler sent his secretary of war, John Spencer, to investigate. Based on Spencer's report, Tyler issued an executive order demanding that the rebels disperse within twenty-four hours and warning them that, if this were not done, he would call on the governors of Massachusetts and Connecticut to send their militia to join federal troops to quash the rebellion. (Interestingly, neither governor contested Tyler's authority to make the request.) The Dorrites soon gave up. Although Dorr was arrested and sentenced to life imprisonment, he was released shortly thereafter, and in 1843 a legally sanctioned convention drafted a constitution providing for white-male suffrage.

The Dorr Rebellion was over, but the efforts to retaliate against Tyler were not. First, some members of the Rhode Island legislature delivered to the House a document charging Tyler with interfering with the suffrage movement in the state. The House then launched an official investigation and requested Tyler produce all pertinent documents. He did, and the criticisms of Tyler dissipated once members of Congress reviewed the documents. Second, Martin Luther's wife filed on his behalf a legal action challenging the authority of a state official, Luther Borden, to arrest him and to search his home. He argued that Borden lacked the authority to arrest and to imprison her husband, because the government from which he claimed his authority was not a "Republican form of government." Daniel Webster represented the charter government and Borden. He argued that the controversy was purely a political matter, which had been settled by the state legislature and which the Court should refrain from reviewing on the merits. In 1849, the Supreme Court by a vote of 8–1 agreed with Webster.[79] In an opinion by Chief Justice Taney, the Court dismissed the lawsuit on the ground that the president and Congress, not the Court, had the sole, final authority to enforce the Republican Guarantee Clause. Ever since, federal authorities have stood by the decision.

AS NORTHERN STATES mobilized for war in 1861, Tyler took his final constitutional stand: He believed that the Constitution derived its authority from the states and therefore the absence of any provision explicitly restricting their right to secession should be construed as leaving to states complete sovereignty over the choice to secede from the Union. He urged his home state of Virginia to secede and served as a member of the Confederacy's Provisional Congress. In November 1861, he was elected to the Confederate House of Representatives but died before taking his seat. Tyler did not live to see a different president, another former Whig, use the presidential powers he had helped to consolidate to preserve the Union and to obscure much of his legacy.

4

Zachary Taylor, 1849–1850

THE POPULAR GENERAL credited with the United States' victory in the Mexican War, Zachary Taylor, is barely remembered as president, much less for anything he did of constitutional significance. Few people know what he did in his fifteen months in office, and most of those who do tend to dismiss him as ill suited for civil leadership or regard his presidency as a failed effort to create an alternative to the two dominant political parties of the era.

In fact, Taylor's presidency cannot be understood without appreciating that one of President Polk's achievements set the central challenge of Taylor's presidency: By securing the admission of Texas as a slave state, Polk ensured that on the day he left office the Senate was split evenly between slave and free-soil states.[1] Taylor's immediate dilemma upon taking office was determining whether and how to maintain this balance.

The hallmark of Taylor's presidency is that he met this challenge head-on. In doing so, he flatly rejected the Whig conception of the presidency. He construed the powers of the presidency as aggressively as Jackson and Polk had.[2] His bold assertions of presidential power produced several surprising, significant precedents regarding the House's powers to investigate and censure, executive privilege, recess appointments, and presidential removal authority. His presidency also influenced the constitutional outlooks of three men who later shaped the fates of the country and the Constitution—Jefferson Davis, Ulysses Grant, and Abraham Lincoln. Taylor's presidency was short but cast a substantial constitutional shadow.

Attacking Whig Principles

Before Taylor agreed to vie for the Whig nomination for president, Whigs had good reason to doubt his commitment to their constitutional convictions. Because Taylor had never been previously involved with politics or a political party, Whigs needed reassurance of his commitment to their principles of legislative supremacy and opposition to the Mexican War of which he had been a part (particularly the use of military force to acquire additional territory for the country). While some prominent Whigs suspected Taylor was like most army officers who favored Whig policies,[3] others were concerned about Taylor's repeated descriptions of himself "as a true republican who put the public interest ahead of party goals"[4] and of his commitment to transcend partisan divisions if he were elected president.[5] In two widely distributed letters written to John S. Allison ("the Allison letters"), Taylor tried to reassure Whigs of his constitutional commitments. In the first Allison letter, Taylor stressed that he was "a Whig, but not an ultra Whig," and repeated his pledges "to act independent of party domination" if he were elected president, not to veto measures "except in cases of clear violation of the Constitution, or manifest haste or want of due consideration by Congress," and to defer to Congress in domestic policymaking.[6] The first Allison letter proved insufficient to reassure Whig voters of Taylor's commitment to their principles, particularly in light of his repeating in another letter, "I am not a party candidate, and if elected cannot be President of a party, but the President of the whole people."[7] In the second Allison letter released two months before the general election, Taylor rejected criticisms that he had "an equivocal attitude towards . . . the Whig party," acknowledged he had been "a Whig in principle" when he was serving in the Mexican War, and suggested he had been nominated because the party considered him "a Whig" but not an extreme one.[8] Taylor pointedly added, "I am not prepared to force Congress, by coercion of the veto, to pass laws to suit me or to pass none."[9]

Notably, Taylor did not mention his commitment to Whig principles in the first public statement he released upon winning the general election.[10] Nevertheless, many Whigs were reassured by Taylor's declaration in his inaugural address that "it is for the wisdom of Congress itself, in which all legislative powers are vested by the Constitution, to regulate [various] matters of domestic policy. I shall look with confidence to the enlightened patriotism of that body to adopt such measures of conciliation as may harmonize conflicting interests and tend to perpetuate the Union which should be the paramount object of our hopes and affections."[11] Some Whigs might have wondered about what might happen if Taylor did not agree that Congress was acting to "perpetuate the Union" or what he meant when he pledged that, in interpreting the Constitution, he would "look to the decisions of the judicial tribunals established by its authority and to the practice of the Government under the earlier Presidents, who had so large a share in its formation."[12] Since neither the courts nor any "earlier Presidents" had upheld a Whig conception of the presidency, his address was hardly a resounding affirmation of Whig principles of governance.

It did not take Taylor long to confirm Whigs' worst fears and reject their orthodoxy on presidential power. In his First—and only—Annual Message, Taylor laid out the single, boldest proposal of his administration—to separately admit California and New Mexico as new states into the Union.[13] Taylor agreed Congress had complete discretion to condition the admission of a new state on any basis that it chose,[14] but he planned to allow the people of California and New Mexico to determine which constitution they each preferred for their admissions to be based on.

The boldness of Taylor's plan derived from its dependence on controversial attitudes about presidential power, congressional discretion, and popular sovereignty. First, Taylor did not defer to congressional leaders' preferences regarding the admission of new states into the Union. Instead, he exercised his authority as president to urge Congress to defer to his proposal and thus to consider separately the applications of California and New Mexico for statehood. Most members of Congress objected to Taylor's plan because they disagreed with him substantively or considered his efforts, even in trying to take the lead rhetorically (or to use the presidency as a bully pulpit), to conflict with their conception of presidents as subservient to congressional will. The fact that Taylor's chief defender in the Senate was the old Democratic warhorse Thomas Hart Benton showed how much his leadership breached Whig principles.

Benton defended Taylor's plan as following the practice of unconditionally admitting new states. In response to demands that the admission of new states be conditioned on accepting slavery, Benton stressed, "I deem it a very material thing, as it is proposed that we should now commence with doing by a new State what is without precedent in the annals of legislation, and which many feel to be a deep indignity to the State, that I shall, by reference to the cases of admission of new States, show that such a thing has never been done before."[15] It did not help Taylor with Whigs that Benton had been one of Jackson's fiercest defenders.

Everyone appreciated that Taylor's plan would tip the balance of power in the Senate (and thus the Union) in favor of antislavery forces.[16] While many Whigs wanted to weaken the slave power in Congress, they disliked Taylor's plan because it preempted Congress from taking the lead in regulating the admission of new states into the Union. Taylor believed, however, a fight in Congress over extending slavery into the territories risked disrupting the Union. He believed his plan avoided that fight and had the further advantage of respecting popular sovereignty, a principle that later became the Democratic Party's central tenet. He was convinced that slavery would not be economically viable in California or New Mexico and that neither state would permit it. Aware that his plan was controversial, he urged that "we should abstain from the introduction of those exciting topics of a sectional character which have hitherto produced painful apprehension in the public mind; and I repeat the solemn warning of the first and most illustrious of my predecessors against furnishing 'any ground for characterizing parties by geographic discriminations.'"[17]

Taylor's resolve to stand by his plan proved "unconquerable"[18] as its merits and constitutionality were debated in Congress until he died unexpectedly on July 9, 1850. His proposal had angered virtually every contingency in Congress except the northern Whigs, who accepted his abandonment of the Whig conception of the presidency in exchange for his opposition to the spread of slavery *and* his support for the Wilmot Proviso. The House had passed the Wilmot Proviso in 1847 and 1848 to outlaw slavery in any federal territory to be acquired from Mexico (excluding Texas, which had been acquired before the Proviso's passage).

Throughout the first half of 1850, Taylor tried unsuccessfully to persuade Democrats and southern Whigs that his plan was the best possible compromise because it gave "the North substance of the Wilmot Proviso but without forcing the South to swallow it as a formally enacted principle."[19] In contrast, southern Whigs, led by Clay, favored a compromise including a fugitive slave law, to which Taylor objected because he believed it would have drawn the federal government into supporting slavery and would have ripped the Union apart. Southern Whigs were outraged by Taylor's threatened veto[20] because they believed, in accordance with the Whig orthodoxy, a president should only veto measures that were clearly unconstitutional and they believed any compromise they fashioned was just the opposite—plainly constitutional. On May 21, 1850, Clay formally broke with Taylor, suggesting that Taylor, "entertaining that constitutional deference to the wisdom of Congress which he has professed, and abstaining from any interference with its free deliberations, ought, without any dissatisfaction, to permit us to consider what is best for our common country."[21]

Taylor warned southern Democrats that they would be worse off if they failed to support his plan. He suggested that their opposition to his plan ran the risk of motivating Congress to approve the Wilmot Proviso, whose constitutionality he had acknowledged to Congress.[22] Nevertheless, some southern Democrats, including Jefferson Davis, then a Mississippi senator, opposed Taylor's plan because it enabled antislavery forces to become a majority in the Senate (they already controlled the House) and provided a backdoor means through which to enact the Wilmot Proviso, which they believed violated the constitutional right to own slaves as property and the principle of popular sovereignty.[23] When other southern Democrats, including John Calhoun in his last statement on the Senate floor,[24] threatened to secede rather than accept Taylor's plan, Taylor issued his own threat—again, without waiting to follow Congress's lead—to stop any movement toward secession through the use of military force.[25]

There are different explanations for Taylor's obstinate refusal to compromise. The first is that it might have reflected his oversensitivity to personal attacks or his deeply engrained response as a soldier to stand his ground. The problem with this explanation, other than its discounting Taylor's well-known ability to improvise on the battlefield, is that it does not explain why Taylor chose the particular ground he did on which to take his stand. A second possible explanation is that Taylor felt compelled to follow the dictates of several antislavery foes, including William Seward, whose support had been critical to Taylor's narrow victory in the 1848 election and which Taylor needed to be reelected in 1852. The problem with this theory is that Seward and Taylor did not have identical views on slavery. Seward opposed slavery more ardently than Taylor, who, unlike Seward, had been a slaveholder.[26] Another possible explanation for Taylor's obstinacy is that he was convinced his plan had the best chance of preserving the Union and averting a civil war. Taylor repeated this theme in meetings with members of Congress and his public addresses, such as in Richmond, where he declared, "As to the Constitution and the Union, I have taken an oath to support the one and I cannot do so without preserving the other, unless I commit perjury, which I certainly don't intend to do. We must cherish the Constitution to the last . . . we must fall back upon Washington's farewell advice, and . . . preserve the Union at all hazards."[27] The defenders of the plan in Congress made this same argument.[28] It is possible that Taylor's obstinacy resulted from a combination of factors.

A second example of Taylor's rejection of Whig orthodoxy on the presidency arose in conjunction with his plan for New Mexico's statehood. Encouraged by Taylor, New Mexico, still under a military governor, had applied for immediate statehood under an antislavery constitution. No sooner had Taylor announced the plan than Texas authorities threatened to acquire, by force if necessary, all the New Mexico territory east of the Rio Grande, including Santa Fe.[29] Texas authorities believed the land belonged to them and wanted to extend the domain of slavery. If the United States decided to intervene militarily to stop Texas, a civil war appeared likely.

Taylor was not deterred. He sent federal troops to Santa Fe and directed the colonel in charge to prepare his troops to rebuff any invasion of New

Mexico.[30] The federal troops garrisoned in Santa Fe kept the Texas forces at bay. A stalemate ensued that was still in effect when Taylor died.

Taylor's decision to send troops to thwart the threatened invasion of New Mexico had significance beyond maintaining the viability of his plan for New Mexico's statehood. Significantly, Taylor had not turned to Congress for any special authorization to order federal troops to Santa Fe. Though there are no documents spelling out Taylor's thinking on the subject, we can infer his possible reasoning from his actions.

Conceivably, Taylor might have had four constitutional grounds for ordering federal troops to New Mexico. The first was his presidential duty under Article II to ensure that the laws be faithfully executed. In this circumstance, the law he might have been trying to preserve had not yet been enacted—the bills for admission of California and New Mexico as states. He might have figured that his authority as president to enforce the laws faithfully empowered him to do whatever he felt was necessary to protect the opportunity for Congress to use its authority to admit new states.

Second, Taylor might have believed, as commander in chief, that he had the constitutional authority to put down a rebellion, and he understood the threat made by Texas to be nothing more than a rebellion because it threatened the integrity (and boundaries) of the prospective state of New Mexico. This argument was the same that Jackson and Polk had used against threats of nullification and secession; and it would be the same ground on which Lincoln would initially rely to order federal troops into action a decade later.

Taylor's third ground might have been that the Constitution barred a state from interfering with a federal instrumentality, including federal territory. New Mexico was federal territory. It belonged to the United States, and Taylor believed that no state could invade a territory of the United States. The principle at stake was the same one that the Marshall Court had recognized nearly three decades before in *McCulloch v. Maryland*[31]—that the Constitution barred a state from exercising authority that could effectively destroy a federal instrumentality. Texas's invading New Mexico would have destroyed the autonomy of a territory of the United States.

Fourth, Taylor might have believed that in unilaterally ordering federal troops, he was acting to avert a civil war and keeping the Union intact. To achieve these ends, Taylor let it be known that, if necessary, he would lead the federal troops to stop a Texas invasion.

The third example of Taylor's rejection of the Whig conception of a weak presidency was how he used his cabinet.[32] In fact, Taylor did not consult Whig leaders on cabinet appointments, much less allow them to dictate his cabinet appointments.[33] Thus, his cabinet had no one representing the north-eastern part of the country or the most progressive wing of the Whig Party. Instead, it consisted entirely of men committed to *his* political agenda and not to that of Whig congressional leaders, including Clay.

To be sure, Taylor followed the preferred Whig practice of requiring his cabinet to unanimously approve all major appointments and major policy initiatives.[34] Vesting the cabinet with such authority was a sharp deviation from the practice that had taken hold, since Harrison's death, of presidents' using their cabinets as sounding boards and principal agents in implementing their preferred policies.[35] Yet Taylor's vesting his cabinet with substantial authority was not as Whiggish as it appeared, since, consisting as it did of men loyal to Taylor, it tended to follow *his* preferences on appointments and policy. When the cabinet deviated from his preferences, he followed his own counsel. Taylor followed the advice of his cabinet only when it coincided with his own views.[36]

If there were any doubt that Taylor was hostile to the Whig conception of the presidency, it should be dispelled by the fact that Whigs joined Democrats in the Senate to block or reject most of his executive branch nominations.[37] Some of Taylor's nominations were blocked as punishment for his persistent refusal to compromise with senators on the matter of California and New Mexico statehood. The fact that Taylor chose not to cut deals on appointments to curry favor with Whig leaders is further evidence of his rejection of the Whig conception of the presidency.

The fourth instance of Taylor's rejection of the Whig conception of the presidency is his unprecedented number of recess appointments made in response to the Senate's blockage of his nominations. Federal authorities before the Civil War had different interpretations of the president's authority "to fill up all Vacancies that may happen during the Recess of the Senate."[38] The clause was designed as an exception to the Appointments Clause, which generally set forth the distribution of powers governing appointments to cabinet or other posts established by Congress. Presidents agreed that the term "all" in the clause meant "all," even Article III judgeships, which had different tenure than officers appointed to political offices. Before 1823,[39] attorneys general and presidents narrowly construed the clause as permitting presidents to fill positions that had become vacant during recesses (which extended for several months).[40] In 1823, Monroe's attorney general, William Wirt, construed the clause broadly to encompass all vacancies that happened to exist, for whatever reason, during a "Recess."[41] Attorneys general over the next two decades reverted back to the narrower construction of the power as being available to fill vacancies arising during recesses.[42] Taylor agreed, however, with Monroe and Wirt that the Constitution authorized presidents to make temporary appointments to any offices that, for whatever reason, were vacant at the time of a recess. Consequently, Taylor made 428 recess appointments, more than all the recess appointments made by the eleven previous presidents.[43] Plainly, Taylor used this authority to fill the vacancies that the Senate had refused to allow him to fill in response to his demand that Congress approve the admissions of New Mexico and California separately as new states. Because Taylor had not asked for an attorney general's opinion on the scope of his recess appointment power, some members of Congress questioned it.[44] Nevertheless, Franklin Pierce's attorney general later adopted the same, broad construction of the scope of the recess appointment authority as Taylor had.[45]

Taylor's views on his removal authority were just as inconsistent with the Whig notion of a weak presidency as had been his views on his recess appointment authority. At the time he entered office, the principle of rotation in office had become more widely accepted than it had been during Harrison's short presidency. While some Whigs complained about the choices Taylor made for his cabinet, Whigs and Democrats generally did not dispute Taylor's constitutional authority to replace Polk's cabinet with choices of his own.[46]

Taylor's remarkable, unilateral decision to remove nearly two-thirds of Polk's appointees during his first full year in office[47] was, however, debated widely in Congress. Members of Congress from both parties contested Taylor's removal authority throughout the Thirty-first Congress, particularly its deviation from the Whig conception of a weak presidency.[48]

Taylor went further to consider replacing his entire cabinet as a response to the biggest scandal of his administration. The scandal resulted from an official decision made by Taylor's attorney general to authorize the treasury secretary to pay the full amount of the interest on a claim against the United States dating back to 1773.[49] When it became known that the interest was five times the size of the principal and that half of the principal and half of the interest was to go to Taylor's war secretary, George Crawford, for his legal services on behalf of the claimants, a public outcry arose. The matter festered for months, while the House considered censuring the three members of Taylor's cabinet involved in the deal and Taylor mused about the necessity of firing his entire cabinet to remove any appearance of corruption within his administration.[50] (Jackson had been the only previous president to claim the inherent authority to remove executive branch officials, even if the Senate had confirmed them.[51] To the extent Taylor's decision to remove his cabinet was known outside the administration, it would have strengthened the important precedent on presidential removal authority that Jackson had set earlier.)

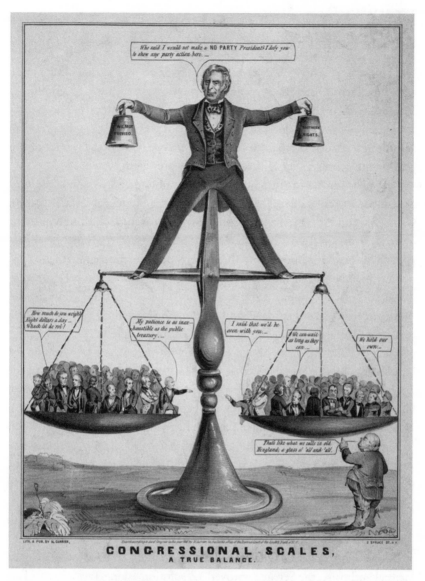

FIGURE 4.1 A satire on President Zachary Taylor's attempts to balance Southern and Northern interests on the question of slavery in 1850. Taylor stands atop a pair of scales, with a weight in each hand; the weight on the left reads "Wilmot Proviso" and the one on the right "Southern Rights." Below, the scales are evenly balanced, with several members of Congress, including Henry Clay in the tray on the left, and others, among them Lewis Cass and John Calhoun, on the right. Taylor says, "Who said I would not make a "NO PARTY" President? I defy you to show any party action here." One legislator on the left sings, "How much do you weigh? Eight dollars a day. Whack fol de rol!" Another states, "My patience is as inexhaustible as the public treasury." A congressman on the right says, "We can wait as long as they can." On the ground, at right, John Bull observes, "That's like what we calls in old Hingland, a glass of 'alf and 'alf."

Source: Library of Congress Prints and Photographs Division, Washington, D.C. 20540 USA

Congressional Pushback

The House and Senate retaliated against Taylor's blows to the Whig notion of the presidency. Their most common response took the form of resolutions. The more than thirty resolutions considered by the House and Senate attempted to restore the perceived imbalance of power between the president and Congress and to establish significant precedents on the scopes of impeachment, censure, oversight, and executive prerogatives.

The first anti-Taylor resolutions that the House and Senate considered were made in response to Taylor's annual message requesting statehood for California and New Mexico. Both chambers approved resolutions requesting more information from Taylor about what he had done to advance his plan,[52] and Taylor quickly responded to them.[53] It is noteworthy that neither Taylor nor any members of the House or Senate disputed either chamber's constitutional authority to approve the resolutions. Rather than question the authority of either chamber to demand information from him, Taylor explained that he had directed that "all measures of domestic policy adopted by the people of California must originate solely with themselves . . . without any interference by the executive," that his plan was designed "to afford to the wisdom and patriotism of Congress the opportunity of avoiding occasions of bitter and angry dissensions among the people of the United States," that if New Mexico became a state, then the Supreme Court would have jurisdiction over its boundary dispute with Texas, and that he pledged not to interfere with the "undoubted right . . . guaranteed to [the people of New Mexico] by the treaty of cession itself."[54] While Taylor disclaimed any interference with California's decision on whether to adopt a pro- or antislavery constitution, it could not be said that he was refraining from interfering—indeed, trying to direct—Congress's disposition of the subject.

In another attempt to retaliate against Taylor's efforts to consolidate presidential authority, the Senate approved a resolution asking Taylor to produce information regarding his postmaster general's removal decisions and appointments.[55] In both his responses, Taylor implicitly accepted the Senate's authority to request such information and submitted, without condition or objection, the requested information.

Next, on June 11, 1850, the Senate unanimously passed a resolution asking Taylor whether he had ordered federal troops in Santa Fe "to hold possession against the authority of Texas, or in any way to embarrass or prevent the exercises of her jurisdiction over that country" and requesting that he produce copies of any correspondence between the War Department and the military in Santa

Fe since Taylor's report in his annual message.[56] Six days later, Taylor responded that he had given no such orders and enclosed the requested correspondence.[57] Once again Taylor implicitly accepted the constitutionality of the requests.[58]

Meanwhile, the House debated censuring Taylor and his cabinet. House members considered different resolutions charging with misconduct the three members of Taylor's cabinet involved in the Galphin scandal. On July 6, 1850, the House voted 91–88 to add to the resolutions under consideration an amendment censuring Taylor for his "connection" with the claim.[59] On the day before Taylor died, the House approved three resolutions censuring Taylor's secretary of war, treasury secretary, and attorney general,[60] but the House tabled the resolutions when a motion was made to reprimand Taylor.[61] No one saw the point in kicking the dying president.

Taylor's acceptance—or lack of objection—to the House censure might have encouraged subsequent presidential rebukes by the House and Senate. Indeed, resolutions as a means of presidential rebuke remained intact after Taylor's presidency. Less than a decade later, President James Buchanan vigorously contested two attempts by the House to censure him, though the House ignored his protests, a House committee in 1860 castigated him for licensing corrupt practices within his administration, and the House in 1858 approved a committee report rebuking Buchanan for improprieties in awarding government contracts.[62]

Shaping Executive Leadership

Both before and during his presidency, Taylor significantly influenced two future presidents—Abraham Lincoln and Ulysses Grant—and future secretary of war and president of the Confederacy, Jefferson Davis. All three learned valuable lessons from Taylor on military strategy and the president's responsibilities, particularly in time of war.

To begin with, the Mexican War provided the principal testing ground for many men who became military leaders for both the Union and Confederate armed forces in the Civil War.[63] Winfield Scott, the commanding general of the army, had several talented young men on his staff, including Robert E. Lee, while Ulysses Grant served as a lieutenant under Scott and Taylor. Years later in his memoirs, Grant acknowledged that he had grown to admire Taylor and emulated his leadership style.[64]

Among Mexican War veterans, none had a closer relationship with Taylor than Jefferson Davis, who had served as a lieutenant under Taylor in the Black Hawk War.[65] After almost a decade of not speaking to each other,[66] the two men reconciled during the Mexican War, after which they forged a close relationship that lasted for the rest of Taylor's life. The two corresponded frequently while Taylor was pondering whether to run for the presidency; after Taylor's election, Davis was one of three senators who helped to plan his inaugural, and Davis frequently advised Taylor while Davis was a Democratic senator from Mississippi and Taylor was president.

Throughout his candidacy for the presidency and in office, Taylor urged Davis to follow his personal and constitutional convictions without fearing the loss of Taylor's respect.[67] Although Taylor had, in his prepresidential correspondence with Davis, sympathized with slaveholders and acknowledged that federal interference with slavery would likely tear the Union apart,[68] the hard line that Taylor took as president on the admissions of California and New Mexico as new states challenged Davis to express his own strident support for secession (which Taylor opposed), federal regulation of the territories (which Taylor recognized but Davis opposed), and slavery (which Davis believed the Fifth Amendment guaranteed as private property).[69] Davis voted to support Senate resolutions requesting further information from Taylor on his plan for statehood for California and New Mexico. While Davis voted to approve the Senate resolution requesting information from Taylor regarding his decision to send federal troops to Santa Fe,[70] Davis made the point, after Taylor's death, of defending Taylor's decision as the only way to preserve the opportunity for Congress to peaceably define the boundaries of Texas and New Mexico.[71]

The most important person whose constitutional views Taylor influenced was Abraham Lincoln. In fact, Lincoln was a faithful Whig until the party died. Although he campaigned for Clay in 1832 and 1844, he campaigned for Taylor in 1848 because he concluded Clay was no longer a viable presidential candidate.[72] In January 1849, Lincoln was finishing his single term as a Whig member of the House when he led the effort to censure Polk for unlawfully precipitating the Mexican War.[73] In 1849, Lincoln turned down an appointment by Taylor as secretary of the Territory of Oregon.[74] On July 25, 1850, Lincoln wrote a lengthy eulogy to Taylor that appeared in two local publications in Chicago.[75] Later, less than three weeks before his inauguration, Lincoln reassured his audience of the "political education" he had received from Taylor that "strongly inclines me against a very free use of [the veto and] any [other means of usurping congressional authority]. As a rule, I think it better that congress should originate, as well as perfect its measures, without external bias."[76]

Lincoln scholar David Herbert Donald suggests that such comments by Lincoln, coupled with his actions as president, indicate that Lincoln really was a Whig who deferred to congressional leadership on most domestic policymaking but believed in strong presidential leadership to address emergencies and war.

It is, however, possible that Donald might overstate Lincoln's devotion to Whig orthodoxy. Indeed, Donald suggests, on "key policies, ... especially those involving the use of war, Lincoln, like Harrison and Taylor before him, departed from the Whig theory of Cabinet responsibility."[77] Lincoln would also almost certainly have been aware of Taylor's rejections of the Whig conception of the presidency, rejections that extended into realms beyond war. In addition, Lincoln's deference to congressional leaders—and cabinet secretaries—on appointments was often conditioned on their compliance with his preferred criteria or made in exchange for their support for certain initiatives.[78] Moreover, Lincoln followed Taylor's broad construction of the president's recess appointment authority, which Lincoln's attorney general adopted in an official opinion in 1862.[79] Indeed, Lincoln is the only nineteenth-century president to have matched Taylor's numbers of recess appointments.

Thus, it might be more accurate to think of Lincoln as something other than a Whig: He was, in all likelihood, a political innovator who took advantage of casting his constitutional philosophy in traditional terms. Rather than initiate an entirely new rhetoric to describe his approach to presidential power, Lincoln appreciated that his exercise of executive power had to be grounded in precedents and language familiar to most Americans. He might have picked up where Taylor had left off in trying to exercise presidential power in ways that transcended partisan divisions for the sake of preserving both the nation and the Constitution.

TAYLOR AND WILLIAM Henry Harrison had much in common. They both were generals and successful Whig candidates for president. Both had to compete against Clay for control of their party and administrations. They were the only two Whigs elected president, and both died in office. Neither man came to the presidency with deeply held commitments to Whig principles, and both challenged Whig orthodoxy. The vice presidents who followed Harrison and Taylor into office each helped to further undermine the Whig conception of a weak presidency. As the next chapter shows, Taylor's successor, Millard Fillmore, was the only genuine Whig to be president, but he forged a constitutional legacy that helped to bury Whig principles of governance once and for all.

5

Millard Fillmore, 1850–1853

NO PRESIDENT PLEASED Henry Clay more than Millard Fillmore. The two men had been friends for many years, and Clay knew from firsthand experience that Fillmore was a loyal Whig. They had worked closely together when Fillmore was the chair of the House Ways and Means Committee and Clay was the Whig leader in the Senate. Fillmore had supported Clay's unsuccessful presidential campaigns, and Fillmore had been chosen as Taylor's running mate to appease southern Whigs, including Clay. Clay got the respect and deference from Fillmore that he believed that Harrison, Tyler, and Taylor had wrongfully denied him.[1]

In the four months between Fillmore's inauguration and Clay's reluctant departure from the Senate because of failing health, Clay served as Fillmore's spokesman in Congress, and the two often met privately to consult on major appointments and policy matters.[2] Before he died, Clay endorsed Fillmore as the Whig presidential nominee, the only time he endorsed anyone before the party's convention.

Yet, as president, Fillmore's constitutional stands destroyed the Whigs. While the constitutional act for which Fillmore is best known—signing the Compromise of 1850 including the controversial Fugitive Slave Act—was consistent with Whig expectations, many of his other actions were not, including his lobbying members of Congress to support the Compromise, his threats to use federal force to stop Texas from invading New Mexico, and his actions to stifle northern states' resistance to the Fugitive Slave Act. Later, Lincoln relied on Fillmore's actions to oppose secession and coordinate federal force to preserve the Union.

Being a Good Whig

The conventional account of Fillmore's fifteen months as vice president emphasizes his alienation from Taylor. It suggests that he had no influence over Taylor, even on appointments in his home state of New York, and criticizes

Taylor's failure not to use Fillmore—once a well-respected Whig leader in the House—to break the impasse in the Senate over Taylor's plan for admitting California and New Mexico as new states.[3] It attributes Fillmore's marginalization to Taylor's conviction that he owed his election and reelection to Fillmore's rival faction in the New York Whig Party led by Seward and Thurlow Weed. Fillmore's unhappiness over Seward's influence is often thought to explain why Fillmore told Taylor, shortly before Taylor died, that he publicly supported Taylor's plan but, if there were a tie vote on the Compromise, he intended to vote for it.[4]

Though historically supportable, this account overlooks the most obvious explanation for Fillmore's apparent disloyalty to Taylor: As vice president, Fillmore was following basic Whig principles. In his capacity as presiding officer of the Senate, Fillmore was acting upon his belief that the Constitution required him to defer to legislative supremacy, particularly from his position as presiding officer of the Senate; and he thus refrained from any active involvement in the debates over Taylor's plan and pledged to accept the evolving Compromise. Taylor was disappointed, but probably not surprised, that Fillmore was more loyal to Whig principles than to him. The fact that Fillmore's stated preference to follow his own construction of his constitutional duty as vice president severed his fragile relationship with Taylor underscores the extent to which Taylor had been following a different conception of presidential power.

Taking the Lead on Backing the Compromise of 1850

The Compromise of 1850 was not a single law but five bills that were separately debated, raised different constitutional issues, and were signed into law in the span of eleven days. The common purpose uniting the disparate bills—admitting California as a new state, abolishing the slave trade in the District of Columbia, organizing New Mexico and Utah as new territories, resolving the border dispute between Texas and New Mexico, and enacting a new fugitive slave law—was to be, as Fillmore said, "a final settlement of the dangerous and exciting subjects which they embraced."[5] The bills signified shifts in the government's approach to the constitutional divisions within Congress and the country over slavery.

First, the Compromise rejected the Wilmot Proviso's prohibition of slavery in the territories in favor of allowing the people of each territory and state the discretion over how to handle slavery.[6] The Compromise reflected Congress's endorsement of the principle of popular sovereignty that was becoming the central tenet of the Democratic Party. In the same vein, the Fugitive Slave Act of 1850 did not commandeer state officials to assist the enforcement of the law. It left the law's enforcement to federal officials and private citizens. States had some discretion to outlaw slavery if they wanted to do so, though federal law obliged them to refrain from assisting escaping slaves or interfering with the enforcement of the fugitive slave law. (More than a century later, the Supreme Court would uphold a state's constitutional immunity to be free of federal coercion.)[7] Moreover, California's admission as a state did not tip the balance of power in favor of antislavery forces in the Senate, as Southerners like Jefferson Davis had feared.[8] In fact, California did not bar the presence of slaves that had been in the state prior to its admission into the Union; and California's representatives and two senators were Democrats who usually supported slavery in the period between California's admission and the Civil War's onset.[9] Similarly, by organizing New Mexico and Utah as new territories without any restrictions on slavery, the Compromise allowed the people of each of these territories to deal with slavery as they saw fit.[10] The Compromise thus became a model for later federal laws affirming popular sovereignty.

The second shift in the federal government's approach to the constitutional issues associated with slavery was evident in the portion of the Compromise granting Texas some of its claims to New Mexican territory and $10 million in exchange for relinquishing others. This bill reinforced Congress's authority as the principal arbiter of border disputes among the states and the territories. In exercising this authority, Congress effectively rejected Taylor's proposal of leaving the dispute for the Supreme Court to resolve. (In fact, shortly before Congress approved this component of the Compromise, the Senate rejected, 42–1, Taylor's proposals to admit New Mexico as a new state and to refer its boundary dispute with Texas to the Supreme Court. William Seward cast the only favorable vote.)

The law signified a novel use of Congress's spending power. It did not follow the conventional path of using federal money to bribe states to forgo doing things they had the constitutional authority to do.[11] Instead, Congress validated the popular government in Texas and rewarded it for not doing something it actually lacked the authority to do. The law, in other words, vested the state with power it did not previously have. In doing so, it illustrated how the spending power could be used to expand states' rights.

The third shift in the constitutional approach adopted in the Compromise was embodied in its most controversial component, the Fugitive Slave Act of 1850. Its passage within the House was universally perceived as flatly rejecting the Wilmot Proviso. (Indeed, neither the House nor the Senate would come close again to approving anything like the Proviso until after the Civil War.) The 1850 Fugitive Slave Act was modeled on the antithesis of the Wilmot Proviso, the original Fugitive Slave Act, which the First Congress had enacted in 1793 and which the Supreme Court had upheld.[12] Proponents of the Fugitive Slave Act of 1850 thus defended its constitutionality on the bases of long-standing historical practices *and* judicial precedent. Southern Democrats claimed that the Constitution required Congress to enact this statute as a means of protecting the ownership of slaves as private property guaranteed to be free from federal interference by the Fifth Amendment's Due Process Clause.[13]

By signing all five measures of the Compromise, Fillmore signed onto their constitutional significance. On the day he became president, Fillmore told Webster, then a key Whig proponent of the Compromise in the Senate, that he was withdrawing Taylor's plan and was willing to accept any reasonable compromise approved by Congress on the subject. Fillmore further signaled his intention publicly by making his first cabinet appointment the selection of Webster as secretary of state. (Webster correctly construed Fillmore's offer to join his cabinet as solid evidence of Fillmore's intention to approve a legislative compromise.)[14] In his first special message to Congress, Fillmore promised his unconditional support for the Compromise.[15]

By accepting and vigorously enforcing the Compromise, Fillmore was following the basic Whig belief that the president should defer to congressional leadership on the slavery question and enforce Congress's preferred policy unless it plainly violated the Constitution. Since Fillmore did not believe the Compromise violated the Constitution, he signed it. Shortly thereafter, he told Hamilton Fish, the Whig governor of New York and an opponent of the Fugitive Slave Act, that, in spite of his personal opposition to slavery and the Fugitive Slave Act, he felt compelled by Whig principles to sign the law.[16] He similarly wrote to Webster, "God knows that I detest slavery, but it is an existing evil [that] we must endure, give it such protection as is guaranteed by the Constitution, till we can get rid of it without destroying the last hope of free government in the world."

Yet Fillmore had not just been a faithful Whig in signing the Compromise. He had not waited passively for the Compromise to come to his desk for his signature. In sharp contrast to his refusal to become involved in Senate debate on Taylor's plan, Fillmore was actively involved in persuading northern Whigs to support the Compromise and shaping Senate negotiations over the Compromise.[17]

As part of his duty to enforce the new law, Fillmore went further to respond to the constitutional arguments made against its enforcement in several states. In fact, nine northern states[18] enacted "personal liberty laws," which forbade state officials (including judges) to participate in the enforcement of the Fugitive Slave Act or prohibited the use of their jails in fugitive slave cases. The laws tried to remedy the defects cited by opponents of the federal law as the reasons for its unconstitutionality. Accordingly, the laws expressly guaranteed to African-Americans, captured pursuant to the Fugitive Slave Act, the two rights that federal law had denied them—the right of habeas corpus and the right to jury trials. Resisting states asserted the right to nullify, or not to comply with, federal laws that they deemed unconstitutional. (Interestingly, the same arguments have been used by states to refuse compliance with federal laws with which they disagreed, including not only prior to the Civil War but also more recently with respect to the Affordable Care Act.)

For the remainder of his time in office, Fillmore used every power that he had as president to rebuff the constitutional attacks made against the law's enforcement. Less than a month after he had signed the Fugitive Slave Act of 1850 into law, a group of local citizens in Lancaster, Pennsylvania, refused to comply with a federal marshal's request for assistance in capturing a fugitive slave. The refusal prompted the marshal to turn to two Pennsylvania judges, who asked Fillmore to order federal troops to assist the marshal in enforcing the law. Fillmore understood that the Constitution's Supremacy Clause made federal law supreme over any state law (or resistance) to the contrary[19] and that he was responsible for ensuring states did not interfere with the enforcement of federal law. Fillmore reassured his cabinet and members of Congress that he had sworn an oath to support the Constitution and that he had the duty to ensure the enforcement of all federal laws that were plainly not inconsistent with it. He told Webster that he would avoid using military force if necessary, "not doubting that there is yet patriotism enough left in every State north of Mason's and Dixon's line to maintain the supremacy of the laws; and being particularly anxious that no State should be disgraced, by being compelled to resort to the army to support the laws of the Union."[20] In the absence of Webster and Attorney General Crittenden, Fillmore's cabinet unanimously advised Fillmore that he had the power and the duty to use military force to support civilian authorities trying to enforce the law. Fillmore instructed the marine commander in nearby Philadelphia to assist local authorities if a federal judge deemed such assistance necessary and informed the federal marshals and commissioners in the area that they would have the same support when needed.[21]

Fillmore delivered the same message to everyone. In November, he reiterated to Fish that his principal duty was to preserve the Union. As resistance to the federal law intensified, Fillmore modified the basis of his actions to include the oath he had sworn to protect the Constitution and the need to protect the integrity of the Union. He explained to Fish that northern Whigs "did not appreciate the dangers to which we are exposed from the South, and the infinite importance of setting an example of maintaining the Constitution in all its parts." Toward this end, he felt the fugitive slave law "must be executed" and "sustained against attempts at repeal."[22] Fillmore was aware of the risk that several southern states might try to secede once Congress admitted California. To stop them, Fillmore said that he was prepared "to bring the full force of the government" to sustain the law in the North. He believed its enforcement would show Southerners his intention to use force if necessary to stop secession and nullification to preserve the Union and the Constitution.

In early December, Fillmore used his First Annual Message to bolster political and constitutional support for the Compromise. He promised that "to the utmost of my ability and to the extent of the power vested in me I shall at all times and in all places take care that the laws be faithfully executed." He further declared, "I deem it my first duty not to question [the Constitution's] wisdom, add to its provisions, evade its requirements, or nullify its commands." He believed resistance to congressional will was unnecessary and destroyed the rule of the law in "a government like ours, in which all laws are passed by a majority of the representatives of the people, and those representatives are chosen for such short periods that any injurious or obnoxious law can very soon be repealed." He defended the Compromise as necessary "to allay asperities and animosities that were rapidly alienating one section of the country from another and destroying those fundamental sentiments which are the strongest supports of the Constitution."[23]

Less than two months later, a group of free African-Americans stormed a Boston courtroom and released a man who had been on trial as a fugitive slave. In response, Fillmore issued a proclamation urging Boston citizens to obey the laws and commanding "all officers, civil and military, and all other persons, civil or military" in the area to aid by all means in their power "in quelling this and other such combinations."[24] Fillmore directed the federal prosecutor in Boston to prosecute anyone who assisted the rescue. In a special message sent to the Senate on February 19, Fillmore requested that Congress facilitate enforcement of the act by amending it to empower him to call state militia into national service without first issuing a proclamation calling on lawbreakers to desist and disperse.[25] Though Congress never acted on the request, it demonstrated Fillmore's willingness to take the initiative in formulating responses to the resistance to federal law.

In May 1851, Fillmore extended his public defense of the Fugitive Slave Act on a five-hundred-mile road trip, along with his cabinet, to celebrate the completion of the Erie Railroad from New York to Dunkirk. Since the people and state legislature of New York had announced their opposition to the Fugitive Slave Act, Fillmore and Webster were pressed along the way to defend the law. Consequently, they became the most conspicuous defenders of the constitutionality of the law. Their public defense of the law is an early instance of a president's using his bully pulpit and cabinet to mobilize public support for a controversial initiative.

Besides defending enforcement of federal law in New York, Secretary of State Webster repeatedly urged enforcing the law in Massachusetts. In October 1850, the owners of two married slaves had hunted them down in Boston, where local abolitionists prevented the marshal from recapturing them. Webster traveled to Boston to support the marshal and persuaded Fillmore to announce that he would use federal troops, if necessary, to enforce the law. The couple was rescued and taken to England before a local court could act upon Webster's request to have them placed in federal custody. In February, Webster traveled back to Boston to intercede on behalf of the law when another crowd stormed a courtroom and freed a man who was on trial as a fugitive slave. Incensed over the lawlessness, Webster published a letter declaring, "No man is at liberty to set up, or affect to set up, his own conscience as above the law, in a matter which respects the rights of others, and the obligations, civil, social, and political due to others from him. Such a pretense saps the foundation of all government."[26] Webster arranged for the indictment of eight men for helping the slave to escape, but a hung jury resulted in their release. After Webster helped to foil a plot to free a fugitive slave from being forced to return to captivity, Fillmore "congratulate[d Webster] and the country upon the triumph of the law in Boston." As in Pennsylvania, judges asked Fillmore to send troops, and Fillmore again directed that federal judges give that authority to marshals and deputies if they deemed it necessary.[27] Webster predicted that Fillmore's steady backing of the fugitive slave law, along with the decisions of state and federal judges to uphold its constitutionality, "will settle the question" of the legality of noncompliance with the law.[28]

In May, Webster left the president's entourage to deliver speeches defending the Fugitive Slave Act in Syracuse, Buffalo, and Albany. In Syracuse, "that laboratory of abolitionism, libel, and treason," Webster denounced people who had "set up themselves over the Constitution, over the laws, and above the decisions of the highest tribunals, and who say [the fugitive slave law] shall not be carried into effect." They have "pledged their lives, their fortunes, and sacred honor!—for what? For the violation, of the law, for the committal of treason to their country; for it is treason, and nothing else."[29] In Buffalo, Webster used the metaphor of a "house divided" (which Lincoln later embellished) to stress the need to "preserve the Union of the States, not by coercion, not by military power, not by angry controversies . . . but by the silken chords of mutual, fraternal, patriotic affection." He conceded the problem was slavery but told the crowd that he had never consented to adding "one foot of slave territory beyond what the old thirteen States had at the time of formation of the Union." He explained "that it was not within the scope or design of the Constitution to admit new States out of foreign territory." He reminded his audience that he had voted against the treaty with Mexico and had wanted "none of her territory, neither California, New Mexico, nor Utah." He declared that if the Compromise had not passed, "civil war would have ensued; blood, American blood, would have been shed; and who can tell what would have been consequences?" Acknowledging the fact that slavery existed in the South, he said, "It must be obvious to every intelligent person that, if Congress possessed power over slavery as it exists in the southern States, any attempt to exercise such power would break up the Union just as surely as would an attempt to introduce slavery in Massachusetts." He explained that the Constitution made federal law supreme over state resistance and promised "to exert any power I had to keep that country together."[30] In Albany, Webster urged the "young men of the United States [to] uphold the institutions under which you were born. . . . [I] believe firmly that this Union, once broken, is utterly incapable [of] being reconstructed in its original character, of being re-cemented by any chemistry, or art, or effort, or skill of man."[31]

In June, Webster went too far. In Virginia, he stressed that, in order to preserve the Constitution, *all* of its parts had to be honored. He argued that, when different parties enter into a compact, none of them may disregard one provision and expect others to obey the rest. Webster maintained that the same principle applied to the fugitive slave law. "A bargain cannot be broken on one side, and still bind the other side." He added, "I am as ready to fight and fall for the constitutional rights of Virginia as I am for those of Massachusetts. [I] would no more see a feather plucked unjustly from the honor of Virginia than I would see one so plucked from the honor of Massachusetts."[32] It did not take long for Webster to realize that his argument supported secession. He subsequently tried to clarify that the Constitution could only be dissolved by revolution. The effort failed, and southern secessionists delighted in citing Webster's speech in defense of a state's constitutional right to secede from the Union.

In the fall of 1851, Clay used his final days in the Senate to rally the nation behind the Compromise and against secession. In response to the Boston riots, Clay asked Mississippi senator Henry Foote, a Unionist Democrat, to meet with Fillmore. Fillmore assured Foote that he would "enforce the laws of the land at all hazards, and put down, with the whole power of the government, if need be, any illicit or violent attempt to counteract or overturn them." At Fillmore's suggestion, Foote met with Webster, who stressed the administration's resolve to use force if necessary to preserve the Union.[33] In his final speech before the Senate, Clay emphasized that the Constitution recognized no right within the states to nullify federal laws or to secede. "You find that whenever you press [secessionists] on these points, they fly from the Constitution and talk about the mode of its formation, its compact character, its being formed by the States." Referring to the obstruction of the fugitive slave law in Boston, Clay said that not since the Whiskey Rebellion had there been "an instance in which there was so violent and forcible obstruction of the United States since the commencement of the Government."[34]

Burying the Whig Conception of the Presidency

The initiative Fillmore took in pushing the Compromise of 1850 through Congress and in its enforcement were hardly his only deviations from Whig governance principles. He deviated in several other areas, including appointments, removals, pardons, and his uses of his cabinet and military force.

First, Fillmore defended the principle of rotation in office. On his second day in office, Fillmore became the first president to accept the resignation of his entire cabinet. None agreed with his support for the Compromise. He then worked systematically with Webster and Clay to "remodel" his administration by removing anyone who had not supported the Compromise.[35] Consequently, he removed the largest number of political appointees of any president up until that time, including over half of the political appointees in the State Department.[36] Fillmore's actions helped to entrench the principle of rotation in office as a fact of constitutional life.

Second, Fillmore used his appointment power to reward people who supported the Compromise and opposed the Wilmot Proviso. An additional criterion for his cabinet selections was a sworn commitment not to become a candidate in the next presidential election. Although Fillmore's appointment preferences were designed to heal the party and unify support for his policies within his administration, his purpose was undercut by his purposeful exclusion of Whigs, particularly from the North, who had supported Taylor and the Wilmot Proviso. Perhaps most importantly, he followed his own counsel in appointing his new cabinet and subcabinet officers. The new cabinet was loyal to Fillmore but not to the party's leaders.

Fillmore followed a similar tack in his one successful Supreme Court appointment. When Associate Justice Levi Woodbury died, Fillmore turned to Webster, but notably not other congressional leaders, for advice. Webster recommended Benjamin Curtis, a prominent lawyer, scholar, and faithful Whig who had opposed the Fugitive Slave Act. Although Democrats held a majority of 35–24 in the Senate, Curtis was easily confirmed by voice vote. Less than six years later, Curtis dissented in *Dred Scott v. Sanford*[37] and resigned in disgust from the Court.[38] His dissent is notable as the most comprehensive and carefully reasoned defenses of the federal government's power to restrict slavery in the territories and of the entitlement of African-Americans to the privileges and immunities of national citizenship.

Fillmore used a different tactic in trying to fill the other vacancy that arose during his presidency. It arose in the summer of 1852 when Associate Justice John McKinley died. In trying to fill the vacancy, Fillmore accepted, as he had with his nomination of Curtis, the need to fill it with someone from the same circuit as the justice being replaced. This time, Fillmore made four different nominations to fill the position, but none succeeded. First, he nominated Whig lawyer Edward Bradford. The Senate was, however, led by Democrats who, eager to keep the vacancy open for the next president to fill, quickly tabled Bradford's nomination. Fillmore next tried to take advantage of the principle of senatorial courtesy—the Senate's historic deference to nominations of one of its own to confirmable offices. He nominated Senator George Badger of North Carolina, a Whig whom Fillmore believed fellow senators would agree to confirm. Instead, the desire to keep the vacancy open for Democrats to fill prevailed, and the Senate postponed further action by a single vote. Fillmore then pushed the Senate harder to adhere to senatorial courtesy by taking the unusual step of nominating a Democrat in a Whig-like attempt to defer to the will of a majority of the Senate. Though the Senate confirmed his nomination of newly elected Democratic senator Judah Benjamin of Louisiana, Benjamin declined the appointment. Days before Franklin Pierce's inauguration, Fillmore nominated Benjamin's law partner, William Micou, a Whig whom he hoped Democrats would find agreeable because of his close association with Benjamin. Again, the Senate tabled the nomination. Fillmore ran out of time, and Pierce got the vacancy to fill.

In using his cabinet, Fillmore further deviated from Whig principles. Whereas Whig orthodoxy called for a president to defer to his cabinet's votes on major policy initiatives, Fillmore made clear from the outset that his cabinet served him and not the other way around. Indeed, Fillmore only consulted with Webster and Attorney General Crittenden on constitutional objections that had been made to the Fugitive Slave Act,[39] and he signed the law without consulting other members of his cabinet. For the remainder of his presidency, Fillmore did not ask his cabinet for advice unless he knew it agreed with him.

Fillmore's deference to his attorney general, John Crittenden, coincided with another deviation from the Whig orthodoxy on presidential power. Two men convicted of violating the Fugitive Slave Act were in prison in the nation's capital and had been required to pay fines to the federal government and two slaveholders. Their prosecution and imprisonment had received widespread attention since their attempts to assist fugitive slaves had been a part of the largest recorded escape attempt by slaves in American history. Represented by Horace Mann (who had also been one of the lawyers for the slaves who had mutinied on the *Amistad*), the men requested a pardon from Fillmore, who asked Crittenden for his opinion. Crittenden opined that Fillmore had the power to release the two men from jail *and* to absolve them from having to pay fines owed to the federal government but that his pardon power did not extend to money owed—even under a federal statute—to private citizens.[40] Fillmore took the advice and freed them from prison and paying federal fines; however, he did not release them from having to pay the fines they had been ordered to pay to the two slaveholders. The fact that Fillmore pardoned the men was no small thing. The pardon literally had undone the various acts he had authorized in signing the Fugitive Slave Act into law and in overseeing the prosecution of the men who sought his pardon. The pardon thus stands in marked contrast to the deference he had shown in signing the Fugitive Slave Act into law and the intense efforts he had waged to secure compliance with it. The pardon was thus an act of independence incompatible with the subservience that faithful Whigs expected from their president.

Fillmore's fifth rejection of the Whig conception of the presidency was one of his first. In his first message to Congress, he declared, contrary to Whig expectations that he would follow Congress's lead, that he had decided on his own initiative to send an additional 750 troops to Santa Fe to stop Texas from invading New Mexico. Echoing Taylor (and foreshadowing Lincoln), Fillmore vowed,

If the laws of the United States are opposed or obstructed in any State or Territory by combinations too powerful to be suppressed by the judicial or civil authorities, ... it is the duty of the President either to call out the militia or to employ the military and naval force of the United States or to do both if in his judgment the exigency of the occasion shall so require. . . . If Texas militia, therefore, march into any of the other States or into any territory of the United States [to] execute or enforce any law of Texas, they become at that moment trespassers; they are no longer under the protection of any lawful authority, and are to be regarded merely as intruders; and if within such State or Territory they obstruct any law of the United States, whether by power of arms or mere power of numbers ... the President ... is bound to obey the solemn instruction of the Constitution and exercise the high powers vested in him by that instrument and by the acts of Congress.[41]

Fillmore's decision was significant. He had not consulted with congressional leaders before making or announcing his decision, and there was no law authorizing him to send troops to New Mexico, even to protect against a threatened invasion of federal land. New Mexico was not yet a territory, so the only laws that Fillmore could have been enforcing were a combination of the Constitution, the Treaty of Guadalupe Hidalgo, and the federal law against treason. In not waiting for specific congressional authorization, Fillmore was making the larger point that the authority at stake was that of the federal government. Through his actions and statements, he was emphasizing that a state lacked the authority to assert, by force or otherwise, the authority vested in Congress by the Constitution to resolve boundary disputes within the United States. This decision, along with Fillmore's arguments against the constitutionality of secession and subsequent decisions to deploy troops to ensure enforcement of federal law, established significant precedents that Lincoln followed in rejecting the legality of secession and ordering federal troops to put down the treason and rebellion threatening the Union and the Constitution.

THE TENSIONS BETWEEN the demands of Whig orthodoxy and the presidency were evident throughout Fillmore's time in office. While Fillmore assumed that the president had unilateral power to order troops to thwart a threat to federal territory, to remove at will federal officials whom the Senate had confirmed, and to follow his own counsel in making nominations, he agreed to sign and vigorously enforce the Compromise of 1850 out of deference to Congress. Such deference did not win back for Fillmore the support he had lost within the Whig Party because of the independence he had shown as president.

Fillmore's ambivalence to Whig principles is also apparent in his indecision about running for reelection. Early in his presidency, he had said he would follow the Whig principle of a president's serving only for a single term,[42] and he maintained this commitment as late as the winter of 1851. When Fillmore made the pledge, it pleased traditional Whigs who construed it as fealty to the party. Northern Whigs were pleased, because they opposed making him their party's nominee for president in 1852. Traditionalists within the party were not happy less than a year later when Fillmore broke his pledge. The turnaround came too late, as he realized he had no hope to secure the party's nomination. No president after Fillmore pledged to serve a single term. It was one of many Whig principles Fillmore helped to bury for good.

6

Franklin Pierce, 1853–1857

IF YOU DRIVE west heading out of downtown Topeka, Kansas, you will cross fifteen streets that are named chronologically for the antebellum presidents. One name is missing. After Topeka became the state capital, the legislature, dominated by the Free Soil Party, decided not to name a street after Franklin Pierce. Instead, they named the fourteenth cross street for Henry Clay. If Pierce is remembered in Topeka, it is ironically because of the deliberate effort to forget him.

Many people dismiss Pierce as one of America's most inept presidents. Nothing before his election promised otherwise: In six years in the House and five in the Senate, he never sponsored any important legislation and rigidly followed the Democrats' party line. When Pierce's wife, Jane, was told that her husband was the Democratic nominee for president, she fainted. She worried that the pressures of the presidency would cause her husband to begin drinking again,[1] while Pierce's college friend, Nathaniel Hawthorne, told Pierce after he won the 1852 presidential election, "I pity you—Indeed I do, from the bottom of my heart!"[2]

The low expectations for Pierce's presidency fell further when, just two months before his inauguration, the railcar in which he, his wife, and their only son, Bennie, were traveling suddenly derailed and fell down an embankment. Bennie was killed as Pierce and his wife watched helplessly. Neither Pierce nor his wife recovered. Jane spent much of her time in the White House alone, writing letters to Bennie and blaming Pierce's political ambitions for her son's death. Bennie's death was clearly on Pierce's mind as he entered the presidency: He referred to his child twice in his inaugural address—once in its opening line and again in the second paragraph when he asked the American people to "sustain me by your strength."[3] For the next three years, Pierce sought solace in a renewed commitment to his religious faith. He refused to work on the Sabbath except for the one occasion he met with congressional leaders to forge the Kansas-Nebraska Act, whose enactment and enforcement were the most consequential constitutional events of his presidency.

In spite of generating low expectations as the second dark horse after Polk to win the Democratic presidential nomination,[4] Pierce benefited in the general election from several factors—his general amiability; the arrogance and stiffness of his Whig opponent, General Winfield Scott; his stature as a Doughface (a northern politician who sympathized with the South and slave-holders); and a flattering campaign biography (written by Hawthorne) that made his exploits as an officer in the Mexican War more heroic than they were. Pierce won a decisive victory in the Electoral College, making him the fifth general to be elected before the Civil War. Yet, with more than three million votes cast in the general election, Pierce received less than 50,000 votes more than his five opponents combined. Once in office, he quickly lost favor with his fellow Democrats, who viewed him as inept, indecisive, and weak. He became the only popularly elected president denied renomination by his party. More embarrassingly, he lost the nomination to his ambassador to Great Britain, James Buchanan. In retirement, his drinking increased, as did the stridency of his criticism of Lincoln for waging war against the South. After Lincoln's assassination, Pierce barely managed to escape a crowd gathered outside his home to lynch him because he had not displayed a flag in mourning for the dead president. Pierce drank himself to death, stubbornly insisting to the end that northern abolitionists caused the Civil War. It took more than fifty years for the citizens of his hometown to erect a statue in his honor.

Pierce's problem was, however, not so much that he was indecisive and vacillating, but rather that he was largely successful in implementing his uncompromising, flawed constitutional vision. He is the first and only president who served a complete term without a single change in his cabinet.[5] He was known as "Young Hickory of the Granite Hills" because he had modeled his presidency and constitutional vision on those of "Old Hickory" Andrew Jackson and "Young Hickory" James Polk. Yet his strict construction was more extreme than either of theirs. He insisted that the Constitution was not neutral on the question of slavery but rather protected the rights of slave-holders and obliged the federal government to enforce laws restricting anti-slavery activities.[6] His unrelenting efforts to implement his strict construction of the Constitution did more than expand the country's continental borders to where they now stand and marshal federal power to protect slavery. His unbending constitutional commitments backfired, producing near–civil war in Kansas, fracturing his party, and fomenting the rise of the Republican Party. Pierce has a substantial constitutional legacy, though it is one that even he drank to forget.

Strict Construction of the Constitution in the White House

The first of Pierce's three significant constitutional legacies is his strict construction of the Constitution. While this mode of constitutional interpretation can be traced back to Jefferson and Jackson, strict constructionists during the first half of the nineteenth century generally agreed that the Constitution's authority derived from the states rather than the people of the United States. Yet they differed over the extent to which the Constitution allowed states to disregard federal laws with which they disagreed or to secede from the Union. While Pierce, before becoming president, had managed to avoid endorsing either the doctrine of nullification or secession, his strict construction of the Constitution required vigorous protection of states' rights and the rights of slaveholders. His persistent espousal of strict construction also signaled that as president he was on the side of southern Democrats in the great constitutional debates of the times.[7] In his inaugural address, Pierce declared that "the Federal Government" should "confine itself to the exercise of powers clearly granted by the Constitution," and he explained that "involuntary servitude, as it exists in different States of this Confederacy, is recognized by the Constitution. I believe that it stands like any other admitted right, and that the States where it exists are entitled to efficient remedies to enforce the constitutional provisions."[8] After reiterating his campaign pledge to stand by the Compromise of 1850, Pierce expressed his belief that "the constitutional authorities of this Republic are bound to regard the rights of the South in this respect as they would view any other legal and constitutional right, and that the laws to enforce them should be respected and obeyed, not with a reluctance encouraged by abstract opinions as to their propriety in a different state of society, but with cheerfulness and according to the decisions of the tribunal to which their exposition belongs." Promising to act on his convictions, Pierce hoped that "the question [of slavery's future] was at rest" and "that no sectional or fanatical excitement may again threaten the durability of our institutions or obscure the light of our prosperity." He was soon proved wrong.

Subsequently, the theme Pierce expressed most consistently in his public addresses was his commitment to strict construction of the Constitution. This commitment is evident in all four of his annual messages to Congress. In each of the first two, Pierce sounded the same theme he had previously espoused as a member of Congress, namely, that strict construction required recognizing funding internal improvements as beyond the power of Congress. In the first message, he reminded Congress of President Jackson's opposition to such funding, and following that example, he questioned the pending proposal of federal aid for a transcontinental railroad: "Is it not the better rule to leave all these works to private enterprise, regulated and, when expedient, aided by the cooperation of the State?"

In each of Pierce's remaining annual messages, he emphasized the fundamental importance of strict construction to the nation's survival. He emphasized that the Constitution's guaranteed protection of states' rights was forged "under a written compact between Sovereign States, uniting for specific objects and with specific grants to their general agent."[9] He explained that the Union, which he often referred to as a "confederation" or "the Confederacy," could survive only by "strictest fidelity to the principles of the constitution as understood by those who have adhered to the most restricted construction of the powers granted by the people and the States."

Pierce's last annual message was his most vitriolic, extreme declaration of the link between strict construction and constitutional protection of slave owners' rights. The stridency was surprising, for he was by then a lame duck and widely dismissed as irrelevant by Congress and the rest of the nation as it prepared for Buchanan's inauguration. Pierce's strict construction of the Constitution lapsed into a shrill political manifesto: He construed James Buchanan's 1856 election as vindicating his conviction that the nation had rejected the idea of sectional parties and instead had affirmed "the constitutional equality of each and all the States of the union as states; they have affirmed the constitutionality of each and all the citizens of the United States as citizens."[10] Moreover, in Pierce's judgment, the American people "have maintained the inviolability of the constitutional rights of the different sections of the Union, and they have proclaimed their devoted and unalterable attachment to the Union and to the constitution, as objects of interest superior to all subjects of local or sectional controversy, as the safeguard of the rights of all." Although Pierce did not explicitly name the newly formed Republican Party, he accused it of pretending to stop the spread of slavery while really being determined "to change the domestic institutions of existing States." He ended with a litany of the ways in which northern aggression "against the constitutional rights of nearly one-half of the thirty-one States" was responsible for *all* the country's sectional troubles.

Pierce's strict construction of the Constitution was not just rhetorical. He also tried vigorously to implement it through his exercise of the presidency's unique powers. He vetoed nine laws on constitutional grounds, five of which Congress overrode. Most of the vetoes involved internal improvement projects, which Pierce explained, as a matter of strict construction, Congress had no constitutional authority to enact. Indeed, his best-known veto clearly reflected this perspective: It involved a bill to set aside twelve million acres of public land to fund institutions for the indigent mentally ill.[11] Dorothea Dix, who would become internationally famous for her efforts to help the mentally ill, had devoted years to building support for the measure. In various forms the bill had been under consideration since 1848, and it enjoyed the support of many Whigs and Democrats in Congress, as well as strong public support and favorable editorial opinion. But in a lengthy veto message Pierce declared the bill unconstitutional. The Constitution did not grant authority to make the federal government "the great almoner of public charity," wrote Pierce. Indeed, he found the bill to be "subversive of the whole theory upon which the Union of these States is founded." Congress failed to override the veto. Most of Pierce's other vetoes involved other internal improvement projects, most of which had been planned for the Northwest, while one nixed a southern project.

Pierce used his judicial and other appointments to entrench his strict construction of the Constitution. In fact, the Senate confirmed all but one of his judicial nominees, who professed strong fidelity to the same constitutional philosophy. Pierce's most influential judicial appointment was his first and only Supreme Court appointment. Because of the Senate's refusals to approve any of Fillmore's three nominations to replace Justice McKinley, who had died in the summer of 1852, Pierce found himself in the first week of his presidency with a Supreme Court vacancy to fill. In an unprecedented move, Justices John Catron and Benjamin Curtis delivered letters from all the justices asking Pierce to appoint John Campbell of Alabama. As a strict constructionist, Campbell shared Pierce's constitutional philosophy, but his nomination commanded bipartisan support because of his reputation as one of the nation's most learned lawyers and best appellate advocates and because of his expressed opposition to secession. Although Campbell had been Chief Justice Roger Taney's choice as a successor, he left the Court after only eight years to join the Confederacy. While on the Court, he consistently defended states' rights from federal encroachment and concurred, as a matter of strict constitutional construction, with the majority in *Dred Scott v. Sanford*.[12] After the Civil War and a short prison term for aiding the Confederate states, Campbell resumed his law practice and reestablished his reputation as a preeminent Supreme Court advocate. Over the next quarter century, Campbell argued forty-three more cases before the Court, including representing the plaintiffs in the first case to test the meaning of the newly adopted Fourteenth Amendment.[13]

Pierce was the first president to vest in his attorney general control over the selection of federal judges, though he reserved the authority to establish guidelines for their selection and to make specific recommendations. Pierce's attorney general, Caleb Cushing, recommended that Pierce nominate only candidates who were Democrats, were "well qualified by experience," and were committed to strict construction of the Constitution and enforcement of the Fugitive Slave Act. With Cushing's help, Pierce appointed fifteen judges to lower courts, two to the Circuit Court for the District of Columbia, one to a special Circuit Court for the District of California, and twelve others to territorial district courts. Each of Pierce's judicial nominees was strongly committed to strict construction of the Constitution[14] and strict enforcement of the Fugitive Slave Act.

Moreover, many of Pierce's major nonjudicial appointments were strict constructionists. Of his seven-member cabinet, the three on whom Pierce most heavily relied were strict constructionists—Caleb Cushing as attorney general, Jefferson Davis as secretary of war, and James Guthrie as treasury secretary.

Implementing Strict Construction through the Cabinet

Pierce's second constitutional legacy consists of his relationship with his cabinet and its consequences. In assembling his cabinet, he was neither vacillating nor indecisive. To the contrary, he understood he had unilateral authority over his cabinet choices and deployed it to the extreme, but his independence and decision not to consult with congressional leaders backfired politically: The cabinet he assembled did not unify Democrats or his administration. It had geographic representation but omitted southern Unionists and many powerful Democrats. Nor did Pierce appoint any moderates to his cabinet. These omissions put the administration at odds philosophically and programmatically with the party's most powerful leaders, including Stephen Douglas of Illinois.

Moreover, Davis and Cushing held extreme constitutional opinions that many Democrats and Whigs rejected. Nonetheless, the Senate confirmed them both. The fact that Democrats held a large advantage in the Senate— thirty-eight of sixty-two seats—helped both Davis and Cushing. Moreover, Davis benefited from senatorial courtesy on which Pierce, himself a former senator, had counted. Since the Senate also confirmed William Marcy, another former senator, as Pierce's secretary of state, Pierce helped to entrench senatorial courtesy further in the balance of power on federal appointments.

To complicate matters, the cabinet as a whole was dysfunctional. At meetings, the best Pierce could do was to moderate, not lead, discussion. Though he often consulted his cabinet on policy options and frequently visited the different departments, forging consensus within the cabinet was impossible. When the cabinet met, members often yelled at each other, and Pierce found it easier to conduct business with cabinet members individually rather than as a group.

As Pierce's secretary of state, New York's William Marcy initially seemed an odd choice. He had been governor of New York and Polk's secretary of war, but he had no meaningful foreign policy experience and was Pierce's third choice for secretary of state. Yet Marcy was instrumental in helping Pierce to keep his campaign promise to energetically extend American influence throughout the Western Hemisphere. In pursuit of these goals, Pierce and Marcy had one great success and one terrible failure. Marcy was a chief architect of the great success, which was the Gadsden Treaty of 1854, named after James Gadsden of South Carolina, whom Pierce had appointed at Davis's suggestion, to negotiate with Mexico to buy at a cost of $10 million 45,535 square miles of territory.[15] The configuration of the tract covered what is now southernmost Arizona and New Mexico and provided the straightest possible path for a transcontinental railroad, which Davis had been proposing to benefit the South and to make it easier to transport the army and supplies to protect the western frontier. The deal did not produce as much additional acreage as southern expansionists had wanted or northern antiexpansionists had feared. Consequently, it did not provoke strong opposition in the Senate, which ratified the treaty.

But Pierce and Marcy failed in their ambitious enterprise to acquire Cuba from Spain.[16] Cuba's annexation was attractive to Democrats who sympathized with Cuban victims of Spanish tyranny, expansionists who valued its strategic location, and Southerners who saw Cuba as another potential slave state. Davis supported Pierce in appointing three prosouthern men, all strict constructionists, to posts that would be enormously important to the acquisition of Cuba—John Mason of Virginia as minister to France, James Buchanan as ambassador to Great Britain, and Pierre Soule of Louisiana as minister to Spain.

The three men produced the Ostend Manifesto,[17] which urged that the United States offer to purchase Cuba for $120 million and asserted that, if Spain refused to sell, the United States "shall be justified in wresting it from Spain, if we possess the power." The manifesto maintained that "Cuba is as necessary to the North American republic as any of its present members, and that it belongs naturally to that great family of States of which the Union is the providential nursery." Besides dooming the negotiations, the manifesto was leaked to the *New York Herald*, which published it. Consequently, the negotiations fell apart, and Pierce and Marcy were publicly humiliated and repudiated the manifesto to save face.[18]

Davis was not the only cabinet officer, besides Marcy, to encourage Cuba's acquisition. It was also the desire of Attorney General Cushing.[19] Whereas Davis could forge friendships across the political aisle, Cushing could not; he was arrogant and disdainful of people with differing views and managed over the course of a political career spanning more than four decades to have been a Whig, a Democrat, and a Republican, picking up enemies across the political spectrum but managing to be elected president of the Democratic National Convention in 1860 and serving as President Grant's minister to Spain a few years after Grant had unsuccessfully nominated him to be chief justice.[20]

Nonetheless, Cushing became one of the most influential attorneys general in American history. Though he initially had no department to oversee, he persuaded Pierce to propose new legislation, which Congress passed, to allow Cushing to become the first attorney general to receive an annual salary so that he could devote his full attention to the job. Cushing expanded the office's jurisdiction to take responsibility for legal issues previously handled by the State Department, and he cleared the backlog of cases left by the former administration. At Pierce's request, Cushing wrote the first complete history of the Office of Attorney General.[21] Cushing's analysis became the standard description of the office. Pierce further suggested that the attorney general should make periodic reports to the president and through him to Congress, prosecute all suits in which the United States had an interest, be given authority to grant pardons, and be in charge of issuing all judicial commissions. By the time Cushing left office, he had written 387 official opinions of the attorney general, the most produced by any attorney general until 1870, the most produced by the attorney general on his own, and the highest rate of productivity of any attorney general at least until 1870.

Many of Cushing's opinions have had significant influence on American law. In one opinion, he anticipated, for example, the Supreme Court's 1983 decision striking down a one-house veto[22] when he concluded that a resolution not enacted into law by a majority in each chamber of Congress and signed by the president as Article I requires for all lawmaking could not bind the executive branch as a legal rule of its own force or as an authoritative interpretation of existing law.[23] In another opinion, he concluded that while

Congress has the power to create "administrative departments" to assist presidents in exercising their constitutional responsibilities, "the great constitutional fact remains that the 'executive power' is vested in the President, subject only, in the respect of appointments and treaties, to the advice and consent of the Senate."[24] In further opining that the president unilaterally had the authority to control all the actions of his subordinates, Cushing adopted a perspective that the Court later ratified in holding that a president has inherent authority to remove any officials performing purely executive functions within the executive branch.[25] Cushing's legal opinions on the president's constitutional authority to appoint or remove any official exercising executive authority are still cited by Justice Department officials (and scholars), particularly for their apparent support of the unitary theory of the executive.

As a strict constructionist, Cushing strongly defended states' rights and the rights of slaveholders.[26] He wrote several presidential proclamations and messages and regularly spoke to the press on behalf of the administration.[27] His most notorious missive is known as "Cushing's Ukase," which he published, with Pierce's approval, when forces opposed to slavery appeared to be gaining an upper hand in the midterm elections to be held in Massachusetts.[28] Triggering the loss of key Democratic support in Massachusetts, Cushing declared that the antislavery movement should be "crushed" and threatened that the president would eradicate "the dangerous element of Abolitionism, under whatever guise or form it may present itself." He subsequently wrote several opinions supporting strict enforcement of the Fugitive Slave Act,[29] and another opinion anticipating arguments adopted by the majority in *Dred Scott v. Sanford*.[30]

Yet it was Davis on whom Pierce relied most heavily.[31] Even though they had only met once before Pierce's election, Davis was one of the first people whom Pierce asked to join his administration. Pierce appreciated that among southern politicians Davis had inherited Calhoun's mantle as the chief spokesperson for states' and slaveholders' rights, even though Davis never endorsed Calhoun's nullification doctrine.

As secretary of war, Davis was energetic and innovative. The department had not been seriously reformed since Calhoun was secretary of war from 1817 to 1825. Davis had several impressive achievements as secretary of war, including increasing the army's size, raising army officers' salaries, upgrading the curriculum and facilities at West Point, streamlining the army's chain of command, improving the quality of officers promoted within the army, upgrading and helping to produce and distribute throughout the corps a new tactics manual, and overseeing substantial progress in building the Washington Aqueduct and expanding the Capitol. But Davis's most significant achievement as secretary of war was establishing that in the chain of command the army's commanding general, Winfield Scott, reported to the war secretary. Scott believed he had no superior but the president, while Davis insisted that he was Scott's superior as the duly authorized person appointed by the commander in chief to run the War Department. After intense bickering, Davis turned to Pierce and Cushing for help. Acting upon an official opinion of the attorney general that unequivocally supported Davis's position,[32] Pierce directed that the secretary of war had command authority over the army's commanding general. The improvements Davis made in the army's organization and command made it better able to defeat his southern forces in the Civil War.

Pierce's personal and ideological affinity for Davis is evident from the fact that in July 1843 Davis was one of three cabinet members whom Pierce took with him on a trip to attend the Exhibition of All Nations in New York City. At each stop along the way, Davis delivered the same public remarks, each time with Pierce in attendance. He spoke about his pride in being an American, stressed the importance of strict construction of the Constitution, and recognized the importance of the "fraternity" of states on which "our Union was founded."[33]

The accomplishments of Pierce's cabinet secretaries came at a price. Their reform efforts produced fractures within the Democratic Party that destroyed his presidency, particularly when combined with the fallout from Pierce's most momentous constitutional judgment as president to break his campaign pledge to stand by the Compromise of 1850.

Enforcing the Constitution to Protect Slavery

Pierce's third constitutional legacy is the political and constitutional fallout from his signing into law and enforcing the Kansas-Nebraska Bill of 1854. Besides the bloody violence it provoked in the Kansas territory, the law was Congress's most significant attempt to leave the question of slavery to state sovereignty.

To understand the bill's constitutional significance, we need to recall that, a year into his presidency, Pierce faced a constitutional conundrum largely of his own making: Strict constructionists, like Pierce, had argued that Congress lacked the power to restrict slavery in the territories, but as a candidate Pierce had sworn to uphold the Compromise of 1850, which, in reauthorizing the original Missouri Compromise, had barred slavery from the territories it covered. By 1854, pressures for organizing territorial governments in Kansas and Nebraska had intensified to the extent it became impossible for Pierce and Congress to ignore them. Although Pierce urged strict enforcement of the fugitive slave law, he preferred not to revisit the Missouri Compromise and thus left the burden for taking action on Congress, where Illinois senator Stephen Douglas chaired the Senate Committee on Territories. Douglas devised a plan to promote settlement of the West and facilitate construction of a transcontinental railroad.[34] After his plan failed to pass the House, Douglas developed a new one allowing settlers in the newly organized territories of Kansas and Nebraska to decide for themselves whether to permit slavery. His objective was to institutionalize popular sovereignty—or local control—over the slavery question. He believed that popular sovereignty held the greatest promise of averting civil war and was at the core of the Kansas-Nebraska Act, his reelection to the Senate in 1857, and his unsuccessful presidential campaign in 1860.

Initially, Douglas planned to say nothing about repealing the Missouri Compromise but instead to report out a bill giving settlers in Kansas and Nebraska the right to draft state constitutions at the time of statehood. Southern Whigs and Democrats told Douglas, however, they would not support the bill unless it implemented genuine popular sovereignty in Kansas and Nebraska—that is, allowed local inhabitants to vote on the slavery question during the territorial years and thus to repeal the Missouri Compromise.

Up until this point, neither Pierce nor his cabinet had participated in the negotiations over Douglas's bill. In a belated response to the policy developing in Congress, Pierce met with his cabinet on Saturday, January 21, 1854, to discuss whether the Missouri Compromise should be repealed. With the backing of a majority of his cabinet,[35] Pierce agreed to bring the question to the Supreme Court, which he expected would declare the Missouri Compromise unconstitutional on the ground that by stripping slave owners of their slaves it violated the Fifth Amendment's ban on seizing private property without due process of law. Pierce liked having the Court take the heat for eradicating the Missouri Compromise.

Later that same day, Douglas agreed to repeal the Missouri Compromise to maintain the support of southern Whigs and Democrats. Because he had to present an amended bill on Monday or face delay, he realized that he had to meet with Pierce the next day, Sunday.

On Sunday morning, Douglas appeared with a group of southern Democratic members of Congress at Davis's residence. They asked Davis to arrange a meeting with Pierce later that day. After being persuaded of the need for urgency, Davis went with the group to the White House and privately urged Pierce to meet with them. Begrudgingly, Pierce agreed.

After listening to the delegation, Pierce agreed to support the bill as amended. He was persuaded that the bill was consistent with the constitutionally protected rights of states and slaveholders and the ideal of popular sovereignty. Determined that Pierce not change his mind, Douglas asked Pierce to write out the portion of the bill repealing the Missouri Compromise. When he did, Pierce transferred responsibility for the bill from Douglas to himself.

Pierce used all the powers of the presidency to secure the bill's passage. In the Senate, the Democratic majority was so large as to make its passage a virtual certainty, but Pierce made supporting the bill a test of loyalty for House Democrats and promised to withhold patronage and other favors he had to bestow from anyone who voted against the bill. When the dust settled, a coalition of more than half the northern Democrats and most Southerners approved the bill by 37–14 in the Senate and by a narrower vote in the House. Eight days later, Pierce signed the Kansas-Nebraska Bill into law.

The rest, as they say, is history: The Kansas-Nebraska Act transformed the constitutional landscape instantaneously. By repealing the Missouri Compromise, President Pierce and Congress were rejecting a landmark piece of legislation and the principle it embodied—Congress's power to bar slavery in federal territories, which had been a constitutional fixture since Monroe's presidency. The Kansas-Nebraska Act embraced the entirely different constitutional principle of popular sovereignty, which, Pierce explained in his Second Annual Message, allowed the states and territories to decide for themselves on whether to allow slavery. Yet this new principle was largely untested. It had worked in Nebraska, where the people overwhelmingly opposed slavery. Pierce, Douglas, and the majority in Congress were betting that popular sovereignty would work in Kansas as long as the losers accepted the results.

The bet was a bust of monumental proportions. While southern Democrats and the people of Nebraska were satisfied, the Democratic Party suffered huge losses in the midterm elections. In the congressional elections, Democrats lost every antislavery state except California and New Hampshire. Losing more than fifty seats in the House, the Democrats went from having a solid majority in the first two years of Pierce's presidency to a minority in its last two years. While Democrats actually increased their seats in the Senate to forty, the gain was illusory: The coalition that had brought Pierce to the White House was shattered, and Democrats who opposed slavery, such as Seward and Ohio's Salmon Chase, left the party.

During the remaining two years of Pierce's presidency, the violence in Kansas intensified, while its ramifications were felt throughout the nation.[36] In the fall of 1854, a territorial government was established, and Pierce appointed the leaders of the new regime, including Andrew Reeder as its first governor and Samuel Lecompte as its first chief justice. Reeder had the authority to set the dates for elections, and the first date he set for electing a congressional delegate was near the end of November 1854. Meanwhile, proslavery residents of Missouri, at the insistence of Missouri's proslavery senator David Atchison, flooded the territory, to vote for a proslavery delegate to Congress, while antislavery residents, mostly settled in the southern part of Kansas, voted for Reeder as their delegate to Congress. Atchison and other Missouri politicians exhorted proslavery residents of Missouri to flood into Kansas to prevent northern abolitionists from taking control of the territory. On March 30, 1855, proslavery settlers voted to select a proslavery legislature, which quickly passed a statute criminalizing antislavery activities. Antislavery residents protested that the proslavery legislature and the bills it passed were illegitimate, because proslavery residents from nearby Missouri had infiltrated the electorate; however, proslavery forces claimed they had fairly won the election to choose the legislature. As Reeder adjudicated claims of voter fraud, his armed guard stood on one side of the room, while proslavery settlers stood on the other side flaunting their weapons. Even though Reeder upheld at least two-thirds of the proslavery settlers' claims, proslavery forces were displeased. To no avail, he suggested a compromise solution—resolving the election in favor of the proslavery residents but requiring the legislature to meet in the state's northern part populated largely by antislavery residents.

After the legislature refused to meet as Reeder directed, Atchison and the proslavery legislature of Kansas urged Pierce to dismiss Reeder. He replaced Reeder with Wilson Shannon, who was a Doughface and former Ohio governor. By the time Shannon arrived in Kansas, antislavery settlers in the north of the territory had formed their own government under what they called the Topeka Constitution. After proslavery residents in the southern half refused to recognize the legitimacy of the Topeka Constitution and reiterated their belief in the legitimacy of the government that they had formed, something had to give. Violence soon erupted. Shannon repeatedly urged Pierce to send federal troops to restore law and order. Pierce did nothing until January 24, 1856, when he formally addressed the controversies percolating in Kansas.[37] Pierce refused to differentiate among the laws the proslavery legislature had passed, insisting that they were all valid and that he would use force if necessary to ensure they were enforced. He condemned the Topeka Constitution and rejected the request of antislavery residents for statehood under it. Pierce further characterized the free-soil movement that had supported the Topeka Constitution and the election of an antislavery governor as "of revolutionary character." If that movement led to organized resistance by force to the federal government or its duly enacted laws, it would be "treasonable insurrection."

In his formal statement, Pierce briefly mentioned the Kansas problems, blaming them on "inflammatory agitation," which for two decades had produced "nothing save unmitigated evil, North and South." Without such agitation, he argued, the Kansas issue would have aroused little emotion. He recommended that as soon as there were enough settlers in the territory they should elect delegates to a constitutional convention to prepare for statehood "through regular and lawful means," and he asked Congress to enact the necessary legislation.

In the same message, Pierce reiterated his view that the Constitution protected the rights of slaveholders, that each state retained its sovereignty under the Constitution, and that each state retained the right to allow slavery within its borders. The Constitution, he believed, further required the return of fugitive slaves to their owners. As he explained, "While the people of the Southern states confine their attention to their own affairs, not presuming officiously to intermeddle with the social institutions of the Northern States, too many of the inhabitants of the latter are permanently organized in associations to inflict injury on the former by wrongful acts." As violence spread through Kansas, Pierce urged the repeal of the Missouri Compromise. Abandoning his campaign pledge to stand by it, he defended its repeal because its continued existence threatened to disrupt the United States. He rejected the possibility that slavery could ever end, proclaiming that the slavery conflict would "inevitably dash itself in vain against the unshaken rock of the Constitution." In his view, the Union was stronger "than all the wild and chimerical schemes of social change which are generated one after another in the unsuitable minds of visionary sophists and interested agitators." He staked his constitutional claim on the side of the South and slaveholders.[38]

Southerners applauded Pierce's message, but it was roundly condemned elsewhere. The recently elected governor of Ohio, Salmon Chase, responded in a special message to the state legislature, and the legislature accepted Chase's recommendation for resolutions of sympathy and support for a free Kansas. Northern states responded similarly to Bleeding Kansas.

Shortly thereafter, Pierce issued a proclamation warning to both sides in Kansas to stop the violence. The House authorized a broad inquiry into the possible causes of the troubles in Kansas and who should be the territory's congressional delegate. It sent a delegation to Kansas to investigate, while Pierce agreed to the House's request to station federal troops at Forts Leavenworth and Riley at the disposition of the territorial governor.[39]

In early May, Chief Justice Lecompte convened a grand jury to indict former governor Reeder and then-governor Charles Robinson, who had been chosen by the antislavery, free-soil movement in the state. After they were indicted for treason, Lecompte ordered their arrest and detention until their trial. When the federal marshal attempted to arrest Reeder while he was meeting with the congressional delegation investigating who should be the territory's congressional delegate, Reeder resisted. Lecompte added a contempt charge to Reeder's indictment. Eventually, Pierce released Robinson and Reeder.

The violence in Kansas spread, at this point, onto the floor of the Senate. On May 19–20, 1856, Massachusetts senator Charles Sumner delivered what he believed was the most important speech of his career. He was right, but for the wrong reason: He not only spoke of a widespread conspiracy involving the Pierce administration to foist slavery on the settlers of Kansas, but also directed insulting personal attacks against Douglas, James Madison, and South Carolina senator Andrew Pickens Butler. Two days after the speech, Congressman Preston, a cousin of Senator Butler, approached Sumner as he was writing at his desk on the Senate floor. Declaring the speech a libel on South Carolina and Senator Butler, Brooks began striking Sumner repeatedly with his walking stick. Sumner was stunned and blinded by the first few blows, after which he wrenched his desk from its mooring and fell onto the Senate floor, bleeding and unconscious. Several members of Congress watched but did nothing to stop Brooks.[40] Although the physical and psychological damage kept Sumner out of the Senate until 1859, he was reelected in 1857. Meanwhile, an investigating committee of the House recommended expulsion for Brooks, but the House censured him instead. Brooks resigned from the House but was reelected to his seat.

When informed that those elected to the legislature under the Topeka Constitution were preparing to meet, Pierce ordered them not to meet (again on the basis he was faithfully executing the law in the form of the Kansas-Nebraska Act). They defied the order, assembling in Topeka where Colonel Edwin Sumner, who led a squadron of the U.S. Army, ordered the legislature to disperse. Shortly thereafter, Davis censured Sumner for acting precipitously, while the House considered whether to add a provision to a new army appropriations bill that forbade the army from being used to enforce the laws of the Kansas territorial legislature unless Congress had declared its validity.

Although the House adjourned before voting on the bill, Congress was called back into session by proclamation and passed it.

After removing Shannon as the territorial governor of Kansas on July 28, 1856, Pierce appointed a new governor, John Geary. Although Geary is generally credited with restoring some law and order to the territory, the proslavery resistance to his efforts intensified. Like Shannon, he constantly received death threats. Yet in November Geary wrote a letter to Pierce requesting that he dismiss Lecompte as chief justice. Although Pierce agreed with Geary's assessment of Lecompte's liabilities, he did not settle on a successor—James O. Harrison—until early December. On December 12, Pierce wrote Geary to commend what he was doing and to urge him to "cultivate kind relations with" another proslavery justice whom Pierce had appointed in Kansas.[41] Pierce submitted Harrison's nomination to the Senate, but he neglected to send a letter dismissing Lecompte. The Senate refused to confirm Harrison since Lecompte remained in office. Meanwhile, in response to a request from the Senate, Lecompte wrote a letter that defended his actions to Cushing and Pierce and that convinced southern senators to reject Harrison. Lecompte thus remained in office for the duration of Pierce's term.

The official, proslavery legislature of Kansas joined Lecompte in harassing Geary. When it first met in Lecompton in January 1857, it formally denounced Geary and secretly voted to override all of his vetoes. In spite of being threatened at gunpoint, Geary vetoed a censure bill that the legislature had passed to prepare for a summer election of delegates to a constitutional convention, and the legislature overrode his veto. Geary resigned on the same day as Buchanan was inaugurated.

As the news of "Bleeding Kansas" spread around the country, public opinion, particularly in the North, became increasingly antislavery. It intensified further when Anthony Burns, a fugitive slave, was arrested in Boston on a trumped-up charge that he had broken into a jewelry store. When a local marshal informed Pierce by wire that an angry mob had failed to break Burns out of jail and that two companies of federal troops were stationed in the courthouse where Burns was being held, Pierce wired back, "Your conduct is approved. The law must be executed."[42] Three days later, the U.S. attorney reported to Pierce that he expected armed resistance and asked if the military expense could be paid if it became necessary for the mayor to further employ the federal troops. Pierce responded, "Incur any expense deemed necessary by the Marshal and yourself, for city military or otherwise, to insure the execution of this law."

Although Richard Henry Dana Jr. ably defended Burns, Commissioner Edward Loring ruled that Burns ought to be returned to his master in Virginia. As reportedly 50,000 Bostonians watched, all available police and federal troops escorted Burns from the courthouse to the ship taking him south. Subsequently, several antislavery men who had attempted to free Burns were indicted for rioting. The trial was postponed until the spring of 1855, when the judge dismissed the indictments on technical grounds. Nonetheless, Burns's extradition intensified criticism of the law throughout the North.[43]

As fallout from the Kansas-Nebraska Act mounted, Attorney General Cushing tried to strengthen the law. In one opinion, he defended federal payments to defense counsel in any case in which a federal marshal was sued by a black for illegal imprisonment.[44] In another opinion, Cushing said slave owners had the right to remove fugitives from all states and organized territories and even from unorganized territorial possessions of the United

FORCING SLAVERY DOWN THE THROAT OF A FREESOILER

FIGURE 6.1 The artist lays on the Democrats the major blame for violence perpetrated against antislavery settlers in Kansas in the wake of the Kansas-Nebraska Act. Here a bearded "freesoiler" has been bound to the "Democratic Platform" and is restrained by two Lilliputian figures, presidential nominee James Buchanan and Democratic senator Lewis Cass. Democratic senator Stephen A. Douglas and President Franklin Pierce, also shown as tiny figures, force a black man into the giant's gaping mouth. The freesoiler's head rests on a platform marked "Kansas," "Cuba," and "Central America," probably referring to Democratic ambitions for the extension of slavery. In the background left is a scene of burning and pillage; on the right a dead man hangs from a tree.

Source: Library of Congress Rare Book and Special Collections Division, Washington, D.C. 20540 USA

States.[45] If no commissioner was available, the owner could recapture his slave without legal process. Later, Cushing declared that a federal marshal in pursuit of a fugitive slave had the authority to enlist able-bodied men "as a posse comitatus" and to request military force if necessary.[46] He found that habeas corpus did not apply in cases involving the lawful arrest of a fugitive slave.[47] Cushing's final opinion as attorney general authorized U.S. postal officials to honor Mississippi law by refusing to deliver abolitionist mail sent from Ohio to that state. While today any such postal policy would be dismissed as violating the First Amendment, Cushing's opinion reflects the lengths to which strict constructionists went to defend the slavocracy.[48]

AFTER THE CIVIL War, the principal place to find any reminders of Pierce's presidency was New Hampshire, which begrudgingly recognized Pierce as the only resident to be president. Although the state's only law school had been named in his honor, it dropped its name and ceased to be private in 2010 when it was rebranded as the University of New Hampshire Law School. Pierce's home state made forgetting him easier.

Pierce's successor vigorously adhered, like Pierce, to strict constitutional construction. President Buchanan agreed that strict construction required upholding the constitutional rights of slaveholders, though he denied that the Constitution protected antislavery activities or authorized the federal government to stem the tide of impending secession, which, like Pierce, he blamed on northern abolitionists rather than anything he had done as president.

7

Chester Arthur, 1881–1885

CHESTER ARTHUR MIGHT have done more than any other president to destroy his own legacy. On the day before he died, he burned his personal papers. Even though he was president for nearly four years, Arthur has no library or museum devoted solely to his presidency, and there are important events during his presidency for which we have no records.

Arthur seemed destined for obscurity. He had held only one political office before he was nominated as James Garfield's running mate in 1880—collector for the Port of New York. While a substantial portion of the federal government's revenue then came from New York's Customs House, Arthur held this job primarily because he could be relied on to use his position to dispense patronage on behalf of his boss and benefactor, Senator Roscoe Conkling of New York. Arthur did not distinguish himself in the job: In 1878, President Hayes dismissed him after an official investigation of corruption in the New York Customs House.

Arthur's dismissal had perhaps the most remarkable unintended consequence of any in American history: It endeared him to Conkling's powerful wing of the Republican Party, which called themselves the Stalwarts because of their steadfast support of the party's traditions, including patronage. Arthur became a martyr, whom Stalwarts pushed as Garfield's running mate; and he became the consensus choice because he was the least objectionable Stalwart, though Conkling urged him to reject the job.[1] The two standard bearers for the Republican Party in the 1880 presidential election were Garfield, who was a war hero, respected member of Congress, and skilled orator; and his running mate, who was a political hack.

In his short six months as president, Garfield shut Arthur out of everything because Arthur had continued to do what he had always done before—Conkling's bidding. In the single, most important constitutional event of Garfield's presidency, Arthur sided with Conkling in a battle in which senatorial courtesy was pitted against the president's power to exercise his nominating authority independently. The prize was the right to nominate someone to fill Arthur's old job. Although Arthur broke a tie vote in the Senate to reject Garfield's nominee for the post, Conkling's victory was short-lived, as Garfield slyly withdrew all his nominations except the one Conkling was blocking, and Conkling's overwhelming interest in aggrandizing himself at the expense of all other business of the government became painfully clear for all to see. Conkling foolishly resigned to protest the move, and the New York legislature refused to reappoint him to the Senate.[2] Conkling appeared to be dead politically until a deranged man, Charles Guiteau, shot Garfield, who died because of his doctors' incompetency. Conkling prepared to return to power with Arthur as his puppet, an amazing occurrence in itself since Conkling could have been—but was not—implicated in Garfield's shooting: Guiteau had proclaimed upon shooting Garfield, "I am a Stalwart. Arthur is president now." It is constitutionally significant that Guiteau is widely remembered for shooting Garfield because he wanted a Stalwart president. It underscores the wisdom of the Twelfth Amendment's ensuring that the president and vice president are from the same party, as a way of decreasing the incentives for assassination, while at the same time it points to the fact that ticket balancing within a party, as was the case with Arthur's selection, can partly undo that salutary effect of the Twelfth Amendment.

Most importantly, Arthur's presidency dramatically demonstrates how the office transforms its occupant. As president, Arthur repeatedly sacrificed his political support in order to fulfill his constitutional commitments. As the first president to sign significant civil service reform into law, he lost the Stalwarts' support but forged, to most observers' surprise, a record of competent, balanced administration.

Reforming Civil Service

The three Republican presidents who immediately preceded Arthur did little to reform the civil service system. Grant generally appointed people who were not the best qualified but were loyal to him. In response, Congress authorized Grant to set regulations for federal employment and to appoint an oversight body.[3] By the end of Grant's administration, the commission was defunct since Congress had not funded it. Even worse, Grant's treasury secretary, Benjamin Bristow, discovered a cadre of federal officials who had defrauded the government of millions of dollars in internal-revenue taxes pertaining to whiskey sales and consumption. Grant refused to allow the perpetrators to be prosecuted and fired the prosecutor. Bristow resigned in protest. Grant's successor, Rutherford B. Hayes, promised serious civil service reform and appointed a leading advocate for civil service reform, Carl Schurz, to his cabinet. Unable to get Congress to enact legislation to reform the civil service, Hayes conducted his own investigation of the New York Customs House and dismissed Arthur.[4] With the exception of his battle to establish his authority over federal appointments in New York, Garfield was ambivalent about merit-based appointments.[5] Everyone believed the prospects of civil service reform died with him.

Everyone was wrong. Arthur did the opposite of what the Stalwarts urged him to do. While Garfield was battling Conkling for the prerogative to name the collector of New York, a major bill to reform civil service—the Pendleton Civil Service Act—had languished in the Senate. Whereas Garfield had not shown any support for the bill and Conkling expected it would die in the finance committee, Arthur declared in his first major address that nothing would "deter me from giving the measure my earnest support."[6] His support never wavered.

Through his first year in office, Arthur understood that the political momentum for reform was overwhelming and that Congress merely had to approve the Senate bill that it already had pending before it. Though he urged Congress to approve civil service reform, Republican leaders were initially unmoved. They continued to oppose reform until the midterm elections of 1882, when the voters punished them for their opposition. In fact, the House experienced one of its largest reversals of control in history: Republicans went from a twelve-seat majority in the House to an almost eighty-seat deficit. While Republicans managed to gain control of the Senate by two seats, Senate leaders got the message. Knowing that Arthur was prepared to sign into law any reform that they approved, they quickly moved the bill onto the Senate floor, where just after Christmas, it passed 38–5, with thirty-three abstentions. Soon thereafter, the vote in the House was 155–47, with eighty-seven abstentions.[7]

The Constitution figured little in congressional debates. Opponents of the Pendleton Act largely focused on policy issues, expressing concerns that the act was merely a scheme to keep Republicans in power or that the exams it required would result in the appointments of bureaucrats who were mediocre or elites who had little in common with most Americans.[8] While few Republicans expressed any enthusiasm for the bill, none voted against it. That Republicans were in no position to impede the momentum of a bill they had long opposed was reflected further in their allowing the bill to bear the name of its Democratic sponsor, George Pendleton of Ohio.

To most historians, the Pendleton Civil Service Act that Arthur signed into law was symbolically rather than substantively important: It covered only about 11 percent of all federal employees, applied to big cities and not rural areas in which the Post Office operated, and had gaping holes that allowed for political assessments and payoffs, two of the evils that civil service reformers had long opposed, to persist.

Yet the Pendleton Act's authorization had serious constitutional ramifications. As the first major reform of civil service ever enacted, its passage constituted a significant blow to the notion that the Constitution vested the president with complete removal power over all executive branch personnel. At the same time, the law was the first step toward the bureaucratic state, which purported to serve society, not political parties. Moreover, the creation of the Civil Service Commission, the board for drafting and administering civil service exams, and the standards for employment and removal of civil servants were based on Congress's exercise of its power to regulate interstate commerce. Today, such enactments seem commonplace, and their constitutionality is not open to serious debate.

Arthur had not just given lip service to the Pendleton Act. He also understood his duty under Article II to "take care to enforce the laws faithfully"[9] as requiring just that: He strongly supported the new order that limited his powers and undermined the patronage system that he had long embodied and brought him to power. The three men whom he appointed to the Civil Service Commission were notable leaders in civil service reform; he issued thirteen executive orders to implement rules and regulations for the civil service that were based on commission recommendations;[10] and the commission praised Arthur more than once for his "constant, firm, and friendly support."[11] The act was also the subject of five attorney general opinions, including one upholding Arthur's power to use recess appointments to fill "all vacancies that may happen in a recess of the Senate, irrespective of the time when such vacancies first occur,"[12] one that recognized the president's inherent authority to make "interim appointments,"[13] and another holding that the question of whether "there are already two or more members of a family in the public service" as provided by the act is a question for the president to decide.[14] Another opinion recognized that another officer could not perform the duties of the treasury secretary even though the incumbent had died.[15] These orders and opinions remain significant executive-branch precedents on the scope and permissible limitations on a president's appointment and removal authorities.

Playing President

While Garfield had won an important victory for the president's independence in nominating confirmable officials, most senators expected Arthur to defer to senatorial courtesy. Moreover, at the time of Arthur's presidency, the extent of a president's removal power over executive officials whom the Senate confirmed was still unsettled. (Indeed, when Hayes dismissed Arthur, Arthur had objected on the ground that Hayes had not complied with the Tenure in Office Act; however, Senate Democrats allowed Hayes to circumvent the act in order to embarrass Conkling.) Arthur appreciated that he would not be able to make appointments unless there were vacancies, and there would be no vacancies unless Congress created some.

Even before Arthur had announced his support for the Pendleton Civil Service Act, he had made one of his most significant constitutional decisions as president: Roughly a month after Garfield's death, Arthur asked Conkling to visit him at the White House. The purpose of the meeting was no secret—to address the question of Conkling's power over the new administration. While neither man ever spoke of what they discussed, it is not hard to figure out from subsequent developments: Conkling made known his desire to be appointed to one of the two or three most important cabinet posts and to have Stalwarts appointed to replace various Garfield appointees, but Arthur declined these requests.[16]

Particularly over his first six months as president, Arthur took great care to signal that he was firmly committed to acting independently rather than remaining Conkling's agent. First, he decided not to remove Garfield's choice of Robertson as collector of New York. Conkling and other Stalwarts pushed Arthur to do this, but Arthur refused. His decision signaled his determination to rise above partisan politics in making appointments or removals. Throughout his presidency, he kept his promise not to remove anyone for personal or partisan reasons.[17]

Arthur's most significant removals were postal officials involved in the Star Route scandal. The Star Routes were federal contracts stamped with asterisks or stars signifying "certainty, celebrity, and security"—terms meant to convey that the persons who received the contracts were supposed to be paid at special rates set by Congress to deliver mail in isolated western areas. The scandal arose from the practice of certain high-ranking postal department officials who fraudulently arranged for their confederates to receive the initial contracts at absurdly low rates but later got Congress to pay for improvements in the routes that were never made, with the funds instead pocketed by the officials involved. Although Garfield had ordered an investigation into the scandal, it was still going when Garfield died. Nine days after becoming president, Arthur ordered the removals of officials involved in the scandals and asked his attorney general to uncover the fraud "earnestly and thoroughly."[18] In the same message in which he had promised to support civil service reform, Arthur pledged to prosecute offenders "with the utmost vigor of the law."[19] Thus, he reaffirmed the president's power to prioritize and direct prosecutions of the law.

Second, Arthur acted unilaterally in making his cabinet appointments. He passed over many mediocre candidates urged upon him by Republican senators and instead made cabinet appointments based on merit. His choices inspired the confidence of Senate leaders that he could be trusted to use his appointment power judiciously and not in a partisan or vengeful manner. Consequently, the Senate easily confirmed all twelve of his cabinet appointments. By appointing two former senators to his cabinet, Arthur astutely used senatorial courtesy to his advantage and ensured that he would have men familiar with the Senate working closely with him. (He had apparently learned the importance of building bridges to the Senate from Garfield's successful gambit to fill Arthur's old job.) Moreover, Arthur directed his cabinet secretaries to make appointments and removal decisions based on "notions of fairness and not simply faction."[20] His appointments angered Stalwarts. Conkling complained that Hayes had been "respectable, if not heroic" in comparison.[21] The angrier Republicans got, the more evident Arthur's willingness to do his duty at all cost became.

Third, Arthur made two excellent Supreme Court appointments. Indeed, he was one of a few presidents who came into office with pending Supreme Court vacancies. The first arose when Justice Nathan Clifford died shortly after Garfield had been shot and was thus unable to act upon the vacancy.

Two months after becoming president, Arthur nominated Horace Gray to replace Clifford. Gray had been strongly recommended by the influential senator George Hoar of Massachusetts[22] and was an astute choice. Justice Samuel Miller, a highly regarded Lincoln appointee, also recommended Gray, who had impeccable credentials—he had served as a state court judge for nearly two decades, including eight years as the chief justice of the Supreme Court of Massachusetts; was widely regarded as an eminent legal scholar and historian; and had been the youngest person to date appointed to the Supreme Court of Massachusetts.[23] His commitment to the Reconstruction amendments made him popular among Republicans. A day after formally receiving the nomination, the Senate confirmed Gray 51–5. He continues to hold the record for the justice who served the longest as a lower-court judge prior to his nomination to the Court.

The next vacancy arose barely two months after Gray's appointment when Justice Ward Hunt resigned from the bench in ill health. Although most people expected Arthur to nominate George Edmunds, a widely respected Vermont senator, he did not. Instead, he offered the job to Conkling. In retrospect, it is unclear why Arthur did this. Perhaps he did it as payback or because Conkling was from the same state as Hunt, or he might have expected Conkling to decline. The press savaged Arthur for lapsing into his old ways. Surprisingly, Conkling said he would take the seat, and the Senate confirmed him in an ironic demonstration of the strength of senatorial courtesy. Five days after his confirmation, Conkling announced that he would not take the oath or seat.[24] This time, Arthur asked Edmunds, hoping to take further advantage of senatorial courtesy. Although quickly confirmed, Edmunds declined. Arthur then turned to Samuel Blatchford of New York. Like Gray's, his credentials were stellar: He had been a widely respected lawyer before being appointed to the district court and had served for fifteen years on the Second Circuit Court of Appeals, on which he had been renowned for his professionalism, legal acumen, and expertise in admiralty law. The Senate greeted the nomination with relief and acclimation. Less than ten days after receiving the nomination, the Senate unanimously approved it by voice vote. Blatchford remains distinctive as the first Supreme Court justice to serve beforehand as both a district and a circuit court judge and as the first person appointed by three different presidents to three different Article III courts, including the Supreme Court. (He is also known among New York lawyers as a founder of the law firm Cravath, Swaine & Moore.)

Arthur had at least two objectives in choosing Gray and Blatchford. First, each man had outstanding professional qualifications. In keeping with his support of civil service reform and his commitment to being independent as president, Arthur—a lawyer himself—did not want to appoint partisan hacks to the Court. While the norm then was not to opt for sitting judges as nominees, Arthur opted to make appointments that the legal community viewed as merit-based. The appointments buttressed Arthur's vow not to appoint partisans or hacks to important posts and clearly benefited the Court itself. Second, with Republicans only having a two-seat margin of control in the Senate, Arthur wanted swift rather than messy confirmations.[25] He achieved this by working within, rather than challenging, existing norms for Supreme Court appointments. Thus, he took various factors into account, including senatorial courtesy and the strength of the nominees' support in the Senate.

On another front, Arthur's attorney general, Benjamin Brewster, wrote two of the earliest opinions on the meaning of the Constitution's ineligibility clause, which provides that "[n]o Senator or Representative shall, during the time for which he was elected, be appointed to any civil office under the authority of the United States, which shall have been created, or the emoluments whereof shall have been increased, during such time."[26] In one, Brewster construed the plain language of the clause to mean that it would preclude the "nomination and confirmation" of someone who was ineligible to be appointed to the position for which he was ineligible since nomination and confirmation were "acts necessary and incipient to steps to an appointment."[27] In the other, Brewster maintained in what he thought was the first opinion on point that Samuel Kirkwood, Arthur's first interior secretary, was ineligible to be appointed to the U.S. Tariff Commission because he had been a member of the Senate at the time it was created. Brewster construed the clause's rule to be "absolute, as expressed in the terms of the Constitution, and behind that I cannot go, but must accept it as it is presented regarding its application in this case."[28] While Brewster was wrong that no prior president had faced the question,[29] his opinion enabled Arthur, yet again, to follow the law rather than do whatever was politically expedient.

Independently Exercising the Veto

Arthur's biographers emphasize the importance of his deployment of his veto authority,[30] though he cast far fewer vetoes—six total, four of which were pocket vetoes[31]—than other presidents in the last quarter of the nineteenth century. Nonetheless, his vetoes were important because they were unexpected. Just as with his support of civil service reform and his cabinet and Supreme Court appointments, he did not exercise this authority to make party leaders in Congress happy. Indeed, he challenged congressional leaders on a few discrete issues, and in doing so demonstrated a capacity of the presidency that we take for granted—the president's using the veto authority to steer legislation in his preferred direction. Moreover, in grounding his vetoes on both constitutional and policy grounds, he followed the precedents established earlier by Jackson and Tyler. Also, it is telling that the Congress only overrode one of his six vetoes. The fact that an unelected, increasingly unpopular president had five out of his six vetoes upheld by Congress underscores an important dynamic within the structure of power at the federal level—namely, the fact that the Constitution requires such a high threshold to override vetoes enables *every president* to exercise significant influence over the policymaking process.

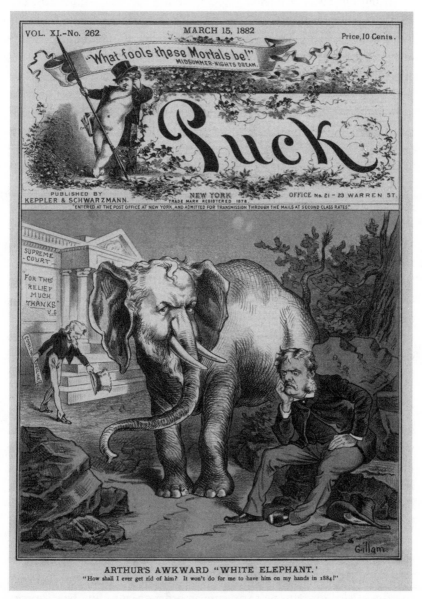

VOL. XI.–No. 262   MARCH 15, 1882   Price, 10 Cents.

"What fools these Mortals be!"
MIDSUMMER-NIGHTS DREAM.

Puck

PUBLISHED BY
KEPPLER & SCHWARZMANN.   NEW YORK   OFFICE No. 21 – 23 WARREN ST.
TRADE MARK REGISTERED 1878
"ENTERED AT THE POST OFFICE AT NEW YORK, AND ADMITTED FOR TRANSMISSION THROUGH THE MAILS AT SECOND CLASS RATES."

ARTHUR'S AWKWARD "WHITE ELEPHANT."
"How shall I ever get rid of him? It won't do for me to have him on my hands in 1884!"

FIGURE 7.1 Print shows President Chester A. Arthur sitting on a rock with a large white elephant that looks like Roscoe Conkling standing next to him; Arthur is wondering how to get rid of the elephant. Uncle Sam, holding papers labeled "Conkling Declines," walks away from the "Supreme Court." Roscoe Conkling turned down Arthur's offer for a position on the Supreme Court.

Source: Library of Congress Prints and Photographs Division, Washington, D.C. 20540 USA
http://hdl.loc.gov/loc.pnp/pp.print

Arthur cast his three notable vetoes in his first full year in office. The first was the most momentous: On April 4, 1882, he vetoed the Chinese Exclusion Bill,[32] which barred Chinese laborers from entering the country for twenty years and denied citizenship to Chinese residents.[33] Restricting Chinese immigration was popular among Republicans, but Arthur believed the policies were "a breach of our national faith"[34] and "undemocratic and hostile to the spirit of our institutions." Congress quickly passed another bill that included several of Arthur's recommendations.[35] In recognition of the fact that the second bill had passed by margins large enough to exceed the two-thirds required in each chamber to override a presidential veto, Arthur signed the bill. Arthur's veto reflected how it might be used to lead Congress, but his belated acceptance of an exclusion bill did not win back the support of Republicans who had pushed the bill. Nor did his veto stem the tide of discrimination against Chinese immigration, since his approval of the second bill effectively acquiesced in the extension of the discrimination underlying it. (Indeed, the law was not repealed until 1943.) Moreover, Arthur's switch of positions on Chinese exclusion underscored the purely political calculations underlying his judgments.

On August 1, Arthur vetoed the 1882 Rivers and Harbors bill.[36] The veto caused a stir in Congress because it was an attack against a pork-filled law, and it invited retribution from party leaders. Nevertheless, he found much of the bill entailed wasteful, illegitimate spending and that much of the bill benefited "particular localities" and thus did not advance the common defense, interstate commerce, or the general welfare.[37] Consequently, he believed the bill went "beyond the powers given by the Constitution to Congress and the President."[38] He argued that the bill established a bad precedent, which might lead Congress to approve even more "extravagant expenditure of public money."[39] Although Congress overrode Arthur's veto,[40] he had evolved from being a political hack to an early opponent of wasteful spending.

In his last year in office, Arthur faced the difficult question of whether to veto a bill that he would have personally liked to sign. The bill involved Fitz John Porter, who had had been a major in the Union Army but had been court-martialed for refusing to execute an order given to him by a superior officer and formally dismissed from the army after President Lincoln upheld the conviction upon review. In 1878, President Hayes assembled a review board to reconsider whether Porter should be reinstated to the army. Though it concluded that Porter should be, both Hayes and Arthur concluded that they did not have the unilateral authority to reinstate him. Indeed, Arthur's attorney general suggested that Arthur had the authority to use his pardon and commutation power to erase the portion of his sentence that had dis-qualified him "forever" "from any office" in the federal government.[41] On May 4, 1882, Arthur used his pardon and commutation powers to remit his sentence, and Congress subsequently passed a bill authorizing Porter's rein-statement. Arthur asked his attorney general for an opinion on its constitu-tionality. On June 23, 1884, he advised Arthur that he believed the bill was unconstitutional because a statute directing the appointment of a specific in-dividual "clearly invades the constitutional rights of the President" and the Senate to exercise their respective nominating and confirmation authorities as each sees fit.[42] Arthur vetoed the bill.[43]

Although historians overlook this veto, it is significant. First, Congress failed to override it. Hence, it underscores the power of a veto even in the hands of a lame-duck president. Second, it illustrates the Constitution's con-straining power. Arthur agreed that the proper thing would have been to rein-state Porter, but he was unable to do it because he could not find a legal way to do it. He felt bound by the Constitution.

Arthur also took seriously his responsibility to propose legislation to Con-gress. In all four of his annual messages, he urged Congress to enact a national bankruptcy law and to protect "by suitable legislation the forests situated upon the public domain." He repeatedly asked Congress to enact a federal statute to direct what should happen if a president were to die or become in-capacitated without a vice president in office. He reminded Congress of the need to determine the meaning of the constitutional phrase referring to a president's "inability to discharge the powers and duties of said office." More-over, in each of his annual messages, Arthur urged Congress not to forget the District of Columbia. He declared, "The denial to its residents of the great right of suffrage in all its relations to national, state, and municipal action imposes upon the Congress the duty of affording them the best administra-tion which its wisdom can devise. The report of the District Commissioners indicates certain measures whose adoption would seem to be very desirable." In all four of Arthur's annual messages, he pressed Congress to enact appro-priate legislation to forgo the turmoil and confusion that had arisen in the aftermath of the 1876 presidential election. Indeed, in the opening of his fourth and final message, he reminded Congress, "Eight years have passed since a controversy concerning the result of a national debate sharply called the attention of Congress to the necessity of providing more precise and def-inite regulations for counting the [presidential] electoral vote. It is of the gravest importance that this question be solved before conflicting claims to the Presidency shall again distract the country, and I am persuaded that by the people at large any of the measures of relief thus far proposed would be preferred to continued inaction." The failure of Congress to enact any of Arthur's proposals demonstrated the limits of Arthur's leadership. Yet his persistence in reiterating his proposals underscored the capacity of the presidency to be forward-looking. Issues arising from the fact that the District of Columbia is not a state persist, and Congress is still considering today whether genuine representation in Congress for the district may be provided by means of a statute or a constitutional amendment. In 1887, the Congress enacted the Electoral Count Act, but it failed to achieve Arthur's purpose, as reflected in its becoming the center of controversy in the immediate aftermath of the 2000 presidential election. The Twenty-third Amendment, which grants to the citizens in the District of Columbia the right to vote in presidential elections, was ratified in 1961. The Twenty-fifth Amendment, which governs presidential incapacity, was not ratified until 1967; scholars and members of Congress still debate the proper line of presidential succession.

Confronting Constitutional Complexity

Four different matters challenged Arthur to confront questions about the Constitution, federal power, discrimination, and minority rights. Three of these arose in the West. The first was the Chinese Exclusion Act, discussed earlier. The second involved the federal government's efforts to stamp out polygamy in the Utah territory. The practice of polygamy among Mormons, who comprised a majority of the population in Utah, had prevented the territory from becoming a state. By the time Arthur came into office, the Supreme Court had upheld a federal law prohibiting polygamy there.[44] Because Mormons controlled the local courts, prosecuting polygamists was practically impossible. Although Garfield had denounced polygamy in his inaugural address,[45] only Arthur was able to accomplish something: In 1882, he signed into law the Edmunds Act,[46] which recodified the prohibitions in other statutes, criminalized polygamy, disqualified polygamists from jury duty, and barred polygamists from holding public office.[47] Through the establishment of a five-person commission to supervise voting in Utah, the act sought to effectively take control of the government from the Mormon majority. Mormons charged discrimination, though neither the president nor Congress recognized any part of the federal Constitution as a basis for their claim. They further protested that Arthur—and Congress— lacked the power to enact a law forbidding their particular religious practice, though Arthur agreed with his attorney general[48]—and the Supreme Court— that Articles I and IV vested Congress with this authority.

What followed was a remarkable struggle between the federal government in Washington and the Mormons over the control of local governmental operations in Utah. Most Mormons in the area resisted complying with the federal law restricting polygamists from voting and overwhelmingly voted to return Mormons to power in the first election held under the Edmunds Act.[49] The new local legislature refused to outlaw polygamy, and Arthur was forced to call for direct congressional control of Utah as a further exercise of its plenary power to regulate federal territories.[50] Although Congress failed to act before Arthur left office, his actions reinforced the Supreme Court's rulings that the First Amendment did not protect polygamy and was not a bar to the federal government's plenary authority over federal territories and statehood.

On a third matter, Arthur extended the efforts that President Hayes had begun to improve the conditions for Native Americans.[51] Arthur and his secretary of the interior, former senator Henry Teller, acknowledged the need to find peaceful ways to incorporate Native Americans "into the mass of our citizens."[52] At Arthur's insistence, Congress created the office of superintendent of Indian schools,[53] increased funding for Indian schools nearly twofold,[54] and established a system of courts with Native American judges who would be responsible for punishing various offenses.[55]

Arthur also took an equally progressive, albeit less successful, stance on the federal government's authority to protect African-Americans from private violence. In 1883, the Supreme Court in *US v. Harris*[56] had held that the federal government did not have the power to make the beatings of several African-Americans a federal offense because they were private actions to which the Constitution did not apply. In response, Arthur said nothing. Later that year, he reacted differently to the Court's decision in *The Civil Rights Cases*[57] overturning the Civil Rights Act of 1875.[58] The law barred racial discrimination in public accommodations. Arthur, like many of the Republicans of his generation, believed the Civil War was fought in large part to eliminate slavery and guarantee equal rights to African-Americans. Accordingly, he asked his attorney general to urge the Supreme Court to uphold the law. But in November 1883 the Court reiterated that the Fourteenth Amendment only applied to state action and determined that the law exceeded the constitutional boundaries of Congress's powers under section 5 of the Fourteenth Amendment.[59] In his Third Annual Message to Congress,[60] Arthur reminded Congress that "the special purpose" of the Fourteenth Amendment was "to insure to members of the colored race the full enjoyment of civil and political rights," referenced the Court's "recent[]" decision, and declared, "Any legislation whereby Congress may lawfully supplement the guarantees which the Constitution affords for the equal enjoyment by all the citizens of the United States of every right, privilege, and immunity of citizenship will receive my unhesitating support."[61] Interestingly, Arthur's rebuke of the Court was the first time since Lincoln that a president had done so. The House did not act on his proposal, and Arthur never had the chance to make good on his promise. It was not until 1964 that a president signed into law a civil rights bill nearly identical to the one struck down in 1883.[62]

IN 1972, RICHARD Nixon made history as the first American president to visit China. The trip was historic because it was an important step toward normalizing relations with China and because it was Nixon who did it. As a man with a long-standing reputation as a strident anticommunist, Nixon was immune to criticism that he was pandering to the Communist government led by Mao Zedong. His visit inspired the phrase, "Only Nixon could go to China," used to refer to a leader's immunity from criticism for doing something he once stridently opposed. The shift is considered to result from a desire to place principle over self-interest.

The same could be said of Arthur: He embodied the patronage system and had long been one of the most ardent opponents of civil service reform. Yet one could say that "only Arthur could have signed serious civil service reform into law," because, as president, he was immune to charges that he switched because of expedience rather than principle. It is a measure of the neglect of Arthur's presidency that no such phrase ever was voiced, much less took hold.

8

Grover Cleveland, 1885–1889

BESIDES THE FACT that Grover Cleveland is the only president to have served two nonconsecutive terms in the White House,[1] most people know nothing about his presidency, much less its constitutional impact. When he won the presidential election of 1884, he became the first Democrat to be elected president since Buchanan in 1856. He was the only Democratic president in the second half of the nineteenth century and the first Democratic president to run for reelection since Van Buren in 1840. Each of the three times Cleveland ran for president he received a plurality of the vote, "a record [of popular support] exceeded only by Franklin D. Roosevelt."[2] He cast more vetoes in his first term than *all* previous presidents combined and cast the second largest number of vetoes of any president (except for Franklin Roosevelt) in American history. He presided over the worst economic downturn in between the two great depressions and the worst period of labor unrest except for the second great depression.

Cleveland has failed, however, to garner much contemporary interest, perhaps because he seems to be a throwback to a distant era, with which most Americans are unfamiliar. Particularly in his first term, he did not conceive of, much less use, the presidency as a bully pulpit. Among the ten presidents who served for more than a term, Cleveland is the least colorful and worst orator. A memorable or pithy quote from Cleveland is nearly impossible to find. The issues on which he staked his first term—the tariff and gold standard—seem arcane and anachronistic. The same could be said of his notion of the presidency as restricted to curbing congressional excesses.

Yet a negative presidency—one that opposes, rather than advances, significant change in the status quo—can be both politically and constitutionally significant. In strongly opposing congressional encroachments, he helped to shift in the president's favor the balance of power over federal appointments, executive privilege, and removals. Indeed, his vigorous defenses of these prerogatives led then-political scientist Woodrow Wilson to alter his opinion that the presidency was a ministerial office subservient to Congress.[3] Wilson concluded that Cleveland was the only significant American president between 1865 and 1898.

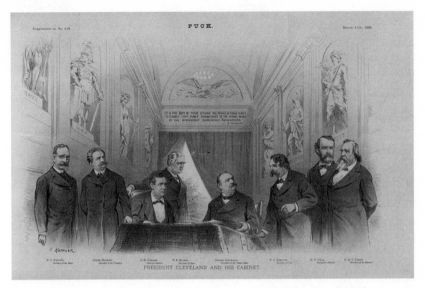

FIGURE 8.1 This shows President Cleveland sitting at a desk between his cabinet members, from the left, "W.C. Whitney, Secretary of the Navy, Daniel Manning, Secretary of the Treasury, A.H. Garland, Attorney-General, T.F. Bayard, Secretary of State, W.C. Endicott, Secretary of War, W.F. Vilas, Postmaster-General, [and] L.Q.C. Lamar, Secretary of the Interior." They are in a hall lined with statues labeled "Navy, War, Justice, State, Treasury, Interior, [and] Post." On the wall at the back of the room is the following quote, "It is the duty of those serving the people in public places to closely limit public expenditures to the actual needs of the government economically administered. G. Cleveland."

Source: Library of Congress Prints and Photographs Division, Washington, D.C. 20540 USA http://hdl.loc.gov/loc.pnp/pp.print

Deferring to Congress

Cleveland entered the presidency with a conception of presidential power that had two basic components. The first was the belief that a president's duty was primarily to enforce the law and not to tell the Congress how to do its job. He reiterated this belief throughout his first term. For example, in his inaugural address, Cleveland pledged "to be guided by a just and unstrained construction of the Constitution, a careful observance of the distinction between the powers granted to the Federal Government and those reserved to the states or to the people, and by a cautious appreciation of those functions which by the Constitution and by the laws have been especially assigned to the executive branch of government."[4] Hence, Cleveland declared that "civil-service reform should in good faith be enforced" even though, as a candidate, he had questioned its utility.

Although Cleveland vowed he would not "meddle" with the lawmaking process,[5] he appreciated that the Constitution vested him with the authority

intry."[26] Five days later, Cleveland caused a furor when he
eed Bill, which had appropriated $10,000 to purchase seed
fter a drought had ruined their crops. He told Congress,

warrant for such an appropriation in the Constitution,
believe that the power and duty of the general govern-
be extended to the relief of individual suffering which is
operly related to the public service or benefit. A preva-
to disregard the limited mission of this power and duty
k, be steadfastly resisted, to the end that the lesson should
enforced that, though the people support the govern-
ernment should not support the people.[27]

Cleveland's clearest expression of his belief that the Consti-
no affirmative duty on the federal government to ameliorate
sibility for economic downturns in the private sector.[28] It is
uren's views decades before and foreshadowed Coolidge's sev-
r.

many pension bills, Cleveland was also acting on the basis of
on-of-powers concerns. Even though Congress had created
Claims in 1855 to handle pension and other kinds of claims
ernment, it did not have jurisdiction over most veterans' pen-
tead, Congress maintained that it had jurisdiction over these
ause of its constitutional duty to receive petitions and because
ead belief among members that the claims raised questions
r Congress than for the courts to decide. Cleveland was more
this perspective, particularly since many of the pensions
raudulent and the process by which Congress was approving
ect. While Cleveland was disposed not to tell Congress how to
omplained that the overwhelming number of claims pressed on
ed it to approve the bills by general consent, usually without a
without any debate. There is nothing arcane or anachronistic
nd's concerns, which continue to be expressed about Congress
aking process.

ple might wonder, however, why Cleveland issued no signing
begin with, the bills, which were presented to him, were deliber-
to force Cleveland to make a choice between signing or vetoing
as no middle ground: The bills plainly granted special benefits of
eland had promised to veto, so his only option was to stick to his

to "recommend to [Congress's] consideration such Measures as he shall judge necessary and expedient."[6] In each of his annual messages, he did so, though he purposely left the details for Congress to work out. Indeed, this is what he did in his first term with respect to three landmark laws. First, in his First Annual Message, he recommended that the

> present condition of the law relating to the succession to the Presidency in the event of the death, disability, or removal of both the President and Vice-President is such as to require immediate amendment. This subject has repeatedly been considered by Congress, but no result has been reached. The recent lamentable death of [Vice President Thomas Hendricks[7]], and vacancies at the same time in all other offices the incumbents of which might immediately exercise the functions of the presidential office, has caused public anxiety and a just demand that a recurrence of such a condition of affairs should not be permitted.[8]

In January 1886, Congress acquiesced and enacted the Presidential Succession Act, which Cleveland quickly signed.[9] A year later, Congress, acting on its own initiative, finally addressed the issues arising in the aftermath of the disputed 1876 presidential election and enacted the Electoral Count Act.[10] Cleveland signed the bill, which is still the principal law governing disputes arising in presidential elections. Its interpretation was at the center of the dispute more than a century later in *Bush v. Gore*.[11]

The third landmark law signed by Cleveland in his first term was the Interstate Commerce Act.[12] The legislation was a response to the Supreme Court's ruling that the states lacked the authority to regulate interstate railroads.[13] In his Second Annual Message, Cleveland told Congress that "the expediency of Federal action" in this field was "worthy of consideration," and Congress passed the Interstate Commerce Act early the next year. The law vested the federal courts with the powers of enforcement and punishment and created a five-member Interstate Commerce Commission, which was authorized to conduct investigations of railroad practices and to ensure that the rates set were "reasonable and just." Though Cleveland had concerns about the constitutionality of "government by commission,"[14] he signed the bill in deference to Congress's judgments. The Interstate Commerce Act is one of the first laws based on the understanding that the Commerce Clause empowers Congress to create federal agencies with jurisdiction over matters relating to the national economy.[15]

The principal exception to Cleveland's preference not to "meddle" with lawmaking was his campaign to stop the production of silver as currency and to lower the federal tariff. A large surplus in the federal treasury and the scarcity of gold coins (which could be used for investments and to pay off private debts) led Cleveland to push Congress to stop producing silver. In his First Annual Message, he asked Congress to repeal the Bland-Allison Act.[16] He also believed that lowering the tariff would be a catalyst for producing lower prices for consumers and reducing the surplus in the federal treasury, which in turn (he believed) drained the amount of currency in circulation. When the House defeated a bill that would have stopped silver production and did not act on legislation to lower the tariff, Cleveland convened a summit of Democratic congressional leaders to discuss the problem.[17] When it failed to produce consensus, Cleveland took the unprecedented step of devoting his Third Annual Message entirely to a single subject—urging Congress to reduce the tariff.[18] In taking this initiative, Cleveland was perhaps on the verge of using the presidency as modern presidents do, as a bully pulpit, for he had made the tariff issue "the only important national topic."[19] But Cleveland did not capitalize on the attention and support his proposal was receiving around the nation. Once a bill was introduced in the House in March 1888, he got no further involved—he did not lobby members of Congress, made no speeches, and issued no statements urging senators to act, even after the House (in which Democrats held a majority of seats) approved the bill in July 1888.[20] The Republicans, who held a slim majority in the Senate, approved an alternative bill but allowed both this and the House's bill to die in conference committee just before the 1888 presidential election.[21] Cleveland's failure to negotiate with Congress over the substance of a bill after it had been formally introduced was undoubtedly a factor in the bill's demise. Later presidents would embrace a different philosophy in which they actively tried to shape congressional debates and outcomes.

The likely reason that Cleveland had meddled with the tariff was his strong belief that the president had the duty to block Congress from enacting legislation favoring special interests, exceeding the boundaries of its powers, or interfering with the independence of the executive branch. Cleveland objected to higher tariffs because he saw them as another form of favoritism for domestic businesses and manufacturers.

Throughout his presidency, Cleveland repeatedly emphasized the president's duty to protect the American people from having the federal government play favorites, spend federal money to give special benefits to certain groups, or exceed the boundaries of its powers. In his inaugural address, he

explained, "It is the duty of
limit public expenditures t
cally administered, because
tribute from the earnings of
public extravagance begets e

In a rare press briefing on
ophy of executive power. He
job as president was "to insis
and legislative branches of th
the legislative branch to see th
and well-defined, which their
He explained that the Constit
recommendations to Congress
meant to be strictly Presidentia
certain executive functions to
ends. The office is one of the co
tors and members have their du
upon the Bible and take the san
does the President."[25]

Cleveland made good on his
legislation that he regarded as unv
of vetoes he cast in his first term is
(including 110 pocket vetoes). Th
vetoes of prior presidents put tog
half—228—were directed at bills a
denials of special pensions to spec
gress passed the Dependent Bill, w
every Union veteran who could cla
by physical labor even if the disabili
Cleveland vetoed the bill. After poi
disability benefits to veterans no ma
even if their injuries had nothing to
that was likely (if history was any g
Cleveland concluded that "the evil th
mously expensive public charity prog
with great responsibility in behalf of t
bring to the consideration of this meas
ment and perform my constitutional d
consequences except such as appear to

interests of the c
vetoed the Texas
grain for farmers

I can find no
and I do not
ment ought t
no manner p
lent tendenc
should, I thi
be constantl
ment, the go

This statement
tution imposed
or to take respo
similar to Van
eral decades lat

In vetoing s
serious separat
the Court of
against the go
sion claims. In
claims both be
of the widesp
better suited f
dubious abou
seemed to be
them was sus
do its job, he
Congress for
quorum and
about Clevel
and the lawn

Some pe
statements. T
ately designe
them. There
the kind Cle

principles and appear to be consistent, *or* to demonstrate compassion and incur goodwill by taking the sides of beneficiaries, who were obviously quite sympathetic. Even Cleveland understood that denying the various bills' beneficiaries would cost him the support of veterans and risk appearing callous and indifferent to the plight of citizens for whom some kind of public assistance was their last hope. Second, Cleveland served at a time when presidential signing statements were not the norm.[29] He agreed with other presidents that the Constitution granted him the authority to sign or veto a bill in full. Third, presidential signing statements did not fit with Cleveland's conception of presidential power. For him, there were no middle grounds in disputes between presidents and Congress; something either was or was not constitutional. For him, any special interest legislation or any protectionist legislation was simply unconstitutional.

Congress upheld almost all of his 414 vetoes (it overrode only two). Hence, his vetoes were effectively the last word on each of the statutes in question. No other presidents, with the possible exceptions of Jackson, Tyler, and Franklin D. Roosevelt, did as much as Cleveland did to secure the president's unilateral authority to veto legislation on whatever grounds he deemed appropriate.

Invigorating Presidential Prerogatives

Cleveland had significant clashes with the Senate that shaped the balance of power over appointments, removals, and executive privilege. By winning most of these, he established enduring precedents in these domains on which other presidents have relied ever since.

Upon entering office, Cleveland was deluged by people seeking offices or pushing people for offices. Since he was the first Democratic president in almost twenty-five years, there was a generation of Democrats who were yearning for their first opportunity to work in a presidential administration. Cleveland attempted to manage the pressure—and to keep faith with his long-standing commitment to the principle of rotation in office—through the articulation of five principles that he announced would guide his appointment and removal decisions. First, he pledged that in the offices filled by presidential appointees for four-year terms, inoffensive and inefficient Republicans should not be removed "during the terms for which they were appointed."[30] Second, if people in minor offices had been good public servants, he promised not to replace them until their terms expired. Third, he declared that "those who have been guilty of offences against our political code" or exhibited what Cleveland called "pernicious partisanship" "should go without regard to the time they have served."[31] Fourth, he promised not to appoint any

Democrats solely because they had been loyal Democrats. He insisted they would have to merit their appointments because of honesty, competency, and devotion to public service. Last, he vowed not to appoint people to federal offices simply because they were his friends.[32]

Notwithstanding these principles, he looked for opportunities to implement his lifelong support for rotation in office. When he came into office, the federal civil service was staffed almost entirely by Republicans, and the law required a finding of "offensive partisanship" or some other kind of misconduct as a basis for removing covered employees. Initially, he tried to handle this by resisting the pleas of party leaders to replace civil servants who were Republican holdovers with Democratic employees, and he even kept a few Republicans in office after their terms expired. But, a year into Cleveland's presidency, power-hungry Democratic leaders and partisans pressured him for more. In fact, he did two things: The first was to keep his promise to wait until the terms of Republicans had expired before he replaced them.[33] This strategy allowed him to appoint Democrats to offices throughout the administration. Second, Cleveland asked his cabinet secretaries to vet the qualifications of civil servants and to root out those who were performing poorly or were "offensively" or "perniciously" partisan. Through this purge, Cleveland achieved a nearly clean sweep of political appointments in the Department of the Interior and the Post Office, in which most of the positions covered by the Pendleton Civil Service Act were located.[34] By the end of his term, Cleveland had replaced two-thirds of the federal bureaucracy with Democrats. Consequently, the National Civil Service Reform League, which had endorsed Cleveland in the 1884 presidential election, opposed his reelection.[35]

The most significant obstacle to fully implanting rotation of office in Cleveland's first term was the Tenure in Office Act. In 1867, it had been redrafted to give the Senate veto power over President Andrew Johnson's removals of civil officers whom the Senate had confirmed.[36] Once Johnson left office, Congress in 1869 amended the act to allow the president to suspend an executive branch officer for any reason (rather than for misconduct or the commission of a crime); to drop the requirement that the president send the Senate "the evidence and reasons"[37] for any suspensions; to allow the president during a recess to suspend executive officers and to replace them with temporary appointments as long as he submitted the names of replacements within thirty days after the Senate had reconvened and the names were subject to Senate confirmation; and to deny a suspended officer the return or expectation to return to his position if the Senate did not concur in his removal.[38] Significantly, this last provision shifted the balance of power on removals: Whereas the 1867 law had upheld the Senate's power to compel presidents to retain people whom they wanted to dismiss, the 1869 version did not. The latter allowed presidents to make nominations to fill vacancies until the Senate approved them.

Cleveland was determined not to allow the Tenure in Office Act to inhibit his discretion over appointments and removals. Once in office, he quickly suspended 643 officials in ostensible compliance with the act's requirements.[39] But, as his nominations to fill the vacant offices came before the Senate, Republicans were ready for battle. Committee chairs told Cleveland that they would approve any nominations for offices in which the dismissals were justified. Consequently, they upheld all of his nominations, and the Senate passed several resolutions directing cabinet secretaries to explain any dismissals and the qualifications of the nominees.[40]

The president leapt into action. Believing that the Senate was intruding upon his unilateral authority over nominations and removals of executive branch officers, he directed his cabinet secretaries to use pro forma responses to the Senate requests and resolutions.[41] The crisis soon came to a head.

On December 26, 1886, Senator George Edmunds, the chair of the Judiciary Committee, asked Cleveland's attorney general, Augustus Garland, to send him the official papers pertaining to George Duskin's suspension as the U.S. attorney for the Southern District of Alabama and to the nomination of his replacement, John Burnett.[42] Although Attorney General Garland had delivered documents regarding Burnett's qualifications, Cleveland directed Garland to refuse to send any materials regarding Duskin's removal.[43] In response, Edmunds drafted a Senate resolution ordering the attorney general to transmit copies of all Justice Department documents from the previous year relating to the office of U.S. attorney for the Southern District of Alabama. On January 26, 1886, the Senate approved the resolution.[44] Three days later, Attorney General Garland sent a letter to Senator Edmunds declining to furnish the requested documents.[45]

On February 17, 1886, the Republican caucus adopted new resolutions.[46] They included a formal censure of Garland for refusing to comply with Senate document requests and a declaration that the Senate would not confirm persons nominated to succeed suspended officers unless the administration furnished reasons for the suspensions. The Senate Judiciary Committee issued a report supporting the resolution.[47] The report explained that the Senate was entitled to information about the suspensions because Congress had created and funded the offices involved and because the Constitution had given the Senate coordinate authority with the president over the appointments, which could only be made with its advice and consent.

The ensuing Senate debates on the resolutions and supporting argumentation revealed political and constitutional difficulties for the Senate. The political problem was that it became apparent that publicizing the department's
internal documents might embarrass some senators more than Cleveland.[48]
Documents revealed that senators were responsible for more than a few of the
disputed removals. Second, several senators stressed that Cleveland had the
independent, unilateral authority to nominate people to fill any vacant offices.[49] Some Republican senators conceded the point or acknowledged that
the Tenure in Office Act probably interfered with the president's entitlement
to suspend or remove executive branch officers who impeded his ability to
discharge his constitutional duties.[50]

On March 1, 1886, Cleveland delivered a special message to the Senate,
which he intended to reach the American people.[51] The message was, as one
biographer notes, "one of the most dignified, concise, and logical of all his
writings."[52] First, Cleveland dismissed as illogical the claim made in the Senate
Judiciary Committee report that because Congress had created an office, the
Senate had the right to dictate its operation. He explained that "these instrumentalities were created for the benefit of the people and to answer the general purposes of government under the Constitutions and the laws, and [they]
are unencumbered by any lien in favor of either branch of Congress growing
out of their construction, and unembarrassed by any obligation to the Senate
as the price of their creation."

Second, Cleveland explained that the president had complete discretion
over which documents to share with the Senate because they were private and
privileged. He explained that the attorney general had been following his
orders when he refused to comply with the request for documents relating to
Duskin's suspension and that he had issued this order "because I regard the
papers and documents withheld and addressed to me or intended for my use
and action [as] purely unofficial and private, not infrequently confidential,
and having reference to the performance of a duty exclusively mine. I consider
them [as] deposited there for my convenience, remaining still completely
under my control." Cleveland suggested further that the "nature and character" of the documents pertaining to Duskin's suspension "remain the same
whether they are kept in the Executive Mansion or deposited in the Department. There is no mysterious power of transmutation in departmental custody, nor is there magic in the undefined and sacred solemnity of Department
files." He went further to suggest that he was "constrained to deny the right of
the Senate to the papers and documents described, so far as the right to the
same is based upon the claim that they are in any view of the subject official, I

am also led unequivocally to dispute the right of the Senate by the aid of any document whatever, or any way save through the judicial process of trial on impeachment, to review or reverse the acts of the Executive in the suspension, during the recess of the Senate, of Federal officials."

Third, Cleveland declared that the Constitution gave the president the sole power of suspension or removal of executive officers. He reminded the Senate that the Constitution required the president "'shall take care that the laws be faithfully executed" and that in exercising this function the president was responsible to the people, not the Senate. He argued that the careful delegation of specific responsibilities to the Senate in the Constitution "should be held, under a familiar maxim of construction, to exclude every right [of the Senate] of interference with Executive functions." Last, Cleveland reviewed the history of the Tenure in Office Act. Without conceding its constitutionality, he noted that Congress had repealed the sections within the act requiring that he report to the Senate his reasons for suspensions or removals.

Public opinion shifted in Cleveland's favor. Major newspapers praised Cleveland and denounced Republicans for their obstruction. On March 12, Senator John Logan of Illinois, a staunch Republican, persuaded seven other Republicans, for the sake of senatorial courtesy, to join in confirming a friend of his as the surveyor-general of Utah.[53] This was the first sign of a crack in the opposition. Two weeks later, the Senate approved a formal censure of Garland by a straight party-line vote, 32–25,[54] but approved by a single vote a resolution declaring it to be the Senate's duty to refuse its confirmation in all like cases.[55] Three Republicans broke ranks to oppose the resolution. Meanwhile, after senators learned that Duskin's term expired several months earlier, they quickly confirmed him, ceased to demand that cabinet secretaries produce documents relating to suspensions or removals, and began to confirm the nominees to replace suspended or removed officials.[56]

Cleveland's final, decisive victory came later that year. In mid-December 1886, Senator George Hoar of Massachusetts introduced a bill to repeal the Tenure in Office Act.[57] The Senate Judiciary Committee favorably reported the bill to the full Senate. Senator Edmunds cast the only dissenting vote. The House approved the bill, and Cleveland signed it into law on March 3, 1887.[58]

The repeal of the Tenure in Office Act had several constitutional ramifications. First, the repeal signaled the law's effective end. No serious effort was made within the Senate to revive it, thereby underscoring the extent to which Congress and the president, rather than the Supreme Court, had the last word on its constitutionality. Second, the repeal reinforced the unilateral authority of the president's nominating and removal authorities. Cleveland began the contest over the Tenure in Office Act with most members of Congress conceding that he had unilateral authority to make nominations to most confirmable offices as he saw fit, and the fight ended with consensus that the president had similarly broad discretion over removing executive branch personnel. Third, Cleveland won an important victory for executive privilege. By backing down in the face of Cleveland's assertions of executive privilege, the Senate reinforced the president's power to define the scope of executive privilege. Fourth, Cleveland's defense reflected his understanding of the capacity of the presidency to leverage public opinion. In all likelihood, Cleveland's success in marshaling public opinion in support of his unilateral nominating and removal authorities might have emboldened him to take the initiative at the end of the year to ask Congress to lower the tariff.[59]

Cleveland's friction with the Senate over appointments was not restricted to the fallout from his support for civil service reform and opposition to the Tenure in Office Act. He also overcame stiff Senate opposition to secure the confirmation of two nominees to the Supreme Court. In doing so, Cleveland broke new ground for the Supreme Court and consolidated the presidency's power over Court appointments.

The first vacancy arose upon the death of Justice William Woods, a Republican appointed by President Hayes. Because Woods had come from Georgia, Cleveland faced pressure to conform to the long-standing norm of replacing a justice from the same region from which the departing justice came. Cleveland was agreeable to following the norm, but the choice of a southern Democrat was likely to provoke opposition within the Senate, because Senator Edmunds was determined as chair of the Judiciary Committee to block a southern Democrat's nomination. Nevertheless, Cleveland proceeded to nominate as Woods's replacement his secretary of the interior, Lucius Lamar, from Mississippi. It was a controversial choice because Lamar was a veteran of the Confederate army (as a colonel he was part of the Confederate army's contingent that surrendered to Grant at Appomattox). Northern Republicans, led by Edmunds, bottled up the nomination for six weeks while they voiced their objections to the nomination on the grounds that he was sixty-two and therefore too old for the Court, had committed treason against the Union as a member of the Confederate army, and had inadequate legal experience (since he had spent most of his career as an elected politician and not practicing law). Cleveland beat down the opposition by taking advantage of senatorial courtesy. Prior to becoming secretary of the interior, Lamar had served in the House for two terms and the Senate from 1876 until his appointment to the cabinet in 1885. He had been easily confirmed as interior secretary to "recommend to [Congress's] consideration such Measures as he shall judge necessary and expedient."[6] In each of his annual messages, he did so, though he purposefully left the details for Congress to work out. Indeed, this is what he did in his first term with respect to three landmark laws. First, in his First Annual Message, he recommended that the

> present condition of the law relating to the succession to the Presidency in the event of the death, disability, or removal of both the President and Vice-President is such as to require immediate amendment. This subject has repeatedly been considered by Congress, but no result has been reached. The recent lamentable death of [Vice President Thomas Hendricks[7]], and vacancies at the same time in all other offices the incumbents of which might immediately exercise the functions of the presidential office, has caused public anxiety and a just demand that a recurrence of such a condition of affairs should not be permitted.[8]

In January 1886, Congress acquiesced and enacted the Presidential Succession Act, which Cleveland quickly signed.[9] A year later, Congress, acting on its own initiative, finally addressed the issues arising in the aftermath of the disputed 1876 presidential election and enacted the Electoral Count Act.[10] Cleveland signed the bill, which is still the principal law governing disputes arising in presidential elections. Its interpretation was at the center of the dispute more than a century later in *Bush v. Gore*.[11]

The third landmark law signed by Cleveland in his first term was the Interstate Commerce Act.[12] The legislation was a response to the Supreme Court's ruling that the states lacked the authority to regulate interstate railroads.[13] In his Second Annual Message, Cleveland told Congress that "the expediency of Federal action" in this field was "worthy of consideration," and Congress passed the Interstate Commerce Act early the next year. The law vested the federal courts with the powers of enforcement and punishment and created a five-member Interstate Commerce Commission, which was authorized to conduct investigations of railroad practices and to ensure that the rates set were "reasonable and just." Though Cleveland had concerns about the constitutionality of "government by commission,"[14] he signed the bill in deference to Congress's judgments. The Interstate Commerce Act is one of the first laws based on the understanding that the Commerce Clause empowers Congress to create federal agencies with jurisdiction over matters relating to the national economy.[15]

The principal exception to Cleveland's preference not to "meddle" with lawmaking was his campaign to stop the production of silver as currency and to lower the federal tariff. A large surplus in the federal treasury and the scarcity of gold coins (which could be used for investments and to pay off private debts) led Cleveland to push Congress to stop producing silver. In his First Annual Message, he asked Congress to repeal the Bland-Allison Act.[16] He also believed that lowering the tariff would be a catalyst for producing lower prices for consumers and reducing the surplus in the federal treasury, which in turn (he believed) drained the amount of currency in circulation. When the House defeated a bill that would have stopped silver production and did not act on legislation to lower the tariff, Cleveland convened a summit of Democratic congressional leaders to discuss the problem.[17] When it failed to produce consensus, Cleveland took the unprecedented step of devoting his Third Annual Message entirely to a single subject—urging Congress to reduce the tariff.[18] In taking this initiative, Cleveland was perhaps on the verge of using the presidency as modern presidents do, as a bully pulpit, for he had made the tariff issue "the only important national topic."[19] But Cleveland did not capitalize on the attention and support his proposal was receiving around the nation. Once a bill was introduced in the House in March 1888, he got no further involved—he did not lobby members of Congress, made no speeches, and issued no statements urging senators to act, even after the House (in which Democrats held a majority of seats) approved the bill in July 1888.[20] The Republicans, who held a slim majority in the Senate, approved an alternative bill but allowed both this and the House's bill to die in conference committee just before the 1888 presidential election.[21] Cleveland's failure to negotiate with Congress over the substance of a bill after it had been formally introduced was undoubtedly a factor in the bill's demise. Later presidents would embrace a different philosophy in which they actively tried to shape congressional debates and outcomes.

The likely reason that Cleveland had meddled with the tariff was his strong belief that the president had the duty to block Congress from enacting legislation favoring special interests, exceeding the boundaries of its powers, or interfering with the independence of the executive branch. Cleveland objected to higher tariffs because he saw them as another form of favoritism for domestic businesses and manufacturers.

Throughout his presidency, Cleveland repeatedly emphasized the president's duty to protect the American people from having the federal government play favorites, spend federal money to give special benefits to certain groups, or exceed the boundaries of its powers. In his inaugural address, he explained, "It is the duty of those serving the people in public place to closely limit public expenditures to the actual needs of the Government economically administered, because this bounds the right of the Government to exact tribute from the earnings of labor or the property of the citizen, and because public extravagance begets extravagance among the people."[22]

In a rare press briefing on January 4, 1886, Cleveland elaborated his philosophy of executive power. He told the press that the most important part of his job as president was "to insist upon the entire independence of the executive and legislative branches of the government, and [to] compel the members of the legislative branch to see that they have responsibilities of their own, grave and well-defined, which their official oaths bind them sacredly to perform."[23] He explained that the Constitution "directed him from time to time to make recommendations to Congress and gave him the power to veto bills, and he meant to be strictly Presidential."[24] Being "strictly Presidential" meant, "I have certain executive functions to perform; when that is done my responsibility ends. The office is one of the coordinate branches of government. The Senators and members have their duties and responsibilities. They put their hands upon the Bible and take the same oath of obligation upon assuming office as does the President."[25]

Cleveland made good on his pledge to be "strictly Presidential" by vetoing legislation that he regarded as unwise or unconstitutional. Indeed, the number of vetoes he cast in his first term is a record for vetoes cast in a single term—414 (including 110 pocket vetoes). This was more than twice the number of all the vetoes of prior presidents put together. Of Cleveland's 414 vetoes, more than half—228—were directed at bills attempting to override the Pensions Bureau's denials of special pensions to specific veterans or their families. When Congress passed the Dependent Bill, which granted a pension of $12 a month to every Union veteran who could claim that he was incapable of earning a living by physical labor even if the disability had not been caused by military service, Cleveland vetoed the bill. After pointing out that the Dependent Bill granted disability benefits to veterans no matter how long (or short) they had served, even if their injuries had nothing to do with their military service, and at a cost that was likely (if history was any guide) to exceed congressional estimates, Cleveland concluded that "the evil threatened by the bill [of creating an enormously expensive public charity program,] is, in my opinion, such that, charged with great responsibility in behalf of the people, I cannot do otherwise than to bring to the consideration of this measure my best efforts of thought and judgment and perform my constitutional duty in relation thereto, regardless of any consequences except such as appear to me to be related to the best and highest interests of the country."[26] Five days later, Cleveland caused a furor when he vetoed the Texas Seed Bill, which had appropriated $10,000 to purchase seed grain for farmers after a drought had ruined their crops. He told Congress,

> I can find no warrant for such an appropriation in the Constitution, and I do not believe that the power and duty of the general government ought to be extended to the relief of individual suffering which is no manner properly related to the public service or benefit. A prevalent tendency to disregard the limited mission of this power and duty should, I think, be steadfastly resisted, to the end that the lesson should be constantly enforced that, though the people support the government, the government should not support the people.[27]

This statement is Cleveland's clearest expression of his belief that the Constitution imposed no affirmative duty on the federal government to ameliorate or to take responsibility for economic downturns in the private sector.[28] It is similar to Van Buren's views decades before and foreshadowed Coolidge's several decades later.

In vetoing so many pension bills, Cleveland was also acting on the basis of serious separation-of-powers concerns. Even though Congress had created the Court of Claims in 1855 to handle pension and other kinds of claims against the government, it did not have jurisdiction over most veterans' pension claims. Instead, Congress maintained that it had jurisdiction over these claims both because of its constitutional duty to receive petitions and because of the widespread belief among members that the claims raised questions better suited for Congress than for the courts to decide. Cleveland was more dubious about this perspective, particularly since many of the pensions seemed to be fraudulent and the process by which Congress was approving them was suspect. While Cleveland was disposed not to tell Congress how to do its job, he complained that the overwhelming number of claims pressed on Congress forced it to approve the bills by general consent, usually without a quorum and without any debate. There is nothing arcane or anachronistic about Cleveland's concerns, which continue to be expressed about Congress and the lawmaking process.

Some people might wonder, however, why Cleveland issued no signing statements. To begin with, the bills, which were presented to him, were deliberately designed to force Cleveland to make a choice between signing or vetoing them. There was no middle ground: The bills plainly granted special benefits of the kind Cleveland had promised to veto, so his only option was to stick to his principles and appear to be consistent, *or* to demonstrate compassion and incur goodwill by taking the sides of beneficiaries, who were obviously quite sympathetic. Even Cleveland understood that denying the various bills' beneficiaries would cost him the support of veterans and risk appearing callous and indifferent to the plight of citizens for whom some kind of public assistance was their last hope. Second, Cleveland served at a time when presidential signing statements were not the norm.[29] He agreed with other presidents that the Constitution granted him the authority to sign or veto a bill in full. Third, presidential signing statements did not fit with Cleveland's conception of presidential power. For him, there were no middle grounds in disputes between presidents and Congress; something either was or was not constitutional. For him, any special interest legislation or any protectionist legislation was simply unconstitutional.

Congress upheld almost all of his 414 vetoes (it overrode only two). Hence, his vetoes were effectively the last word on each of the statutes in question. No other presidents, with the possible exceptions of Jackson, Tyler, and Franklin D. Roosevelt, did as much as Cleveland did to secure the president's unilateral authority to veto legislation on whatever grounds he deemed appropriate.

Invigorating Presidential Prerogatives

Cleveland had significant clashes with the Senate that shaped the balance of power over appointments, removals, and executive privilege. By winning most of these, he established enduring precedents in these domains on which other presidents have relied ever since.

Upon entering office, Cleveland was deluged by people seeking offices or pushing people for offices. Since he was the first Democratic president in almost twenty-five years, there was a generation of Democrats who were yearning for their first opportunity to work in a presidential administration. Cleveland attempted to manage the pressure—and to keep faith with his long-standing commitment to the principle of rotation in office—through the articulation of five principles that he announced would guide his appointment and removal decisions. First, he pledged that in the offices filled by presidential appointees for four-year terms, inoffensive and inefficient Republicans should not be removed "during the terms for which they were appointed."[30] Second, if people in minor offices had been good public servants, he promised not to replace them until their terms expired. Third, he declared that "those who have been guilty of offences against our political code" or exhibited what Cleveland called "pernicious partisanship" "should go without regard to the time they have served."[31] Fourth, he promised not to appoint any

Democrats solely because they had been loyal Democrats. He insisted they would have to merit their appointments because of honesty, competency, and devotion to public service. Last, he vowed not to appoint people to federal offices simply because they were his friends.[32]

Notwithstanding these principles, he looked for opportunities to implement his lifelong support for rotation in office. When he came into office, the federal civil service was staffed almost entirely by Republicans, and the law required a finding of "offensive partisanship" or some other kind of misconduct as a basis for removing covered employees. Initially, he tried to handle this by resisting the pleas of party leaders to replace civil servants who were Republican holdovers with Democratic employees, and he even kept a few Republicans in office after their terms expired. But, a year into Cleveland's presidency, power-hungry Democratic leaders and partisans pressured him for more. In fact, he did two things: The first was to keep his promise to wait until the terms of Republicans had expired before he replaced them.[33] This strategy allowed him to appoint Democrats to offices throughout the administration. Second, Cleveland asked his cabinet secretaries to vet the qualifications of civil servants and to root out those who were performing poorly or were "offensively" or "perniciously" partisan. Through this purge, Cleveland achieved a nearly clean sweep of political appointments in the Department of the Interior and the Post Office, in which most of the positions covered by the Pendleton Civil Service Act were located.[34] By the end of his term, Cleveland had replaced two-thirds of the federal bureaucracy with Democrats. Consequently, the National Civil Service Reform League, which had endorsed Cleveland in the 1884 presidential election, opposed his reelection.[35]

The most significant obstacle to fully implanting rotation of office in Cleveland's first term was the Tenure in Office Act. In 1867, it had been redrafted to give the Senate veto power over President Andrew Johnson's removals of civil officers whom the Senate had confirmed.[36] Once Johnson left office, Congress in 1869 amended the act to allow the president to suspend an executive branch officer for any reason (rather than for misconduct or the commission of a crime); to drop the requirement that the president send the Senate "the evidence and reasons"[37] for any suspensions; to allow the president during a recess to suspend executive officers and to replace them with temporary appointments as long as he submitted the names of replacements within thirty days after the Senate had reconvened and the names were subject to Senate confirmation; and to deny a suspended officer the return or expectation to return to his position if the Senate did not concur in his removal.[38] Significantly, this last provision shifted the balance of power on removals: Whereas the 1867 law had upheld the Senate's power to compel presidents to retain people whom they wanted to dismiss, the 1869 version did not. The latter allowed presidents to make nominations to fill vacancies until the Senate approved them.

Cleveland was determined not to allow the Tenure in Office Act to inhibit his discretion over appointments and removals. Once in office, he quickly suspended 643 officials in ostensible compliance with the act's requirements.[39] But, as his nominations to fill the vacant offices came before the Senate, Republicans were ready for battle. Committee chairs told Cleveland that they would approve any nominations for offices in which the dismissals were justified. Consequently, they upheld all of his nominations, and the Senate passed several resolutions directing cabinet secretaries to explain any dismissals and the qualifications of the nominees.[40]

The president leapt into action. Believing that the Senate was intruding upon his unilateral authority over nominations and removals of executive branch officers, he directed his cabinet secretaries to use pro forma responses to the Senate requests and resolutions.[41] The crisis soon came to a head.

On December 26, 1886, Senator George Edmunds, the chair of the Judiciary Committee, asked Cleveland's attorney general, Augustus Garland, to send him the official papers pertaining to George Duskin's suspension as the U.S. attorney for the Southern District of Alabama and to the nomination of his replacement, John Burnett.[42] Although Attorney General Garland had delivered documents regarding Burnett's qualifications, Cleveland directed Garland to refuse to send any materials regarding Duskin's removal.[43] In response, Edmunds drafted a Senate resolution ordering the attorney general to transmit copies of all Justice Department documents from the previous year relating to the office of U.S. attorney for the Southern District of Alabama. On January 26, 1886, the Senate approved the resolution.[44] Three days later, Attorney General Garland sent a letter to Senator Edmunds declining to furnish the requested documents.[45]

On February 17, 1886, the Republican caucus adopted new resolutions.[46] They included a formal censure of Garland for refusing to comply with Senate document requests and a declaration that the Senate would not confirm persons nominated to succeed suspended officers unless the administration furnished reasons for the suspensions. The Senate Judiciary Committee issued a report supporting the resolution.[47] The report explained that the Senate was entitled to information about the suspensions because Congress had created and funded the offices involved and because the Constitution had given the Senate coordinate authority with the president over the appointments, which could only be made with its advice and consent.

The ensuing Senate debates on the resolutions and supporting argumentation revealed political and constitutional difficulties for the Senate. The political problem was that it became apparent that publicizing the department's internal documents might embarrass some senators more than Cleveland.[48] Documents revealed that senators were responsible for more than a few of the disputed removals. Second, several senators stressed that Cleveland had the independent, unilateral authority to nominate people to fill any vacant offices.[49] Some Republican senators conceded the point or acknowledged that the Tenure in Office Act probably interfered with the president's entitlement to suspend or remove executive branch officers who impeded his ability to discharge his constitutional duties.[50]

On March 1, 1886, Cleveland delivered a special message to the Senate, which he intended to reach the American people.[51] The message was, as one biographer notes, "one of the most dignified, concise, and logical of all his writings."[52] First, Cleveland dismissed as illogical the claim made in the Senate Judiciary Committee report that because Congress had created an office, the Senate had the right to dictate its operation. He explained that "these instrumentalities were created for the benefit of the people and to answer the general purposes of government under the Constitutions and the laws, and [they] are unencumbered by any lien in favor of either branch of Congress growing out of their construction, and unembarrassed by any obligation to the Senate as the price of their creation."

Second, Cleveland explained that the president had complete discretion over which documents to share with the Senate because they were private and privileged. He explained that the attorney general had been following his orders when he refused to comply with the request for documents relating to Duskin's suspension and that he had issued this order "because I regard the papers and documents withheld and addressed to me or intended for my use and action [as] purely unofficial and private, not infrequently confidential, and having reference to the performance of a duty exclusively mine. I consider them [as] deposited there for my convenience, remaining still completely under my control." Cleveland suggested further that the "nature and character" of the documents pertaining to Duskin's suspension "remain the same whether they are kept in the Executive Mansion or deposited in the Department. There is no mysterious power of transmutation in departmental custody, nor is there magic in the undefined and sacred solemnity of Department files." He went further to suggest that he was "constrained to deny the right of the Senate to the papers and documents described, so far as the right to the same is based upon the claim that they are in any view of the subject official, I am also led unequivocally to dispute the right of the Senate by the aid of any document whatever, or any way save through the judicial process of trial on impeachment, to review or reverse the acts of the Executive in the suspension, during the recess of the Senate, of Federal officials."

Third, Cleveland declared that the Constitution gave the president the sole power of suspension or removal of executive officers. He reminded the Senate that the Constitution required the president "'shall take care that the laws be faithfully executed" and that in exercising this function the president was responsible to the people, not the Senate. He argued that the careful delegation of specific responsibilities to the Senate in the Constitution "should be held, under a familiar maxim of construction, to exclude every right [of the Senate] of interference with Executive functions." Last, Cleveland reviewed the history of the Tenure in Office Act. Without conceding its constitutionality, he noted that Congress had repealed the sections within the act requiring that he report to the Senate his reasons for suspensions or removals.

Public opinion shifted in Cleveland's favor. Major newspapers praised Cleveland and denounced Republicans for their obstruction. On March 12, Senator John Logan of Illinois, a staunch Republican, persuaded seven other Republicans, for the sake of senatorial courtesy, to join in confirming a friend of his as the surveyor-general of Utah.[53] This was the first sign of a crack in the opposition. Two weeks later, the Senate approved a formal censure of Garland by a straight party-line vote, 32–25,[54] but approved by a single vote a resolution declaring it to be the Senate's duty to refuse its confirmation in all like cases.[55] Three Republicans broke ranks to oppose the resolution. Meanwhile, after senators learned that Duskin's term expired several months earlier, they quickly confirmed him, ceased to demand that cabinet secretaries produce documents relating to suspensions or removals, and began to confirm the nominees to replace suspended or removed officials.[56]

Cleveland's final, decisive victory came later that year. In mid-December 1886, Senator George Hoar of Massachusetts introduced a bill to repeal the Tenure in Office Act.[57] The Senate Judiciary Committee favorably reported the bill to the full Senate. Senator Edmunds cast the only dissenting vote. The House approved the bill, and Cleveland signed it into law on March 3, 1887.[58]

The repeal of the Tenure in Office Act had several constitutional ramifications. First, the repeal signaled the law's effective end. No serious effort was made within the Senate to revive it, thereby underscoring the extent to which Congress and the president, rather than the Supreme Court, had the last word on its constitutionality. Second, the repeal reinforced the unilateral authority of the president's nominating and removal authorities. Cleveland began the contest over the Tenure in Office Act with most members of Congress conceding that he had unilateral authority to make nominations to most confirmable offices as he saw fit, and the fight ended with consensus that the president had similarly broad discretion over removing executive branch personnel. Third, Cleveland won an important victory for executive privilege. By backing down in the face of Cleveland's assertions of executive privilege, the Senate reinforced the president's power to define the scope of executive privilege. Fourth, Cleveland's defense reflected his understanding of the capacity of the presidency to leverage public opinion. In all likelihood, Cleveland's success in marshaling public opinion in support of his unilateral nominating and removal authorities might have emboldened him to take the initiative at the end of the year to ask Congress to lower the tariff.[59]

Cleveland's friction with the Senate over appointments was not restricted to the fallout from his support for civil service reform and opposition to the Tenure in Office Act. He also overcame stiff Senate opposition to secure the confirmation of two nominees to the Supreme Court. In doing so, Cleveland broke new ground for the Supreme Court and consolidated the presidency's power over Court appointments.

The first vacancy arose upon the death of Justice William Woods, a Republican appointed by President Hayes. Because Woods had come from Georgia, Cleveland faced pressure to conform to the long-standing norm of replacing a justice from the same region from which the departing justice came. Cleveland was agreeable to following the norm, but the choice of a southern Democrat was likely to provoke opposition within the Senate, because Senator Edmunds was determined as chair of the Judiciary Committee to block a southern Democrat's nomination. Nevertheless, Cleveland proceeded to nominate as Woods's replacement his secretary of the interior, Lucius Lamar, from Mississippi. It was a controversial choice because Lamar was a veteran of the Confederate army (as a colonel he was part of the Confederate army's contingent that surrendered to Grant at Appomattox). Northern Republicans, led by Edmunds, bottled up the nomination for six weeks while they voiced their objections to the nomination on the grounds that he was sixty-two and therefore too old for the Court, had committed treason against the Union as a member of the Confederate army, and had inadequate legal experience (since he had spent most of his career as an elected politician and not practicing law). Cleveland beat down the opposition by taking advantage of senatorial courtesy. Prior to becoming secretary of the interior, Lamar had served in the House for two terms and the Senate from 1876 until his appointment to the cabinet in 1885. He had been easily confirmed as interior secretary because his colleagues considered him to be erudite, a gifted orator, and honest.[60] The goodwill of his former colleagues enabled Lamar's Supreme Court nomination to get to the floor in spite of a negative recommendation from the Republican-controlled Judiciary Committee. With Republicans controlling the Senate by the narrow margin of 39–37, every little bit helped: Lamar was barely confirmed, 42–38, a result made possible because of the crossovers of three senators who respected Lamar and did not want "a ban against all Confederate veterans."[61] Lamar was the first Southerner confirmed to the Court since Pierce appointed Lamar's distant cousin John Campbell in 1853; the first Democrat-appointed Supreme Court justice since Nathan Clifford in 1858; and "the first with a background of legislative and executive service in *both* the Union and the Confederate governments."[62]

Cleveland's second opportunity to fill a Supreme Court vacancy came two months after Lamar's confirmation when Chief Justice Morrison Waite died. Cleveland decided to adhere to the tradition of selecting a chief justice from outside the Court. He also wanted to appoint someone from Illinois, which produced more Supreme Court litigation than any other state except New York but was not represented on the Court at the time. When Cleveland's first choice, Illinois Supreme Court justice John Scholfield, declined the opportunity because he did not want to move to Washington, Cleveland turned to a confidante, Chicago lawyer Melville Fuller, who had repeatedly rejected other appointments, including as solicitor general. Although Fuller lacked a national reputation, he was widely respected in Illinois and had strong support from the state's two Republican senators and President Lincoln's son, Robert Todd Lincoln, a prominent lawyer in Illinois. In spite of this support, Judiciary Committee chair Senator Edmunds wanted the appointment for a friend. He therefore tried to focus the hearings as much as possible on three possible problems—Fuller's apparent opposition to the Court's decision sustaining the issuance of legal tender notes in peacetime, Fuller's criticism of Lincoln's actions during the Civil War, and Fuller's possible misconduct in handling some legal affairs. Though Edmunds resisted divulging the names of people charging Fuller with unethical conduct, he relented to the public pressure to allow Fuller to see the documentation so that he could respond.[63] With Republicans on the committee opposing Fuller, the committee agreed as a compromise to send Fuller's nomination to the full Senate without a recommendation.[64] On the Senate floor, Edmunds argued that Fuller could not be trusted to keep "the results of the Civil War safe," while Illinois's two Republicans defended Fuller's war record and character.[65] Democrats sat by silently while Republicans debated the nomination among themselves. After three hours of discussion, the Senate confirmed Fuller 41–20. With his confirmation, Fuller became the first chief justice who had never previously held a federal office, only the second Democrat (after Taney) appointed as chief justice,[66] and the first to be commissioned "Chief Justice of the United States."[67]

With the confirmations of Lamar and Fuller, Cleveland established several enduring precedents on Supreme Court appointments. First, he deftly used senatorial courtesy to break an impasse over Lamar's appointment. Second, he extended the tradition of appointing someone from outside the Court as chief justice. Third, both appointments underscore that preoccupation with a justice's likely ideological commitments is a long-standing concern in confirmation hearings. In fact, Cleveland was extending the long-standing practice of presidents to try to shape the Court through their appointments. Fourth, Fuller's confirmation demonstrates that a nominee's lack of prior judicial and governmental experience is not necessarily disqualifying. Other factors, including character, substantial legal experience, judgment, and bipartisan support, can be important.

Both of President Cleveland's appointments helped to initiate an era in which the Supreme Court was disposed to enforce sharp limitations on federal and state authority to interfere with private enterprise. By the end of Fuller's tenure, the Court had made history by striking down not only the 1894 income tax that had been supported by both Cleveland and a Democratic Congress[68] but also progressive economic regulations that it found had violated a constitutionally protected right to contract. The new era took its name from one of these opinions, *Lochner v. New York*,[69] which the next two Democratic presidents—Woodrow Wilson and Franklin Roosevelt[70]—were determined to bury through their twelve Court appointments.

DURING THE 1888 presidential election, Cleveland bet his reelection on the tariff, and he lost, barely. Over the next four years, he carefully cultivated support from Democratic Party leaders and won the next Democratic nomination for president. By winning the presidential election later that year against the incumbent, Cleveland became the first, nonincumbent president to regain the office. The 1892 election made Cleveland the third and last ex-president to be elected to a national political office (the first was John Quincy Adams to the House and the other was Andrew Johnson to the Senate). While Van Buren was the only other former president to run for the presidency after having been defeated for reelection, Cleveland's successes in regaining his party's presidential nomination *and* winning the presidency back again demonstrated the capacity of an ex-president to remain politically relevant.

9

Benjamin Harrison, 1889–1893

IT IS EASY to understand why most people know almost nothing about Benjamin Harrison except perhaps that he is the only grandson of a president to be elected president in his own right. He was uncharismatic and had trouble connecting with the general public. He never won a direct election, was twice defeated for governor of Indiana, and lost the popular vote both times he ran for president. The people who worked closely with him complained about his "lack of imagination, . . . absence of personal magnetism, and [r]eserved, icy, and aloof manner."[1] Rather than nurture the support of party leaders, he angered them by appointing only one of them to his cabinet, James Blaine, as secretary of state; however, Blaine disliked him so much that he challenged Harrison for the 1892 Republican presidential nomination. Thus, Harrison alienated the people he needed to unify his administration,[2] to support his reelection, and to protect his legacy once he left office. Moreover, he was uninspiring as a speaker and obsessed with the details of policy issues rather than the big picture. His wife's death in the closing days of the 1892 presidential election made him largely indifferent to its outcome and his future. His legacy has been further obscured because he was one of fifteen men who served for one term or less as president, the fourth of five Republicans elected president in the last half of the nineteenth century, one of the twelve generals elected president, and one of twenty-five presidents who were lawyers.[3]

Yet there is a reason that the historian Henry Adams, who disliked Harrison personally, ranked him among our best presidents.[4] In his single term, Harrison fortified rotation in office; signed landmark Commerce Clause enactments including the Sherman Anti-Trust Act; transformed the federal judiciary by making four Supreme Court appointments in a single term and by sanctioning the creation of two enduring features of the federal court system—the federal circuit courts of appeal *and* the Supreme Court's discretionary control over its docket; and established one of the most important precedents upholding presidential authority to take noncongressionally

FIGURE 9.1 Caricature of President Benjamin Harrison, as a very short person, with large head, seated at a desk, wearing the big hat of his grandfather William Henry Harrison, also a president. On a bust perches Secretary of State James G. Blaine, shown as a raven, presumably croaking "Nevermore." Harrison and Blaine were at odds over the proposed McKinley Tariff.

Source: Library of Congress Prints and Photographs Division, Washington, D.C. 20540 USA

authorized action to do what is necessary to ensure that the laws are faithfully executed. Though Harrison seems remote and bland to contemporary Americans, many of his constitutional judgments remain relevant.

Bolstering Unilateral Exercise of the Nominating Power

By the time Harrison took the oath of office on March 4, 1889, rotation in office had largely been secured. While the Supreme Court had not addressed this issue directly, presidents from Jackson through Cleveland had agreed that the Constitution vested presidents with the unilateral authority to remove high-ranking executive branch officials, including the entire cabinet, on whatever basis they deemed appropriate. Yet, some significant challenges remained, ones that had confronted previous presidents, including his grandfather.

One of the main challenges, the Senate's desire to dominate the federal appointments process, was not new to Harrison. He knew from firsthand experience as a senator about senators' desires to distribute federal patronage within their states. In his one term as senator, Harrison had acted the same as other senators in pressing for the appointments of his preferred candidates to federal offices in his home state. While Harrison had voted for the Pendleton Act, he appreciated that it limited a president's authority to remove certain personnel in the executive branch and reduced the opportunities for patronage.

Once elected, Harrison was stunned by the intensity and extent of pressure placed on him to abdicate authority over appointments to Republican Party leaders and senators. The pressure began but did not end with his cabinet choices. Since Harrison was the first Republican president since Lincoln to come into office after a Democratic administration, Republican Party leaders and senators were eager to regain their control over the distribution of patronage. Harrison underestimated the amount of time he was forced to devote to appointments. He was pressed to spend up to six hours a day on appointments, and he, like many other presidents before him, complained incessantly about the unceasing demand of office seekers. The demand was so oppressive that he often complained it made him feel like a "hunted animal."

Harrison did more than complain about these pressures. As president-elect, he began to think about appointments from a different perspective than he had as a senator. He realized that as president he alone had to take the responsibility for his appointments, and he assiduously defended his prerogative to nominate people based on his, rather than senators', preferred criteria.

Republican Party leaders and senators badly misread Harrison's demeanor. Many had assumed Harrison would continue to be what he seemed to have been as a senator—a good party man. While Harrison generally equated the nation's best interests with those of his party, he never suffered fools gladly. He obsessively focused on details, relished hard work, was resentful when others told him what to do, was impatient with subordinates and matters he considered to be beneath him, and stubbornly held his ground whenever he thought he was right. Opposed to delegating responsibility for making major appointments, he appointed too small a staff to assist managing the huge demand for appointments. He resented the time he spent on appointments because it interfered with business he thought was more important, and his appointments invariably made more enemies than friends.

Harrison was convinced, however, that the cabinet was instrumental to the success of his administration. He thus made sure, before asking anyone to join his cabinet, that the candidate understood that "each member of my official family will have my full confidence and I shall expect his in return." Drawing on his experience as a senator, Harrison tried to ameliorate possible Senate hostility to his cabinet choices by taking advantage of senatorial courtesy. Hence, he appointed two former senators to his cabinet—James Blaine as secretary of state and William Windom as treasury secretary.[5] The Senate unanimously approved them both, as it did the rest of his cabinet. Harrison was pleased that the cabinet was committed to his priorities, and its quick confirmation further entrenched within the constitutional culture Senate deference to the nominations of their colleagues to cabinet posts *and* to presidents' cabinet choices generally.

The fact that the Senate had unanimously confirmed Harrison's cabinet did not mean, however, that senators had forgotten Harrison's refusal to follow their advice in assembling it. He angered senators more by refusing to defer to the candidates that Republican senators and party officials wanted for federal offices besides the cabinet posts. Even before he became president, Harrison had acknowledged, "I was nominated at [the Republican convention] without the smallest promise of any sort relating to federal appointments and I am now absolutely without any promise or entanglements of any sort."[6] Republican senators could not have been pleased with Harrison's declaration in his inaugural address that "all applicants will be treated with consideration; but I shall need, and the heads of Department will need, time for inquiry and deliberation."[7] The implication was clear that Harrison expected people within *his* administration to help him with appointments and to make sure that the people whom *he* appointed would perform their jobs as he would like. As Harrison's private secretary, Elijah Halford, recalled, Harrison carefully avoided "even a semblance of a bargain, for under no circumstances would he be bound by any promise, express, or implied, either during the campaign or later."[8] He told senators that he "could not consent to the surrender of the personal responsibility for appointments which the Constitution enjoined, and he would have proper inquiries initiated on his own behalf, and he hoped the result would be to corroborate the judgment of the senators."[9]

Although Harrison had promised civil service reform as a candidate, he was not naïve about its prospects. He knew, as well as anyone, that genuine civil service reform would antagonize the Republican Party leadership. The only people likely to be pleased with this pledge were reform-minded Republicans, who were not a major force in the party or the Senate. Although Harrison pledged to reform the spoils system in his public messages, he took almost no initiative on this front over the next four years. His most notable effort to facilitate civil service reform was to fill two of the three seats on the Civil Service Commission with two ardent supporters of civil service reform, one of whom was the brash, thirty-year-old Teddy Roosevelt of New York. Although Roosevelt's seemingly boundless energy and exuberance for reform brought national attention to his efforts, Harrison was not alone in regarding Roosevelt as a nuisance rather than a help. Harrison fielded numerous complaints about Roosevelt, whose recommendations he generally ignored. Roosevelt grew disenchanted with Harrison, who, he believed, "had never given the Commission one ounce of backing."[10]

It did not take long for the friction between Harrison and party leaders to take its toll. To be sure, Harrison took pride in the fact that the Senate, besides unanimously approving all his cabinet nominations, rejected none of his major appointments. Yet he understood that "[n]o President can conduct a successful administration without the support of Congress, and this matter of appointments, do what he will, often weakens that support." Several Republican senators, irked over their loss of control over patronage, deliberately thwarted many of Harrison's legislative priorities, including the first major civil rights bill since Reconstruction and a major bill to fund public education throughout the country. The Senate rejected the education bill (even though it had passed a nearly identical one in 1888) and took no action on the voting rights law Harrison wanted. Not coincidentally, "only half the states from which the original cabinet hailed would give Harrison a majority of their votes for re-nomination" in 1892.[11] The loss of support he incurred within his party because of his independence proved costly: Harrison, who had barely won Cleveland's home state of New York to win in 1888, lost that state—and his bid for reelection—four years later.

Pushing Congress

The first two years of Harrison's presidency coincide with what has been called "the billion-dollar Congress," marking the fact that it was the first legislative session in which Congress approved enactments requiring the appropriation of more than a billion dollars. Unlike Cleveland, Harrison was proactive throughout the session, attempting through various initiatives—public addresses and informal dinners, interaction, and receptions with legislative leaders—to cultivate support for his legislative initiatives. Harrison was thus acting directly contrary to his grandfather's pledge not to become part of the legislative process. Harrison thrust himself into the middle of it.

Of the major enactments approved in that session, none was more significant than the Sherman Anti-Trust Act, the first federal antitrust law enacted. Prior to the 1888 presidential election, state common law and statutes provided the only legal constraints on the unfair trade practices of business, particularly the problematic, often unethical ways in which big businesses tried to destroy their competition. Both the common law and the state statutes had been ineffective against the anticompetitive practices of trusts. A dangerous, new phenomenon in the financial sector, trusts were special arrangements by which the stockholders in several companies transferred their shares to a single set of trustees. In exchange, stockholders received a certificate entitling them to a specified share of the consolidated earnings of the jointly managed companies. Trusts had several advantages over preexisting financial arrangements, enabling trustees to operate the trusts like monopolies, since they would be effectively running the component companies. The popularity of trusts grew, and they soon dominated several major industries by destroying their competition through price-fixing and other dubious means. By 1888, the public clamor for federal intervention to address the dangers posed to free enterprise and competition by trusts—particularly the Standard Oil trust[12]—had become so strong that both major parties and their candidates pledged to combat trusts.

Harrison's commitment to fighting trusts was evident from the outset of his administration. In his inaugural address, he emphasized that the federal government needed to play a greater role in monitoring the practices of big businesses: "When organized, as they often are, to crush out all healthy competition and to monopolize the production or sale of an article of commerce and general necessity, they are dangerous conspiracies against the public good, and should be made the subject of prohibitory and even penal legislation."

The day after Harrison's message had been delivered to the Senate, several senators, including John Sherman, the chairman of the Senate Finance Committee, introduced various antitrust bills in response to Harrison's request and popular demand. Like Harrison, Sherman had originally wanted to outlaw monopolization in "production" as well as trade, but most members of Congress believed that the Constitution restricted Congress's power to regulate business practices that related to matters of interstate or foreign commerce. Sherman's bill was substantially amended to outlaw every contract, combination, trust, or conspiracy "in restraint of trade or commerce" and to impose fines of up to $5,000 and up to a year in prison. The Senate quickly and overwhelmingly approved the bill, 52–1. The bill went to the House, where, after conference with the Senate, it was approved with no dissent, though eighty-five representatives did not vote. The bill enacted by Congress was not as tough as Harrison would have liked, but he signed it into law on July 2, 1890.

The bill was vaguely worded on purpose, and members of Congress, not surprisingly, differed on its rationale (complicating its subsequent interpretation). On the Senate floor, Senator Sherman argued that the bill helped rather than hurt business, while Senator Hoar suggested that it was not a violation of the bill if a company "got the whole business because nobody could do it as well." Merely being more efficient than other businesses in particular fields or dominating a particular industry did not, in Senator Hoar's opinion, constitute an unlawful "restraint of trade." Moreover, the act's supporters attributed different objectives to the bill, some suggesting that its goal was to increase competition, while others suggested it was to lower prices. While it was clear that the Sherman Anti-Trust Act was not specifically directed at trusts, it did not define critical terms such as "trust," "combination," "conspiracy," and "monopoly," and it pointedly left unclear which particular business practices, other than price-fixing, were unlawful "restraints of trade." Consequently, it fell to the federal courts, particularly the Supreme Court, to clarify the scope and meaning of the new federal antitrust law. But the Court could only clarify the scope of the act if an appropriate case came before it, and prosecutions were extremely difficult to initiate. Moreover, the attorney general—William Henry Harrison Miller (a law partner but no relation of the president)—did not consider enforcing the new law to be a priority, and Congress had failed to appropriate funds to support antitrust investigations and prosecutions. More than a year after the law was in force, Harrison urged the attorney general to advise US attorneys to lay the law "alongside any combinations or trusts within your district, and if by such measurement, it is found that those trusts or combinations are infractions of the law, prosecute vigorously." In the thirty-two remaining months of Harrison's presidency, the administration initiated seven antitrust actions (four civil and three criminal). (Cleveland's second administration initiated eight cases, but McKinley's administration initiated only three.) Three of these cases were concluded by the time Harrison left office, and the federal government won only the first of these. In his last annual report, Attorney General Miller complained about the difficulties in enforcing the act, including its narrow construction by federal judges. Several years later the Supreme Court maintained the trend and narrowly construed the law partly because of Harrison's transformation of the Court.[13]

Shaping the Courts and the Law

As reflected in the initiatives he took in the field of antitrust, Harrison was, by training and temperament, a first-rate lawyer. Indeed, he had gained so much notice from his highly successful law practice in Indianapolis that President Grant had appointed him the lead defense counsel for army personnel in one of the most important civil lawsuits challenging the legality of military detentions during the Civil War.[14] Although the Supreme Court rejected Harrison's defense of the president's controversial policy of trying civilians in military tribunals rather than civilian courts, Harrison convinced the trial judge on remand to award Milligan just $5 even though the Court had found he had been illegally arrested and imprisoned.

Harrison's interest in law led him to become involved in a number of issues involving the administration of justice. In his First Annual Message, he urged Congress to create "intermediate courts having final appellate jurisdiction of certain classes of questions and cases."[15] Congress did not act until early 1891, when the Supreme Court's backlog of pending cases had reached an all-time high and was considerably higher than the number the justices said they could competently handle annually. Although Congress had no constitutional obligation to create the intermediate courts that Harrison had requested, it agreed on their necessity and thus used its Article I power to "constitute inferior tribunals to the Supreme Court" to enact the Circuit Court of Appeals Act of 1891.[16] The act established the framework of the modern federal court system, including the terminology by which the federal circuit courts of appeals are known today.[17] Consequently, the Court's caseload quickly shrank; it had fewer than 400 new cases to handle in 1891 and less than 300 in 1892. Moreover, the act introduced the "then revolutionary, but now familiar principle of discretionary review of federal judgments on writ of certiorari,"[18] the process through which the Court chooses which state or federal court judgments to review.

While the act restructured the Supreme Court's docket, it presented Harrison with the opportunity to pack the circuit courts to an unprecedented degree. As Lee Epstein and Jeffrey Segal explain, "Republicans, who controlled both Houses and the presidency, enacted the bill on March 3, 1891—just a day before the Democrats would take over the House (but not the Senate and the White House). Accordingly, Republicans were able to expand the bench when their party was in power and then, because they controlled the presidency and the Senate, fill the new seats with partisans."[19] In fact, the act created a total of ninety new judgeships. Harrison personally screened prospective nominees to pick judges who had been loyal Republicans, had substantial practice or judicial experience, were skeptical of extensive congressional regulations of areas traditionally left to state regulation or of economic affairs, and were disposed to protect property rights and rights to contract. By the end of his term, Harrison had nominated more judges to lower federal courts than had any president before then, and the circuit judges he had appointed effectively had "final" say, by virtue of Congress's plenary power, to regulate the jurisdiction of the federal courts, in most cases.

Just as, if not more, importantly, Harrison transformed the Supreme Court through the unusually large number of appointments he made in a single term, the differences those appointments made to the Court's decision making, and how he had made them. While Harrison's grandfather is one of four presidents who never had the opportunity to make any Supreme Court appointments, Harrison made four appointments to the Court. Only four other presidents made more appointments to the Court in a single term—Washington, Lincoln, Taft, and Franklin Roosevelt. Harrison's appointments altered the Court's ideological balance, transforming several areas of constitutional law. Moreover, in making each of these appointments, Harrison took his time and formulated selection criteria that emphasized previous experience as a judge, loyal service to the Republican Party, and commitment to "freedom of contract, absence of governmental restraint on business activities, and the sanctity of property."[20] He secured Senate confirmation of his preferred nominees by successfully maneuvering around several norms that had previously dominated the selection process.

Harrison's first opportunity to fill a vacancy arose when Justice Stanley Matthews died in March 1889. Since the Senate did not plan to convene to vote on a replacement until December, Harrison had plenty of time to make his decision. His objective was "to get the best man and [not to] be very concerned by geography" in spite of the norm to replace justices with people who came from the same circuit or region.[21] Harrison told friends he was considering three possible nominees—Henry Hitchcock, then the president of the American Bar Association; David Brewer, Justice Stephen Field's nephew and an Eighth Circuit Court judge who had been a judge for fourteen years on the Kansas Supreme Court; and Judge Henry Brown of the US District Court in Detroit. Harrison narrowed the choice to Brewer and Brown, each of whom had demonstrated the conservative judicial philosophy Harrison demanded of his Supreme Court appointees. Harrison chose Brewer because he had more extensive judicial experience than Brown, and Harrison had been impressed by Brewer's humility and generosity in recommending that Harrison nominate Brown rather than himself. Although Matthews had come from Ohio and Republicans held only thirty-nine of the Senate's sixty-six seats, Harrison's careful deliberations and lobbying paid off: The Senate confirmed Brewer 53–11.

Harrison's next opportunity arose shortly thereafter when Associate Justice Samuel Freeman Miller died. Though Harrison had already decided to nominate Brown for the seat, he did not make the announcement immediately. He waited for two months during which he methodically built support for Brown. Brown became so well known in the Senate that senators did not bother to record the vote when they confirmed him within a few days of his nomination.

Although Brown's and Brewer's appointments helped to loosen geography as a prerequisite for Supreme Court selection, Harrison confronted different norms when Justice Joseph Bradley of New Jersey died in January 1892. This time, Harrison decided to compromise and thus fill the vacancy with someone who came from the same circuit. He could find, however, no acceptable nominee from New Jersey. Instead, Harrison decided the nominee should be from nearby Pennsylvania because it had not been represented since Justice William Strong had retired in 1880. Harrison knew that if he were to choose a nominee from Pennsylvania, he would have to contend with powerful Republican senator Matthew Quay, who had opposed Harrison's initiatives and nominations because Harrison had refused to give Quay complete control over the patronage in his state. Rather than placate Quay, Harrison challenged his power; he nominated a candidate favored by the anti-Quay faction in Pennsylvania, George Shiras, a prominent Pittsburgh lawyer whom James Blaine (a cousin) and Andrew Carnegie had urged Harrison to nominate. Besides opposition from Quay (and the fact that Shiras lacked judicial experience), the nomination faced another complication: Shiras had turned sixty earlier that year and thus violated a norm that discouraged presidents from nominating anyone over sixty because they might be prone to leave the Court as soon as they could take advantage of the law that allowed Supreme Court justices to retire at full pay at the age of seventy with ten years of service. Senator Quay managed to delay any decision on the nomination for six months, but he relented because of the strong support that Shiras had received from former senators Blaine and Harrison as well as Carnegie. In addition, Senate Democrats were disposed to support Shiras because they were happy to frustrate Quay and they liked Shiras's politics. Nor did it hurt Shiras's chances that when his nomination came before the Senate, Republicans controlled eight more seats than they had since the last time a Supreme Court nomination had arisen and Quay had lost power.[22] Although the Senate confirmed Shiras, the nomination infuriated Quay, who backed Blaine for the 1892 Republican Party nomination for president. Even so, Harrison was renominated and won Pennsylvania in his rematch with Cleveland.

Harrison's last opportunity to fill a Supreme Court vacancy arose when Associate Justice Lucius Lamar died on January 23, 1893. By this time, Harrison was a lame duck, Cleveland's inauguration was less than two months away, and Harrison had to face a norm, which persists to this day, of the opposition party's trying in the Senate to keep a Supreme Court vacancy available for the incoming president to fill. Harrison understood that Democrats wanted Cleveland to fill the vacancy, and he knew that the incoming Senate would be under the control of Democrats, who would reject a Republican nominee similar to the ones Harrison had previously selected. Harrison's solution was to take advantage of senatorial courtesy, and he nominated Howell Jackson, a Democrat and former senator from Tennessee. The nomination was a masterstroke, since Jackson had endeared himself to Republicans by recommending Brown's appointment to Harrison, and Brown was returning the favor by urging Harrison to appoint Jackson. Moreover, Jackson had previously proven himself to Harrison with a decision that upheld the prosecution of three Tennessee men indicted for conspiring to interfere with the civil rights of five federal marshals. Harrison praised Jackson, "You were a believer in the nation and did not sympathize with the opinion that a United States marshal was an alien officer, or that election frauds or any other infraction of the federal statutes were deserving of naught but indignant condemnation and punishment."[23] Jackson's nomination had something for everyone, and the Senate confirmed him by voice vote sixteen days after receiving the nomination. Jackson was the first Democrat appointed by a Republican president to the Court since Lincoln appointed Stephen Field.

All four justices appointed by Harrison left their marks on constitutional law, particularly in a dramatic series of opinions decided over a four-month period in 1895. First, Brewer, Brown, and Shiras joined the Court's unanimous opinion upholding the power of a U.S. attorney to obtain an injunction, in spite of the absence of any statutory authorization, to break the Pullman Strike of 1894 and to imprison the strike's leader, Eugene Debs.[24] Next, in *United States v. E.C. Knight Co.*,[25] Justices Brewer, Shiras, and Brown joined the Court's decision to severely restrict the reach of the Sherman Anti-Trust Act. The Court ruled that the American Sugar Refining Company had not violated the act, even though it controlled more than 80 percent of the production of processed sugar in the United States. The Court held that the Sherman Anti-Trust Act did not apply to manufacturing, over which, it found, Congress lacked any regulatory authority. In *Pollock v. Farmers' Loan and Trust Company*,[26] Justices Brewer and Shiras joined three other justices to hold the income tax unconstitutional. Three months later, Justice Jackson died. In 1896, Justice Brown wrote the Court's opinion in *Plessy v. Ferguson*[27] upholding state-mandated segregation in public transportation. By then, Harrison was no longer president and made no comment on the ruling.

Securing the President's Inherent Authority to Act

Harrison's fourth constitutional legacy is based on a seemingly innocuous decision that became the basis for the principle now widely accepted that presidents have, even in the absence of explicit congressional authorization, the power to do what is necessary to enforce the law. The decision arose out of a feud involving Justice Field and a former chief justice of the California Supreme Court, David Terry. The story of the feud is so dramatic that it is easy to miss the brief moment in which Harrison became involved, even though his involvement produced one of the most important precedents on the scope of a president's inherent authority to enforce the law.

In the late 1850s, Field had briefly sat with Terry on the California Supreme Court; however, in 1859, Terry resigned to fight a duel against Senator David Broderick, whom Terry killed. Field replaced Terry as chief justice. Four years later, President Lincoln appointed Field to the Supreme Court.

Almost twenty years later, Terry married Sarah Hill, who was then suing the estate of Senator William Sharon of Nevada, to whom she claimed to have been secretly married. Sharon had denied Hill's claim and filed a federal court action to dismiss the purported marriage contract on the ground that it had been forged. Meanwhile, Susan filed for divorce, and the state court ruled in her favor and ordered Sharon to pay alimony. Sharon died in 1885, but the federal lawsuit continued with Field, in his capacity as a circuit justice, presiding over the proceedings. During a deposition, Sarah pulled out a pistol and threatened to shoot one of Sharon's lawyers. Field ordered that Sarah be disarmed when attending depositions and that an officer of the court be present to ensure she did not interrupt the proceedings. On December 26, 1885, the circuit court, without Field present, ruled in favor of Sharon's executor. The state court proceedings continued, and the California Supreme Court in January 1888 affirmed the decree of divorce but substantially reduced the alimony owed to Sarah. Meanwhile, Sharon's heirs asked the federal court to require Sarah to deliver her marriage contract for cancellation.

Contemporaneous records agree that, when Field upheld the executor's claims, David and Sarah Terry were present and that both loudly complained. It appears that Terry likely brandished a knife and struck a marshal and that his wife had a loaded revolver in her satchel. When the dust settled, Field held them both in contempt of court. He sentenced Mr. Terry to a six-month prison sentence and Sarah to three months in jail. They swore to get revenge.

It was at this moment that Harrison became briefly involved: After returning to Washington, Justice Field met with Harrison and his attorney general. Field told them both about the threats, and they both agreed there was convincing evidence that Field was in danger. With no law expressly authorizing him to do so, Harrison assigned a guard, Deputy Marshal David Neagle, to travel with Field on his train trip back west and as he rode circuit.

When the train stopped in Fresno, Field got off to get breakfast. In fact, the Terrys lived in Fresno, and they appeared in the restaurant while Field ate breakfast. Sarah left almost immediately after seeing Field, but David sat at a nearby table. After a short while, Terry stood to leave, but accounts diverge on what happened next. Some kind of altercation occurred as Terry passed Field's table, and in the midst of it, Neagle fired his pistol twice, killing Terry. Neagle claimed he had identified himself, had seen Terry brandish a knife, and asked Terry to desist. Other witnesses were unsure what Neagle said or if Terry had a knife (though some people claim Sarah hid it).

Because there were no federal laws immunizing U.S. marshals while performing their duties and authorizing presidents to assign marshals to protect justices, Neagle and Field were charged with murder. Field quickly posted bond, was released on his own recognizance, and got the charges against him dismissed. Although a federal appellate court granted Neagle's writ of habeas corpus, the State of California claimed jurisdiction in the case and appealed the federal appellate court's decision to the Supreme Court. Field abstained from the case, but his nephew, David Brewer, did not. Instead, Justice Brewer—and Harrison's two other appointees—joined the Court's 6–2 decision sustaining the legality of Neagle's actions *and* Harrison's decision to authorize protection for Field, in spite of the absence of any statutory authorization to do so. The Court found that, in appointing Neagle, Harrison had acted "as the principal conservator of the peace of the United States" and pursuant to his constitutional "duty" to ensure that the laws be faithfully executed. The president was not obliged to rely either on the states or some specific authorization of federal law to secure federal interests from physical and legal threats.[28] Neagle was freed without a trial. Every subsequent president relies on the case to support his inherent authority to take whatever actions are necessary to protect federal interests.

One of the most interesting things about the case is how little thought Harrison and his attorney general apparently gave to the decision to appoint a bodyguard for Field. Neither made any contemporaneous record of the decision nor commented later. There was no Justice Department opinion on the issue. Yet the decision has had an enduring impact on constitutional law. It is similar to the decisions presidents have made every day, with little thought, no or little written record, and with little or no thought given to what the courts might do. Most such decisions never reach the Supreme Court, but when they do, as in Neagle's case, the Court generally upholds the presidential judgments long after they have been made and changed lives in the meantime.

IN THE EIGHT years he spent as an ex-president before he died, Harrison published two books on constitutional law. Both are forgotten. The first contains six public lectures on constitutional law that he delivered at the newly established Stanford University.[29] The other largely consists of articles he wrote for the *Ladies' Home Journal*. The book provides insights into what Harrison believed were his most significant presidential decisions. He devoted four chapters to the presidency, including an extensive discussion of senatorial courtesy and the president's nominating authority. The last two chapters focused on the federal judiciary. He concluded that the bar "should always give its powerful aid to support the influence of the courts, for the Judicial Department is the 'keystone' of our Government, and assaults upon it threaten the whole structure of the stately arch." Modern readers are likely to find Harrison's insights platitudinous, including his recognition—well before Roosevelt's famous Court-packing plan and modern disputes over the blockage of judicial nominations—of the overriding importance of appointments and courts to the American system of justice.

10

Grover Cleveland, 1893–1897

IF A SECOND chapter on Grover Cleveland is surprising, you have forgotten he served two separate terms as president. The discontinuity between
his terms is significant, because it means that, unlike the sixteen other presidents who have served more than a single term, Cleveland was unable to
seamlessly transition into power or directly build on his prior actions. In his
second term, Cleveland had to react like any first-term president following a
president with whose policies and priorities he disagreed. Moreover, he
adopted a radically different understanding of presidential power in his second term. In his first term, he had refused to "meddle" with the lawmaking
process once a bill had been introduced, but in his second term he aggressively deployed his presidential powers so as to bend Congress to "his imperial
will."[1] He consolidated presidential power over appointments, removals,
vetoes, foreign affairs, lawmaking, mobilizing public opinion, and protecting
federal operations from private interference. It was as if there were two different Clevelands, the first seeming antiquated and the second embodying
many aspects of the modern presidency.

The Emergence of the Modern Presidency

The marked shift in Cleveland's understanding of executive power was evident from the start of his second term. In his second inaugural address, he
acknowledged the severe "degradation" of the nation's currency, "the danger
of depreciation in the purchasing power of the wages paid to toil," and "our
present embarrassing situation as related" to deteriorating economic conditions.[2] He vowed "none of the powers with which [the executive branch of
the Government] will be withheld when their exercise is deemed necessary to
maintain our national credit or avert national disaster."

Over the next year, the economic devastation was unprecedented: Over
fifteen thousand businesses and more than five hundred banks failed, nearly 20
percent of the nation's factory workers lost their jobs, farm prices fell sharply, and

the nation's gold supply shrank. As the panic mounted, Cleveland, citing the special authority given to him by the Constitution to schedule special sessions of Congress,[3] ordered one "so that the people may be relieved through legislation from present and impending danger and distress."[4] The day after the session opened, Cleveland sent a special message to Congress addressing "existence of an alarming and extraordinary business situation, involving the welfare and prosperity of all our people."[5] He proposed to solve the economic crisis by having Congress repeal the Sherman Silver Purchase Act,[6] which Harrison had signed into law and required the federal government to purchase silver using notes backed by silver or gold.

Cleveland went further. He became personally involved in the lawmaking process. The circumstances were unlike those in his first term: The Democratic Party controlled both houses of Congress for the first time since Reconstruction,[7] and Cleveland believed the economic downturn was a genuine crisis. He further believed, much like Jackson and Van Buren, that there should be complete separation between the government and the banking industry and that currency issues should be left to the marketplace. Like Taylor, Cleveland believed it was all or nothing—Congress should repeal the Silver Purchase Act or fail trying. He heavily lobbied Democrats in Congress and threatened to use patronage to compel their compliance.[8] Many senators protested that presidents "had never before . . . used [their appointment powers] to command votes for a particular legislative measure."[9] Although William Jennings Bryan, then a young congressman from Nebraska, warned Cleveland that his threat was going to "injure the party,"[10] Cleveland called Bryan's bluff and did not appoint any Bryan supporter to federal office. He took the further step of publicly denouncing a filibuster led by prosilver Democratic senators to stop the repeal, and his threat not to make any further patronage appointments until the Senate approved the unconditional appeal thwarted a compromise proposal suggested at the last minute by thirty-seven of the forty-four Senate Democrats.[11] In the end, Cleveland got what he wanted. On August 28, the House approved the repeal bill largely along party lines. On October 30, 1893, the Senate approved the repeal bill 48–37, with most Republicans voting for it. Cleveland signed the bill.

Cleveland's push for repeal cost him politically: It split his party, many of whose leaders complained about Cleveland's arrogance and bullying. Cleveland was unable to use his success with the repeal to cultivate other legislative successes. It increased the likelihood that Congress would not do what he wanted when next he asked.

Within a year of the repeal, Cleveland's awkwardness in implementing his new understanding of executive power became apparent. He had initially pushed Congress to lower the tariff, which the McKinley Tariff Act[12] had raised to an unprecedented high in 1890. Both Cleveland and the chair of the House Ways and Means Committee, William Wilson, had drafted the initial bill. It was one of the few times—other than the Kansas-Nebraska Act—that Congress considered enacting a bill written by the president; and Cleveland again threatened party members that he would deny them the patronage they wanted unless they supported the bill. Cleveland remained closely involved in the House proceedings, and the House eventually approved Cleveland's desired bill. But the bill met considerable resistance in the Senate. After it was amended more than six hundred times, the Senate approved it, though its final version did not include, or diluted, most of the House's bill.

In the midst of the Senate debate, Cleveland allowed Congressman Wilson to publicize a letter that he had written to Wilson defending the amended bill. In the letter, Cleveland declared, "Every true Democrat and every sincere reformer knows that the bill in its present form and as it will be submitted to the conference falls short of the consummation for which we have long labored. . . . Our abandonment of the cause or the principle upon which it rests means party perfidy and party dishonor."[13] While House members generally ignored the comment, but many senators did not. One of the bill's sponsors, Democratic senator Arthur Gorman, lambasted Cleveland for impugning the integrity of Democratic senators and for exceeding his constitutional authority. Gorman maintained that Cleveland had violated the spirit of the Constitution and failed to heed the passage in Washington's Farewell Address in which he cautioned against encroachments of the executive upon the Congress's prerogatives.[14] Cleveland's ploy backfired, as Democratic senators rallied to Gorman's, not Cleveland's, side.

To Cleveland's dismay, the House accepted all the Senate's amendments to the bill, which it approved (with many members abstaining). Even though Cleveland suggested the bill was "not in line with honest tariff reform,"[15] he allowed it to become law because he believed that it was not unconstitutional and that it was better than the McKinley tariff bill, which would have remained in force otherwise.

Although several members of Congress[16] challenged Cleveland's strategy, he was praised in several newspapers around the country.[17] Cleveland's push for repeal was a principal factor in its success, which became a precedent that other leaders duly noted,[18] though his aggressive use of power had further cost him political support within his own party.

After leaving office, Cleveland described the circumstances at the time of his push for the repeal as an "emergency," a period in which "there had intervened a growing apprehension among the masses of our own people concerning the Government's competency to continue gold redemption" amid "the dark surroundings."[19] Cleveland's rhetoric was not accidental; it underscored the exigencies that justified his aggressive use of power. Moreover, his decision to sell gold bonds as part of his plan to save the economy had not been authorized by Congress; it was a unilateral exercise of power that was justified because of an "emergency" and his "appeal to Congress for legislative aid was absolutely fruitless."[20] Cleveland's actions to restore the gold supply were *all* done on the basis of his inherent presidential authority to ameliorate or solve the economic crisis and comprised a significant precedent for future, unilateral presidential action in similar circumstances.[21]

Yet Cleveland's actions underscored the limits of how far presidents may push Congress. His failure is another striking example of the fallacy of the myth that most nineteenth-century presidents were weak. The problem was not that Cleveland was weak, indecisive, or passive. The problem was the opposite: As president, Cleveland had acted upon the belief that the Constitution authorized him to steer, if not take charge of, the lawmaking process, particularly in an emergency, and his actions produced consequences beyond his control.

Cleveland took responsibility for another by-product of the Wilson-Gorman Act. One provision from the House bill that was included in the amended bill was the provision for a 2 percent tax on personal incomes over $4,000 and on all corporate profits above operating expenses and costs.[22] Cleveland appreciated that the provision was the first individual income tax enacted by Congress and that some members of Congress opposed taxing individuals rather than just corporations.[23] Cleveland accepted the provision as part of the compromise to get the tariff reduction he wanted.

However, in 1895, the Supreme Court in *Pollock v. Farmers' Loan and Trust Company*[24] struck down the income tax provision as unconstitutional. Even though Cleveland's attorney general had argued that the tax was similar to the levy authorized by Congress during the Civil War, the Court, in an opinion by Chief Justice Fuller, concluded 5–4 that it was a direct, not an excise, tax, and therefore it could only have been levied (or apportioned) on a per capita basis.[25] Cleveland condemned the decision. *Pollock* was particularly unpopular in the West and the South, where people denounced the "Cleveland Court" and *Pollock* as exemplifying Cleveland's bias in favor of big business.[26] Less than fifteen years later, due partly to another forgotten president's efforts, *Pollock* was overruled through the Sixteenth Amendment.[27]

"WHO DARES GIVE BATTLE WITH ME?"

FIGURE 10.1 Cartoon showing Grover Cleveland dressed as a gladiator holding sword and shield.

Source: Library of Congress Prints and Photographs Division, Washington, D.C. 20540 USA
http://hdl.loc.gov/loc.pnp/pp.print

Presidential Initiatives in Foreign Affairs

Two important foreign affairs decisions bookended Cleveland's second term. The first involved the possible annexation of Hawaii. On January 20, 1887, the Senate had ratified the treaty Cleveland had negotiated with the Hawaiian kingdom.[28] It gave permission to the United States to build a naval base at Pearl Harbor, a move that fit Cleveland's objective to maintain American influence there. Even so, Cleveland did not support the annexation of Hawaii. In January 1893, Harrison became involved after a revolution replaced the native ruler with an American citizen, Sanford Dole, who had helped the coup. Acting on his own initiative, the U.S. minister in Hawaii, John Stevens, approved the coup and ordered marines to assist local rebels in bringing it about. After the revolution succeeded, Stevens recognized the legitimacy of Dole's provisional government and proclaimed Hawaii an American protectorate, which Harrison's secretary of state recognized.[29] Shortly thereafter, Harrison negotiated a treaty for Hawaii's annexation and submitted it to the Senate for ratification.[30]

The Senate Foreign Affairs Committee did not act, however, on the treaty before Cleveland's inauguration. While Harrison hoped that Cleveland would treat the treaty as a fait accompli, he did not. Five days after his inauguration, Cleveland recalled the treaty from the Senate.[31] No one questioned Cleveland's authority to recall the treaty, though Harrison was displeased.[32] Rather than approve the treaty, Cleveland appointed James Blount, a former chair of the House Foreign Relations Committee, to undertake a fact-finding mission to determine whether a majority of Hawaiians supported annexation and the United States had been complicit in overthrowing the Hawaiian monarchy. On July 11, 1894, Blount released his final report, which found, among other things, that most Hawaiians opposed annexation and that the American minister in Hawaii had been improperly involved in the coup and abused his authority in involving the marines in the rebellion and in issuing his proclamation of the protectorate.[33]

Undoing the coup was easier said than done. Up to this point, Cleveland had acted unilaterally in withdrawing the treaty and ordering Blount to investigate. But the deposed queen, whom Cleveland intended to return to power, wanted to behead Dole, who refused to abdicate. Cleveland concluded he could no longer do it alone, and on December 18, 1893, he formally asked Congress to solve the dilemma.[34] Cleveland told members of Congress that the treaty of annexation favored by the previous administration had "contemplated a departure from unbroken American tradition in providing for the addition to our territory of islands of the sea more than two thousand miles removed from our nearest coast."[35] He commended the matter to "the extended powers and wide discretion of Congress," and promised to support any legislative solution "which is consistent with American honor, integrity, and morality."[36]

Although most members of Congress supported Dole, the Senate approved a resolution declaring that the United States should take no further action to annex Hawaii and to restore the monarchy.[37] Without commenting on the resolution's constitutionality, Cleveland acknowledged Dole as a "great and good Friend" and his proclamation establishing the Hawaiian Republic.[38]

Cleveland was not obliged to refer Hawaii's annexation to Congress or to defer to Congress, but he did. Through his actions, he reinforced the principle that the president could not unilaterally annex territory. His actions established a precedent upholding the joint responsibility of the president and Congress over annexation, and his threat to veto legislation facilitating annexation[39] was a strong reminder that any decisions about annexation were not possible without the president's approval.[40]

Cleveland's involvement in the long-standing boundary dispute between Venezuela and the colony of British Guiana illuminates further his understanding of the allocation of power over foreign affairs. In spite of American pressure dating back to Cleveland's first term, Great Britain persisted in refusing to submit the territorial dispute between its colony and Venezuela to arbitration.[41] After reiterating his request for international arbitration in his Second Annual Message[42] and issuing a series of increasingly forceful requests to the British government, Cleveland approved a special dispatch by his secretary of state, Richard Olney.[43] The message in the dispatch became known as the Olney Doctrine, which, for the first time, extended the Monroe Doctrine throughout the Western Hemisphere, particularly Latin America. In the dispatch, Olney explained that the United States had long been concerned about "British aggression upon Venezuelan territory," that international law allowed a nation to "justly interpose in a controversy" to prevent a result that threatened "its own integrity, tranquility, or welfare," and that the Monroe Doctrine provided the justification for American intervention in the dispute between Venezuela and British Guiana as long as there was proof that Great Britain had genuinely threatened its independence and integrity.[44] Olney explained the purpose of the Monroe Doctrine as proclaiming that "no European power or combination of European powers shall forcibly deprive an American state of the right ... of self-government and of shaping for itself its own political fortunes and destinies." He further characterized the Monroe Doctrine as declaring that threats against the territorial independence of any American state should be treated as against "the safety and welfare of the United States."[45] Olney suggested that the only way that the United States could be assured there was no threat to Venezuela's independence or integrity was to refer the dispute to international arbitration. After demanding to know whether Great Britain "will consent or will decline to submit the

Venezuelan boundary question in its entirety to impartial arbitration,"[46] he concluded, "Today the United States is practically sovereign [in the Western Hemisphere], and its fiat is law upon the subjects to which it confines its interposition. [The] infinite resources [of the United States] combined with its isolated position render it master of the situation, and practically invulnerable as against any and all other powers." Although the message was offensive, the British did not respond until December 7, 1895,[47] at which time it declared that it considered the Monroe Doctrine inapplicable and reiterated its refusal to submit the matter to arbitration.

Ten days later, Cleveland took the extraordinary step of delivering a special message. In one of the strongest presidential endorsements and extensions of the Monroe Doctrine, he declared that the

> doctrine upon which we stand is strong and sound, because its enforcement is important to our peace and safety as a nation, and is essential to the integrity of free institutions and the tranquil maintenance of our distinctive form of government. It was intended to apply to every stage of our national life, and cannot become obsolete while our Republic endures. If the balance of power is justly a cause for jealous anxiety among the governments of the Old World and a subject for our absolute non-interference, nonetheless is the observance of the Monroe Doctrine of vital concern to our people and their Government.[48]

Cleveland dismissed the British government's claim that the doctrine was inapplicable on the ground that in fact it "finds its recognition in those principles of international law which are based upon the theory that every nation shall have its rights protected and its just claims enforced."[49] After recounting the British government's refusal to accede to American requests to submit "their dispute to impartial arbitration," he requested Congress make "the necessary investigation" and "an adequate appropriation" to finance a special commission to determine the proper boundary between Venezuela and Guiana.[50] Cleveland warned that, once the commission issued its report, "it will in my opinion be the duty of the United States to resist by every means in its power as a willful aggression upon its rights and interests the appropriation by Great Britain of any lands or the exercise governmental jurisdiction over any territory which . . . we have determined of right belongs to Venezuela. In making these recommendations, I am fully alive to the responsibility incurred, and keenly realize all the consequences that may follow."[51] Congress acceded to Cleveland's request, and the British government eventually agreed to arbitration once it was convinced that Cleveland was not bluffing. In 1899, the arbitration tribunal awarded nearly all of the disputed territory to Great Britain.

Cleveland's involvement in steering the Venezuelan border dispute to international arbitration was constitutionally significant because he demonstrated that the president is uniquely capable of shaping a policy that guides future administrations in foreign affairs. It was all the more remarkable because of his unilateral efforts to assert American interests in a circumstance in which it was not a party. Congress could not stop him, and subsequent presidents have followed his modifications to the Monroe Doctrine. Moreover, members of Congress shared his conception of the president's role, as reflected in the absence of any serious protest over his actions and the quickness of Congress's approval of his request for the funding of a commission to investigate the dispute. He had pushed the boundaries of executive power without breaking them.

Reshaping Federalism

In his first term, Cleveland had pledged to respect state sovereignty, but in his second term economic circumstances forced him to reconsider his attitudes about federalism. Initially, he maintained that the federal government had no constitutional authority to address local disruptions caused by labor protests; he believed that the Constitution vested only the states with the authority to maintain law and order in their respective jurisdictions. But when faced with the economic depression of 1893, Cleveland changed his mind: With labor unrest increasingly threatening the operations of the federal government, particularly the postal service, Cleveland was persuaded that the federal government had the constitutional authority to act. The event crystallizing these concerns was the Pullman Strike.

With sharp declines in profits, George Pullman, the director and owner of the Pullman Car Company, reduced the wages of his employees 20 percent but did not correspondingly reduce the prices of utilities and food that his workers were forced to buy from the company as a condition of their employment. After Pullman dismissed some workers who had asked for reductions in rents or increases in wages, 80 percent of his workforce went on strike. In late spring, Pullman closed the shops where his employees bought their food and clothing. They all went on strike, which the American Railway Union (the ARU) supported. At the direction of ARU membership and its leader, Eugene Debs, the strike went national on

June 26, 1894. In an effort to ensure that the strike got the attention of the federal government, the railroad owners joined Pullman cars to trains that carried the mail, so the stoppage virtually ended mail service in twenty-seven states and territories. By July 1, Chicago was besieged by massive demonstrations.

It was at this point that a consortium of twenty-four railroad company executives asked Attorney General Olney to intervene. A few months away from becoming secretary of state, Olney had agreed to swear in an army of deputies to keep the trains moving. After violence broke out between the deputies and the striking workers, Olney cited the Sherman Act and the federal judiciary's equity power to enjoin "a public nuisance"—the strike—from threatening "a public injury."[52] Relying on the Sherman Act, the circuit court ordered union officials and all persons conspiring with them to cease stopping any trains operating in interstate commerce or carrying mail;[53] however, Cleveland was hesitant to order the federal troops to intervene without more pressing necessity.[54] Meanwhile, striking workers destroyed rail cars and other private property, and Attorney General Olney pressed Cleveland to send troops to Chicago. When informed that violence had erupted between the federal troops and the striking workers and the destruction of private property was increasing, Cleveland met with his cabinet to tell them that he believed he had the constitutional and federal statutory authority to order federal troops to protect liberty or property or obstruction of the federal government's operations.[55] The cabinet unanimously agreed.[56] Later the same day, Cleveland ordered four thousand federal troops to enforce the injunction and thereby restore the mail service between Chicago and the West Coast.

Before ordering federal troops into Chicago, Cleveland did not consult with Illinois's governor, John Altgeld. Altgeld was outraged. On July 5, he telegrammed Cleveland that he believed that the federal intervention ordered lacked legal and constitutional justifications. Altgeld suggested that federal intervention required Cleveland to request beforehand the governor's permission and that in the absence of such permission the Constitution required "the immediate withdrawal of the Federal troops from active duty in this State."[57] A few hours later, Cleveland telegraphed Altgeld that the federal government did not need his permission to protect U.S. mail and the flow of interstate commerce. Cleveland told Altgeld that federal troops had been ordered into Chicago "in strict accordance with the Constitution and laws of the United States upon the demand of the Post Office Department" and that the use of troops had been "deemed not only proper but necessary" to ensure delivery of the mail and counteract conspiracies "against commerce between the States."[58] The next day, Governor Altgeld telegraphed that "not even the autocrat of Russia could possess, or claim to possess, greater power than is possessed by the executive of the United States, if your assumption is correct." He suggested that the only proper authorities to act were the state and local authorities. Almost immediately, Cleveland responded, "While I am still persuaded that I have neither transcended my authority nor duty in the emergency that confronts us, it seems to me that in this hour of danger and public distress, discussion may well give way to active efforts on the part of all in authority to restore obedience to law and to protect life and property."[59] He explained he had sent federal troops after he had been convinced "that the process of the Federal courts could not be executed through the ordinary means, and upon competent proof that conspiracies existed against commerce between the States."[60] The federal troops stopped the violence and arrested Debs for violating the injunction. Through similar injunctions and the deployment of additional federal troops, Cleveland put down strikes and disorder in the western states.

That was not the end of the affair. Over the next year, Governor Altgeld took his case to the public. He successfully portrayed Cleveland as the puppet of big corporate interests and blocked his efforts to win a third nomination for president in 1896.[61] In the meantime, Debs asked his lawyer, Clarence Darrow, a protégé of Altgeld (who would later become his law partner), to defend him in his criminal trial for contempt of court for violating the injunction. Darrow asked the Supreme Court for a writ of habeas corpus. He told the Court that the injunction was unconstitutional because there was no specific federal law enacted by Congress authorizing its issuance. The absence of any such law meant that it was impossible for Debs to have had notice of the offense with which he could be charged. Attorney General Olney responded that if a court had the power to enjoin individuals from committing particular actions, it had the authority to define the scope of an offense, enjoin a group of people from encouraging others to commit that offense, and hold in contempt anyone who disobeyed the injunction.

The Supreme Court unanimously agreed with Olney, denied the writ, and upheld the constitutionality of Cleveland's actions and the injunction.[62] First, the Court recognized an even broader constitutional basis for the president's actions than even that for which Olney had argued. In his opinion for the Court, Justice Brewer declared,

[T]he entire strength of the nation may be used to enforce in any part of the land the full and free exercise of all national powers and the security of all rights entrusted by the Constitution to its care. The strong arm of the national government may be put forth to brush away all obstructions to the freedom of interstate commerce or the transportation of the mails. If the emergency arises, the army of the Nation, and all its militia, are at the service of the Nation to compel obedience to its laws.[63]

Such broad authority derived from not only federal statutes but also the public nuisance doctrine. Second, the Court upheld the equity jurisdiction of the federal courts to prevent unlawful interference with interstate commerce. It upheld injunctive relief on the basis of the federal government's "property" interest "in the mails" and the fact that "[e]very government, entrusted by the very terms of its being, with powers and duties to be exercised and discharged for the general welfare, has a right to apply to its own courts for any proper assistance in the exercise of the one and the discharge of the other, and it is no sufficient answer to its appeal to one of those courts that it has no pecuniary interest in the matter."[64] Justice Brewer went further to recognize the inherent authority of judges to issue injunctions "against the assaults of the lawless, or to enforce its orders, judgments, or decrees against the recusant parties before it" and that a court of equity even had the authority to punish by contempt any actions that violated criminal law.[65] In so ruling, the Court, in the opinion of one scholar, "placed the Supreme Court's imprimatur on the growing use of labor injunctions. More significantly, in [the case] the Fuller Court had a major impact on remedial jurisprudence by opening the door for more extensive use of injunctive power by the government."[66]

The most enduring part of this opinion is its affirmation of a president's broad inherent power. The Court upheld the first presidential deployment of federal troops to end a strike and to restore law and order in the absence of a formal appeal from a state governor. The decision did more than vindicate the legality of Cleveland's actions. There was no statute specifically authorizing the federal government to break the railroad strike, so the decision upholds inherent presidential authority to keep the economy, or at least the nation's railroads, operating by any means necessary.

Bolstering Presidential Prerogatives

In his second term, Cleveland aggressively deployed his veto, nominating, and removal authorities. His total number of vetoes—170—in his second term was less than half his number in the first; however, no president cast more vetoes in a single term than Cleveland did in his first, and the second term total of 170 vetoes ranks as the fifth most cast by any president in a single term. Moreover, Cleveland's second-term vetoes were unusual because most of them—128—were pocket vetoes, the largest number of pocket vetoes cast by any president except for Franklin Roosevelt. The fact that Cleveland cast more pocket vetoes than regular vetoes in his second term was unusual as well; indeed, he was the second of only three presidents to have done so in American history. The only president other than Grant and Cleveland to cast more pocket vetoes than regular vetoes has been Dwight Eisenhower. While Franklin Roosevelt holds the record for the most presidential vetoes ever cast, Cleveland cast more per term: His vetoes for two terms remains the largest number of presidential vetoes cast in two terms, and the fact that in his second term Congress overrode only five of them reaffirmed the extent to which the veto power enables a president, even an unpopular one, to keep Congress from having the last word on policymaking.

In exercising his nominating authority, Cleveland pushed back harder against senatorial courtesy in his second term than he had in his first term. Although nearly every nineteenth-century president had complained about being inundated by office seekers,[67] Cleveland was the first president to issue an executive order addressing the problem. A few months into his second term, he issued a directive "to decline from and after this date all personal interviews with those seeking appointments to office, except as I on my own motion may especially invite them. The same considerations make it impossible for me to receive those who merely desire to pay their respects except on the days and during the hours especially designated for that purpose."[68] This order saved Cleveland's time to do other business and established a precedent for subsequent presidents to create alternative mechanisms for handling appointments not requiring their personal involvement with the application process for political appointments.[69]

Moreover, Cleveland's independence in deploying his nominating authority was put to test when he tried to fill two Supreme Court vacancies in his second term.[70] On July 7, 1893, Justice Blatchford died. Because Blatchford was from New York, its powerful Democratic senator, David Hill, believed that he had the prerogative to name Blatchford's replacement.[71] Cleveland did not, however, want that to happen. Hill and Cleveland had long been political foes: Hill had led the anti-Cleveland faction within New York, and as governor of New York, he had made sure that Cleveland lost New York in his 1884 reelection bid. Consequently, Cleveland nominated William Hornblower, a well-respected Princeton graduate and leader of a prominent New

York law firm, to fill the vacancy. But the Senate rejected his nomination because Hill's Senate colleagues wanted to vindicate the principle of senatorial courtesy. Next, Cleveland nominated Wheeler Peckham, a well-respected New York lawyer and former New York Bar Association president, whom Hill opposed because Peckham had opposed Hill's reelection as New York governor in 1888 and approved a critical report on his preferred nominee. Once again, Hill persuaded his Democratic colleagues to reject the nomination to vindicate senatorial courtesy. Cleveland changed his strategy. Rather than nominate a third New Yorker, Cleveland employed a different form of senatorial courtesy to defeat Hill's resistance: He nominated the Democratic majority leader of the Senate, Edward Douglass White of Louisiana. Neither anti-Catholic bias (which had the potential to hurt White as the second Catholic nominated to the Court) nor Hill could stop the nomination. White was so popular and beloved in the Senate that it confirmed him unanimously on the same day that it received his nomination.

The contest between Cleveland and proponents of senatorial courtesy was not over. When Justice Howell Jackson of Tennessee died on August 8, 1895, Cleveland did not nominate a replacement from Tennessee or the South. This time, Cleveland surprised Senator Hill by asking him whether he would approve of the nomination he had in mind, the brother of Wheeler Peckham, Rufus, who had served as a district attorney, corporation counsel for New York, and judge on the New York Supreme Court and Court of Appeals. Cleveland was not, however, merely acquiescing to Hill's power. Since White's confirmation, Democrats had lost seats in the Senate in the 1894 midterm elections, and Hill thus no longer could count on his Democratic colleagues to defeat whomever Cleveland nominated. Hence, he wrote to Cleveland to approve the nomination, even though Rufus Peckham had been one of Cleveland's political allies. Cleveland nominated Peckham, whom the Senate confirmed by voice vote.

The practice of reserving Supreme Court seats for particular states ended with White's appointment. Indeed, Hornblower and Wheeler Peckham were the last two Supreme Court nominees blocked because of geographic objections. While geography was a problem for some later nominations, it was not for the same reason as it had been with Hornblower or Wheeler Peckham—it became pertinent later to ensure a previously unrepresented part of the country was represented on the Court.[72]

The final authority that Cleveland pushed hard in his second term was his removal power. Cleveland's support for the civil service system did not prevent his deciding to remove Republicans from a wide range of political offices and to replace them with loyal Democrats. Although the Tenure in Office Act had been repealed, Republicans tried to hold onto political offices on the ground that they were constitutionally entitled to complete their terms. Cleveland did not agree and proceeded to remove many Republican officials before their terms expired. The conflict between Cleveland and the dismissed appointees came to a head in the case of Lewis Parsons. On May 26, 1893, Cleveland wrote to Parsons to inform him that he had been dismissed as the U.S. attorney for the Northern District of Alabama. On the same day, the Senate confirmed Parsons's successor, Emmet O'Neal. Nevertheless, Parsons wrote back to Cleveland that he believed that his commission "authorizes me to hold . . . office for the definite term of four years from the date therefore, fixed by law" and that Cleveland as president "had no power to remove me" and therefore "respectfully declined to surrender the office."[73] Although O'Neal filed a successful lawsuit with a local circuit court to obtain possession of the contents of the local U.S. attorney's office, Parsons filed a separate lawsuit with the Court of Claims for his salary to be paid. The Court of Claims refused, and Parsons appealed to the Supreme Court.

In a unanimous opinion, the Court rejected Parsons's claim. In his opinion for the Court, Justice Rufus Peckham reviewed the history disputes between presidents and Congress over presidential removal power and determined that Parsons's argument was absurd. He was convinced the outcome Parsons desired had

> never been the intention of Congress. On the contrary, we are satisfied that its intention, in the repeal of the tenure of office sections of the Revised Statutes, was again to concede to the President the power of removal, if taken from him by the original Tenure in Office Act [of 1820], and by reason of the repeal to thereby enable him to remove an officer when, in his discretion, he regards it for the public good, although the term of office may have been limited by the words creating the statute. This purpose is accomplished by the construction we give to [the federal law defining the length of a district attorney's term of office], while the other construction turns a statute meant to enlarge the power of the President into one circumscribing and limiting it more than it was under the law which was repealed for the very purpose of enlarging it.[74]

With *Parsons*, Cleveland secured the distinction of being the only president to have had his exercises of power upheld twice by the Supreme Court, each time unanimously, within a single term. With *Parsons*, a president's authority to dismiss an executive official on his own initiative was more firmly established than ever before. Whereas Cleveland in his first term had persuaded Congress to repeal the Tenure in Office Act, his attorney general had persuaded the Court that there was nothing in federal law restricting a president's power of removal over executive officials who had been confirmed by the Senate. With this victory, the Cleveland administration had managed to bring all three branches of the federal government together in support of the president's unilateral removal authority over executive officials whom the Senate had confirmed. Almost thirty years later, the Court set the matter entirely to rest, citing *Parsons* as a basis for its striking down the Tenure in Office Act.[75] No other president did as much as Cleveland to settle the president's independent authority to remove political appointees within the executive branch.

CLEVELAND LEFT THE presidency in 1897 but not before leaving the Democratic Party the year before to endorse a third-party candidate who supported the gold standard. Though the Supreme Court decision in *Plessy v. Ferguson* came down during his last year in office, Cleveland made no comment, perhaps reflecting his lack of interest in civil rights, the possibility he thought the decision unremarkable, his preoccupation with the economy, or some combination of these factors.

Yet Cleveland proved again there was life after the presidency. He devoted his remaining years to a different kind of service: In 1897, he retired to Princeton, New Jersey, where he lectured in public affairs and joined the Board of Trustees at Princeton University. Cleveland became the board's president and worked closely with Princeton's president, Woodrow Wilson, whom he regarded as temperamental and untrustworthy. As board president, Cleveland sided with Princeton's Graduate School dean, Andrew West, in his fight with Wilson over the building of a graduate residence hall near the center of campus. Cleveland also wrote extensively for the *Saturday Post* and published three books.[76]

West ultimately outmaneuvered Wilson. Stung by the defeat and loss of support at Princeton, Wilson turned to politics.[77] Cleveland died before Wilson was elected the next Democratic president after Cleveland. Wilson's presidency soon eclipsed the one that had convinced him of the potency of presidential powers.

11

William Howard Taft, 1909–1913

EVEN WILLIAM HOWARD Taft said he had forgotten his presidency. A few years after achieving his lifelong ambition of becoming chief justice of the United States, Taft told a friend he no longer remembered being president.[1] Taft, of course, had not really forgotten. He was emphasizing how much more he enjoyed being chief justice than president. He had become president begrudgingly, never enjoyed politicking,[2] and suffered one of the worst electoral defeats of any incumbent president (winning only two states and eight electoral votes).[3] Taft's trouncing in the 1912 election branded his presidency as a failure. Afterward, he was as eager as the country to move on—he to teach law at Yale, and the nation to Wilson's inauguration. In the turbulent years afterward, Taft's single term has faded from the nation's memory.

Taft's presidency is, however, important for reasons beyond his distinction as the only person to be both chief justice and president. He is one of a few presidents to have successfully pushed for the ratification of more than one constitutional amendment.[4] He is the only president to have served as secretary of war and an Article III judge beforehand and is one of only five men who were elected to the presidency directly from the cabinet.[5] He is the first lawyer elected president in the twentieth century and one of only six presidents handpicked by their predecessors.[6] He is the fifth of six men whose first popularly elective office was president,[7] and he came to the presidency with one of the most extensive records of public service ever.[8] He was the first president of the forty-eight contiguous states. His six appointments to the Supreme Court are the second most that a president made in a single term, and he ranks third behind Washington and Franklin Roosevelt in the total numbers of Supreme Court appointments made. Taft is the only former president to have taught full-time as a law professor after leaving office.

Most importantly, Taft's presidency has a rich constitutional legacy. While he was the last president to conceive of the presidency as largely subservient to Congress in policymaking, he reinforced the president's unilateral powers over nominations and removals and role in guiding the constitutional amendment process. He perfected criteria for picking judges and is the model for any president bent on transforming the federal judiciary into a bulwark of protection against invasions of private property rights and an overbearing national government.

Rejecting the Stewardship Theory of the Presidency

One of the most distinctive aspects of Theodore Roosevelt's presidency was his philosophy of executive power. Roosevelt followed the stewardship theory of presidential power, which held the president had the authority to do anything that he believed was in the public's best interest as long as the Constitution did not expressly prohibit it. Since there were few ways in which the Constitution expressly restricted presidential action, Roosevelt encountered few practical limitations on doing what he wanted as long as he had the support of the American people.

Taft had nearly the opposite conception of presidential power. He considered himself a strict constructionist who maintained that each branch had limited authority. It was no accident that a major theme he sounded in his inaugural address was his commitment to strict separation of powers. He sounded the same theme a decade after leaving the presidency when he declared, "We have a government of limited power under the Constitution, and we have got to work out our problems on the basis of law."[9] On Taft's view, a president only had the authority to do something if the Constitution or Congress authorized it.

Not long after leaving office, Taft distinguished his conception of the presidency from Roosevelt's by explaining, "The true view of the executive function is . . . that the President can exercise no power which cannot reasonably and fairly be traced to some specific grant of power or justly implied or included within such express grant as necessary and proper to its exercise. Such specific grant must be either in the Constitution or in an act of Congress passed in pursuance thereof. There is no undefined residuum of power which he can exercise because it seems to him to be in the public interest."[10] Taft believed Roosevelt's conception of power had no limits, and he ridiculed Roosevelt's efforts to liken himself to Lincoln. He suggested that Lincoln's exercise of executive power had to be understood not only within the context of "the stress of the greatest civil war in modern times" but also in light of the fact that "Mr. Lincoln always pointed out the source of the authority which in his opinion justified his acts." "[T]here was," in Taft's assessment of Lincoln, "always a strong ground for maintaining the view which he took."[11] Taft maintained, however, that "the view of [Mr. Roosevelt], ascribing an undefined residuum of power to the President, is an unsafe doctrine" and "might lead under emergencies to results of an arbitrary character, doing irreparable injustice to private right. The mainspring of such a view is that the Executive is charged with responsibility for the welfare of all the people in a general way, that he is to play the part of a Universal Providence and set all things right, and that anything that in his judgment will help the people he ought to do, unless he is expressly forbidden not to do it." Taft minimized the danger posed by a president like Roosevelt because "the good sense of the people has ultimately prevailed and no danger has been done to our political structure and the reign of law has continued. In such times when the Executive power seems to be prevailing, there have always been men in this free and intelligent people of ours, who apparently courting political humiliation and disaster have registered protest against this undue Executive domination and this use of the Executive power and popular support to perpetuate itself." Taft recognized that the people could check presidential usurpations of power through their choice of president (as they apparently had done with him); furthermore, "Even if a vicious precedent is set by the Executive, and injustice done, it does not have the same bad effect that an improper precedent of a court may have, for one President does not consider himself bound by the policies or constitutional views of his predecessors."[12]

Whereas Roosevelt likened himself to Lincoln, Taft claimed Cleveland as a model and cited him with approval in his 1925 book on presidential powers.[13] The differences between Roosevelt's and Taft's conceptions of executive power were as great as their models and were evident throughout Taft's presidency.

First, before winning the 1908 presidential election, Taft distinguished his conception of executive power from that of Roosevelt. In his speech accepting his party's presidential nomination, Taft, then Roosevelt's secretary of war, declared that "the chief function of the next administration, in my judgment, is distinct from, and a progressive development of that which has been performed by President Roosevelt. The chief function of the next administration is to complete and perfect the machinery"[14] that had been put in place by Roosevelt.

Second, Taft criticized Roosevelt's persistent appeals for public support. He viewed such appeals as unnecessary and inappropriate. Taft did not believe a president's constitutional authority derived from, or could be enhanced by, such appeals. Moreover, such appeals were out of character to Taft, who had never served in an elective office before becoming president. Before becoming president, he had no firsthand experience in interacting with the public and soliciting, cultivating, and maintaining electoral support; he only had to report to his superiors. As president, he was for the first and only time in his life accountable to the public for his decisions.

Taft explained that his resistance to presidential appeals to public support derived from the fact that he had a judicial rather than an executive temperament. By this, he meant he was temperamentally suited to think like a judge—to consider the different arguments, to make decisions, and then to explain his decisions through reasoned elaboration. He also blamed losing his reelection on his nonpolitical preferences: "My tastes had been and still are judicial."[15] He meant that he was unaccustomed to doing the glad-handing required of presidents. He strongly disapproved of Roosevelt's bypassing Congress to appeal directly to the American people to authorize his decisions, and he rarely appealed to the public. When he did, he considered his audience to be Congress rather than the public.

Taft further believed that, as president, he had a limited role in lawmaking. In 1915, he explained that "our President has no initiative in respect to legislation given him by law except that of mere recommendation, and no legal or formal method of entering into the argument and discussion of the proposed legislation while pending in Congress."[16] He considered presidential power to be "limited so far as it is possible to limit such a power consistent with that discretion and promptness of action that is essential to preserve the interests of the public in times of emergency or legislative neglect or inaction."[17]

In practice, Taft refrained from trying to steer the lawmaking process. Even when it came to the issue that Taft considered among the most important of his term—the tariff—he refused to take the lead from Congress. Instead, he deliberately avoided participating in the "tariff-writing" process[18] until after the bill had been approved by the House and the Senate and was in the conference committee,[19] by which time it was too late for him to get the public interested, much less mobilized.[20] When Taft later claimed credit for the bill, it sounded hollow because he had been on the sidelines through most of the lawmaking process.[21] His efforts to sell the bill to the public as one of his major accomplishments in office backfired: They appeared to be self-serving, infuriated insurgents within the party who felt insulted by his praise for their opponents' achievements, and failed to win the support of the voting public, which had lost interest by the time Taft began to defend his efforts. Taft's constitutional reluctance to become too closely involved in the lawmaking process cost him dearly.

Similarly, Taft's messages to Congress differed substantially from those of Roosevelt. Roosevelt carefully crafted his messages for public consumption and had no compunctions about bypassing Congress to cultivate the public support that he needed to bolster his authority and ram his preferred policies through Congress. In sharp contrast, Taft considered the press to be a nuisance; he saw journalists as an obstacle to discharging his duties. Taft also crafted his annual messages as if they were judicial opinions. Hence, they were written in copious detail, so much so that he ended up becoming the only president to deliver his annual messages in installments. Whereas Roosevelt's messages were designed to strengthen his relationship with the public, Taft's had the opposite effect: Releasing his messages in installments alienated the public, which increasingly viewed him as remote, uncaring, and ill suited to be president.

Taft's successor, Woodrow Wilson, believed Taft had made a huge mistake in failing to take advantage of his annual messages to dictate the terms of national policy debates. Whereas Taft squandered his chance to mobilize public opinion, Wilson understood he had the means to place himself at the center of national debate on the most important issues of the day by delivering his annual message in person to a joint session of Congress. Subsequent presidents have followed Wilson's model.

Even subsequent Republican presidents who saw themselves as strict constructionists did not question, as did Taft, the scope of the "residuum of power" of the presidency that Roosevelt claimed to exercise. While Taft tried to show that a narrow conception of presidential authority was compatible with a strict construction of the Constitution, subsequent strict constructionists who were president—such as Nixon, Reagan, and George W. Bush—conceived of presidential power more broadly than Taft did. He thus became a model for later Republican presidents to avoid rather than to emulate.

Third, the differences between the Roosevelt and Taft conceptions of executive power were especially apparent in conservation. They both cared deeply about conservation but disagreed on the power they had to achieve it. Indeed, Taft strongly disapproved of Roosevelt's "use of the executive order to accomplish his purposes and promised during his campaign to regularize Roosevelt's actions by appropriate legislation,"[22] and considered Roosevelt's conservation policy to operate without proper legal authorization. For instance, through a series of executive orders, Roosevelt had withdrawn lands from northwest settlements along waterways in order to grant permits to allow the building of hydroelectric power plants without congressional approval. Because Taft believed that only "Congress, not the executive, could withdraw lands for conservation purposes and that he would not violate the law even to achieve reform,"[23] he asked Congress to enact a law empowering him to withdraw public land from settlement for the purposes of conservation.[24]

The ramifications of these different approaches to conservation were significant. On the one hand, executive orders last longer than a single presidency only if future presidents leave them intact or they are not overridden through legislation. In contrast, legislation is harder to change once it is enacted. Thus, Taft enabled Congress to recapture some of its authority and to remain a central player in fashioning and maintaining conservation policy.

On the other hand, the two different conceptions of presidential power reflected different management styles, which had the unintended consequence of producing one of the worst administrative crises of Taft's presidency. Roosevelt appointed people who were loyal to him, and he disliked delegating supervisory authority. He often bypassed cabinet secretaries in order to work with the people who were able to directly implement his preferred policies. This approach undermined cabinet officers but enhanced the authority of subordinates, who were critical to the implementation of Roosevelt's ideals. Taft expected his cabinet secretaries to administer their respective departments and disagreed with "Roosevelt's assert[ion] that unless Congress had acted to prohibit his actions, the president might create forest services, charge for electric power on rivers on federal land, and otherwise use the bureaucracy to implement national programs. Taft found this method distasteful when he was secretary of war, and he intended not to countenance it within his administration."[25]

Taft further believed that Roosevelt had abused his presidential authority by appointing conservationists to administrative offices "who regard laws as obstacles,"[26] and he asked Congress to make Roosevelt's executive orders legally proper by enacting them as law. Indeed, Taft chose not to reappoint Roosevelt's secretary of the interior, James R. Garfield (President Garfield's son), because he had supported Roosevelt's efforts to establish conservation policy through the alternative means of executive orders. Taft picked Richard Ballinger as secretary of the interior because they both disapproved of "Roosevelt's freewheeling use of the executive power to circumvent the will of Congress."[27]

Shortly after Ballinger's appointment, he and Taft had their views on executive power tested. The challenge came from Gifford Pinchot, a Roosevelt loyalist whom Taft had kept as the head of the Forestry Service in the

Agriculture Department and who often clashed with Ballinger over the proper ways to implement conservation policies.[28] Taft and Ballinger believed that the department only had the powers vested in it by Congress and that the secretary was the only department official with whom the president should communicate, while Pinchot believed that Roosevelt had given him special authority to bypass Congress when necessary. Pinchot met with Taft twice to complain about Ballinger's decision to overturn Roosevelt's decisions to bar private entry to public lands that Roosevelt had set aside for hydroelectric power sites. Taft sided with Ballinger and told Pinchot that Congress, not the president, had the authority to withdraw lands for conservation purposes.[29] Pinchot was displeased and decided to discredit Ballinger so that he would be removed from office and his removal would expose Taft's deviations from Roosevelt's conservation policies. Pinchot's opportunity came in the midst of an ongoing investigation into whether Ballinger acted inappropriately in approving the sale of public land in Alaska to a former law client whose claim he had temporarily approved while he was in charge of the General Land Office in the Roosevelt administration and had allowed to be reinstated when he became secretary of the interior. Although the investigator, Louis Glavis, presented his report in person to Taft and his attorney general, George Wickersham, they concluded otherwise. Taft ultimately dismissed Glavis for his overzealousness in pressing the matter. Glavis brought the matter to the attention of Pinchot, who leaked it to the press and published the details of his investigation in *Collier's* magazine. While Taft publicly expressed support for Ballinger and Pinchot in anticipation of the congressional investigation into the charges against Ballinger, Pinchot wrote a letter to the chair of the Senate Committee on Agriculture and Forestry, Jonathan Dolliver. After Senator Dolliver read the letter into the Congressional Record,[30] Taft consulted with his cabinet, which unanimously agreed that Taft should dismiss Pinchot, and he wrote a termination letter to Pinchot.[31] Pinchot was pleased, because he believed his firing would draw attention to the different approaches of Taft and Roosevelt to conservation. He was delighted even more when Congress convened a joint committee to investigate Pinchot's dismissal and the charges against Ballinger. The committee did not question Taft's authority to dismiss Pinchot, and Taft and Wickersham did not object to its investigation since they agreed it had oversight authority and believed it would clear them both.

The ensuing investigation exonerated Ballinger but seriously embarrassed and caused political damage to Taft. First, it found that Ballinger had allowed private businesses to exploit public lands in the West in direct contravention of Taft's conservation policies. This finding contradicted Taft's claim that he shared Roosevelt's commitment to conservation. Second, Glavis and Collier's lawyer, Louis Brandeis, discovered that Taft and Attorney General Wickersham had tried to bolster their support of Ballinger by backdating a report to make it appear as if it had been issued before, rather than a month after, the public letter in which Taft exonerated Ballinger.[32] Taft never forgave Brandeis, and he testified years later against Brandeis's nomination to the Supreme Court. Third, the scandal exposed the different approaches of Taft and Roosevelt to presidential power—namely, Taft's disposition to allow Congress to take the lead on conservation and Roosevelt's to take the initiative himself.

The differences between the two men's conceptions of executive power were reflected further in their attitudes about the national budget. Roosevelt largely took an ad hoc, or indifferent, approach to budgetary affairs, while Taft prioritized fiscal responsibility. On December 17, 1909, he asked Congress to authorize a systematic study of the federal government's budget.[33] Seven months later, it did.[34] Taft's request was the first of its kind, and the ensuing appropriation was the first time that Congress both authorized a comprehensive analysis of the federal budget and agreed to support a specific, executive inquiry into budgetary affairs. The appropriation funded the Commission on Economy and Efficiency, which issued recommendations for making the national government more efficient. Over the course of his presidency, Taft sent Congress 110 reports on how to save the government money and improve its efficiency.[35]

In his last year in office, Taft requested Congress enact legislation establishing a national budget. He explained that the president had "very definite" budgetary responsibilities under the Constitution: "To the end that the Congress may effectively discharge its duties the article of the Constitution dealing with legislative power provides that a 'regular statement and account of receipts and expenditures of all public moneys shall be published,' and the article dealing with the Executive power requires the President 'from time to time to give to the Congress information on the state of the Union and to recommend to their consideration such measures as he shall deem necessary and expedient.'"[36] Accordingly, Taft proposed a scheme in which the president prepared and submitted the national budget to the Congress. He explained that "the President, as the constitutional head of the administration, may lay before the Congress, and the Congress may consider and act on, a definite business and financial program." Taft believed such a method would provide the American people and Congress information they needed on how appropriations were made and decided. In response, Congress cut the commission's budget, reduced its size, and enacted legislation blocking Taft from acting unilaterally in monitoring the budget and from weakening congressional authority over appropriations.[37] Taft quickly signed the bill into law.[38]

Taft did not, however, stop trying to persuade Congress to develop more progressive, efficient budget policies. Six days before leaving office, he submitted a final budget to the Congress with a powerful message:

> Under the Constitution, the power to control the purse is given to Congress. But the same paragraph, which makes it the duty of the Congress to determine what expenditures shall be authorized also requires of the administration the submission of "a regular statement and account of the receipts and expenditures"—i.e., an account of stewardship. The Constitution also prescribes that the President shall from "time to time give to the Congress information of the state of the Union and recommend to their consideration such measures as he shall judge necessary and expedient." Pursuant to these constitutional requirements I am submitting for your consideration a concise statement of financial conditions and results as an account of stewardship as well as certain proposals with estimates of revenues and expenditures in the form of a budget.[39]

In the short term, Taft enabled Congress to strengthen its authority over the budget, while eventually his proposals became a template for the modern budget. Shortly after Taft left office, Congress enacted the Federal Reserve Act of 1913,[40] which marked the first delegation by Congress of significant authority over the budget. Congress went further in the Budget and Accounting Act of 1921,[41] which established the Bureau of the Budget and required that it report to the president and the General Accounting Office, which was required to report to Congress.

Sixth, Roosevelt and Taft had different approaches to antitrust reform and prosecution. As president, Roosevelt was personally involved and thus responsible for steering antitrust prosecutions.[42] Rather than seek reform from Congress, Roosevelt decided to clarify the law through his own interpretations and enforcement decisions. In contrast, Taft put his attorney general in charge of antitrust enforcement. The result was that the Taft administration brought more antitrust cases than did the Roosevelt administration—seventy-five suits in four years as compared to forty suits under Roosevelt.[43] One of the most controversial cases Attorney General Wickersham brought was against U.S. Steel. Because Roosevelt had consented to the formation of the trust, Wickersham's filing made it appear as if Roosevelt had approved an illegal monopoly, and Roosevelt was forced to testify before Congress to explain his administration's policy not to oppose the formation of U.S. Steel.[44] Roosevelt never forgave Taft for the embarrassment, and their relationship completely disintegrated, even though Wickersham had successfully defended Roosevelt's antitrust prosecutions of Standard Oil and the American Tobacco Company before the Supreme Court. Taft's aggressive antitrust policies cost him significant support within the business community, and Congress never acted on his proposals to clarify antitrust law.[45]

Last but not least, Taft's narrow conception of executive authority extended to the veto power. Roosevelt cast eighty-two vetoes, while Taft cast only thirty-nine. Taft reserved vetoes for bills that he considered to be plainly unconstitutional or very bad policy, though his total number of vetoes still ranked the fifth most among presidents as of the time he left office.[46] Among the most notable of Taft's vetoes were two that he cast just before leaving office. He vetoed a House Resolution that would have admitted the territories of New Mexico and Arizona as states into the Union, because Arizona's constitution at the time provided for judicial recall, a policy that he believed was "so pernicious in its effect, so destructive of independence in the judiciary, so likely to subject the rights of the individual to the possible tyranny of a popular majority, and therefore to be so injurious to the cause of free government, that I must disapprove a constitution containing it."[47] When Arizona amended its constitution in response to Taft's veto, he signed the bill, making it the forty-eighth state in the country. Otherwise, Congress did not override any of Taft's vetoes, with the sole exception of his veto of the Webb-Kenyon Act, which prohibited the shipment in interstate commerce of intoxicating liquors intended for sale in dry states. Taft believed the law unconstitutionally vested authority in the states that only Congress had the authority to exercise.[48] Taft also took exception to the predominant view in Congress that the Court should be given the opportunity to express its views on the enactment's constitutionality because it had the primary authority to determine the meaning of the Constitution. As he explained (in language reflecting his judicial temperament), "I dissent utterly from this proposition. The oath which the Chief Executive takes, and which each Member of Congress takes, do not bind him any less sacredly to observe the Constitution than the oaths which the Justices of the Supreme Court take. [I]n spite of the popular approval of this bill, I have not felt justified in signing it, because I feel that under principles of proper constitutional construction it violates the interstate commerce clause of our fundamental law."[49] Taft's message underscored his narrow construction of Congress's Commerce Clause powers.

FIGURE 11.1 Illustration showing Uncle Sam inspecting a large alarm clock with the face of President Taft and a ringer labeled "Roosevelt Policies"; the hand on the clock shows it is nearing the end of Taft's "First Year" in office.

Source: Library of Congress Prints and Photographs Division, Washington, D.C. 20540 USA http://hdl.loc.gov/loc.pnp/pp.print

Packing the Courts

By the time he became president, Taft had thrice turned down Roosevelt's offers to be appointed to the Supreme Court.[50] Each time, Taft declined so he could complete his present job, though he was unhappy watching others attain the position he most wanted for himself.[51]

As a former judge and one of the most distinguished lawyers to become president, Taft understood the function of the courts and knew exactly the kinds of justices he wanted to appoint. Because he believed that a president's greatest impact on the Constitution was made through his appointments to the Supreme Court, he left nothing to chance and personally controlled the selections of his nominees to the Court.

Indeed, Taft came into office having a grim assessment of the state of the Court: "The condition of the Supreme Court is pitiable, and yet those old fools hold on with a tenacity that is most discouraging."[52] He thought that it was "most discouraging to the active men on the bench" that the Court needed to be "rehabilitated."[53] To fix the Court, Taft planned to appoint men whom he personally knew, were relatively young (so they could serve for years), had judicial experience and unquestionable integrity, and were strongly committed to protecting private property rights (through the rigorous enforcement of the Fifth Amendment's Takings Clause and the Fifth and Fourteenth Amendment's Due Process Clauses) and to construing narrowly the scope of Congress's power to regulate interstate commerce.

Taft's first opportunity to make an appointment arose when Rufus Peckham died. Taft quickly nominated a close friend, Horace Lurton, with whom he had sat on the Sixth Circuit Court of Appeals. Though Lurton was sixty-five, Taft believed he had the right constitutional outlook and, with sixteen years on the federal appellate court, the requisite experience. Taft was also pleased that Lurton was a southern Democrat and would therefore fit into his plans to expand his party's base into the South. With Republicans firmly in the majority in the Senate, Taft figured the numbers were in his favor, and they were—the Senate confirmed Lurton unanimously.

Taft's second opportunity to appoint a justice came less than a year later when Justice Brewer died. Just as with his first nomination, Taft knew exactly whom he wanted to nominate—Charles Evans Hughes, the two-term governor of New York, who was forty-eight and once a rival for the Republican presidential nomination. Hughes responded immediately to Taft's offer in a long letter.[54] The Senate moved faster than before: In an executive session that lasted five minutes, it unanimously confirmed Hughes.

Less than three months later, Chief Justice Melville Fuller died. The Court's senior justice, John Marshall Harlan I, desperately wanted to become chief justice, but Taft strongly opposed nominating Harlan, whom he regarded as lazy and unproductive.[55] Taft had difficulty making the decision because he wanted to fill the position himself. He told confidantes, "I am having more of a burden of responsibility in respect to the selection of judges than any president since Washington."[56] Yet Taft recognized a different opportunity for himself as well; he told Justice Moody at the time, "I shall have the appointment of probably a majority of the Supreme Court before the end of my term, which, in the view of the present agitation in respect to the Constitution, is very important."[57] To ease his burden, he asked Attorney General Wickersham to poll the Court. The outcome was unanimous—the justices favored their colleague, Edward Douglass White. Taft liked the fact that White had been on the Court for seventeen years, and he liked White's voting record. After agonizing for more than seven months, Taft nominated White. The Senate confirmed White less than an hour after Taft named him, and he became the first chief justice nominated from within the Court. Taft privately lamented, "There is nothing I would have loved more than being Chief Justice of the United States. I cannot help seeing the irony in the fact that I, who desired that office so much, should now be signing the commission of another man."[58]

Although at sixty-six White would be the oldest man to date to become chief justice, his age was not a problem for Taft. One reason that Taft chose White over Hughes (whom he promised to consider seriously as chief justice)[59] might have been that Taft figured that he would have a better chance of becoming chief justice if White were appointed, since he was likelier to die sooner. In fact, White did, and Taft persuaded Warren Harding, who was then president, to nominate him to replace White.

Three days after the Senate confirmed White as chief justice, Taft announced his choice to fill the seat vacated by White's elevation. He chose Willis Van Devanter. Taft liked that Van Devanter was only fifty-one, and he admired the strong conservative views that Van Devanter had expressed as chief justice of Wyoming's Territorial Supreme Court (the precursor to the Wyoming Supreme Court) and as a judge on the Eighth Circuit Court of Appeals for eight years. Enjoying strong support from the business community and western senators, Van Devanter was confirmed by a voice vote without any dissent.

Before the year ended, another vacancy arose when Justice William Moody resigned because of poor health. Taft turned to his third southern

Democrat, Joseph Lamar (a cousin of Lucius Lamar), who for seven years had been a judge on the Georgia Supreme Court, on which he demonstrated the constitutional outlook Taft admired. Once again, the Senate approved the nomination unanimously.

Taft got his last chance to make an appointment when Justice Harlan died on October 14, 1911. Though Harlan was from Kentucky, Taft did not feel bound to nominate someone from the same region or state. He chose Mahlon Pitney from New Jersey. At fifty-four, Pitney had spent eleven years on various New Jersey courts, on which he had demonstrated the judicial commitments that Taft had wanted to see on the Court. But this time, the Senate was not quite so cooperative. Democrats questioned Pitney's credentials and constitutional commitments, and for one of the first times in history, organizations— labor unions—tried to mobilize opposition to the nomination. The labor unions based their opposition on opinions that had upheld labor injunctions and other obstructions to unionization and labor protests. The opposition managed to delay a vote on the nomination for a month before the Senate confirmed Pitney 50–26.

In spite of the care Taft had taken to make his Court appointments, they did not all fulfill his expectations. Taft was pleased with the voting records of Van Devanter, White, Lurton,[60] and Lamar, though the last two did not serve long—each died within five years of his appointment. Taft's respect for Hughes grew while he was an associate justice, but Hughes left the Court in 1916 to run for president. Taft was displeased, however, with Pitney. After overlapping with Pitney for a year on the Court, Taft considered him a "weak member" to whom he "could not assign cases."[61] Nonetheless, the fact that Taft correctly forecast his appointees' judicial philosophy ensured that other Republican presidents interested in making similar appointments would use similar criteria in picking their nominees.

Taft also took his lower-court appointments as seriously as he took his Supreme Court appointments. His principal criteria were legal acumen and judicial philosophy. In four years, he made fifty-one appointments to the lower federal courts. While this was not as many as Teddy Roosevelt had made, it was the second largest number made by a president up until that time, amounted to 45 percent of the judges then sitting, and helped to make the lower courts a bulwark for protecting private property rights. The most famous of these was one of his first appointees, an Albany lawyer named Learned Hand, who had been strongly recommended by the president of the New York bar to Attorney General Wickersham for a federal district court judgeship. Initially, Taft was pleased with Hand's performance, but he earned Taft's enduring enmity by publicly supporting Roosevelt rather than Taft for the presidency in 1912. Hand further irked Taft through his increasing criticism of economic due process, to which Taft and his Supreme Court appointments were strongly devoted. Taft subsequently blocked Hand's appointment to a higher court until 1924, at which time another forgotten president was persuaded that Hand was the "best man" to be appointed to the U.S. Court of Appeals for the Second Circuit.[62]

Evading the Ineligibility Clause

In one of his last acts as president, Teddy Roosevelt established an important precedent on the meaning of the Ineligibility Clause in the course of working with Congress to salvage Taft's nomination of Philander Knox as secretary of state. Knox had earned Taft's respect after having served as the attorney general for Presidents McKinley and Roosevelt and later as a popular senator from Pennsylvania, a position that Taft figured would help to secure Knox easy, quick confirmation because of senatorial courtesy.

Taft was wrong. With his inauguration just weeks away, the *New York Times* uncovered a problem with the nomination—Congress had voted on February 26, 1907, to increase the salary for secretary of state, but at the time of the vote Knox was a senator, and "the Constitution plainly prohibits any member of Congress from appointment to office under the Federal Government the salary of which office has been increased during the term for which he was elected."[63] As a strict constructionist, Taft was in a quandary. The Ineligibility Clause seems to be phrased in absolute terms with no apparent exception: "No Senator or Representative shall, during the Term for which he was elected, be appointed to any civil Office under the authority of the United States, which shall have been created, or the Emoluments whereof shall have been [in]creased during such time . . . "[64] By traditional modes of constitutional interpretation, a constitutional provision should be construed as excluding any rights, conditions, or exceptions other than those expressly set forth therein. While Roosevelt was happy to resolve the issue unilaterally, most members of Congress thought the critical question of what if anything to do fell within its, not his, jurisdiction. The Senate Judiciary Committee quickly rallied around the solution of resetting the salary prior to vote on February 26, 1907. President-Elect Taft perceived the problem as a mere technicality and thought that the Senate's solution was perfectly appropriate (and the same as Congress had enacted a few years before to salvage President McKinley's nomination of Senator Walcott to the Monetary Commission).

Accordingly, Taft telegraphed Knox that he had "no doubt that [the passage of the Senate bill] will remove all the difficulties of the situation in light of its purposes."[65] Taft reasoned that the proposal removed the technical bar. One day after the *Times'* report, the Senate voted unanimously (and with no debate) to approve the Judiciary Committee's proposal.[66] The House debate was more intense, with some members defending the Senate's proposal as effectively removing the constitutional barrier but others maintaining that the Senate's proposal made the written Constitution's directives into a nullity, since they could be so easily maneuvered around. The House passed the bill, 173–115, after a special procedural rule, four roll calls, and a whole day's debate.[67] Roosevelt signed the bill, which became a model for future presidents to follow when appointing members of Congress to officers on whose salaries they had voted while serving in Congress.[68]

Protecting Economic Liberties

Nothing was more important to Taft in constitutional law than the Constitution's protection of economic liberties. Taft was president during the *Lochner* era, which took its name from the Court's decision in *Lochner v. New York*[69] overturning a New York state law protecting the health of bakers by regulating the number of hours they could work. During this period, the Court struck down over a hundred laws for exceeding the scope of Congress's power to regulate interstate commerce or, as it did in *Lochner*, for violating a fundamental right to contract. Throughout his public life, Taft fiercely defended the Constitution's recognition of a fundamental right to contract, or economic due process, based on the liberty component of the Due Process Clauses of the Fifth and Fourteenth Amendments. On Taft's view, this right severely restricted government's ability to regulate, or interfere with, private economic affairs. As his veto of the Webb-Kenyon Act reveals, he maintained, like many conservative judges and leaders of the era, that state sovereignty precluded Congress from regulating a wide variety of local activities, including manufacturing.

Nevertheless, Taft supported some broad constructions of Congress's Commerce Clause authority partly because of his willingness to defer to congressional judgments as long as they were not plainly unconstitutional or terrible policy. For example, he signed the Mann-Elkins Act into law. The law expanded the jurisdiction of the Interstate Commerce Commission (ICC); created a specialized court, the Court of Commerce, to hear appeals from the ICC; and for the first time placed the telephone and telegraph industries under the regulatory power of the ICC.[70] Taft also signed bills into law creating the Industrial Bureau, the Bureau of Mines, and separate Departments of Commerce and Labor; limiting work on federal projects to eight hours a day; and strengthening the Pure Food and Drugs Act. In addition, he signed into law the bill authorizing the Children's Bureau[71] and, in appointing a woman to lead the bureau, became the first president to appoint a woman to lead a federal agency.[72] Although a principal purpose for most of these bills had been to improve the efficiency of the federal government, these bills, as well as the Mann-Elkins Act, affirmed the Commerce Clause as the principal source of authority for creating and expanding federal instrumentalities.

Moreover, Taft signed into law the nation's second law regulating campaign finance, which was based on the Commerce Clause—the Federal Corrupt Practices Act.[73] It restricted the amounts of money that private corporations could contribute to political campaigns.[74] The bill was amended in 1911 to extend its requirements to U.S. Senate candidates and primary elections, to require financial disclosures by candidates for the first time, and to set limits on candidates' expenditures on their campaigns, but ten years later the Supreme Court held that Congress's authority to regulate elections did not extend to regulating party primaries and nominations and struck down the 1911 amendment's spending limits.[75] In 1925, Congress revised the law to extend its coverage to multistate parties and election committees and required that financial disclosures be made quarterly; the Court upheld the act's reporting requirements in 1934 and its spending limits on federal elections in 1941.[76] It remained in this form as the primary federal law governing campaign finance until 1971, at which time it was repealed and replaced by Congress with an elaborate scheme in which the Federal Election Commission was given a key role in monitoring the contributions made to and the expenditures made by or on behalf of political candidates.[77] The Federal Corrupt Practice Act has since been cited frequently by the Supreme Court as among the first in a long line of congressional enactments regulating different aspects of campaign finance, including requiring candidates to disclose contributions made to their campaigns, and remains a fixture of federal election law.[78]

Another significant statute Taft signed into law was the infamous Mann Act.[79] The act made it a felony to transport knowingly any woman or girl in interstate or foreign commerce for prosecution, debauchery, or "other immoral purposes," or to coerce a woman or girl into such immoral acts. Even though federal criminal statutes were quite rare in 1910 and many conservatives opposed the Mann Act because it displaced state police powers, the law encountered little opposition in Congress. In 1913, the Supreme Court upheld the constitutionality of the Mann Act.[80] Initially, the law was used to prosecute prostitution, white slavery, and men who took women across state lines for consensual sex but was later amended to cover child pornography and all sexual exploitation.

Thus, Taft's construction of the Commerce Clause was not so narrow that it precluded many laws that are familiar to Americans today. Indeed, as president, he applied the same understanding that he later expressed as chief justice: the Court should "not substitute its judgment for that of Congress in [matters pertaining to the regulation of interstate commerce] unless the relation of the subject to interstate commerce and its effect upon it are clearly non-existent."[81] This understanding is the basis for modern economic regulations, including minimum wage regulations.[82]

Supporting Amendments to the Constitution

Few presidents have been as successful in securing constitutional change as Taft. First, he believed that "new kinds of taxation" were necessary to eliminate the growing federal deficit. At the time, his options were limited: One was to ratify a constitutional amendment overturning the Court's decision in *Pollock v. Farmers' Loan and Trust Company* striking down an income tax, and the other was to support a corporate tax, which *Pollock* did not address. In a special message to Congress, Taft asked for both options: He proposed a 2 percent federal income tax on corporations via an excise tax and asked Congress to draft a constitutional amendment authorizing an income tax.[83] On July 12, 1909, Congress overwhelmingly passed a resolution proposing the Sixteenth Amendment, whose text Taft had approved beforehand.[84] The amendment was sent to the states for ratification, and, on February 25, 1913, Secretary of State Knox certified that the Sixteenth Amendment had been ratified.[85]

Next, Taft reluctantly supported ratification of the Seventeenth Amendment, which altered the means by which senators were elected. Prior to its adoption, the Constitution provided that state legislatures chose senators; however, this mode of selection was widely believed to foster political corruption, and the Seventeenth Amendment was proposed as a solution by making senators directly accountable to the people rather than a smaller, more elite group consisting of friends and allies. Though Taft was skeptical of direct democracy because it might lead to tyranny of the majority, he recognized the overwhelming popularity of the progressive movement in favor of the Seventeenth Amendment and introduced it in Congress, where it was only able to achieve the two-thirds approval required in the Senate after Vice President James Sherman cast the tie-breaking vote in favor of its ratification.[86] Taft followed the amendment through most of the ratification process, which did not become final until shortly after Wilson's inauguration.

Third, Taft's veto of the Webb-Kenyon Act proved to be an early salvo in a protracted dispute over the scope of federal authority to prohibit intoxicating liquors. Though Congress had overridden Taft's veto of the Webb-Kenyon Act and the Supreme Court had upheld its constitutionality, there were lingering concerns about the extent of the federal government's authority to ban intoxicating liquors, particularly in light of the Court's holding that states retained authority to ban the sale of liquor absolutely within their borders. To remove any doubts, Congress approved a resolution adopting the Eighteenth Amendment, which the states ratified on January 16, 1919. The amendment became unpopular and difficult to enforce, and organized crime quickly took control over the manufacture, sale, and distribution of alcoholic beverages. It was repealed in 1933.

ALTHOUGH TAFT HAD failed to replicate and extend Roosevelt's record of reform, he was the first president to adapt strict construction of the Constitution to the modern world. Later presidents who were strict constructionists held similar positions on many issues, though some claimed broader presidential but narrower congressional powers than Taft did. Yet those who yearn for a Supreme Court that vigorously protects state sovereignty and property rights are likeliest to find their ideals instantiated in the Courts that Taft assembled as president and presided over as chief justice.

Calvin Coolidge, 1923–1929

NO COMMENT BETTER captures Calvin Coolidge's presidency than Dorothy Parker's cutting remark on learning of Coolidge's death, "How could they tell?" The problem with Coolidge's presidency was it left more of an image to be satirized than a record of positive acts to defend. His pride in championing inaction as a principled stance made him an easy target, particularly as the prosperity the nation enjoyed during his presidency lapsed into the Great Depression. Few people have since remembered, much less taken seriously, what Coolidge did as president.

Yet Coolidge's constitutional impact is significant. He shaped the balance of power on appointments and foreign affairs and supported landmark laws regulating broadcasting and commercial aviation. Most importantly, he was the first twentieth-century president to advance two constitutional convictions important to modern conservatives—the first that the Constitution restricted governmental power to regulate the economy, and the second that the federal government's limited powers include cultivating the moral character of Americans. Thus, Coolidge conceived of legislative power in ways that resonate more with modern conservatives than did Taft, though Taft's conception of judicial power seems more like that of contemporary Republicans than does Coolidge's. Years later, Ronald Reagan and George W. Bush would both meld these two conceptions in their respective presidencies.

Shaping the Modern Conservative Presidential Administration

Of the six Republican presidents from McKinley through Hoover, Coolidge has had the greatest impact on presidential administration. While Coolidge served longer and enjoyed greater electoral success than these other presidents, several other factors explain his impact on presidential power.

To begin with, Coolidge advanced a philosophy of governance that has been commonly associated with conservative constitutionalists ever since.

Though he initially pledged to adhere to President Harding's policies, he increasingly advanced his own distinct constitutional philosophy. He construed presidential power more broadly, but congressional power more narrowly, than Taft and was the first president to champion the need for "lower taxes, less government, and more freedom." Because of this, President Reagan decided, shortly after his inauguration, to honor Coolidge by replacing the portraits of John Adams and Truman in the upstairs of the White House with one of Coolidge.[1]

Reagan believed Coolidge was "one of our most underrated presidents."[2] He explained, "I am an admirer of Silent Cal and believe he has been badly treated by history. . . . He served his country well and accomplished much." Reagan admired Coolidge because he "cut taxes four times. We had probably the greatest growth and prosperity that we've ever known. [I have] taken heed of that, because if he did nothing, maybe that's the answer [for] the federal government."[3]

The constitutional and political pronouncements of Reagan and George W. Bush and other contemporary conservatives echo those of Coolidge.[4] Coolidge objected to an activist federal government that stretched its powers beyond their limits at the expense of state sovereignty. For example, Coolidge in his Fourth Annual Address called "for reducing, rather than expanding, government bureaus, which seek to regulate and control the business activities of the American people."[5] He rejected the need for the federal government to generally address social and other problems: "Unfortunately, human nature cannot be changed by an act of the legislature. . . . It is too much assumed that because an abuse exists it is the business of the federal government to remedy it."[6] He believed the Constitution left social problems to be resolved in the private sector.[7]

The remark most commonly associated with Coolidge's philosophy of governance—"the chief business of the American people is business"[8]—is a corollary derived from his conviction that the protection of private property was central to the constitutional order. For instance, in his inaugural address, he declared, "It is not property but the right to hold property, both great and small, which our Constitution guarantees. All owners of property are charged with a service. These rights and duties have been revealed, through the conscience of society, to have a divine sanction. [The] result of economic dissipation to a nation is always moral decay."[9] He explained further that "our most important problem is not to secure new advantages but to maintain those we already possess. Our system of government made up of three separate and independent departments, our divided sovereignty, composed of Nation and State, the matchless wisdom that is enshrined in our Constitution, all these need constant effort and tireless vigilance for their protection and support."[10] Citizens who want their rights "respected under the Constitution and the law" should "set the examples themselves of observing the Constitution and the law."[11] Coolidge believed that the framers protected private property as an integral part of their vision to implement the classic libertarian ideal that people are free to act as they please as long as they do not hurt others.

Yet Coolidge did not believe that government only had the powers to protect national security and to maintain law and order. He believed that government had the power to help citizens develop their moral character rather than solve social problems. While the distinction between the two seems slippery, Coolidge had no problem distinguishing them. For him, building character involved the government in doing something that benefited everyone and not playing favorites, whereas fixing social problems entailed having the government trying to redress social inequities that it did not create or have any constitutional obligation to fix.

Indeed, this theme was so important to Coolidge that in his First Annual Message he urged Congress to establish a federal department to encourage character development and education. He further proposed constitutional amendments to set a minimum wage for women and to restrict child labor. In explaining these initiatives, he suggested that "there is an inescapable personal responsibility for the development of character, of industry, of thrift, and of self-control. These do not come from the Government, but from the people themselves. But the Government can and should always be expressive of steadfast determination, always vigilant, to maintain conditions under which these virtues are most likely to develop and secure recognition and reward."[12] Otherwise, he believed, states, not the federal government, had the power and responsibility to address social inequities. Coolidge explained in 1926 that "we must . . . recognize that the [federal government] is not and cannot be adjusted to the needs of local government. It is too far away to be informed of local needs, too inaccessible [to respond] to local needs."[13] The government's job was "not to run things but to help them run themselves."[14] Thus, for Coolidge, the constitutional guarantee of private property provided the conditions for the proper cultivation of the American character. Closely connected to this theme was Coolidge's belief that reducing federal interference with business enabled business to be more profitable, and the more profitable it was the more firmly it set the foundations for refining the American character.

Another constant theme in Coolidge's speeches was federalism. In his Third Annual Message, he explained, "The functions which the Congress are to discharge are not those of local government but of National Government. The greatest solicitude should be exercised to prevent any encroachment upon the rights of the States or their various political subdivisions. Local self-government is one of the most precious possessions. It is the greatest contributing factor to the stability, strength, liberty, and progress of the Nation."[15] He believed that "society is in [more] danger from encumbering the National Government beyond its power to [to regulate] than from leaving [l]ocal communities to bear their burdens and remedy their own evils."[16] In his judgment, smaller government engendered greater respect for private property rights. In his judgment, the American people control their own freedom and the ownership of their own property. He believed that "neither of these can be impaired except by due process of law. The wealth of our country is not public wealth, but private wealth. It does not belong to the Government, it belongs to the people. The Government has no justification in taking private property except for a public purpose. It is always necessary to keep these principles in mind in the laying of taxes and in the making of appropriations. No right exists to levy a dollar, or to order the expenditure of a dollar, of the money of the people, except for a necessary public purpose duly authorized by the Constitution. The power over the purse is the power over liberty."[17]

By linking the protection of private property to restricting government spending and taxation, Coolidge extended Taft's arguments from more than a decade before. In his Fourth Annual Message, Coolidge reemphasized the nation's commitment to federalism. He reminded Congress, "It is too much assumed that because an abuse exists it is the business of the National Government to provide a remedy. The presumption should be that it is the business of local and State governments. Such national action results in encroaching upon the salutary independence of the States and by undertaking to supersede their natural authority fills the land with bureaus and departments which are undertaking to do what it is impossible to accomplish and brings our whole system of government into disrespect and disfavor."[18] The solution was for the American people to understand that "permanent success lies in local, rather than national action. Unless the locality rises to its own requirements, there is an almost irresistible impulse for the National Government to intervene. The States and the Nation should [realize] that such action is to be adopted only as a last resort."[19]

Separation of powers, like federalism, was designed to facilitate the same objective—preserving ample space within which the American people could flourish. In 1926, he explained,

> [The Constitution's framers intended] to establish a free government, which must not be permitted to degenerate into the unrestrained authority of a mere majority or the unbridled weight of a mere influential few. They undertook to balance these interests against each other and provide the three separate independent branches, the executive, the legislative, and the judicial departments of the government, with checks against each other in order that neither one might encroach upon the other. These are our guarantees of liberty. As a result of these methods enterprise has been duly protected, the people have been free from oppression, and there has been an ever-broadening and deepening of the humanities of life.[20]

That Coolidge never stated his constitutional views more clearly than he did in these statements was a shortcoming. He is the last president to write his own speeches and deliberately made them short. Indeed, one scholar found "the length of the average Coolidge sentence to be 18 words, compared to 26.6 words for Lincoln and 51.5 for Washington."[21] Coolidge gave subsequent generations fewer words and images to remember and thus left them with the task of teasing out of his sparse rhetoric his particular construction of the Constitution. Both the relative paucity of the material that he produced as president and the nature of what has been left have hindered the formation or maintenance of a meaningful legacy in constitutional law.[22]

Nonetheless, Coolidge shaped presidential administration through his carefully orchestrated publicizing of his objectives. While Teddy Roosevelt revolutionized the presidency's capacity to use his office as a bully pulpit, Coolidge took the concept a step further. In spite of his distaste for interacting with the press, he recognized the institutional advantage of a president's using the press to bypass Congress and to speak directly to the American people.[23] Hence, Coolidge held press conferences twice a week, regularly made off-the-record comments to the press, and generally tried to use the press to facilitate public awareness of—and support for—his administration.[24] Indeed, Coolidge was the first president to have his State of the Union broadcast nationally. As his chief of staff, Bascon Slemp, observed, Coolidge governed through "direct reliance upon the mass of the people."[25]

Coolidge understood he needed popular support for his initiatives and bypassed Congress and reached the public through his interaction with the press.

At the same time, Coolidge used his power to make agency appointments to keep regulatory agencies under his control. Executive agencies are, by definition, under the control of the president, who may appoint and remove their directors. The same is not true for independent agencies, to which presidents may appoint their directors but have little or no removal power over them. But Coolidge recognized that while he did not have formal authority to dissolve the agencies and commissions, he had authority to appoint as the heads of these agencies and commissions people who opposed or were highly skeptical of the basic missions of the agencies that they were appointed to administer. Coolidge's concerted strategy was to weaken agencies through such appointments as well as by withholding or restricting their resources. As senators became aware of Coolidge's strategy, they refused to confirm the people he had nominated to lead agencies. In response, Coolidge made "recess appointments to the regulatory agencies of men who would serve him but could not be confirmed in office."[26] As a result, regulatory agencies ended up doing little or nothing while Coolidge was president. Led by his appointees, federal regulatory agencies did not change policies, were denied resources to do their work, or adopted policies of allowing the businesses within their jurisdictions to regulate themselves.[27] For example, in response to the steadily expanding jurisdiction of the Federal Trade Commission, Coolidge appointed commissioners who created "a trade practice conference division within the commission staff to encourage industrial self-regulation." Subsequently, regulation "in the Coolidge era [was] thin to the point of invisibility."[28] Through his nomination and recess appointment authorities, Coolidge systematically weakened federal regulatory agencies.[29]

Confronting Corruption

Because he inherited Harding's scandal-ridden administration, Coolidge became the first twentieth-century president to address the constitutional and political fallout from the misconduct of high-ranking, executive branch officials whom he had not appointed. Throughout Coolidge's presidency, Congress conducted several investigations of corruption in the executive branch. Among these were two Senate hearings on allegations of corruption within the Veterans' Bureau and on the leasing of naval oil reserves at Teapot Dome in Wyoming and Elk Hills in California to private developers. Before these investigations were concluded, the Senate initiated another inquiry, the focus of which was on alleged misconduct by Harry Daughtery, who had been Harding's campaign manager and attorney general. There were additional hearings on possible corruption committed not only by Coolidge's treasury secretary, Andrew Mellon, but also the chief of the Office of the Alien Property Custodian. In these investigations, Senate leaders asserted their power to oversee and check the president and other high-ranking executive branch officers. The investigations ultimately tested the respective authorities of the executive and legislative branches to investigate and sanction the misbehavior of high-ranking executive branch personnel.

On February 12, 1923, the Senate began its investigation into Charles Forbes's possible misconduct as Veterans' Bureau administrator.[30] Forbes had allegedly arranged with private contractors to build overpriced hospitals, to stock them with overpriced equipment, and to sell the equipment later for substantial profits. Forbes supposedly received kickbacks on all these transactions. Shortly after the Senate began its investigation of Forbes, Harding, at the urging of Attorney General Daugherty, demanded his resignation. Over the next month, Forbes left the country to avoid prosecution, and two administration officials—Charles Cramer, Forbes's general counsel, and Jess Smith, an assistant to Daugherty, killed themselves. The investigation grabbed national headlines, and the impetus for further investigation was irresistible.

Harding's death on August 2, 1923, prompted the Senate Select Committee on Veterans' Bureau Investigation to delay the start of its hearings until October 14, 1923. Although Forbes was the principal focus of the hearings, Coolidge was a target, since Democrats and progressive Republicans blamed him for allowing "predatory interests" to take control of his administration.[31] Although Forbes denied any wrongdoing, the committee concluded that he was responsible for defrauding over $200 million from the federal government. A year after the hearings, Forbes was indicted, convicted, and sentenced for bribery and corruption.

Forbes's prosecution was significant for two other reasons. The first was its timing—it followed the Senate hearings on Forbes's misconduct. The Constitution provides that "the Party convicted [and removed by the Senate] shall nevertheless be liable and subject to Indictment, Trial, Judgment and Punishment according to law."[32] This language has been read as presuming, if not requiring, that an impeachable official should have his misconduct addressed initially through the impeachment process and only be subject to criminal prosecution after leaving or being removed from office. This clause, thus, could be read as requiring impeachment before criminal prosecution.

The fact that Forbes's prosecution followed Congress's hearings and his resignation reinforces this reading of the Constitution.

The prosecution of Forbes did not, however, deflect growing concerns about Daugherty's misconduct. The Senate's investigation into Forbes's misconduct raised questions about Daugherty's relationship with the Veterans' Bureau under Forbes's directorship (even though Daugherty had pushed for Forbes's prosecution). These questions were added to those already circulating about Daugherty's integrity. Indeed, a resolution to impeach Daugherty had been filed in 1922 for his failing to enforce anti-trust, war-profiteering, and prohibition laws; abusing the pardon privilege; hiring corrupt cronies; exercising undue influence in ending strikes; and authorizing surreptitious surveillance of unfriendly members of Congress. Though the impeachment effort failed, many members of Congress were determined to force Coolidge to dismiss him.[33]

But Forbes's misconduct and the Senate's growing discontent with Daugherty were overshadowed by the Teapot Dome scandal, which ranks second only to Watergate in the amount of attention it has received among presidential scandals. More has been written about the Teapot Dome scandal than any other aspect of Harding's or Coolidge's administration.[34]

Nonetheless, the Senate hearings on Teapot Dome had underappreciated constitutional consequences. The first was Coolidge's decision to appoint two special counsels to investigate and prosecute crimes arising from the affair. Coolidge made the decision to preempt Senator Thomas Walsh, who was chairing the Senate investigation, from introducing a resolution urging Coolidge to appoint special prosecutors to look into the scandal. Coolidge understood that the people in charge of the prosecution had to be independent from the political parties or the attorney general who was under investigation. Hence, Coolidge signed the joint resolution authorizing the appointments of two special counsels.[35] The fact that he did not challenge the resolution provided important support for the constitutionality of joint inquiries into executive branch misconduct.

The appointments were historic. Never before had a president appointed two counsel to investigate a criminal matter within his own administration. Prior to Coolidge's presidency, the appointments of special prosecutors had not worked out well, most famously failing when President Grant ordered his attorney general to fire the special prosecutor investigating corruption within his administration in the reporting of whiskey production.[36] Consequently, Coolidge became the first president who appointed special prosecutors to investigate a single scandal *and* allowed them to complete their mission with no interference at all on his part. After the Senate resisted his first two choices as prosecutors, he appointed two others—Atlee Pomerene, a former Democratic senator from Ohio, and Owen Roberts, a former prosecutor and prominent lawyer from Philadelphia. The Senate confirmed Pomerene 59–13; two days later, it confirmed Roberts 68–8.[37] Naval Secretary Edward Denby, who was one of the targets of the investigation, resigned the same day.

The subsequent prosecutions were significant for several reasons. First, they, like Forbes's prosecution, followed the Senate investigation. They thus fortified the growing precedent in support of prosecuting officials after they left office. Second, by all accounts, the special prosecutors conducted exemplary investigations and prosecutions of the targeted officials. Fall became the first cabinet official to be jailed for misconduct in office, while Daugherty and Edward L. Doheny, one of the oil lessees, were tried but not convicted. Harry Sinclair, also one of the oil executives who had paid money to Fall and Denby for the private leases, was convicted of contempt of Congress for refusing to appear before the committee for contempt of court, was fined $1,000, and went to prison for three months. In the course of his trial for contempt of Congress, Sinclair authorized private detectives to spy on the jury, for which the trial court found him to be in contempt of court. Sinclair challenged the trial judge's ruling, but the Supreme Court, in a landmark ruling, upheld the authority of the trial judge to hold Sinclair in contempt of court for jury tampering.[38] The reputation the prosecutors developed for doing their jobs without demonstrating any partisanship undoubtedly helped them later when they needed bipartisan support for subsequent appointments by Herbert Hoover—Roberts as an associate justice of the Supreme Court and Pomerene to lead the Reconstruction Finance Corporation.

Another constitutional consequence of the Teapot Dome hearings was Congress's persistence in approving censure resolutions against high-ranking executive branch officials. Among the resolutions approved were Senate Joint Resolution 54 (suggesting that Fall and Denby were guilty of violating federal law in the granting of oil leases and directing the president to submit his appointments of special prosecutors to the Senate for approval);[39] a Senate resolution calling for the resignation of Navy Secretary Denby;[40] Senate Resolution 108 (urging Coolidge to direct the treasury secretary to turn over to the Public Lands Committee the income tax returns of the three principals in the Teapot Dome scandal);[41] and a Senate resolution to investigate Daugherty and the Justice Department for failure to prosecute corruption.[42]

While members of Congress believed these resolutions derived from their oversight powers and authority to express themselves freely on matters of public concern, Coolidge denounced them all as unconstitutional. On the day that the Senate passed the resolution urging Denby's dismissal, Coolidge published an extensive critique. "No official recognition," he declared, "can be given to the passage of the Senate resolution relative to their opinion concerning members of the Cabinet or other officers under executive control." He said that any action he took regarding the Teapot Dome matter had to be based on the advice of his special counsel, not the directives of Congress. Citing Presidents Madison and Cleveland, Coolidge added, "The President is responsible to the people for his conduct relative to the retention or dismissal of public officials. I assume that responsibility.... I do not propose to sacrifice any innocent man for my own welfare, nor do I propose to retain in office any unfit man for my own welfare."[43] Coolidge also vigorously contested the legality of Resolution 180, which he believed violated the protections accorded to tax returns by the Revenue Act of 1921 (as well as directly encroached upon his inherent authority to remove executive officials).[44] To avoid a constitutional conflict, Coolidge suggested altering Treasury Department rules to allow the committee's representatives to inspect the requested tax returns. Congress ignored his suggestion, though it provides a basis for subsequent presidents' objections to similar resolutions.

Fourth, the Select Committee requested that Coolidge's chief of staff appear before the committee to explain whether he aided Fall during the investigation. He agreed to testify and thus became the first presidential chief of staff to testify before a Senate committee about possible misconduct in office. When asked whether he had communicated with the White House on a trip he took to Florida to visit with a newspaper publisher who was also suspected of assisting Fall, Slemp refused to answer: "All communications that I would make to the White House I would have to reserve as confidential."[45] Slemp's activities remained a subject of concern to the committee until the publisher confirmed that none of their communications had anything to do with the investigation. Coolidge relieved concerns further by appointing a special committee to advise the administration on how best to use the naval oil services, replacing the officials forced out of the administration with well-known, trustworthy individuals, and establishing a cabinet-level Federal Oil Conservation Board to study oil conservation.

As the Public Lands Committee's hearings on the Teapot Dome scandal unfolded, a Senate Select Committee began hearings on the possible misconduct of Attorney General Daugherty. The hearings had several constitutional consequences. The first was the fact that the simultaneous congressional hearings on the various scandals within the administration strongly bolstered the Senate's authority of oversight of corruption within the executive branch.

Second, Daugherty was only the second attorney general to be the focus of a congressional investigation for misconduct, though he refused to testify on the ground that compelling him to appear would interfere with the Justice Department's administration. He further refused to allow the investigating committee access to Justice Department files. The refusal was grounded not on any privileged basis but rather his need to be insulated from harassment by Congress.[46] The fact that Daugherty claimed no clear constitutional (or legal) basis for the refusal further undermined his support within the administration and Congress.

A third consequence of the hearings was Coolidge's firing of Daugherty. Before the hearings, Coolidge had refused to acquiesce to congressional pressure to dismiss Daugherty, even though he had reason to believe that Daugherty had become mentally unhinged as a result of the intense congressional scrutiny.[47] After two heated meetings with Daugherty, Coolidge decided he had to do something. The opportunity arose when Daugherty refused to appear before the committee and to provide it access to pertinent Justice Department documents. For Coolidge, this was the last straw, since Daugherty was refusing to comply with Coolidge's directive that he cooperate with the investigation. In late March 1924, Coolidge dismissed him for mishandling the Senate investigation of his misconduct.[48] It was the most significant dismissal of a cabinet officer since Andrew Johnson's firing of his war secretary, which provoked Congress to retaliate by impeaching and nearly removing him from office.[49] Daugherty joined a long line of other officials whom Coolidge dismissed, including William Burns, the first director of the Bureau of Investigation within the Justice Department.[50] Coolidge replaced Burns with his deputy, J. Edgar Hoover.

Coolidge's decisions to dismiss high-profile executive officials including Daugherty and Burns reinforced the long-held view of presidents that they had the inherent authority to fire high-ranking executive officials, including cabinet members. When Coolidge became president, it was widely accepted that a president had such authority to ensure faithful execution of the laws; a president needed the power to remove subordinates within the executive branch to ensure that they followed his directives. The decision tracked the arguments that the Coolidge administration had made before the Supreme Court in December 1923 in a case called *Myers v. United States.*[51]

Myers is widely known among lawyers as an important Supreme Court decision upholding a president's inherent authority to discharge executive branch officials. Though the case involved President Wilson's discharge of a postmaster, it fell to the Coolidge administration to challenge the constitutionality of a provision in an 1876 postal appropriations act restricting President Wilson's authority to discharge a postmaster unilaterally. (The defense illustrates how presidents from different parties agreed on the constitutional issues at stake.) Coolidge's solicitor general pressed the act's unconstitutionality before the Court. This was unusual because the Justice Department is generally charged with defending the constitutionality of a federal statute, but this case involved a clash between a federal law and a president's inherent authority. Consequently, the Court scheduled re-argument in the case to allow Senator George Wharton Pepper to defend the constitutionality of the statute before the Court. In the re-argument before the Court, the Coolidge administration reiterated its argument that through this act Congress was unconstitutionally attempting to usurp a president's power to direct the exercise of executive power by removing people who were impeding his ability to discharge his constitutional responsibilities faithfully. Pepper told the Court that the president was obliged constitutionally to execute the laws enacted by Congress and that if Congress had the authority to create offices, it had the authority to place conditions on appointments to or removals from them. The Court agreed that the act unconstitutionally interfered with a president's inherent authority to discharge officials performing purely executive functions within the executive branch.[52]

Yet *Myers* is widely misunderstood. It is commonly cited—mistakenly—as overturning the Tenure in Office Act. It did not. While Court mentioned the Tenure in Office Act, it did not rule on its constitutionality. Instead, the Court struck down the removal provision of the postal appropriations act. Because the Court's reasons for doing so were equally applicable to the Tenure in Office Act, the Court and scholars have since assumed that it too was deemed unconstitutional, though Cleveland actually had brought about its demise years earlier.

Another reason that the Senate's Daugherty hearings were significant was the Senate resolution approved after they had ended. By a vote of 70–2, the Senate condemned Daugherty for his misconduct. The resolution was consistent with prior resolutions condemning various high-ranking officials for misconduct. It was yet another precedent supporting the power of Congress to censure public officials through such resolutions.

Fifth, Daugherty's prosecution after his resignation from the Justice Department fits into the same pattern of criminal prosecutions of other former Harding officials for misconduct after they left office. The pattern is significant support for the authority of Congress to initiate proceedings against sitting or former executive branch officials and for criminal proceedings to follow those proceedings.[53] This pattern generally held until the post-Watergate era, in which federal criminal prosecutions of public officials began more commonly to precede impeachment or congressional investigations.

Last, a significant constitutional issue arose when Daugherty's brother, Mally, refused to comply with a Senate subpoena to testify. The committee cited Mally for contempt of court, a crime for which he could be imprisoned. Mally filed a lawsuit challenging his citation. The case went to the Supreme Court, which, in a landmark ruling, unanimously upheld the inherent constitutional authority of congressional committees to issue and enforce subpoenas in the course of overseeing the administration of the laws. The Court declared that "the power of inquiry—with process to enforce it—is . . . essential and appropriate . . . to the legislative function."[54] This was the first case upholding the inherent authority of Congress to enforce its subpoenas to serve investigative purposes. Even more striking was language in the opinion suggesting this authority may override refusals to testify based even on claims of executive privilege.

There were several other congressional investigations into possible misconduct in the Coolidge administration, though they were important less for their political fallout than for what they revealed about the power of Senate Committee chairs. Article I, section 5, of the Constitution vests both chambers of Congress with the authority "to determine rules for their proceedings."[55] Each chamber has used this authority to establish committees and to vest them with particular jurisdiction. The authority of the chairs of the committees derives in part from these general delegations as well as the informal norms within the Senate. In Coolidge's second term, there were two committee chairs who directly challenged Coolidge's authority and strongly asserted their own. The first was Senator William Borah, a Progressive Republican from Idaho. By Coolidge's second term, Borah had advanced in seniority within the Senate. As the chair of both the probe into the Alien Property Custodian and the powerful Senate Foreign Committee, Borah could be counted on as an ally only as long as Coolidge courted his favor. Borah persistently made his presence—and his opinions—felt within the White House, especially in the realm of foreign affairs. For example, in the midst of a period of tense relations between the United States and Mexico resulting from the United States' involvement in revolutionary uprisings in Nicaragua, Borah secured the unanimous passage of a Senate resolution recommending arbitration with Mexico.[56] While the resolution is yet another instance of the

Senate's exercise of its power to express itself through such measures, Borah publicly defended himself against the charge that he was breaching the president's authority: "As Chair of the Senate Foreign Relations Committee, I have a right to get my information from any source I wish. This I propose to do, and I know of no power that can stop me."[57]

Another committee chair creating problems for the Coolidge administration was Senator James Couzens, a Republican from Michigan.[58] Early in 1924, Couzens persuaded his colleagues to initiate an investigation of the Internal Revenue Service for giving tax rebates to large corporations. His objective was to expose the conflicts of interest Andrew Mellon had as treasury secretary in formulating tax policies. Couzens took over the investigating committee when the first chair resigned under pressure from Coolidge, who, upon Mellon's urging, had written an open letter to the Senate criticizing the hearings for serving no beneficial purpose. Attaching a letter from Mellon, Coolidge argued that, as a result of the Senate's allowing "one senator [to] essentially conduct[] an investigation of the government, the Constitutional guarantee against unwarranted search and seizure breaks down, the prohibition against what amounts to a government charge of criminal action with the formal presentment of a grand jury is evaded, the rules of evidence which have been adopted for the protection of the innocent are ignored, and the Department becomes the victim of vague, unformulated and indefinite charges, . . . Against the continuance of such conditions, I enter my solemn protests and give notice that in my opinion the departments ought not to be required to participate in it."[59] Coolidge's criticisms backfired: Senate leaders defended Couzens and criticized Coolidge for overreaching. Senator Thomas Walsh, for example, told colleagues that Coolidge's message was "the most arrogant sent by any executive to a parliamentary body since the days of the Stuarts and Tudors."[60] Senator Reed described Coolidge's letter as "such an insult as one branch of the government could not accept from another." He urged the Senate to expunge Coolidge's letter from the record. Senator Carter Glass, a Democrat and President Wilson's treasury secretary, told the Senate that Coolidge's and Mellon's letters "constitute the most extraordinary breach of official etiquette that has ever occurred in the history of the Republic."[61]

Couzens was not deterred. As chair, he extended the hearings, during which he urged Mellon's impeachment. Though no impeachment materialized, the hearings were important because they "end[ed] secrecy about the [tax] rebates [granted by the administration] and led to providing Congress with a permanent staff of tax experts" who could advise members of Congress on the complex legal issues involved.[62]

Controlling Appointments

Coolidge used his appointment powers to reshape his administration and the judiciary. While he initially had pledged to keep Harding's cabinet in place, Coolidge systematically put his own stamp on key appointments. One of his first opportunities to reshape Harding's cabinet came after he dismissed Daugherty. Coolidge nominated the dean of Columbia Law School, Harlan Fiske Stone, to replace Daugherty. While Coolidge and Stone had been friends at Amherst College, the main reason he picked Stone to run the Justice Department was to restore its integrity and reputation.[63] Within a year, Stone did just that. (President Ford followed the same strategy when he appointed Edward Levi, the president of the University of Chicago, to restore the department's integrity in the aftermath of Watergate.)

Coolidge also handled judicial appointments differently than Harding. Whereas Harding had primarily based his judicial appointments on nominees' likely judicial philosophy, Coolidge "developed his own criteria. . . . He generally was guided by the degree of unanimity of political and bar leaders in the court district or circuit involved, the Justice Department's assessment of the candidates' professional qualifications and experience, and for circuit court selections, the principle of representation from the states in the circuit."[64] Coolidge strongly resisted senatorial courtesy and, in the process, made some excellent circuit court appointments, including Augustus Hand and Thomas Swan, the dean of Yale Law School, to the Second Circuit Court of Appeals and John Parker to the Fourth Circuit. Coolidge appointed more lower-court judges than any president before him.

Among Coolidge's judicial appointments, two had unusual impact on the law. Appointed to the federal district court in 1909, Learned Hand had tried without success to persuade Presidents Taft and Harding to appoint him to the Second Circuit. Coolidge's willingness to place merit over ideology in appointing Hand to the federal court of appeals still has ramifications in American law. Hand served on the Second Circuit until 1951, nearly three decades, during which he wrote landmark opinions in numerous areas, including torts, contracts, commercial law, and the First Amendment.[65]

The other judicial appointment made by Coolidge with special impact was his nomination of Harlan Fiske Stone to the Supreme Court. The appointment was significant not just because of the influence Stone would wield for decades as an associate justice and later as chief justice, but also because he was the first Supreme Court nominee to testify before the Senate Judiciary Committee. When Stone's nomination to the Court was first made, it met stiff resistance from Montana's two senators. Stone had agreed, based on a Justice Department investigation, to ask a federal grand jury to indict one of Montana's senators, Burton Wheeler, for practicing law before a government agency while a public official and for defrauding the U.S. government. The case was pending at the time of his nomination to the Court, and Senator Wash, the other senator from Montana, was on the Judiciary Committee. Immediately after Coolidge nominated Stone, Walsh asked Coolidge to recommit the nomination, a highly unusual request given that the nomination had been made in the middle of the legislative session. After Coolidge resubmitted the nomination, Senator Walsh requested Stone's appearance before the Judiciary Committee to explain why the Justice Department indicted Wheeler. Stone appeared before the Committee and adeptly handled Walsh's intensive questioning. After his appearance, Senator Walsh conceded, "The very excellent impression I formed of him ... before the time, was confirmed by his demeanor before the Committee."[66] On the floor, Walsh voted against Stone's nomination, but the Senate overwhelmingly confirmed him.[67]

Coolidge's choice to replace Stone as attorney general was less politically astute than his choice of Stone to replace Daughtery. He chose Charles Beecher Warren. Before the Senate, Warren's nomination quickly fell apart. Coolidge had failed to consult Senate leaders beforehand, and Warren had been a longtime representative of the Sugar Trust, which was under indictment at the time for violating antitrust laws. Warren embodied the corporate misbehavior that many politicians wanted the administration to prosecute.[68] Nonetheless, Coolidge expected confirmation since there was a Republican majority in the Senate and expanding Senate deference to presidents on cabinet appointments. The Senate Judiciary Committee reported the nomination favorably to the Senate floor, but Republican leaders misread the Senate's mood. Warren was roundly criticized for his conflicts of interest. The Senate's initial vote was a tie, but by the time Vice President Dawes awoke from a nap and returned to the Senate to break it, he was too late, since Democratic senator Lee Overman had changed his mind and the final vote was 41–39 against the nomination.[69] It was the first time in the twentieth century that the Senate rejected a cabinet nomination and the first time since 1868 the Senate had rejected a nominee for attorney general. Both decisions angered Coolidge. Hoping that he could get Overman's vote back, Coolidge miscalculated again. He renominated Warren. He delivered a statement to the Senate expressing his hope "that the unbroken practice of three generations of permitting the President to choose his own Cabinet will not now be changed, and that the opposition to Mr. Warren, upon further consideration, will be withdrawn in order that the country may have the benefit of his excellent qualities and the President may be unhampered in choosing his own method of executing the laws."[70] In the Senate's second debate over Warren's nomination, the sole focus was on the Senate's authority. Warren lost by a larger margin this time, and the Senate established an important precedent upholding its independent judgment on cabinet nominations. Coolidge got the message. He next nominated Vermont's attorney general John Garibaldi Sargent, whom the Senate confirmed unanimously.

Bolstering Unilateral Exercises of the Pardon and Veto Powers

Coolidge's strong exercises of his veto and pardon authorities belie his image as Silent Cal. The statistics alone underscore how much he embraced these powers: He issued 1,545 pardons, the second most pardons (after Wilson) issued by a president before Franklin Roosevelt; and he cast fifty vetoes, the fourth largest number cast by any president before Franklin Roosevelt and the most cast by any president, except for Teddy Roosevelt, from 1900 to 1933.

The Constitution grants the president the explicit authority to grant pardons or commute sentences for federal offenses.[71] The framers vested presidents with this authority to enable the chief executive to be merciful and to mete out justice. The pardon power enables presidents to correct the mistakes made by prosecutors within the executive branch and to check injustices arising from the enforcement of federal criminal law. Presidents generally construed this power as subject only to their discretion and were careful not to overuse it.[72]

Coolidge took seriously his responsibility as the only federal official with the authority to grant reprieves or pardons for federal crimes. He made his most notable pardons shortly after becoming president when he pardoned thirty-one people who had been convicted and imprisoned for having criticizing the Wilson administration's involvement in World War I.[73] Harding had provoked criticism when he commuted the sentence of Eugene Debs, a controversial leader of the Socialist Party who had been imprisoned for urging people not to comply with the draft. No less controversial, Coolidge's pardons demonstrated his resolve to be his own man and were unusual because they had been issued before they were requested and against the attorney general's advice.[74]

Some of Coolidge's most forceful statements made about the scope of presidential authority and the relationship among the branches were made, however, in the course of exercising his veto authority. He did not narrowly construe the veto power as Taft did. Instead, he believed his veto authority made him an equal partner in the lawmaking process. He believed, like Jackson and Tyler, that the veto could be exercised against laws that he considered to be bad policy or unconstitutional. It was especially important to Coolidge as a means to curb congressional overreaching and protect presidential prerogatives. For example, in his veto message on the Bonus Bill, Coolidge complained that the cost of the bill was too high for the federal government to bear. According to his figures, the bill would cost the nation over $2 billion within a twenty-year period. Coolidge explained that he had vetoed the exorbitant government expenditure because "[t]he prosperity of the Nation, which is the prosperity of the people, rests primarily on reducing the existing tax burden. No other action would so encourage business."[75] The House and Senate each soon voted to override the veto.[76]

In another contest of wills with Congress, the Supreme Court agreed with Coolidge. This dispute arose over Coolidge's decision to use the controversial practice of a "pocket veto"—allowing a bill to expire without signing it after Congress has adjourned. In Article I, the Constitution provides that "[i]f any bill shall not be returned by the President within ten days (Sundays excepted) after it shall have been presented to him [for signature or veto,] the Same shall be a Law, in like Manner as if he had signed it, unless the Congress by their Adjournment prevent its Return, in which case it shall not be a Law."[77] Though begun by Madison, the practice had been strongly condemned as unconstitutional by Whigs when Jackson used it. In 1926, Congress passed a law allowing American Indians in the state of Washington to bring claims based on the loss of their tribal lands to the Court of Claims. On June 26, 1926, Congress sent the bill to Coolidge, but ten days later Coolidge had not returned the bill to Congress with either his signature or a veto. Several Indian tribes filed a lawsuit in the Court of Claims against Coolidge, lost, and appealed the Court of Claims decision to the Supreme Court. By the time the case was argued Hoover was president, but the Court agreed unanimously with Coolidge's position in what became known as the Pocket Veto Case.[78] The Court recognized the practice was long-standing and determined that adjournment is any recess taken by Congress that "'prevents' the President from returning the bill to the House in which it originated within the time allowed." In reaching its conclusion, the Court relied in part on a memorandum prepared by the attorney general "showing the results of an exhaustive research of governmental archives for the purpose of disclosing the practical construction placed upon the constitutional provision here involved in reference to so-called 'pocket vetoes.'"[79] The Court reasoned that a broad construction of "adjournment" in Article I was necessary to bar Congress from scheduling recesses to shorten the amount of time a president had to consider a bill's merits.

Two other vetoes were equally controversial. Each was cast against a different version of the McNary-Haugen Bill, which Congress twice passed. The bills provided support for farm prices by establishing the Federal Farm Board, whose purpose was to buy certain surplus crops for resale abroad, either storing them until prices rose on the world market or dumping them at a loss. In the veto message accompanying his veto of the first version of the law on February 25, 1927, Coolidge expressed concern that it would not benefit all farmers as a whole and would injure the public welfare. Coolidge explained that "government pricing, once started, has alike no justice and no end. It is an economic folly from which this country has every right to be spared." He emphasized that "as a direct tax on certain vital necessaries of life [the bill] represents the most vicious form of taxation," because it served the special interests of some farmers at the expense of others.[80] This veto message was the first presidential statement against price fixing as a federal policy.

Although Congress sustained Coolidge's first veto of the McNary-Haugen Bill, Congress enacted the same law a year later, so it came back a second time to Coolidge. Again, he vetoed it. In his veto message of May 23, 1928, Coolidge incorporated a twenty-three-page opinion of the attorney general, issued the day before and explaining Attorney General Sargent's conclusions that Congress's authority to regulate interstate commerce did not include the "power to fix the prices at which merchandise may be bought and sold" and the delegation of authority to the Farm Board to set prices was unconstitutional because it was "legislative in character" rather than a directive with detailed "rule of law laid down for their guidance and observance."[81] In his veto message, Coolidge added that "the only sound basis for further Federal Government action on behalf of agriculture would be to encourage its adequate organization to assist in building up marketing agencies and facilities in the control of the farmers themselves. . . . Such a program [is] in accordance with the American tradition and the American ideal of reliance on and maintenance of private initiative and individual responsibility, and the duty of the Government is discharged when it has provided conditions under which the individual can achieve success."[82] The Senate failed to override the veto, and Coolidge's stand against government subsidies became a model for conservative constitutionalists to follow.

Implementing the Commerce Clause

When Coolidge became president, the Commerce Clause, which empowered Congress to regulate interstate commerce, had long been the source of most congressional enactments, particularly expansions in federal programs. In line with his views on property rights and the need for smaller, less intrusive federal programs, as well as the views of many scholars of the era,[83] Coolidge believed that the national government lacked the authority to regulate such things as farm prices and workers' hours and wages. He believed that Congress's power to regulate interstate commerce should not be used as a police power to regulate the morals of the citizenry or to regulate local, intrastate manufacturing. For example, in his Fourth Annual Message, he requested "reducing, rather than expanding, government bureaus which seek to regulate and control the business activities of people."[84]

There were, however, three significant exceptions to Coolidge's resistance to expanding federal authority pursuant to the Commerce Clause. Each was historic.

First, beginning with his First Annual Message,[85] Coolidge systematically set out to improve national defense through the development of a national air force. He eventually persuaded Congress to study the idea, to subsidize airmail service and experiments in designing and constructing aircraft, and to establish a Bureau of Civil Aviation in the Commerce Department.[86] In 1926, Congress enacted the Air Commerce Act,[87] which placed civil aviation under the Commerce Department's direction and approved the nation's first two commercial air routes.[88]

Second, Coolidge signed into law the nation's first federal regulation of radio broadcasting. Initially, commercial broadcasting was a small part of the industry, and the stations broadcasting often aired on overlapping frequencies. The industry lobbied the federal government for support, but it got none until Coolidge became president. As he declared, "This important public function has drafted into such chaos as seems likely, if not remedied, to destroy its great value."[89] Coolidge agreed with Commerce Secretary Hoover that Congress should establish a special board to study the problem within his department.

Congress agreed, and Coolidge signed the Radio Act into law in 1927.[90] It declared the airwaves public property and therefore subject to federal control pursuant to Congress's Commerce Clause power. It also established a five-person panel, the Federal Radio Commission, within the Commerce Department, to issue broadcast licenses and assign frequencies. The commission adopted policies that bolstered the power of a few large corporations to establish "a well-rounded program including a variety of musical options, news, weather, and family programming." Over the next few decades, the Radio Act erected a foundation for modern broadcast regulation.

A third important law signed by Coolidge involved federal disaster relief. Two terrible floods in 1927—one in the Midwest and the other in New England—challenged Coolidge's general refusal to expand federal relief programs. Indeed, the Mississippi flood was the worst natural disaster in American history until Hurricane Katrina hit the Gulf Coast in 2005. Nonetheless, Coolidge was highly skeptical of disaster relief. He believed that it was generally the responsibility of local or state government and that it could disrupt the federal budget. He made his reservations explicit in his Fourth Annual Message, in which he (begrudgingly) asked Congress to provide for federal flood control projects along the Mississippi River.[91] Congress began to consider legislation increasing flood control relief beyond what Coolidge requested. At each step in its consideration of flood relief, Coolidge opposed what Congress was doing. Congress ignored Coolidge, who complained about being excluded from the drafting or reconciliation. In April 1927, he told an aide that the bill approved by the Senate was "the most radical and dangerous bill that has had the countenance of the Congress since I have been president."[92] After the House approved a different bill, Coolidge summoned the congressional leaders together to forge a compromise—a far cry from Cleveland's refusal to get involved at all in the lawmaking process. Eventually congressional leaders forged a compromise that satisfied even Coolidge. The final bill authorized about $500 million in assistance and reaffirmed the responsibility of the Army Corps of Engineers for administering federal flood control assistance. Coolidge could have objected that the bill cost too much, but the political support for the bill was widespread. He could also have questioned whether the federal government possessed the authority, particularly since he could have followed the example set by Cleveland's veto of the relief bill for Texas drought victims. Ultimately, he did none of these things and instead signed two bills providing the largest expenditures for disaster relief until the federal response to Hurricane Katrina.[93]

Leading in Foreign Affairs

When he became president, Coolidge had no interest in foreign affairs. Accordingly, he initially left decisions on foreign affairs to the discretion of his secretary of state, Charles Evans Hughes; however, he increasingly assumed a leadership role in the field. He ultimately supported two foreign policy initiatives, which influenced the balance of power between the president and the Senate over treaty ratifications.

The first involved the World Court. President Harding had opposed joining the League of Nations but supported joining its judicial arm, the World Court. He agreed with other prominent Republicans that impartial judges would provide a more stable and fair guarantee of international peace than partisan, self-interested diplomats. The protocol for the United States to join the World Court was pending before the Senate when Harding died.

Initially, Coolidge told Theodore Roosevelt Jr., "[M]y predecessor submitted [the protocol] to the Senate. No action is called, therefore, by me as an Executive."[94] The matter lingered in the Senate throughout the 1924 campaign. By the election, Coolidge found it impossible to resist the mounting pressure to do more to secure the agreement. Hence, in his Second Annual Message, delivered in December 1924, he addressed the claim that subjecting the United States to the World Court's jurisdiction would be unconstitutional because it would place the government of the United States under the control of an authority that the Constitution did not recognize. Coolidge reassured the nation that "our country shall not be bound by advisory opinions which may be rendered by the Court upon questions which we have not voluntarily submitted for its judgment."[95] Just before Coolidge's inauguration, the House expressed its support for American membership in the Court by a vote of 303–28, with one hundred members abstaining.[96] The vote was symbolic, since the House had no formal role in treaty ratifications. Although more than a few House members questioned the constitutionality of the House's vote, the House Committee on Foreign Affairs issued a report citing extensive historical and legal support for the House's involvement. Besides citing to many framers who acknowledged the House's duty to approve laws to carry out the obligations of treaties, the report claimed further support in the House's explicit powers (specifically to make appropriations, to regulate foreign commerce, and to alter domestic law "to carry treaties into effect"); its unique capacity "to express the preferences of the people more adequately than any other," which gave it "not only a right but a duty to express itself upon certain international policies"; and numerous precedents upholding the power of the House to take action on treaties "by legislation rather than by treaties," including the March 1, 1845, joint resolution approved by Tyler that the Republic of Texas "may be erected into a new State in order that the same may be admitted into the Union."[97] Although one hundred representatives abstained from the final vote, they never explained why. Their silence did nothing to weaken the House's case for future involvement in the sanctioning of international agreements besides treaties.

Coolidge's problem was that senators opposing the protocol had devised a strategy for stopping it: They drafted several amendments designed to reduce the protocol's appeal both domestically and abroad. Some senators balked at the actions of their colleagues to alter the treaties negotiated by the president; they insisted the president alone had the authority to negotiate and therefore determine the terms of a treaty. Most other senators disagreed. They insisted that, in giving their "Advice and Consent" on treaties, as explicitly authorized in Article II, they could, among other things, attach conditions or make alterations to treaties—that these latter actions constituted their advice on treaties and that their consent was predicated on the acceptance of this advice. Coolidge could have countered, but did not, that "Advice and Consent" no more authorized the Senate to change a treaty than the same language empowered the Senate to substitute a different nominee for the president's. By the time the protocol came before the Senate for debate, President Coolidge had publicly endorsed all the conditions, including the fifth, which provided that "we are not to be bound by advisory opinions without our consent." In effect, Coolidge respected the fact that under the Constitution the Senate had the final say. He took no action and made no public comments as the Senate debated the protocol. Cloture was barely invoked, and the Senate approved the protocol with the five conditions, 76–17,[98] though the fifth had been modified to require that no advisory opinion could be rendered without giving interested nations advance notice and a chance to require a public hearing on the question.

After the Senate vote, it was apparent that debating the protocol was meaningless. When a conference of signatories gathered in Geneva to consider the reservations in September 1926, Coolidge directed his representatives not to press the other signatories to support its conditions. Though the signatories agreed to four of the conditions, they rejected the fifth. They offered to negotiate with the United States, but Coolidge rejected the offer. "I do not believe," he said, "the Senate would take favorable action on any such proposal, and unless the requirements of the Senate resolution are met, I can see no prospect of this country adhering to the Court."[99] The Senate took no further action, and the protocol died. The end results were that the United States failed to join the World Court under Coolidge and the defeat of the protocol reinforced the Senate's authority over treaty ratifications.

Coolidge had more success in securing the ratification and international support for the Kellogg-Briand Pact. This was an international agreement drafted by then-Secretary of State Kellogg and his French counterpart to outlaw war as a means to settle international conflicts. Initially, Coolidge had been ambivalent about the pact, but he warmed to it as public pressure mounted in its favor during the presidential campaign of 1928. On August 15, 1924, he told a crowd that the agreement "holds a greater hope for peaceful relations than was ever before given to the world. If those who are involved in it, having started it will finish it, its provisions will prove one of the greatest blessings ever bestowed upon humanity." For a man not prone to hyperbole and for a lame duck, the shift in his tone and position were striking. To make sure everyone got the message, he made the ratification of the agreement an important part of his last annual message, in which he referred to the pact as "[o]ne of the most important treaties ever laid before the Senate of the United States." In making the case for ratification, he reassured Congress that the agreement "does not supersede our inalienable sovereign right and duty of national defense or undertake to commit us before the event to any mode of action which the Congress might decide to be wise if ever the treaty should be broken. But it is a new standard in the world around which can rally the informed and enlightened opinion of nations to prevent their governments from being forced into hostile action by the temporary outbreak of international animosities."[100] As Coolidge's term wound down, Secretary of State Frank Kellogg and Vice President Dawes lobbied senators to ratify the treaty. Kellogg and Dawes enlisted Senator Borah to convince senators to accept an explanatory report of the Foreign Relations Committee that would have specifically denied being a statement of reservations and instead summarized the Senate's feelings regarding the treaty. After agreeing to the compromise, the Senate ratified the treaty 85–1, with no reservations.[101] Whereas Coolidge had chosen to sign the protocol endorsing the World Court with no fanfare, he signed the Kellogg-Briand Pact with both his cabinet and leading senators in attendance. The ratification of the treaty was another dramatic exercise and consolidation of the Senate's treaty power, while Coolidge demonstrated that a president or his advisers may negotiate with senators over ratification. For his work on the pact, Kellogg received the Nobel Peace Prize in 1933 and thus became the second official within the Coolidge administration to win the prestigious prize.

Even though forty-seven countries joined the pact after its ratification, it proved meaningless. It allowed for no sanctions and had the unforeseen effect of giving German leaders a basis for mobilizing popular discontent with the efforts of other European nations to maintain dominance over Germany and for helping to create a path by which Germany was able to drag Europe and the United States into World War II.

ALTHOUGH HE HAD been remarkably adept at preserving the constitutional (and political) order he had inherited from Harding, Coolidge's presidency ended as it began—in virtual silence. By the time he left office, the presidency had lost luster for him. He had taken repeated beatings in fighting with Congress and was severely depressed after his son Cal had died during the 1924 presidential election.[102] Coolidge told his father that "the power and glory of the Presidency went with [Cal]."[103] His lack of interest in running for another term—and in Hoover as a successor—ensured the 1928 presidential election had little bearing on his legacy.

After Hoover's inauguration, Coolidge withdrew almost entirely from politics. When Hoover ran for reelection in 1932, Coolidge did little to help him. He was largely forgotten when he died two months before Franklin Roosevelt's inauguration, as the nation waited anxiously for a solution to the Great Depression.

13

Jimmy Carter, 1977–1981

MANY PEOPLE MIGHT dispute the claim that Jimmy Carter is a forgotten president. Some readers lived through his presidency and voted for or against him. Others have probably been invested in supporting or criticizing his performance in office. Many others might question his inclusion because, as the appendix shows, he rates near the middle rather than the bottom of public familiarity with his presidency.

Nonetheless, I include Carter for several reasons. First, most Americans alive today were not born until after Carter's presidency. If folks are familiar with Carter's presidency, it is largely on the same basis on which they are familiar with the presidency of any of the other men in this book—because of what they have read or heard about it from others. Second, my inclusion of Carter is largely predictive, that is, I expect in time that he may likely be forgotten because of the attributes he shares with many other presidents included in this book. Indeed, most Americans actually know little about Carter except perhaps for his activities as an ex-president or his crushing defeat by Ronald Reagan in the 1980 presidential election (the worst electoral defeat of an incumbent president in the twentieth century).[1] People have thus already largely forgotten, or dismissed, Carter's distinctions in office—as the first Evangelical, the first person from the Deep South, and the first governor since Franklin Roosevelt to be elected president, the only Democratic president from 1969 until 1993, and the only president to have served a full term without the opportunity to make a nomination to the Supreme Court. Carter, like Taft, has had his postpresidential activities outshine his activities as president. His distinction as the only former president to win the Nobel Peace Prize has merely made his presidency seem less significant.

The propriety of including Carter became especially evident to me in 2011. On August 2, 2011, President Obama had reached a last-minute deal with Congress to avert a default on the federal government's debt. In the days leading up to the deal, news reports described Obama as the first president to confront such a crisis and speculated about the "unprecedented" constitutional options he should use if he had to act alone to avoid the first default on the national debt. The reports were wrong: Obama was not the first president to face this predicament or to consider his authority under the circumstances. No one mentioned an earlier president who had faced but averted the same crisis twice—Jimmy Carter.

While Carter's involvement in averting a debt crisis is but one of many ways we have overlooked his constitutional impact, it surrounds us. In many areas of constitutional law, including affirmative action and the First Amendment, we live in a world that Carter helped to shape, and he influenced the balance of power over international agreements and appointments and disciplining of lower-court judges. Carter had a view of presidential power closer to that of either Teddy or Franklin Roosevelt than to Taft's or Cleveland's in his first term; Carter is recognizably a modern president who construed—and exercised—the inherent powers of the presidency as broadly as possible. Thus, his presidency shows how the office's capacity for efficiency and energy works to its advantages in extended conflicts with Congress, regardless of a president's (un)popularity. Last but not least, Carter demonstrated the importance of constitutional clarity and coherence to the presidency. He promised more widespread governmental reform than perhaps any president since Franklin Roosevelt, but without a coherent, compelling constitutional vision to tie his reforms together, he lost control over his presidency's narrative and allowed others to define his constitutional legacy. While this factor may not have had much if anything to do with his failure to be reelected, it is not insignificant and illuminates how incoherence—the failure to control or define one's narrative—makes it easier for a president's foes to define, distort, or bury his constitutional legacy.

Mishandling the Presidential Transition

The Constitution says nothing about presidential transitions, leaving them to be worked out informally among national leaders and subject to whatever support Congress chooses to make. Before the Twentieth Amendment's ratification in 1933, presidents-elect had four months to prepare their administrations before inauguration, while presidents-elect after its ratification[2] have had roughly two months to organize their administrations by Inauguration Day. When Carter was elected, there were no laws directing how he should handle the two months of transition and thus it was entirely up to him to develop a plan of action for this period.

The choices Carter made regarding his transition undermined his administration's effectiveness. First, he never developed plans for an effective transition. Before Election Day, he had not assembled a transition team or developed a plan for his White House's organization, agenda, and appointments of key staff and cabinet officials. Immediately after Election Day, Carter arranged a loose assortment of advisers to assist his transition. But he put no one in charge of staffing the new administration, developing its agenda, and devising a strategy for achieving his agenda. These oversights were partly the result of Carter's reluctance to delegate, a reluctance that persisted through his entire presidency. Making matters worse, Carter ordered complicated, time-consuming procedures to review most matters while still reviewing almost everything himself. Organizing the staffing of the administration went slowly because Carter decided that there had to be at least one minority candidate and one female candidate for every cabinet-level post. The transition was further impeded because Carter's closest advisers differed over which of them had final say over which matters. Nearly two weeks after Election Day, Carter placed Hamilton Jordan in charge of presidential appointments. Even though one key adviser suggested Carter should have his White House staff in place by Thanksgiving and his cabinet secretaries announced by Christmas, Carter did neither. He did not complete his cabinet until early January 1977, making him the slowest newly elected president to do so since Eisenhower in 1952.[3]

When Carter settled on his key appointments, they did not appear much different than they would have without his cumbersome review procedures: While most of his cabinet secretaries came from outside his personal network, many key advisers did not, and only a few high-ranking appointees had significant experience with the operations of their departments or units or with working with Congress.[4] Carter's choices of cabinet secretaries posed problems, because he chose them largely because of their management experience, and they had no personal loyalty to Carter. The ensuing conflicts between Carter and most of his cabinet were inevitable, undermined his administration's efficiency, and "isolated him from the diversity of viewpoints that might have better informed his leadership and furnished the White House with a broader perspective."[5]

Carter further hindered his transition by deciding to be his own chief of staff. The Constitution is silent on the White House's organization, leaving it to the discretion of each president (with funding by Congress). Carter's initial plan was to implement a "spokes-in-the-wheel" system under which cabinet secretaries and the White House staff would have direct access to him.[6]

The scheme proved disastrous. For most of his presidency, Carter was inundated with paperwork because no one was in charge of the paper flow in the White House. Nor did Carter devise a plan for implementing his directives. Members of Congress implored him to proceed incrementally and establish legislative priorities before he took action, but to no avail. Early in his presidency, he explained, "Everybody has warned me not to take on too many projects so early in the administration, but it's almost impossible for me to delay something that I see needs to be done."[7] Because of his resolve to be his own chief of staff and to set numerous priorities at the outset of his presidency, he appeared less in public than other post–World War II presidents had in their first ten weeks in office.

Yet another transition decision that undermined the effectiveness of his administration was his decision "to govern without being beholden to established political leaders."[8] Carter was the first Democratic president in nearly a decade but was a political outsider. He was not steeped in the culture of the nation's capital and was not close to or familiar with many established leaders of his party. He believed that the American people wanted a president determined to transcend the petty partisanship that culminated in Watergate and reduced public confidence in the lawmaking process. He thus ignored the counsel of Washington insiders and saw no middle ground between leading and being led by Congress, a choice the Constitution leaves to each president. His decision to push Congress—and to bypass it when it refused to do what he wanted—increasingly alienated congressional leaders.[9]

Several examples illustrate Carter's governance problems and their consequences. The first was in the realm of foreign affairs. From the outset of his administration, he insisted on being his own secretary of state, but he left unclear which other officials were empowered to speak for his administration. This approach produced confusion abroad as officials within his administration sent conflicting messages about the administration's priorities and led to constant infighting among the officials responsible for foreign affairs matters, particularly between Secretary of State Cyrus Vance and National Security Adviser Zbigniew Brzezinski, to whom Carter increasingly turned for advice. When Carter did not consult Vance on his plan to send American forces secretly to free American hostages in Iran, Vance embarrassed Carter by resigning in protest.

The second example of the deleterious effects of Carter's poor transition planning involved the firing of the U.S. attorney in Philadelphia, David Marston. In order to make appointments, Carter needed vacancies, but he had no plan for ensuring that the needed vacancies arose. He and his staff expected that Republicans appointed by Presidents Nixon and Ford to executive offices requiring Senate confirmation, such as U.S. attorney positions within the Justice Department, would follow the examples of their predecessors since the 1930s and tender their resignations. Though most U.S. attorneys offered to resign, Marston, a Ford appointee, did not. Echoing the claims of officials under the Tenure in Office Act, Marston maintained he was entitled to complete the term of office to which the Senate had confirmed him. Carter and Attorney General Griffin Bell disagreed and instead dismissed Marston. The problem was timing: They did not dismiss Marston until nearly ten months after Carter's inauguration and only after Democratic representative Joshua Ellsberg of Philadelphia had pushed Carter to replace Marston. Had Carter or Bell checked before firing Marston, they would have discovered that Marston was investigating Ellsberg, but neither did. Firing Marston undermined Carter's oft-stated commitment to high ethical standards in government.[10]

The third area in which Carter's transition faltered involved Vice President Walter Mondale. Besides making the vice president the presiding officer of the Senate and empowering him to break tie votes in the Senate, the Constitution is silent about a vice president's duties. For most of American history, presidents ignored their vice presidents and gave them few responsibilities. As part of his governmental reforms, Carter promised to give Mondale unprecedented authority. Though he left Mondale out of the transition, Carter included Mondale within his inner circle and designated him as one of four administration officials to be given a daily national security briefing. Throughout Carter's presidency, Mondale gave Carter candid advice and served as a liberal counterpoint to Carter's and his other close advisers' more conservative perspectives. Perhaps more importantly, Mondale assumed a significant role in overseeing the implementation of presidential initiatives. Unlike other vice presidents, Mondale was not a passive leader in the Senate. Though he sometimes privately disagreed with Carter, he consistently used his influence within the Senate and with liberal interest groups to advance Carter's initiatives. Although he became a model followed by subsequent presidents who have delegated substantial responsibilities to their vice presidents, many people, both inside and outside of the administration, did not approve of Mondale's influence or stature and took their displeasure out on Carter.

A final consequence of Carter's poor planning is that tensions within the cabinet forced Carter to use his removal powers to radically reorganize it. With his popularity sinking, Carter decided to reenergize his administration. On July 15, 1979, he delivered a major speech designed to remind the American people of his leadership and rally public support for his energy initiatives.[11]

Whatever good the speech did Carter, he undid it two days later when he asked more than thirty officials, including his entire cabinet, to submit "pro forma resignations" so he could decide which people to retain.[12] The next day, he announced that he had accepted the resignations of five cabinet officers.[13] It was the most significant cabinet shake-up in the twentieth century. While no one questioned Carter's authority to reorganize his cabinet, his actions reinforced the growing sense that his administration was falling apart. Carter responded to the fallout by appointing his first chief of staff, but his choice of Hamilton Jordan backfired. Jordan alienated senior administration personnel when he asked them to complete a questionnaire requesting them "to grade their own senior subordinates on their work habits, interpersonal relations, and loyalty to the White House. The questionnaire was not only insulting in tone but also made it seem that another bloodletting—this time reaching into middle management—was imminent and that allegiance to the administration would be at least as important as competence in deciding who was fired."[14] Carter was unable to undo the political damage that he had done to his own administration.

Perhaps the most significant consequence of Carter's poor transition planning is that subsequent presidents have uniformly rejected Carter's example. As soon as he won the Republican presidential nomination, Ronald Reagan organized a special unit that worked throughout the general election and afterward to get his administration ready for Inauguration Day. While Bill Clinton did not organize a transition team until he won the 1992 general election, he had one in place almost immediately afterward; and it worked tirelessly to prepare Clinton and his team for the day they assumed power. President Obama emulated Reagan by opting to have his transition planning begun before he won the general election. Carter's missteps symbolized the necessity for a president to be proactive, rather than to be passive, in transition planning.

Improving Presidential Administration

In spite of his poor transition planning, Carter generally improved presidential administration. Indeed, one of his first initiatives was to seek congressional support for reorganizing his administration. Initially, Democratic congressional leaders opposed the plan because they did not want to lose their traditional role in overseeing administrative organization. But Carter believed that the president knew best how to increase the administration's efficiency, and he was determined to reduce congressional interference with the administration's internal affairs. After strong lobbying from Carter, Congress approved the plan, the first significant congressional reorganization of the executive branch since Franklin Roosevelt's administration.

Shortly after the cabinet overhaul, Carter and Jordan appointed Alonzo McDonald, an expert on management, to reappraise the administration's organization. Based on his recommendations,[15] the White House achieved an unprecedented degree of centralized control over the administrative order.[16]

Moreover, Carter issued 320 executive orders, more than George W. Bush dispensed in eight years and more than Reagan or Clinton each issued in his first term. Many of Carter's orders focused on improving White House and executive branch efficiency.[17] On Carter's recommendation, Congress enacted the Paperwork Reduction Act, which established the Office of Information and Regulatory Affairs (OIRA) in the Office of Management and Budget and required its director to be nominated by the president and subject to Senate confirmation.[18] Subsequently, every president's attitudes about regulation are evident in his guidelines for OIRA to follow in reviewing proposed regulations.

Carter's persistent efforts to push Congress to reform government strained his working relationship with Democratic leaders in Congress. Although Carter raised the debt ceiling nine times, he twice encountered significant resistance, reflecting his strained relations with Congress—and his own party. First, in 1977, Congress approved an increase only days before the default deadline and four days after the government had begun operating on emergency funds.[19] Two years later, legislation to raise the debt ceiling was tied to a balanced budget plan that failed. Just before the deadline, the increase was approved only after the Treasury Department had implemented a comprehensive scheme to postpone certain payments to avoid default.[20] This time, with Carter's popularity collapsing but the next cycle of elections approaching, Democrats rallied to his defense, and default was avoided by a nearly straight party-line vote. The near defaults reflected Carter's tense relations with Congress, and the tensions, not the near misses, became the story.

Influencing Federal Judicial Selection

Carter had significant impact on judicial selection in several ways. The first involved the Supreme Court. The fact that he had no Supreme Court appointments made it easier for President Reagan to build directly upon the four appointments made by Nixon to thwart Warren Court decisions expanding minority and criminal defendants' rights at the expense of state sovereignty.

An obvious target for Reagan was the Supreme Court's 1973 decision in *Roe v. Wade*.[21] Initially, there was no Republican backlash to the opinion. Indeed, the initial, public response to *Roe* was largely silence. When, for instance, the Senate held confirmation hearings on President Ford's nomination of John Paul Stevens to replace the retiring William O. Douglas, not a single senator asked Stevens about *Roe*. Yet, by the time Reagan was campaigning for the presidency, the Republican platform had called for overruling *Roe*; and as president, Reagan made *Roe* a principal example of the Court's liberalism and pledged to appoint justices who would overturn *Roe*, among other cases. The question is what had happened in the meantime.

The answer is Carter. Carter opposed abortion himself and did not publicly defend *Roe*. Throughout his presidency, he consistently opposed federal funding for abortions. At the same time, he was determined to diversify and improve the quality of the federal judiciary, which led him to put more people on the bench who were actually supportive of *Roe*. When Reagan condemned this practice and intensified his criticism of *Roe*, Carter made no response. The silence was deafening. It left *Roe* largely undefended (except by some Democratic congressional leaders) in public debates during the 1980 presidential election. Reagan largely occupied the void and co-opted some of Carter's base, which had voted for him in 1976 because of his Evangelical Christian background. Carter was left in the awkward position of having his reelection depend on people who supported *Roe* but were unhappy with Carter because of his failure to vigorously support it. His pro-life convictions opened the door for the Republican Party to become the anti-*Roe* party, and the Democratic Party, partly by default, became the party of *Roe*.

The ensuing dynamic was ironic since the Court had decided *Roe* 7–2, with four members of the majority appointed by Republican presidents. This fact was not lost on Reagan's advisers, who understood that two of the four Republicans in the *Roe* majority (Justices William Brennan and Lewis Powell) were Democrats appointed by Republican presidents. Reagan was convinced that more care had to be taken to ensure that future justices would hew closely to the party line. Carter's reelection defeat coincided with a loss of Democratic control of the Senate that made it easier for Reagan's first three Court nominations to be confirmed by Republicans who wanted them to overturn *Roe*.

Meanwhile, Carter's clashes with the Senate over his lower-court appointments had several consequences. The first involved senatorial courtesy. In fact,

Carter is only one of two presidents who at the outset of their presidencies directly challenged senatorial courtesy on judicial appointments, though he had no more success than the first president who tried—Herbert Hoover.[22] On entering office, Hoover had declared that he intended to end the practice of awarding judicial appointments based on senatorial courtesy and instead vowed to raise the standards and requisite qualifications for lower-court appointments. He met with swift opposition from Republican senators who did not want to relinquish their chance to dispense favors to important constituents. Without their support, Hoover had little chance for the Senate to confirm his judicial nominations, since liberal and Progressive senators were disposed to oppose his nominations. Things got worse for Hoover, as the resistance to his reforms and judicial nominations intensified over time. He eventually abandoned his objectives.

As a candidate and shortly after becoming president, Carter and Attorney General Bell proposed radical reforms of judicial selection. They announced a plan for Democratic senators to use merit selection panels to assist them in recommending highly qualified, more diverse nominees for federal district and circuit court judgeships.[23] Carter's initiative met resistance from many Democratic senators, including the chair of the Senate Judiciary Committee, James Eastland. Eastland's opposition ensured that Carter's proposed legislation to create merit selection panels never made it to the floor of the Senate. In response, Carter decided to act alone, and he issued an executive order establishing his own nominating commissions for circuit court appointments.[24] He urged senators to set up nominating commissions for district court judgeships. In time, there were panels in over thirty states. Nevertheless, many senators refused to establish commissions, and their relationships with Carter degenerated over the remainder of his presidency. Carter's decision to bypass the Senate with his executive order reinforced the president's unilateral authority over judicial nominations and limited senatorial courtesy more than ever before, but the consolidation of his authority over judicial nominations alienated Senate leaders, including Ted Kennedy, who blocked Carter's national health care legislation in the Senate and later unsuccessfully challenged him for the 1980 Democratic presidential nomination.

Second, Carter's judicial appointments have become the benchmark for every subsequent president's judicial appointments. Carter appointed more women and minorities to federal judgeships than any previous president, and the percentages of his appointments of women and minorities to federal judgeships provide the benchmark by which the diversity of every subsequent president's judicial appointments has been measured ever since.[25] Moreover, 57 percent of his judicial appointees were rated "exceptionally well qualified" or "well qualified" by the American Bar Association, the highest marks for any president's judicial nominees since the ABA had begun rating judicial nominations in the 1950s.

Carter's judicial appointees provide an additional benchmark against which other presidents' choices are measured: The average age of his circuit court appointees was fifty, younger on average than those of any prior president. Subsequently, the average ages of the circuit court appointees of each of the next four presidents were increasingly lower. The pattern was no accident as each of these presidents recognized the growing importance of appointing relatively young people to the federal courts of appeal because they would be able to serve actively as the last resort for a relatively long time after the presidents who appointed them left office and would provide a deep bench from which the next president(s) of their parties could pick Supreme Court justices. Barack Obama is the only president after Carter to appoint circuit judges whose average ages have at least thus far exceeded those of Carter.

Third, Carter is often singled out as a major reason for the apparently broken state of federal judicial selection. Many conservatives blame Carter for beginning the "politicization" of judicial selection in the modern era by appointing so many judges who favored making federal courts the engines of social change.[26] They have similarly charged every subsequent Democratic president with the same objective—namely, in their view, to pack the courts with people eager to implement liberal policies and values through their decisions. Indeed, the clashes between Carter and the Senate over his appointees foreshadowed an important shift in the appointment process: The approval rates for the judicial nominees of every president since Carter have gone progressively down from a high for Carter (at 92 percent for his district and for circuit court nominees to just below 70 percent for President Obama's lower-court nominees as of the end of March of his third year in office).[27]

Fourth, Carter's judicial appointees have influenced constitutional law, two especially. One was Columbia law professor Ruth Bader Ginsburg, whom President Carter appointed to the U.S. Court of Appeals for the District of Columbia. The other was Carter's last circuit court appointee, Harvard law professor Stephen Breyer, who had been majority counsel to the Senate Judiciary Committee under Chairman Ted Kennedy. Both served as appellate court judges for more than a decade before President

Clinton elevated them to the Supreme Court, where they have been stalwart members of its liberal wing.

Misusing the Pardon Power

Presidential pardons expanded dramatically under Franklin Roosevelt whose 3,687 pardons, commutations, and rescinded convictions were the most made by a single president. Carter's 566 pardons, commutations, and rescinded convictions rank him nineteenth among presidents, though no subsequent president has exceeded his total.[28] While most presidential pardons are uncontroversial and receive little or no public attention, Carter was so politically inept in making some of them that they reinforced the perception of his incompetence in office. Given that he had no obligation to make any in the first place, his choices sometimes revealed the gaps between his values and those of most Americans.

For example, in his very first executive order, Carter boldly attempted to heal national wounds.[29] The day after his inauguration, he kept his campaign pledge to grant unconditional amnesty to an estimated 10,000 Americans who had been convicted, were under indictment, or gone abroad to avoid the draft and service in the Vietnam War. The plan backfired.[30] It angered veterans' groups, who agreed with Senator Barry Goldwater that Carter's action "[w]as the most disgraceful thing that a President has ever done."[31] Carter created more controversy when he nominated Ted Sorenson to head the CIA. Because Sorenson had registered for the draft as a conscientious objector and admitted to removing classified information while working for President Kennedy, the nomination was opposed by Republicans and Democrats who believed Carter was doing too much to appease the war's critics. They persuaded Carter to withdraw the nomination.

Similarly, in an effort to move the nation beyond Watergate, Carter commuted the criminal sentence of G. Gordon Liddy, a Nixon aide who had been criminally sentenced for participating in burglarizing the Democratic headquarters. But the pardon conflicted with his promise of raising his administration to new ethical heights.

Last, Carter is often mistakenly credited with pardoning Jefferson Davis. In fact, he signed a joint resolution restoring U.S. citizenship to Davis.[32] Though the joint resolution was not Carter's idea and passed unanimously, Carter said nothing, and there was no public reaction other than a few critical newspaper editorials. Subsequently, Carter has gotten the credit, perhaps because his failure to speak clearly allowed others to speak for him.

Taking Charge of Foreign Affairs

Foreign affairs are a rich aspect of Carter's constitutional legacy. The Constitution makes the president uniquely responsible—and accountable—for representing the nation abroad, negotiating international agreements on behalf of the United States, handling international crises, and protecting American interests threatened abroad. Thus, for anything that went right—or wrong— in foreign affairs, Carter got credit or blame. Since Carter was determined to be active in this realm, he gave the American people plenty to evaluate.

First, his failure to make clear divisions of authority among his foreign policy advisers bears further scrutiny. Its ramifications were evident in his administration's response to the fall of the shah in Iran, including whether to give the shah asylum, to support the new regime, to negotiate with the forces taking Americans hostage, or to use military force to free the hostages.

Second, when the Soviet Union invaded Afghanistan, Carter responded with several initiatives to punish the Soviets. Perhaps the most controversial was his decision, over the objections of his staff, to boycott the Olympics, which were scheduled for later that year in the Soviet Union.[33] The problem was that he had no direct authority to do this and provoked a long fight with American athletes that the White House eventually won "after threatening legal action against them and the United States Olympic Committee."[34] The tactic largely backfired as numerous commentators and athletes criticized Carter for not understanding the limitations of his own authority and for politicizing the games.

Third, Carter's unilateral actions to establish trade with Communist-led China strained relationships with congressional leaders and raised serious questions about the scope of his authority to unilaterally withdraw a treaty. Acting unilaterally, Carter announced his plan to grant full diplomatic status to the People's Republic of China.[35] As a step in that direction, he unilaterally withdrew the Sino-American Mutual Defense Treaty,[36] which had been signed between the United States and the Republic of China and been ratified by the Senate. The Constitution mentions only the prerequisites for treaty ratification but says nothing about treaty withdrawal. Carter inferred from this silence the unique authority to withdraw treaties from his authorities (based on both the design of the Constitution and long-standing historical practices) to recognize foreign powers and to be the nation's sole representative in international affairs and negotiating treaties.[37] Nonetheless, congressional leaders were angry that Carter had not consulted with them. Senator Goldwater argued that the Senate's explicit authority to ratify treaties implicitly authorized it—not the president—to withdraw a treaty. He persuaded several colleagues to join him in filing a lawsuit challenging Carter's unilateral rescission of the treaty.[38] While Carter claimed ample historical support for his actions, he asked Congress to approve legislation normalizing trade relations with China.[39]

Goldwater's legal challenge reached the Supreme Court. Carter's solicitor general urged the Court to dismiss the lawsuit on the ground that its claims were nonjusticiable, that is, they raised questions that the Constitution clearly vested within the final, nonreviewable discretion of the political branches.[40] Although a majority of the Court dismissed the lawsuit without hearing oral argument,[41] the justices split evenly over their reasons. The case has become a classic example of the kind of political dispute that the Court lacks the authority to decide.

Fourth, in one of the most vivid examples of his being both the president and his own secretary of state, Carter, putting aside many other issues, decided in 1977 to focus much of his energy on securing the ratification of two treaties to turn control of the Panama Canal over to the Panamanians. He personally lobbied senators, appealed directly to citizen groups, and flew several contingents of senators to Panama so they could survey the circumstances themselves and be briefed by local authorities. In the first few months of 1978, the Senate ratified each treaty by a one-vote margin. Although Carter demonstrated that he was politically savvier than his critics maintained, the ratification of the treaties did not "win over any important friends or forge any blocs of support for the White House at home, and . . . actually strengthened Carter's opponents," who "exited the Senate battle with renewed energy at the grassroots level and with greater organizational strength" and used this as an example of Carter's willingness to weaken American influence within Central America. Meanwhile, Carter "had expended a great deal of political capital, including with Republican moderates like Senate Minority Leader Howard Baker who were not very keen on the treaties and who didn't want to make more deals" with Carter.[42]

In another initiative based on his authority to be the nation's sole representative in international affairs, Carter organized a secret meeting at Camp David between Prime Ministers Menachem Begin of Israel and Anwar Sadat of Egypt. After thirteen days, the two leaders, once bitter political foes, agreed to a "Framework for Peace in the Middle East," which outlined basic goals for settling their differences over a homeland for the Palestinians. Initially, the public reaction to the accord was positive. A year later, both Begin and Sadat received the Nobel Peace Prize shortly before they signed a treaty to formalize their agreement. Although the Israeli Knesset approved the framework, Begin agreed to construct new settlements on the West Bank in violation of the perceived spirit of the accord and Sadat was assassinated in 1981 by radical Egyptian elements that objected to his supporting Israeli objectives.

Yet another Carter initiative had significant ramifications for presidential authority with respect to foreign affairs. In response to Nixon's efforts to use the FBI and Central Intelligence Agency to spy on his political enemies, Carter used his unilateral power to reorganize executive agencies to restrict the CIA's and FBI's respective intelligence capabilities and responsibilities.[43]

To strengthen the limitations placed on the CIA, Carter issued Executive Order 12036, which extended an executive order from President Ford[44] restricting the CIA to performing domestically a "coordinating" role with the FBI to identify domestic threats to national security. Carter's executive order "instituted far-reaching changes in the structures and procedures of the intelligence community. [His order] established a remodeled and much more rigorous decision-cycle for covert action."[45] Prior to Executive Order 12036, it had been unclear whether U.S. intelligence agencies could conduct warrantless physical searches within the United States for intelligence purposes. Carter revised Ford's order to provide that investigating activities "for which a warrant would be required if undertaken for law enforcement rather than intelligence purposes shall not be undertaken against a United States person without a judicial warrant, unless the president has authorized the type of activity involved and the Attorney General has both approved the particular activity and determined that there is probable cause to believe that the United States person is an agent of a foreign power."[46] This change complicated procedures for conducting warrantless searches and resulted in the president's need to personally authorize such searches domestically.[47]

Carter's Executive Order 12036, like his other initiatives to broker peace in the Middle East and to authorize the failed mission to free Iranian hostages, extended long-standing precedents from earlier presidents supporting their unilateral authority to reorganize executive branch agencies and to rescind treaties, to recognize foreign powers, and to forge international agreements to which the United States is not a party—or taking emergency actions against other powers—that the president believes are in the nation's best interests.[48] As the first Democrat to serve as president since Lyndon Johnson had been forced out of office because of his stewardship of the Vietnam War, Carter was vulnerable to attacks that he too might not understand foreign policy. While Carter was not afraid to make decisions, they often reinforced the growing sense many Americans had that his approach to foreign affairs was ad hoc and that he was being led by events more than he was using his powers to lead them.

Reshaping Federal Jurisdiction

Like most of his predecessors, Carter took to heart the president's authorization in Article II to "recommend to their Consideration, such Measures as he shall judge necessary and expedient." He believed that the public expected a president to propose initiatives to Congress and to be an active participant in the legislative process. He also construed Congress's regulatory authority broadly. Thus, he signed into law many landmark enactments reshaping federal jurisdiction.

To begin with, one of Carter's enduring legacies is airline deregulation. With bipartisan support in Congress,[49] Carter signed into law the Airline Deregulation Act,[50] which transformed the industry by allowing competitive fare setting and new companies to enter the market and phasing out the Civil Aeronautics Board. Though the industry is subject to federal aviation standards and expanded security regulations, Carter undid one of Coolidge's most significant expansions of federal regulation.

Environmental regulation was a second field in which President Carter significantly reshaped the regulatory landscape. First, he signed into law a special fund to clean up toxic waste (Superfund).[51] The law reinforced the long-standing understanding of the power of Congress to spend money as long as it was done "for the general welfare."[52] Whereas there had been a long history of federal relief for natural disasters, this bill provided the most extensive federal relief to date for cleaning up man-made disasters.[53]

Another significant environmental initiative that Carter signed into law was the Alaska National Interest Lands Conservation Act,[54] which set aside for protection almost 56 million acres of lands and rivers in Alaska. In the absence of congressional action, Carter relied on the Antiquities Act[55] to buttress his authority to issue several proclamations transforming large tracts of federally owned land in Alaska to be national monuments.[56] Since Carter understood that it would be much easier for the incoming president to withdraw his proclamations than it would be for Congress to enact a new law on the subject, he intensified his efforts to get Congress to act. In late November 1980, Congress enacted the law, which Carter signed.[57] The law reaffirmed the federal government's long-standing authority to protect federal lands from development.

A third field in which Carter took the lead in reshaping the law was terrorism. In keeping with his unilateral efforts restricting the CIA from domestic surveillance, Carter urged Congress to enact the Foreign Intelligence Surveillance Act (FISA).[58] FISA restricted unconsented, or warrantless, surveillance within the United States. It required intelligence agencies, for the first time, to obtain a "prior judicial warrant for all electronic surveillance for foreign intelligence or counterintelligence purposes in the United States in which communications of U.S. persons might be intercepted."[59] The bill, which Carter proposed in his second and third States of the Union,[60] received bipartisan support within Congress and was signed into law in 1978. The bill was part of the legal regime governing foreign intelligence operations in the United States until the PATRIOT Act amended it after the September 11, 2001, attacks.

A fourth field that Carter substantially reshaped was government ethics. Coming into office in the aftermath of Watergate, Carter vowed to raise the ethical standards for government service.[61] The centerpiece of the legal reform that he championed was the Government in Ethics Act.[62] It imposed new, unprecedented requirements on the president and other high-ranking governmental officials to make public disclosures of gifts and income, imposed restrictions on lobbying, created the Office of Government Ethics to work with the attorney general to investigate possible ethical violations, and established an Office of Independent Counsel, who would be appointed, at the request of the attorney general, by a special three-judge panel.

One of the first independent counsels, Alexia Morrison, was appointed to investigate possible wrongdoing by then-Assistant Attorney General Ted Olsen, who filed a lawsuit challenging the constitutionality of her appointment. In an opinion by Chief Justice Rehnquist, the Supreme Court determined that (1) the independent counsel's appointment mechanism was constitutional because the Appointments Clause of Article II specified that a court may appoint "inferior officers" and that the independent counsel was an "inferior officer" (because of her limited duties and tenure) and (2) the independent counsel's investigative and prosecutorial responsibilities did not "unduly interfere" with a president's ability to fulfill his oath of office.[63]

In the only dissent, Justice Scalia forcefully argued that the statute deprived the president of his constitutional entitlement to control the exercise of all executive power.[64] His dissent is the most elaborate defense of the unitary theory of the executive. As he explained, the theory posits that the

Constitution vests all executive power in the president for two reasons: First, this arrangement ensures the exercise of executive power is under the control of a politically accountable official—the president. Second, it ensures uniformity in the exercise of executive power because one person will be in charge of its enforcement. Justice Scalia warned that an independent counsel was politically unaccountable and that Congress had created the office as a way to harass presidents whom it lacked the courage to impeach.

Subsequently, sixteen independent counsels were appointed to investigate possible wrongdoing by various executive branch officials, including the next three presidents. Two of the most controversial were Lawrence Walsh, who was charged with investigating several officials including President Reagan for illegally diverting federal resources to assistant rebels in Nicaragua, and former judge and solicitor general Kenneth Starr, who was asked to investigate possible perjury and efforts to obstruct justice by President Bill Clinton, among others. The investigations and prosecutions run by their offices generated so much political backlash that it convinced Clinton and congressional leaders to allow the independent counsel law to lapse.[65]

The story of the collapse of the independent counsel law is significant for several reasons. First, it is another reminder that the Court often does not have the last word in constitutional law. The Independent Counsel Act joins the Alien and Sedition Acts and the National Bank charter, each of which the political branches, rather than the courts, had taken the initiative to end. Second, the independent counsel law confirmed Justice Scalia's dire predictions. For example, the independent counsel arrangement had perverse, unpredictable incentives. The supporters of the law creating independent counsel underestimated the ease with which investigations were triggered and the incentives to prolong them as long as possible.

In another field, Carter authorized the most important law enacted pertaining to judicial discipline, the Judicial Conduct and Disability Act of 1980.[66] The act transformed the handling of judicial misconduct and disability, including misconduct falling short of an impeachable offense and physical or mental disabilities impeding judges' abilities to do their jobs. The law created special mechanisms for judges to police themselves, including the Judicial Conference, which consisted of the chief justice and the chief judges of each circuit and which was authorized to impose certain sanctions for dilatory, disabled, and misbehaving judges. The Judicial Conference was empowered to send referrals to the House requesting that it initiate impeachment inquiries into particular matters.

The debates over the law focused on several constitutional issues. The first was whether it was unconstitutional for Congress to vest Article III judges with the power to discipline themselves, including reassigning or temporarily suspending judges. Some members of Congress believed that by specifying impeachment as the means for disciplining certain kinds of misconduct, the Constitution excluded any other arrangements. They argued further that the referral mechanism empowered judges to make decisions, such as initiating impeachments, reserved to the House. Second, some skeptics believed that the referral mechanism, in addition to the oversight and disciplinary authority vested in the Judicial Conference, undermined judicial independence because the act gave judges the means by which they could retaliate against colleagues whom they disliked or with whose decisions they disagreed. Some judges, including one appointed by President Carter, openly questioned the constitutionality of the law.[67]

The majority in the House and the Senate and Carter believed otherwise. They maintained that judges inherently have some powers to address judicial misconduct that produces delays and impedes the functioning of courts within their jurisdiction.[68] They maintained that judges have vested interests in guaranteeing the integrity of their branch as a whole and thus could be depended on to vigilantly monitor their own integrity. Moreover, the law's supporters did not believe the referral mechanism replaced or impeded the independent judgment of the House on whether to initiate an impeachment inquiry. Subsequently, several courts considered but rejected constitutional challenges to the law.[69] From 1980 to 2011, the Judicial Conference investigated charges of possible misconduct against more than a dozen judges and made nine referrals to Congress to initiate impeachment proceedings, four of which led to formal impeachments and removals of federal judges.[70] The act remains the principal mechanism for addressing federal judges' serious health and ethical problems.

Last but not least, Carter was instrumental in expanding the federal government's size and responsibilities. Congress, upon his initiative, established the Departments of Energy and Education.[71] Both at the time and since, establishing these departments has met resistance from conservatives who argued that federal intervention into the domains of energy and education exceeded the scope of federal authority as originally conceived and tread into areas traditionally regulated by local or state governments. The opposition was unavailing, as Congress and Carter believed otherwise.[72] Subsequent presidents and Congresses have fortified the constitutional foundations of these departments by periodically staffing and funding them.

Impacting Civil Rights

Among Carter's most important priorities as president were civil rights. Indeed, his presidency coincided with the first case in which the Supreme Court considered the merits of a constitutional challenge to a graduate school's affirmative action admissions program, *Regents of the University of California v. Bakke*.[73] Carter was thus the first president to defend affirmative action in higher education.

The constitutionality of affirmative action was one of the most divisive constitutional issues of the modern era. It involved the question of whether the Fourteenth Amendment's explicit guarantee that "[n]o state ... shall deprive to any person within its jurisdiction the equal protection of the laws"[74] barred a public university from using race as either a factor or the principal or sole basis on which to grant admission to minority applicants. There was no doubt among America's leaders, even when the Fourteenth Amendment was first ratified, that at the very least it outlawed laws expressly disadvantaging African-Americans because of their race. In the early twentieth century, much of the debate about the Fourteenth Amendment had focused on whether a law disadvantaging *anyone* on the basis of the race violated equal protection. In *Brown v. Board of Education*, the Warren Court settled the matter by striking down state-mandated segregation in public schools.[75] Since *Brown*, the Court, which had assumed a central role in interpreting the Fourteenth Amendment, had not yet addressed the question of whether an African-American could have his race used as an advantage in the distribution of some government services. This question raised the additional issue of whether a Caucasian could make a claim not to have his race used against him in a public university's admissions process. By the time *Bakke* came before the Court, these questions were the tip of the iceberg, for there were a host of public programs giving advantages to African-American applicants because they belonged to a race of people who had been historically discriminated against because of their race.

Initially, Carter tried to stay out of the controversy, except for directing officials in his administration to strongly endorse affirmative action in principle; however, the pressures to become involved were immense. While none of the federal government's affirmative action programs were at issue in *Bakke*, the president could not ignore the obvious—that *Bakke* presented the most politically salient equal protection case since *Brown*. Americans sharply divided over the constitutionality of affirmative action programs, and everyone expected Carter to stake out a position in the case. Carter found it impossible to stand on the sidelines.

He also recognized that the case, no matter how it was resolved, had serious ramifications for federal affirmative action programs. While the Fourteenth Amendment does not apply to the federal government, the Supreme Court had held in 1954 that the Fifth Amendment, which applies to the federal government, had an equal protection component similar to the one in the Fourteenth Amendment.[76] Even if Carter agreed with the Court's decision, he still had to decide whether, according to his own, independent construction of the Constitution, federal programs satisfied the Fifth Amendment's equal protection component.

When administration officials failed to agree on the constitutionality of affirmative action, Carter became the principal defender of affirmative action in college and graduate school admissions. In several news conferences, he acknowledged personally reviewing the administration's brief in the case, and he answered questions about the administration's position in the case.[77] Once the Court rendered its 5–4 decision upholding the use of race as one of many factors in the University of California graduate admissions process, Carter declared that the Court had vindicated the administration's use of race as a factor in awarding various governmental benefits or contracts.[78] He issued a memorandum directing the heads of executive departments to comply with his understanding of the decision.[79]

Carter's memorandum was important for several reasons. First, it reaffirmed the president's authority to render his own constitutional interpretations. Carter was not obliged to respond to the Court's decision. But he chose to speak in his own voice. Even then, he could have disagreed with the Court, as Lincoln had done with *Dred Scott v. Sandford*.[80] But Carter did not disagree.

Second, Carter's memorandum and other public statements transformed the national debate on affirmative action. It opened the door to Reagan and the Republican Party to take the opposing view. Carter's personal involvement aligned the Democratic Party with an interpretation of the Constitution that upheld government use of affirmative action at least in some circumstances. In response, Reagan defended a view of the Constitution as "color-blind" and rejected Carter's position in favor of interpreting the Constitution as prohibiting the use of race by the government altogether as a basis for governmental action. In the next presidential election, independent and Republican voters, particularly in the South, flocked to the party of Lincoln—and Reagan.

Carter's intervention in the case increased the likelihood of his personally assuming the political risks of upholding affirmative action. Carter's decision was not the first time a president had shaped the administration's case before the Court. Van Buren had done it in the *Amistad* case and Eisenhower in *Brown v. Board of Education*.[81] *Bakke*, like the other two cases, involved the contentious question about the federal government's power to make laws based on race, and Carter's intervention came at a price. Like Van Buren, Carter lent himself and his administration to the appearance of allowing politics, rather than the law, dictate the arguments in the case. Had Carter not been involved, the decisions over the brief would have stemmed from professionals in the Justice Department and could not have been attacked as having been driven by political considerations. Once Carter became involved, critics could charge, as they did with Van Buren, that the president had chosen to politicize a constitutional case. As the only elected official within the administration, the president is uniquely vulnerable to the charge of acting on a partisan rather than a neutral basis, such as the law.

Third, Carter reaffirmed the relevance of presidential support to the implementation of a judicial decision. Presidential opposition to a judicial decision reinforces the unilateral authority of each branch to interpret the Constitution, while presidential approval of a decision reinforces the Court's authority and bolsters the public support needed for contested decisions to endure.

Last but not least, Carter decided, in the aftermath of *Bakke*, to be less equivocal in his support of affirmative action by approving a controversial plan of the Federal Communications Commission to increase minority ownership of radio and television stations. Although the Court upheld the plan,[82] it later overruled its decision and thus Carter's initiative.[83] Carter's high-profile support for affirmative action kept the controversy alive, and subsequent Democratic presidents and Congresses have been challenged to maintain the same constitutional commitment that Carter made.

Carter's presidency also coincided with the rise of the women's rights movement and became embroiled in the controversial, constitutionally salient issues that it brought to the forefront. On abortion rights, Carter was pro-life and consistently opposed federal funding of abortions except in cases of rape and incest.[84] Yet he supported the Equal Rights Amendment. When the amendment appeared unlikely to win state ratification within the requisite time, he urged an extension of time,[85] which Congress granted.[86] But with the extension, Carter seemed to be under less pressure to push hard for the ERA. It fell three states short of the number needed for ratification. Women's rights activists blamed Carter for its failure. They complained that his help came too late and his message of support was muddled. Once again, Carter's constitutional vision lacked clarity.

Altering Public Perceptions of the Presidency

The Constitution says nothing about the presidency's trappings. It says nothing about how presidents should dress, conduct themselves publicly, or interact with the public. Carter's efforts to reshape public perception of the presidency had mixed success but have been instructive to later presidents.

First, Carter, more than any previous president, used television to speak directly to the American people. Each time a presidential initiative needed an important boost from the public, Carter scheduled a presidential address on television to appeal for support from the American people.[87] Unfortunately, Carter's most important speech was his worst, the "Malaise speech."[88] Although he hoped the speech would reenergize his presidency by winning public support for his energy initiatives in Congress, it undercut public confidence in his judgment when he retooled his entire cabinet immediately in its aftermath. Carter was ridiculed for blaming the public for the "crisis in spirit" in the country. Rather than being remembered for the energy plan for which it was trying to build public support, the speech reminded everyone of the essential, but missing, ingredient he needed as president to get things done—the American people's support. (By the end of his administration, he acknowledged, "The President is given a broad responsibility to lead but cannot do so without the support and consent of the people. . . . I know from experience that Presidents have to face issues that are controversial, broad in scope, and which do not arouse the support of a natural political majority.")[89] Subsequent presidents have understood the indispensability of technological advancements as the means by which they can build the public support they need to do what they want.

Second, in response to Nixon's abuses of power, Carter tried to make the presidency more informal and transparent.[90] Following the models of "Jefferson, Jackson, Lincoln, [and] Truman [who] minimized the pomp and ceremony and the pride [that] accrues sometimes to the Presidency,"[91] Carter sought to use the public as a sounding board on his initiatives. He was the first president to bring a pollster full-time into the White House, a move that he believed would help to keep him regularly informed of the public support for his initiatives.[92] At his inauguration, he wore a sweater rather than formal attire and walked down Pennsylvanian Avenue rather than ride in a motorcade because he wanted to show "that I trusted the American people and they respected me. [It] was a symbolic expression of my trust in my own integrity and in my own safety [and] a demonstration that there was no separation encapsulated in a big black limousine between the incumbent President and the people of our country."[93] He subsequently met regularly with voters in informal settings and invited over a dozen citizens to meet with him at Camp David to provide feedback on how he was doing as president.

The informalities did not endure. Reagan did not believe the American people wanted to abandon the formalities of the office, and he restored much of the pomp and circumstance that Carter had removed from the presidency in order to restore public respect for the presidency at home and abroad. Nor did Reagan consider transparency to be as important as Carter believed. Reagan thought it could detract from rather than enhance the prestige, authority, and effectiveness of the office.

Third, Carter spoke more openly about religion than any prior president. Twenty years earlier, John F. Kennedy had declared that he would not allow his Catholic faith or the pope to dictate what he did as president.[94] In contrast, Carter openly practiced his religion. Besides becoming the first president to regularly teach a Sunday school class, he was the first president to acknowledge that he took certain positions because of his faith and that Jesus Christ was the driving force in his life.[95] He told Americans that his faith led him to make human rights a major priority of his administration, to stridently oppose interest group politics, to advocate personal responsibility and morality in public affairs, to oppose abortion funding by the federal government, to promote social justice, and to make the United States "a beacon of light for human rights throughout the world."[96] His election mobilized religious conservatives. He further believed that his candor about his faith was consistent with the First Amendment and did not interfere with his presidential obligations.[97] Subsequent presidents have similarly acknowledged the importance of religion in their lives.[98]

Last, Carter altered the role of the First Lady in the constitutional scheme. The Constitution vests no authority in a president's spouse simply because she is the president's spouse. Nor does the Constitution bar a president from seeking informal advice from anyone he pleases. Presidents have assumed that the only check on their freedom to get informal advice is their political accountability, and they have only differed in the extent to which they have sought such counsel. For example, John Adams relied heavily on his wife, while Franklin Roosevelt assigned special responsibilities to his wife.[99] After World War II, presidents from Truman through Ford did not assign them substantive responsibilities. Carter broke this pattern. His wife, Rosalynn, often appeared on his behalf at public events, visited seven Latin American countries as an official envoy of the United States, conducted high-level negotiations with foreign leaders on various issues, participated in National Security Council briefings, promoted the ERA, testified before Congress to increase funding for the mentally ill,[100] drafted speeches for the president, and advised him on many issues, including appointments. While some people complained Rosalynn was not elected president and not entitled to wield any of its authority, every president since Carter has relied on his spouse for special assignments. Their model is Jimmy Carter.

IN SPITE OF Carter's achieving most of his initiatives, his presidency illustrates the cost of constitutional incoherence. Reform was the central theme of Carter's presidency, but he failed to keep the public meaningfully informed about, much less in support of, his initiatives. He understood that he needed public support to achieve his goals, particularly to change the old ways of doing things, but his failure to articulate a consistently compelling, coherent constitutional vision deprived the American people of not only something to support but also something to remember.

Conclusion

THE STORIES OF the thirteen forgotten presidents in this book reveal several significant patterns in the presidency's impact on constitutional law. First, they illuminate the rich array of presidents' constitutional activities. Presidents, even forgotten ones, address a broader range of constitutional issues than courts address, most of which are never subject to judicial review. The forgotten presidents helped to construct the meaning and scope of constitutional practices regarding such varied matters as federalism, vetoes, pardons, international agreements, civil rights, appointments, the organization of the executive branch including the White House, and removals. Even the failures of forgotten presidents had significant constitutional consequences. For example, the Whig conception of the president as subservient to Congress collapsed because several forgotten presidents undermined it. Its collapse was an important step to Lincoln's presidency and the gradual accumulation of presidential powers into the modern era.

Another important pattern suggests that it will likely become easier to discover presidents' constitutional legacies. The advent of the Internet and the twenty-four-hour news cycle, coupled with the establishment of presidential libraries and archives, ensures that presidents' public constitutional acts and statements will be recorded permanently and in a form that is easily accessible. With every public act of a president recorded and available on the Internet and unparalleled media scrutiny of presidential activities, a president cannot erase his legacy if he wanted to.

The relatively easy availability of information about a presidency does not ensure, however, that people will avail themselves of it or fully appreciate its constitutional significance. There may be too much information for people to consume, and many people may be more interested in speculating or opining on presidential motives than in closely analyzing historical records. Some presidents might also be outside of our political time. Presidencies are historically, politically, socially, and legally contextualized. The more removed we are from the specific contexts in which particular presidents functioned, the more remote their presidencies become and the more likely their constitutional impact will be forgotten. Forgetting a presidency and its constitutional impact may, however, take years. Presidents are unlikely to be forgotten in their lifetimes. Most forgotten presidents served more than a century ago, suggesting we will not know for quite some while which, if any, contemporary presidents will be forgotten.

Third, it is apparent that certain factors may counterbalance the remoteness of a president's constitutional legacy. For example, the longer a president serves the likelier he will engage with constitutional issues that will be salient for more than a generation. Hence, we can expect that George W. Bush will not be forgotten because, even apart from his distinction as the second son of a president to be elected president in his own right, he was the first president to respond to the terrorist attacks against the United States on September 11, 2001. As long as the attacks and the United States' involvement in the wars in Afghanistan and Iran in their aftermath are remembered, he will be associated with them. Similarly, we can expect that Barack Obama will be remembered not just because he is the first African-American to become president but also because his presidency coincided with the convergence of many constitutionally salient issues, including but not limited to his responses to the worst economic downturn since the Great Depression, the overhaul of the health care system and its affirmation in the Supreme Court, his conflicts with Congress over the debt ceiling and judicial appointments, the ending of the Afghanistan and Iraq wars, the killing of Osama Bin Laden, and a dramatic expansion of gay rights.

Fourth, and perhaps most importantly, the forgotten presidents illuminate the extent to which the presidency shapes presidents at least as much as they shape it. The office channels presidents into protecting its prerogatives. Forgotten presidencies demonstrate how various constraints and incentives drive presidents to adapt to the institutional needs of the office and how, by design, the presidency, even under reputedly inept presidents, expanded in power.

The stories of the forgotten presidents shatter the myth that most nineteenth-century presidents were weak and ineffective. By strongly asserting presidential prerogatives, they provoked strong congressional backlashes and often undermined their political support. For instance, Franklin Pierce's strong defense of the Kansas-Nebraska Act split his party and intensified the divide separating slavery's defenders and opponents. While he blamed abolitionists for fomenting rebellion, his aggressive tactics in enforcing the Kansas-Nebraska bill in order to protect the rights of slaveholders drove antislavery

Democrats out of the party and strengthened the need for a more unified front to defend against the spread of slavery.

The most important lesson of the forgotten presidents is, however, that the Constitution genuinely matters. It is widely assumed that the few, limited means for keeping presidents in check include press coverage, congressional oversight, impeachment, and presidents' concerns about reelection and history's judgment. But presidents are also constrained from completely building the world anew. They inherit an assortment of powers at a particular moment in history and are not fully free to do with them as they please. The presidency draws its occupants into performing the role and tasks of the presidential office, to take it as it is rather than as they would like it to be, to think and act presidentially, and to protect and make sacrifices for the presidency. By virtue of their office, presidents are consumed with their constitutional impact.

We forget what presidents always remember—that our Constitution is no longer pristine. It has been tested by one generation after another. It has not been unfazed by those who came before, including forgotten presidents, and we will not pass it to the next generation in the same shape that we inherited from the past.

The final lesson is that presidents cannot perform their duties, much less construct constitutional legacies, on their own. No one wields presidential powers without the staffing and resources of their administrations, and presidents can forge constitutional legacies only if people care about them and tell their stories. A president's constitutional legacy depends on allies, other leaders including later presidents, supporters, historians, members of Congress, students, and even opponents and critics. Without all these perspectives, a president alone cannot keep the memory of his constitutional impact alive. Without an audience, even a president will be forgotten.

Appendix

I considered many variables for measuring the extent of public familiarity with presidents' constitutional legacies. Some were unwieldy, such as street names. Others were measurable, such as the names of schools or colleges, but they were largely geographically bound. People know the names of the schools or colleges named after presidents near where they live but rarely know the names of ones located outside their daily routines. Other variables, such as postage stamps, were measurable but had little arguable pertinence. While there are polling data on public familiarity with American leaders, they are overinclusive, since they indicate that most Americans are unfamiliar with the names of most presidents, much less their constitutional legacies.

I settled on seven variables, which were measurable and pertinent to public familiarity with presidents' constitutional legacies. The first was how long ago a president served in office. The variable reflects the number of years since a president entered office. This is pertinent because changes in technology have affected the quality and availability of the means for memorializing a president's public statements. Today, everything a president says or does is preserved for posterity, usually in many forms, which are accessible to almost everyone. Moreover, formal archiving is a relatively recent phenomenon, so that the more recent a presidency the more voluminous the material is likely to be. Thus, more recent presidents will be more likely to be remembered by the general public, all other things being equal (which of course may not be).

Second, the frequency of a president's appearance in the most popular American history textbooks used in middle and high schools is important because middle and high school history classes are among the first and arguably most critical places where young people learn about presidents' achievements and legacies. It follows that familiarity with certain presidents is developed during childhood and adolescence. Therefore, the presidents discussed the most in middle and high school textbooks are likely to achieve greater familiarity with the average American during childhood.

I coded the second variable as follows: I gave a president a mark for each sentence in each of a representative sampling of textbooks that discusses him by name or obvious pronoun. I used a cross section of textbooks from different authors and publishers and designed for different groups that I selected from the American Textbook Council's list of the most commonly used textbooks within American middle and high school curricula. The textbooks surveyed were Joyce Appleby, Alan Brinkley, and James Macpherson, *American Journey* (McGraw Hill, 2008); Robert Dallek, Jesus Garcia, Donna Ogle, and C. Frederick Risinger, *American History* (McDougal Little, 2007); James West Davidson, *American History of Our Nation: Beginnings through 1877* (Prentice Hall, 2007); and Daniel Boorstin, *A History of the United States* (Prentice Hall, 1997).

Third, I calculated the average number of books about particular presidents in twelve university libraries. I substantiated this variable in two ways. First, the number of volumes represents the market for each president; less familiar presidents are unlikely to have a significant market share. The market is more likely to demand the stories of renowned presidents or even those popular through vilification. Second, it is more difficult to be familiar with something when there is less information available about it. Presidential familiarity can be captured by the sheer extent of biographies. Thus, I gave one count to each volume in the nation's ten largest university libraries—Harvard, Yale, University of Illinois–Champaign, University of California–Berkeley, University of Texas–Austin, Stanford, University of Michigan, Columbia, UCLA, and University of Wisconsin–Madison. I added two other libraries, Duke and UNC–Chapel Hill, to ensure greater geographic diversity.

The fourth variable, presidential libraries, was a dummy variable. Presidential libraries foster and promote presidential legacies. Thus, a president who has a presidential library is more likely to retain familiarity because an organization is devoted to educating the public about his stature. Because presidential libraries are a relatively modern creation, they are imperfect. While every president has an official historic site, there are only nineteen official presidential libraries, including John Quincy Adams, Hayes, Lincoln, and McKinley. The absence of a library likely inhibits learning about a presidency and reinforces ignorance about it.

Fifth, I measured presidential greatness. The opposite of greatness is insignificance. The further a president is from greatness the more insignificant his presidency. I derive my ranking of presidential greatness from William J. Ridings and Stuart B. McIver's *Rating the Presidents* (Carol Publishing Group, 1997), which polled more than 700 presidential experts to rank presidents.

The sixth variable was personality. The principal work on which I modeled my testing of personality was Dean Keith Simonton, "Presidential Style: Personality, Biography, and Performance," 55 *Journal of Personality and Social Psychology* 928–36 (1986). I used two of Simonton's variables, creativity and charisma, because they are likely to influence the probability that a president will be remembered. Charisma makes a president appealing to the public and the press, who are instrumental to maintaining his legacy and image. Creativity reflects a president's ability to initiate new legislation or craft creative solutions to difficult problems. I calculated one personality variable by adding both measures together.

My final variable was rhetoric. I assumed that public speaking is the medium of choice and that people will more likely remember presidents who established bonds of familiarity through their rhetorical skills. I supposed presidents who delivered bland, unimaginative, or dull speeches were more likely to be forgotten.

I considered measuring rhetoric in different ways. For example, I considered but rejected measuring the quantity of a president's public statements, because this likely has little if any bearing on the words or images that moved people during or after a presidency. Rhetoric is a skill that requires special talent, and thus my objective was to find some indicia of the extent to which a president had it. I also considered but rejected surveying historians because their scores could be based on many other qualities, such as greatness. Nonetheless, one interesting, recent study of the presidency is Robert W. Merry's *Where They Stand: The American Presidents in the Eyes of Voters and Historians* (2012), which surveys how historians and others have rated presidents. I found especially interesting how presidents ranked in terms of the numbers of times Merry mentions them in the book; the thirteen presidents who rank the lowest in terms of how often he mentions them are Garfield and William Henry Harrison (twice); Tyler and Arthur (four); Hayes, Fillmore, and Pierce (five); Taylor, Ford, and Benjamin Harrison (six); Van Buren (seven); and Taft and John Quincy Adams (nine). As readers will see, there is a significant degree of overlap between the presidents who are mentioned least in the latter study and the presidents whom I deem to be forgotten.

Consequently, I created a composite variable for rhetoric, using three quantifiable qualities—speech length, imagery, and identification words—that are theoretically indicative of effective rhetoric. For my understanding of these terms, I relied on Ryan Lee Teten's *The Evolutionary Rhetorical Presidency: Tracing the Changes in Presidential Address and Power* (2011). Teten demonstrates that speech length and identification words vary by president. The rhetoric literature suggests that less verbose speeches, such as the Gettysburg Address, tend to be more effective. I borrowed data about speech word count from Teten, who tabulated the number of words communicated for each president's State of the Union addresses. If a president served two terms, I averaged the two.

Teten also provides an analysis of "identification rhetoric." Through the use of certain terms, such as pronouns, presidents are "able to speak to the people and [to] convince them that he is on their side, on the same page with them, and has the interests of the greater whole in mind" (39). This technique is meant to "build consensus and agreement by creating identification between the citizens of the United States and himself; if they identify with what he says, he will receive greater support and have the ability to proceed further with policy objectives." I measured this variable as the number of times a word of identification appeared in a State of the Union address, relative to all other words.

Another study, Cynthia G. Emrich, Holly H. Brower, Jack M. Feldman, and Howard Garland, "Imagines in Words: Presidential Rhetoric, Charisma, and Greatness," 46 *Administrative Science Quarterly* 527–57 (2001), hypothesizes that speech imagery indicates effectiveness because it provides a basis for connecting with the audience. The study separately tabulated the frequencies of image-based words and concept-based words in presidential inaugural addresses. Thus, considering the importance of imagery and identification, I constructed a variable that was an average between the imagery score of the landmark and inaugural speeches.

A significant issue with rhetoric is that each measure within the composite excluded some presidents. The latter study omitted Gerald Ford, John Tyler, Andrew Johnson, Millard Fillmore, and Chester A. Arthur because they were never elected to deliver inaugural addresses, while the former study omitted Garfield and William Henry Harrison because of their brief tenures. A missing value would serve to remove these presidents from the composite index. Therefore, I imputed the missing value within the rhetoric variable, using the president's other qualities. Basically, statistical imputation assumes that there is a relationship among a group of variables. Using how others with a full set of values relate to the missing values, the method assigns a value to the missing ones based upon the studied relationship. I chose this method because it offers a solution that produces conservative estimates that are unlikely to disturb the model's predictive ability. Imputation provides a theoretical validation for using these new values, as opposed to an arbitrary assignment.

Readers will find two different charts showing the results of my calculations of these variables. The first, figure A.1, measures presidential presence in middle and high school textbooks and university libraries. For each president in this figure, there are two columns; the left column represents volumes in university libraries and the right represents presence in textbooks.

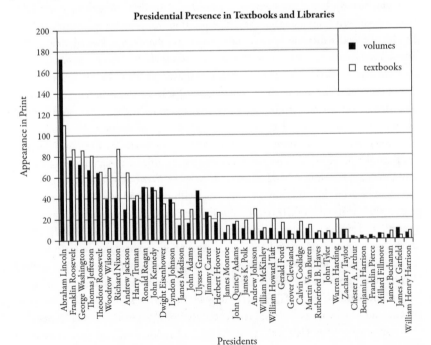

Presidential Presence in Textbooks and Libraries

The four presidents with the fewest volumes about them in the major university libraries that I surveyed—Arthur, Benjamin Harrison, Fillmore, and Pierce—are in this study. Indeed, almost all the presidents in this book are in the lower half of presidents based on this metric. While Taft and Carter are near the middle of presidents on this scale, the volumes on each of them devote significant attention to their unusually active postpresidential careers. Carter also benefits from the enhanced archival requirements in the 1970s.

The second figure, A.2, shows the composite score for each president on public familiarity. The left or y-axis posits levels of familiarity on a range from 0 to 4, and the right or x-axis lists presidents in decreasing order of their familiarity. Hence, the president with the highest composite score (or most public familiarity) is on the far left of the x-axis, and the president with the lowest on the far right of the x-axis.

Several findings are noteworthy. First, the data suggest that the public is unfamiliar with most presidents, though Carter is the only president in this study ranking in the top half of presidential familiarity.

Second, the presidents in this book do not comprise the bottom thirteen based on this data. More than a handful of presidents appear to have less public familiarity than the presidents in this study, though I did not include these other presidents for several reasons. Some of the latter have higher scores than the presidents I included on certain factors I consider to be important (such as the frequency of their being mentioned in history textbooks). Several of the other presidents I did not include are marked by dramatic events that have made them more distinctive than several presidents I chose for this study. For instance, Monroe is well known for the Monroe Doctrine, while Buchanan often gets attention for being rated the worst president.

Third, I appreciate that Carter is not as forgotten as many other presidents whom I did not include. I explain elsewhere in the book why I have included Carter, though it bears repeating that public familiarity with Carter has a lot to do with his being a more

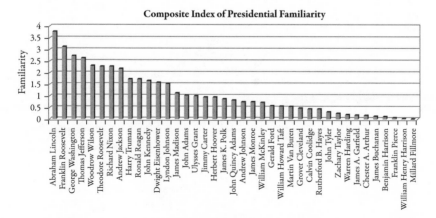

Composite Index of Presidential Familiarity

The Presidents

recent president, with his still being alive, and with his being an unusually active ex-president. Because I believe that Carter lost control of his narrative more than did any other post–World War II president, he, more than any of these others, has had his narrative—the story of his presidency—left for others to tell.

Last, the final rankings of presidents, in terms of presidential familiarity, seem reasonable. The least forgotten president is Lincoln, while the most forgotten is Fillmore. Though William Henry Harrison served barely a month as president, he is the second most forgotten because he has some notoriety as the first president to die in office. Fillmore has no such distinction. He did not die in office and followed another president who, by dying in office, garnered greater distinction. Fillmore served for roughly two years during which he was overshadowed by the political forces and more charismatic, energetic, and eloquent leaders with which he had to contend. It is telling that, after the many speeches Fillmore made to defend his administration's enforcement of the Fugitive Slave Act, his rhetoric has not been memorable. This is because he was not a good orator, he was speaking to largely hostile crowds, he was conflicted about the course he had set, and subsequent defenses of federal supremacy were made for nobler causes. His efforts were not lost to history, but the tide of history cast them aside as failures. They have since been eclipsed by more dramatic events and bolder, more successful, more colorful personalities. Such is the fate of a forgotten president.

Bibliographical Essay

Writing this book has been a journey through several fields. My principal quest was to find something that was not there or, more precisely, to find events that happened but that have been neglected in the annals of constitutional law. I began by refamiliarizing myself with three sets of materials: First, I reviewed popular constitutional law textbooks, histories, and treatises to reacquaint myself with their relative emphases. Second, I reread popular histories of the United States and different eras of American history, including John Morton Blum's *The Republican President* (1954), *The Progressive Presidents: Roosevelt, Wilson, Roosevelt, Johnson* (1980), and *The National Experience* (1963), written by Blum et al.; Richard Hofstadter's *The American Political Tradition and the Men Who Made It* (1948) and *The Age of Reform: From Bryan to FDR* (1955); Alan Nevins's eight-volume history of the United States from 1847 through 1865; Leonard W. White's classic administrative history of the United States; and more recently published histories, including Michael F. Holt, *The Rise and Fall of the American Whig Party: Jacksonian Politics and the Onset of Civil War* (Oxford University Press, 1999), Merrill D. Peterson, *The Great Triumvirate: Webster, Clay, and Calhoun* (Oxford University Press, 1987); Daniel Walker Howe, *What Hath God Wrought: The Transformation of America, 1815–1848* (Oxford University Press, 2007), and Sean Wilentz, *The Rise of American Democracy: Jefferson to Lincoln* (Norton, 2005). Third, I reviewed the presidential studies literature, including Richard Neustadt's *Presidential Power and the Modern Presidents: The Politics of Leadership* (1960); Stephen Skowronek's *The Politics Presidents Make: Leadership from John Adams to Bill Clinton* (1997); Fred Greenstein's *The Presidential Difference: Leadership Style from FDR to Barack Obama* (2009) and *Inventing the Job of President: Leadership Style from George Washington to Andrew Jackson* (2009); Jeffrey Tulis's *The Rhetorical Presidency* (1987) and *The Constitutional Presidency* (2009); and Robert W. Merry's *The American Presidents in the Eyes of Voters and Historians* (2012).

I then examined additional materials to uncover the unsung, discounted, or overlooked constitutional accomplishments of arguably forgotten presidents. First, I combed through the manuscript collections at the Library of Congress for each of the presidents in this book.

Second, I consulted the wonderful, online databases with links to presidential papers, public statements, and orders. These included the Miller Center at the University of Virginia; the Presidency Project at the University of California–Santa Barbara; and the Avalon Project at Yale Law School. If a note lacks a full citation, it refers to an item that is available in presidential papers at the Library of Congress and at least one of these databases. Moreover, the Library of Congress and the National Archives have databases covering a wide range of historical materials, including images. Heinonline has excellent databases for federal statutes and official opinions of the attorney general.

Third, of the presidents I discuss, Carter is the only one with an official library. It is a treasure trove of documents, recordings, and videos.

Fourth, I checked various compilations of the communications of presidents, including *A Compilation of Messages and Papers of the Presidents, 1789–1897* (James D. Richardson, ed., 1900), *Letters of Zachary Taylor from the Battlefields of the Mexican War* (William H. Samson, ed., 1908), and *Letters of Grover Cleveland, 1850–1908* (Alan Nevins, ed., 1933); and the communications of members of Congress, who figure prominently in this study, including *The Papers of Henry Clay* (J. F. Hopkins et al., eds., University of Kentucky Press, 1959–92); *The Works of Daniel Webster*, 6 volumes (Edward Everett, ed., Little, Brown, 1853); *The Writings of Daniel Webster*, 18 volumes (J. W. McIntyre, ed., 1903); *The Private Correspondence of Henry Clay* (Calvin Colton, ed., 1855); John C. Calhoun, *Basic Documents* (John M. Anderson, ed., State College, Pa.: Bald Eagle Press, 1952); and *The Works of John C. Calhoun* (Richard K. Cralle, ed., 1854–57).

Fifth, I have read many books and articles about presidents who were likely candidates for this study, including but not limited to the presidents in this book. I also read the books and other publications written by the presidents I deem forgotten and memoirs, books, and articles written by people who served under them, including but not limited to cabinet officers. I also studied pertinent social histories.

There are also many other excellent secondary materials on presidents. Among these are the American Presidency Series, published by the University Press of Kansas, and the American Presidents series, edited by Sean Wilentz and the late Arthur Schlesinger Jr. and published by Times Books. I cite to other noteworthy biographies in the notes.

In reading the aforementioned materials, I tried to pay close attention to everything: If there were disagreements or inconsistencies between accounts, I searched for primary materials (which I often found) to resolve the conflicts. If there were no conflicts or disagreements in different historical accounts, I insisted on verifying a common legend or statement. Along the way, I confirmed much of what historians (and others) have said about the forgotten presidents in this book, but I found some events that are not in conventional narratives of these presidents and some mistaken assertions, which I have corrected.

Notes

INTRODUCTION

1. Stephen Skowronek, *The Politics Presidents Make: Leadership from John Adams to Bill Clinton* (Cambridge: Belknap Press of Harvard University Press, 1997).
2. Id. at xi.
3. Stephen Skowronek, *Presidential Leadership in Political Time: Reprise and Reappraisal* vi (2nd ed., Lawrence: University Press of Kansas, 2011).
4. See, e.g., 2 Bruce A. Ackerman, *We the People: Transformations* (Cambridge: Belknap Press of Harvard University Press, 1998).
5. Abraham Lincoln, the Gettysburg Address, November 19, 1863.

CHAPTER 1

1. The minister to Great Britain was then considered as important as the secretary of state, and Van Buren wanted to ingratiate himself with Jackson. He became Jackson's heir apparent as a result of the Senate's rejection of his nomination.
2. The Deposit-Distribution Act of 1836 set forth the scheme for regulating federal deposits.
3. Martin Van Buren, Inaugural Address, March 4, 1837, in *Inaugural Addresses of the Presidents of the United States from George Washington 1789 to George Bush 1989* 69, 69–78 (Washington, D.C.: U.S. Government Printing Office, 1989).
4. Martin Van Buren, Special Message to Congress, September 4, 1837.
5. Id.
6. Major L. Wilson, *The Presidency of Martin Van Buren* 88 (Lawrence: University Press of Kansas, 1984) (citation omitted).
7. Cong. Globe, 25th Cong., 1st Sess., at 118 (October 2, 1837).
8. Id.
9. Id. at 119.

10. Id. (citation omitted).

11. U.S. Const., art. I, sec. 8, cl. 18 (empowering Congress "[t]o make all Laws which shall be necessary and proper for carrying into Execution the foregoing Powers, and all other Powers vested by the Constitution in the Government of the United States, or in any Department or Officer thereof").

12. 17 U.S. 316 (1819).

13. Wilson, *Presidency of Martin Van Buren*, at 73 (citation omitted).

14. Id. (citation omitted).

15. The independent treasury consisted of a system of subtreasuries, in which federal funds could be deposited and loaned out on easy terms to fuel more speculation.

16. Merrill D. Peterson, *The Great Triumvirate: Webster, Clay, and Calhoun* 272 (New York: Oxford University Press, 1987) (citation omitted).

17. Id. at 97.

18. Id. at 96.

19. Id. at 97.

20. Id.

21. Id. at 100.

22. See Knox v. Lee, 79 U.S. 457 (1871).

23. Congress passed the relief measures that Van Buren had proposed, including granting import merchants more time to pay overdue duty bonds.

24. Sean Wilentz, *The Rise of American Democracy: Jefferson to Lincoln* 498 (New York: Norton, 2005).

25. See Daniel Walker Howe, *What Hath God Wrought: The Transformation of America, 1815–1848*, at 507 (New York: Oxford University Press, 2007).

26. Before the special session, the treasury secretary received the attorney general's opinion upholding his power to use money under the treasury's control to meet certain federal exigencies. See "Recall of Money's Deposited with the States," 3 Op Att. Gen. 227 (May 22, 1837).

27. Wilson, *Presidency of Martin Van Buren*, at 140 (citation omitted).

28. U.S. Const., amend. X (providing the "powers not delegated to the United States by the Constitution, nor prohibited by it to the States, are reserved to the States respectively, or to the people").

29. See Peterson, *The Great Triumvirate*, at 274 (citation omitted).

30. Calhoun made these statements in a letter to the *Edgefield Advertiser*. See id. (citation omitted).

31. Id. at 276 (italics in original).

32. Van Buren, Inaugural Address, at 69, 69–78.

33. Whigs construed Van Buren's support for the gag rule as an unprecedented, impermissible executive encroachment on a House prerogative.

34. By the time the Court had resolved the matter, only thirty-nine Africans were alive.

35. Wilson, *Presidency of Martin Van Buren*, at 155.

36. U.S. v. Libellants and Claimants of the Schooner *Amistad*, 40 U.S. (15 Pet.) 518 (1841).

37. Van Buren's attorney general produced two opinions pertaining to the *Amistad* case. See "Amistad and What Should Happen with the Property of the Ship," 3 Op. Att. Gen. 484 (November 2, 1839) (advising Van Buren "to issue his order to the marshal, in whose custody the vessel and cargo are, to deliver the same to such persons as may be designated by the Spanish Minister to receive them"); "Expenses on Account of the Amistad Negroes," 3 Op. Att. Gen. 510 (April 11, 1840) (concluding that no prior acts of Congress prohibiting slave trade could be used for the "safekeeping and support" of the "negroes taken out of the Amistad"). Subsequently, Tyler's attorney general, Hugh Legare, opined on the division of the salvage for the *Amistad*. See "What Is to Happen with the Money Awarded for the Salvage of the *Amistad*," 4 Op. Att. Gen. 17 (April 6, 1842) (concluding the salvage decreed in the case should be given to "those who were actually on board of [the ship] at the time of the capture").

38. Wilson, *Presidency of Martin Van Buren*, at 156.

39. The full Court was unable to hear the case because one justice declined to participate and another, Justice Philip Barbour, had died a few days before oral arguments. At the same time that Adams and Baldwin were arguing their case, the Senate was divided over whether to allow Van Buren to fill the vacancy. "[B]ecause of [their defective strategy, absenteeism, and crossed signals,] the Whigs were ultimately outmaneuvered by the Democrats, who managed a bare quorum with most of the Whigs absent and forced a favorable 22–25 vote to confirm Van Buren's nomination of Peter Daniel to fill the seat." Henry Abraham, *Justices, Presidents, and Senators: A History of U.S. Supreme Court Appointments from Washington to Bush II* 104 (4th ed., Lanham, Md.: Rowman and Littlefield, 2007). Thus, Van Buren filled Supreme Court vacancies on one of his first and last days in office.

40. Compliance with the Supreme Court's order was left to President Harrison. In complying with the order, Harrison upheld an important exercise of judicial review over executive action.

41. Wilentz, *Rise of American Democracy*, at 474 (citation omitted).

42. Wilson, *Presidency of Martin Van Buren*, at 157 (citation omitted).

43. See Leonard Baker, *John Marshall: A Life in Law* 745 (New York: Macmillan, 1974). Many historians are skeptical that Jackson made the remark.

44. Wilson, *Presidency of Martin Van Buren*, at 157 (citation omitted).

45. "Attorney General's Opinion on the Testimony of African Americans in a Court Martial," 3 Op. Att. Gen. 523 (April 27, 1840).

46. See Ted Widmer, *Martin Van Buren* 121 (New York: Times Books, 2005).

47. "Existence of War with the Seminoles," 3 Op. Att. Gen. 307 (March 9, 1838).

48. Id.

49. Id.

50. The evacuation of the Cherokees that the army oversaw in the fall and winter of 1839–40 is called the "Trail of Tears," because more than a third of the evacuated

Indians died on the journey. Outraged by the policy, Van Buren's favorite niece told him that she hoped he lost reelection because of it.

51. Martin Van Buren, Proclamation of January 5, 1838.

52. Martin Van Buren, Special Message to Congress, January 5, 1838.

53. Wilson, *Presidency of Martin Van Buren*, at 159.

54. The Neutrality Act of 1838 authorized civilian officials to arrest the flow of people, arms, supplies, and vehicles illegally across the borders. It did not authorize the president to stop groups from organizing and planning to assist the rebellion or the end of British rule in Canada. See 5 Stat. 212–14 (March 10, 1838).

55. Wilson, *Presidency of Martin Van Buren*, at 152.

56. After delays implementing the first commission that had been signed on September 11, 1838, the two countries entered another convention on April 11, 1839. Delays persisted, and the commission was not established until August 25, 1840. By the time the commission awarded money to claimants, Van Buren was out of office.

57. In early 1839, violence threatened to erupt in an area of northern Maine known as the Aroostook Valley. The Peace Treaty of 1783 had left undecided the exact boundary between Maine and Canada, and conflicts over the boundary persisted for years. In January 1839, Canadian authorities arrested a Maine land agent and imprisoned him in New Brunswick. New Brunswick's lieutenant governor declared that American forces should leave the area, while the governor of Maine assembled his own forces to free the captive American. Leaders in Congress wanted war and passed a law giving Van Buren special funds and the authority to mobilize 50,000 American troops to settle the matter. He declined the authority that the law gave him and instead negotiated a peaceful settlement with British authorities, thereby reinforcing the primacy of the president in military and foreign affairs.

58. Wilson, *Presidency of Martin Van Buren*, at 188.

59. Id. at 188–89.

60. Martin Van Buren, Letter to Citizens of Elizabeth City, Virginia, July 31, 1840, *Richmond Enquirer* (August 7, 1840).

61. Leonard W. White, *The Jacksonians: A Study in Administrative History, 1829–1861*, at 309 (New York: Macmillan, 1954) (citations omitted).

62. See House Document 13, 25th Congress, 3rd Session (December 10, 1838); House Document.

63. 25th Congress, 3rd Session (January 4, 1839).

64. House Report 313, 25th Congress, 3rd Session (February 27, 1839).

65. Wilson, *Presidency of Martin Van Buren*, at 128–37.

66. Id.

67. Martin Van Buren, Executive Order (March 31, 1840).

68. 5 U.S. 137 (1803).

69. See An Act for the Relief of George Dawson, Chap. 273, 24th Congress, 6 Stat. 662 (July 2, 1836).

70. "Acts of Postmaster General—How Far Conclusive," 3 Op. Att. Gen. 1 (1836).

71. Records of the U.S. Senate at the National Archives, Records of the Committee on the Judiciary, Cong. Globe, Chapter 13.5 (January 1837).

72. See Kendall v. United States, 37 U.S. 524, 535 (1838).

73. Id. at 524.

74. Id. at 610.

75. Id. at 525.

76. Id. at 613.

77. Id.

78. Id.

79. See Steven G. Calibresi and Christopher S. Yoo, *The Unitary Executive: Presidential Power from Washington to Bush* (New Haven: Yale University Press, 2008).

80. After the Court's decision, the contractor sued Kendall personally for the money that it had lost because of the delay in resolving the dispute. Although a jury found Kendall liable, Congress passed a law abolishing imprisonment for debts, thus sparing him the indignity of going to prison because of his failure to pay the jury verdict. In the meantime, Kendall appealed the judgment. In 1845, the Supreme Court overturned the jury verdict on the ground that at the time Kendall denied the claim he was acting in his official rather than his personal capacity. See Kendall v. Stokes, 44 U.S. 87, 99 (1845). After the ruling, Congress agreed to cover Kendall's expenses in fighting the lawsuit.

81. 24 Cong. Ch. 42, 5 Stat. 187 (1837).

82. 24 Pub. Res. 2, 5 Stat. 199 (1837).

83. "Pensions Claimed by Mrs. Susan Decatur," 2 Op. Att. Gen. 200–201 (1837).

84. 14 Pet. 497 (1840).

85. Id. at 515.

CHAPTER 2

1. The classic biography of Harrison is Freeman Cleaves, *Old Tippecanoe: William Henry Harrison and His Times* (New York: C. Scribner's Sons, 1939). Before becoming president, Harrison had served as governor of Indiana Territory (1800–1812); brigadier general, U.S. Army (1812–13); major general, U.S. Army (1813–14); member, U.S. House of Representatives (1816–19); U.S. senator (1825–29); minister to Colombia (1828–29); and clerk, County Court of Pleas of Cincinnati (1835–40).

2. For an excellent discussion of the 1836 and 1840 presidential elections, see Gail Collins, *William Henry Harrison* 73–111 (New York: Times Books / Henry Holt, 2012).

3. The other Ohioans elected president are Ulysses Grant, Rutherford Hayes, James Garfield, William McKinley, William Howard Taft, and Warren Harding. Benjamin Harrison was born in Ohio but resided in Indiana at the time of his election.

4. The other presidents who made no Supreme Court appointments were Taylor, Andrew Johnson (1865–69), and Carter.

5. Arthur M. Schlesinger Jr., *The Age of Jackson* 391 (Boston: Little, Brown, 1945).

6. William Henry Harrison, Inaugural Address (March 4, 1841), 4 *A Compilation of the Messages and Papers of the Presidents, 1789–1897* 9 (James D. Richardson, ed., Washington, D.C.: Government Printing Office, 1897).

7. Id. at 10.

8. See Letter from William Henry Harrison to Henry Clay, November 15, 1840, in Henry Clay, *The Private Correspondence of Henry Clay* 446 (Calvin Colton, ed., New York: A. S. Barnes, 1855).

9. This quote appears in several respected accounts of the period between Harrison's election and his death. See, e.g., Merrill D. Peterson, *The Great Triumvirate: Webster, Clay, Calhoun* 299 (New York: Oxford University Press, 1987); George Rawlings Poage, *Henry Clay and the Whig Party* 16–17 (1936; Gloucester, Mass.: Peter Smith, 1965); Glyndon G. Van Duesen, *The Life of Henry Clay* 338–39 (Boston: Little, Brown, 1937).

10. Letter from Henry Clay to President William Henry Harrison, March 13, 1841, in *Private Correspondence of Henry Clay*, at 450–51.

11. Letter from President William Henry Harrison to Henry Clay, March 13, 1841, in *Private Correspondence of Henry Clay*, at 452–53.

12. Id.

13. Letter from Henry Clay to President William Henry Harrison, March 15, 1841, in *Private Correspondence of Henry Clay*, at 453–54.

14. Id.

15. Harrison, Inaugural Address, March 4, 1841.

16. See Leonard D. White, *The Jacksonians: A Study in Administrative Practice, 1829–1861* 300–346 (New York: Macmillan, 1954).

17. Id. at 309.

18. Cleaves, *Old Tippecanoe*, at 296 (quoting *Richmond Whig*, October 30, 1835).

19. See White, *The Jacksonians*, at 310.

20. Senate Doc. 26, 27th Cong., 1st Sess., p. 2 (March 20, 1841).

21. "Diary of Thomas Ewing, August and September 1841," *American Historical Review* 18 (1912–13), at 98.

22. White, *The Jacksonians*, at 311 (citations omitted).

23. U.S. Const., art. II, sec. 2.

24. Dumas Malone, 2 *Jefferson and His Time* 269–79 (Boston: Little, Brown, 1948–81).

25. White, *The Jacksonians*, at 92.

26. See Poage, *Henry Clay and the Whig Party*, at 16–17.

27. White, *The Jacksonians*, at 93.

28. Parmelee, "Recollections of an Old Stager," 47 *Harper's New Monthly Magazine* 754 (1873).

29. Id.

CHAPTER 3

1. The Senate voted 32–1 to approve the Force Bill, 4 Stat. 632 (1833). Tyler cast the only negative vote.

2. Robert V. Remini, *Henry Clay: Statesman for the Union* 583 (New York: Norton, 1991) (citation omitted).

3. U.S. Const., art. II, sec. 1, par. 6.

4. See Ruth C. Silva, *Presidential Succession* 39–41 (Ann Arbor: University of Michigan Press, 1951).

5. See Carl Brent Swisher, *Roger B. Taney* 269–72 (1935; Hamden, Conn.: Archon Books, 1961).

6. See Edward P. Crapol, *John Tyler: The Accidental President* 10 (Chapel Hill: University of North Carolina Press, 2006).

7. See Edwin C. Corwin, *The President, Office and Powers, 1787–1957* (4th ed., 1962).

8. Id.

9. Id. at 10.

10. John Tyler, Address Upon Assuming the Office of President of the United States (April 9, 1861), 4 *A Compilation of the Messages and Papers of the Presidents, 1789–1897* 36–39 (James D. Richardson, ed., Washington, D.C.: U.S. Government Printing Office, 1897).

11. Crapol, *John Tyler*, at 12–13.

12. Cong. Globe, 27th Cong., 1st Sess. 3, 4 (1841). See also Norma Lois Peterson, *The Presidencies of William Henry Harrison and John Tyler* 49–50 (Lawrence: University Press of Kansas, 1989).

13. Cong. Globe, 27th Cong., 1st Sess. 4 (1841).

14. Crapol, *John Tyler*, at 10 (citation omitted in original).

15. Peterson, *Presidencies of Harrison and Tyler*, at 50 (citation omitted in original).

16. Crapol, *John Tyler*, at 10.

17. Before the Twenty-fifth Amendment, seven other vice presidents succeeded to the presidency: Millard Fillmore (1850), Andrew Johnson (1865), Chester Arthur (1881), Theodore Roosevelt (1901), Calvin Coolidge (1923), Harry Truman (1945), and Lyndon Johnson (1963).

18. U.S. Const., amend. XXV (providing, "In case of the removal of the President from office or of his death or resignation, the Vice-President shall become President").

19. Tyler did not veto every Whig bill. Among the bills he signed was the nation's first bankruptcy law.

20. Whigs maintained that the veto should be used only to obstruct legislation that was plainly unconstitutional. Webster and Clay had condemned the pocket veto as a particularly despicable usurpation of legislative authority. In 1832, Webster, in a speech before the Republican National Convention, described the pocket veto as "the silent veto" and "a great practical augmentation" of presidential power. He warned that it could "turn that which the Constitution intended only as an extraordinary remedy for extraordinary cases into a common means of making executive discretion

paramount to the discretion of Congress, in the enactment of laws." Daniel Webster, 2 *Writings and Speeches* 117–18 (October 12, 1832). Clay made similar arguments against Jackson's pocket veto of a bill. Senate Doc. 323, 23rd Cong., 1st Sess. pp. 1–2 (May 2, 1834) (declaring, "By retaining this bill, and not returning it to the Congress which passed it, the qualified veto of the President was converted, in effect, into an absolute veto"). For the debate over the scope of a president's veto authority in this period, see generally Leonard D. White, *The Jacksonians: A Study in Administrative History, 1829–1861*, at 30–33 (New York: Macmillan, 1954).

21. Peterson, *Presidencies of Harrison and Tyler*, at 53 (citation omitted).

22. John Tyler, Address upon Assuming Office of the President of the United States, April 9, 1841.

23. See generally Peterson, *Presidencies of Harrison and Tyler*, at 304 (citations omitted).

24. John Tyler, Address to Joint Session of Congress, May 31, 1841.

25. Although much scholarly attention has been devoted to Tyler's vetoes, he backed most Whig initiatives. See note 19.

26. Id. at 69.

27. John Tyler, Veto Message, August 16, 1841.

28. John Tyler, Protest to the House of Representatives, September 9, 1841, Journal of the House of Representatives.

29. Cong. Globe, 27th Cong., 2nd Sess. 634, 637 (1842).

30. Distribution required giving a certain percentage of the proceeds from the sales of federal lands to the states in which they were located and the remainder to be distributed among the states pursuant to a ratio based on their representation in Congress. The funds were supposed to be used for internal improvements.

31. Henry Clay, *The Papers of Henry Clay*, vol. 9, *The Whig Leader, January 1, 1837–December 31, 1843* 736 (Robert Seager II et al. eds., Lexington: University of Kentucky Press, 1988).

32. John Tyler, Veto of Tariff & Land Distribution Bill (August 9, 1842), at 186.

33. Id. at 188.

34. Cong. Globe, 27th Cong., 2nd Sess. 873 (1842).

35. Id.

36. Id.

37. Cong. Globe, 27th Cong., 2nd Sess. 873–75.

38. Tyler's vetoes became enduring precedents. They foreshadowed the principle adopted by the Rehnquist Court more than a century later that Congress may not coerce or command a state to adopt a policy or to execute a policy with which it disapproves.

39. Peterson, *Presidencies of Harrison and Tyler*, at 86 (citing Interview with John Tyler, Jr., at *Lippincott's Monthly Magazine* 417, 417–18 (1888)).

40. Of the twenty-one people who served in Tyler's cabinet, thirteen were Whigs, and eight were Democrats. The turnover in the cabinet was not, however, all Tyler's doing.

In February 1844, Tyler and several dignitaries were present at a demonstration of the unveiling of the USS *Princeton*'s new weapon, which was then supposed to be the largest naval gun. On the third discharge, the weapon exploded at the breech and killed several spectators, including the secretary of state and navy secretary.

41. Wirt served the longest of any attorney general (from 1817 through 1829).
42. 1 Op. Att. Gen. 631 (1823).
43. See "Power of President to Fill Vacancies," 3 Op. Att. Gen. 673 (October 22, 1841).
44. John Tyler, Protest to the House of Representatives about Appointments, March 23, 1843, Journal of the House of Representatives.
45. John Tyler, Address of April 9, 1841.
46. Carl Russell Fish, *The Civil Service and the Patronage* 150 (New York: Longmans, Green, 1905).
47. 3 Op. Att. Gen. 673, 676 (1841).
48. 4 Op. Att. Gen.1–2 (1842). See also "Appointment and Removal of Inspectors of Customs," 4 Op. Att. Gen. 165 (March 24, 1843); "Appointment and Removal of Inspectors of Customs," 4 Op. Att. Gen. 165 (March 24, 1843).
49. Two examples are the House and Senate resolutions requesting Tyler to identify officials whom he had removed from office. Buchanan had sponsored the resolution that the Senate approved, while the House approved an identical resolution on July 16, 1841. Tyler did not oppose either resolution, since he construed them as merely requesting information that was already public.
50. John Tyler, Letter to the House of Representatives about the Northern Border, February 26, 1842, Journal of the House of Representatives, at 447.
51. Tyler's Protest to the House of Representatives, March 23, 1842.
52. Tyler's reference to the Senate in this portion of the protest was purposeful. The Senate, unlike the House, has a role in the appointments process—namely, to give its advice and consent to presidential nominations. This power arguably gave special license to the Senate to inquire into information pertaining to a nomination, but the House had no corresponding power.
53. Journal of the House of Representatives, 113, July 29, 1841.
54. John Tyler, Special Message, January 31, 1843.
55. Tyler, at 224.
56. Though Tyler selected Gilmer, a former Virginia governor, to serve as secretary of the navy, Gilmer died in the explosion on the USS *Princeton*.
57. Cong. Globe, 27th Cong., 2nd Sess. 894–901. See also Carlton Jackson, *Presidential Vetoes, 1792–1946* 71–72 (Athens: University of Georgia Press, 1967).
58. Journal of the House of Representatives, 27th Cong., 2nd Sess., 1343, 1346–52, August 17, 1842. See also Josh Chafetz, "Executive Branch Contempt of Congress," 76 *University of Chicago Law Review* 1083, 1133–34 (2009).
59. John Tyler, Veto of Tariff & Land Distribution Bill, August 9, 1842.
60. The House's resolution declared that the president's protest would not be accepted and was in derogation of the rights of the House. 2 *Hinds' Precedents of the House of*

Representatives (Washington, D.C.: U.S. Government Printing Office, 1907), sec. 1590, pp. 1039–40.

61. The majority opposing the impeachment resolution consisted of an assortment of representatives, including Democrats who did not want to approve any Whig initiatives, ardent supporters of Tyler, and Whigs who disliked Clay.

62. See, e.g., Peterson, *Presidencies of Harrison and Tyler*, at 149.

63. See Michael J. Gerhardt, *The Federal Appointments Process: A Historical and Constitutional Analysis* 56, 106 (rev. ed., Durham: Duke University Press, 2003).

64. It is unlikely that Buchanan's delays in responding to Tyler's nomination were meant to prevent Tyler from filling the post. They were probably the results of Buchanan's ambitions and awkward timing. When Buchanan was considering whether to join the Court, he was also negotiating with President-Elect Polk to become secretary of state. Buchanan figured that this post was a better platform than the Court from which to mount a successful run for president. Polk wanted, however, assurances from Buchanan and his other cabinet officers that they would put aside presidential ambitions to serve in the cabinet. Concerned that Buchanan could not give these assurances, Polk urged Buchanan to join the Court. Eventually, Buchanan told Polk he would join the cabinet, and their relationship throughout Polk's term was tense.

65. Tyler nominated five different people to fill the two vacancies, one of whom the Senate confirmed. Because he nominated several people more than once, Tyler made a total of nine nominations, of which the Senate approved only one.

66. Lincoln was the first of ten presidents to follow Tyler's example in nominating someone from the opposition party to the Supreme Court. The others who did the same were Benjamin Harrison, Taft, Wilson, Harding, Hoover, Franklin Roosevelt, Truman, Eisenhower, and Nixon.

67. The message noted that five-sixths of the ships using the harbor in the islands came from the United States and that American citizens owned more property on the islands than the citizens of any other nation.

68. John Tyler, Special Message of December 20, 1843, at 212.

69. Peterson, *Presidencies of Harrison and Tyler*, at 141.

70. Special Message of December 20, 1843, at 214.

71. 5 Stat. 539 (1842). For the modern version of the McLeod law, *see* 28 U.S.C. sec. 2241.

72. Letters from John Calhoun to Richard Pakenham, April 18 and 27, 1844, in 5 John C. Calhoun, *The Works of John C. Calhoun* 330–47 (Richard K. Cralle, ed., New York: D. Appleton, 1854–57).

73. The admission of Texas as a new state did not follow the usual process that territories followed before being admitted as new states into the Union. Usually, Congress initially enacted an "organic act" in which it recognized an area as a U.S. territory. Then, it enacted an "enabling act" allowing inhabitants to form a convention to establish a state constitution and government. Finally, Congress passed an "act of admission" approving the state constitution and recognizing the territory as

a state "on equal footing" with others. Rather than follow these steps, Congress passed a joint resolution to approve the annexation of Texas that included the proviso that the Republic of Texas "passed its own ordinance on January 1, 1846." Donald E. Fehrenbacher, *The Slaveholding Republic: An Account of the United States Government's Relations to Slavery* 265 (Ward M. McAfee, ed., New York: Oxford University Press, 2001). After Tyler signed the joint resolution, the Texas constitutional convention approved the annexation and drafted a state constitution. Citizens of the Republic of Texas then approved the Texas constitution and annexation, and Congress accepted its constitution. Id. Webster argued that the usual process for transforming a territory into a state did not apply, because Texas was a foreign nation. Others believed that Mexico had taken Texas from the United States and that annexation provided the means for welcoming it back into the Union.

74. Article IV provides in part, "New States may be admitted by Congress into this Union." U.S. Const., art. IV, sec. 3. The long-standing assumption has been that, unless the Constitution specifies a supermajority vote for a congressional action, the default rule for congressional action is a majority vote in each chamber.

75. Benson's resolution declared that "a state formed out of the present Republic of Texas" should be admitted into the Union as soon as a new treaty with Texas could be negotiated. See Peterson, *Presidencies of Harrison and Tyler*, at 229–57.

76. 48 U.S. 1 (1849).

77. Tyler's other constitutionally significant decisions include his upholding the restriction of slavery in the District of Columbia and the gag order in the House.

78. For the correspondence between Tyler and Governor King, see 4 George Raywood Devitt, compiler, *A Compilation of the Messages and Papers of the Presidents, 1789–1902, a Supplement* [1897]–1902, 286–307 (Washington, D.C.: Published by authority of Bureau of National Literature and Art, 1903).

79. Luther v. Borden, 48 U.S. 1 (1849).

CHAPTER 4

1. President Polk reportedly declared in his first cabinet meeting that he had four objectives for his administration—reducing the tariff, establishing an independent treasury, settling the Oregon boundary, and acquiring California for the United States. He achieved all four of his goals along with leading the country through a successful war with Mexico, which secured U.S. control over Texas.

2. While Polk made three Supreme Court appointments, Taylor made none.

3. See, e.g., Washington Hunt to Thurlow Weed, January 1, 1848, in Thurlow Weed Barnes, *Memoir of Thurlow Weed* 165 (Boston: Houghton, Mifflin, 1884) ("I think General Taylor's friends will be able to say that he is strongly in favor of peace, and will be content with a moderate acquisition of territory; that he will take less than any other man that is strong enough to be elected; and more than all that, will leave all legislative questions to the decision of Congress").

4. Michael F. Holt, *The Rise and Fall of the American Whig Party: Jacksonian Politics and the Onset of Civil War* 271 (New York: Oxford University Press, 1999).

5. Taylor to Dr. R. C. Wood, September 27, 1847, in *Letters of Zachary Taylor from the Battlefields of the Mexican War* 131–37 (William H. Samson, ed., Rochester, N.Y.: Genesee Press, 1908); Taylor to Wood, February 18, 1848, in id., at 226–31.

6. Taylor to John Allison, June 28, 1848, in Holman Hamilton, *Zachary Taylor*, vol. 2, *Soldier in the White House* 79–81 (Indianapolis: Bobbs-Merrill, 1951).

7. See id. at 120 (citation omitted).

8. Taylor to John Allison, September 4, 1848, in id. at 121–24.

9. Id.

10. See Taylor to R. C. Wood, December 10, 1848, in *Letters of Zachary Taylor*, at 131–37.

11. Taylor, Inaugural Address, March 5, 1849, in 5 *A Compilation of Messages and Papers of the Presidents, 1789–1897* 6 (James D. Richardson, ed., Washington, D.C.: U.S. Government Printing Office, 1900).

12. Id. at 5.

13. First Annual Message, December 4, 1849.

14. Although the usual path toward statehood required the preliminary steps of Congress's designating a particular area as a territory and empowering it to create a state constitution, northern Whigs disagreed with Democrats and many southern Whigs over the proper construction of Congress's Article IV power "to make all needful Rules and Regulations respecting the Territory or other Property belonging to the United States." U.S. Const., art. IV, sec. 3. Northern Whigs construed this clause as giving Congress authority to regulate federal territories in any way it saw fit, while southern Whigs and Democrats read it as only giving such plenary power to the federal government over territories that the United States owned at the time of ratification.

15. Cong. Globe, 31st Cong., 1st Sess., at 704 (April 11, 1850).

16. Id. at 358–59 (February 14, 1850).

17. Zachary Taylor, Annual Message, December 4, 1849.

18. Elbert B. Smith, *The Presidencies of Zachary Taylor and Millard Fillmore* 121 (Lawrence: University Press of Kansas, 1989) (quoting Brown) (citation omitted).

19. Id. at 60.

20. See, e.g., Cong. Globe, 31st Cong., 1st Sess. A-165 (Clay said that Taylor had given him "an authentic assurance of [his] adherence exclusively to his own particular scheme"); Letter from Thurlow Weed to Hannibal Hamlin, August 8, 1876, in Charles Eugene Hamlin, *Life and Times of Hannibal Hamlin* 202 (Cambridge: Riverside Press, 1899) (suggesting, "Had General Taylor lived, the 'Compromise Bill' including the Fugitive Slave Law, would have encountered a veto").

21. Cong. Globe, 31st Sess. A-615 (May 21, 1850). Clay chided Taylor for sticking with his "peculiar plan" rather than deferring to Congress. Id. Three days before Taylor died, Clay confided to his wife that "the breach between the Administration and me . . . is getting wider and wider." Henry Clay to Lucretia Clay, July 6, 1850.

22. See Taylor, Inaugural Address, at 26–30. See also Letter from Robert Toombs to John Crittenden, April 23, 1850, in Urich Bonnell Phillips, *The Life of Robert Toombs* 64–65 (New York: Macmillan, 1913) ("When I came to Washington, as I expected, the Whig party expecting to pass the Proviso, and that Taylor would not veto . . . I saw Gen. T. and talked fully with him on the subject, and while he stated he had given and would have given no pledges either way, about the Proviso, he gave me clearly to understand that if it was passed he would sign it"). Before the election, Taylor had privately communicated that he accepted the constitutionality of the Wilmot Proviso based on the Northwest Ordinance of 1787 and the Missouri Compromise of 1820. Taylor to R. C. Wood, September 27, 1848, in *Letters of Zachary Taylor*, at 131–37.

23. See, e.g., Cong. Globe, 31st Cong., 1st Sess. 250 (Senator King, D.-Ala.) (January 29, 1850), 419–20 (Senator Davis, D.-Ms.) (February 25, 1850).

24. In his last Senate speech, Calhoun argued that the admission of California "would compel us [Southerners] to infer that you intend to exclude us from the whole of the acquired territories, with the intention of destroying, irretrievably, the equilibrium between the two sections." Accordingly, he proposed amending the Constitution to restore to the South "the power she possessed of protecting herself before the equilibrium was destroyed." John C. Calhoun, *Basic Documents* 323–24 (John M. Anderson, ed., State College, Pa.: Bald Eagle Press, 1952).

25. For one of several reports recounting conversations in which Taylor threatened to use military force to end secession, see, e.g., Barnes, *Memoir of Thurlow Weed*, at 177–79.

26. On March 11, 1850, Seward argued that slavery violated a "higher law than the Constitution" and the Constitution itself. He declared that slavery was "only a temporary, accidental, partial, and incongruous" institution, while freedom was a "perpetual, organic, universal in harmony with the Constitution." Cong. Globe 260–69 (March 11, 1850). Shortly before Taylor died, Seward announced he supported Taylor's plan. See id. at A1021–A1024 (statement of Sen. Seward) (July 2, 1850).

27. 1 Hamilton, *Zachary Taylor*, at 294–98 (quoting Taylor) (citation omitted).

28. See, e.g., Cong. Globe, 31st Cong., 1st Sess. A446–A450 (April 8, 1850) (statement of Sen. Thomas Hart Benton, D.-Mo.). See also id. at A242–A248 (statement of Sen. Hannibal Hamlin, D.-Me.) (March 5, 1850).

29. See K. Jack Bauer, *Zachary Taylor: Soldier, Planter, Statesman of the Old Southwest* 294 (Baton Rouge: Louisiana State University Press, 1985).

30. There is no executive order or proclamation on record in which Taylor directed federal troops to thwart a Texas invasion into New Mexico. There are correspondence and memoirs from the period—or later—confirming the steps Taylor took to defend New Mexico as a "possession of the United States" against invasion by one of the United States. See, e.g., General A. Pleasonton to Thurlow Weed, September 22, 1876, in Barnes, *Memoir of Thurlow Weed*, at 180 (recounting conversation with

Taylor in which Taylor told Pleasonton, "I am glad that you're going to New Mexico. I want officers of judgment and experience there. These southern men in Congress are trying to bring on civil war. . . . [T]ell Colonel Monroe [that] he has my entire confidence, and if he has not force enough out there to support him . . . I will be with you myself").

31. 4 Wheat. (17 U.S.) 316 (1819).

32. One of Taylor's first decisions as president was to expand the cabinet to include the new position of secretary of the interior.

33. See generally Bauer, *Zachary Taylor*, at 249–62.

34. Holt, *Rise and Fall*, at 419–21.

35. See generally Leonard White, *The Jacksonians: A Study in Administrative History, 1829–61* 85–86 (New York: Macmillan, 1956).

36. See, e.g., Smith, *Presidencies of Taylor and Fillmore*, at 56. With respect to judicial appointments, Taylor "placed bipartisan cooperation ahead of the independence of his office and local party interests." Kermit Hall, *The Politics of Justice: Lower Federal Judicial Selection and the Second Party System, 1829–61* 78–90 (Lincoln: University of Nebraska Press, 1979).

37. Holt, *Rise and Fall*, at 421.

38. U.S. Const., art. II, sec. 2, cl. 3.

39. For an overview on how the recess appointment authority has been construed historically, see T. J. Halstead, "Recess Appointments: A Legal Overview," CRS Report (July 26, 2005).

40. Id. at 2–4.

41. 1 Op. Att. Gen. 631, 633–34 (1823).

42. See, e.g., 2 Op. Att. Gen. 525 (1832); 3 Op. Att. Gen. 673 (1841); 4 Op. Att. Gen. 361 (1845); 4 Op. Att. Gen. 523 (1846).

43. See Carl Fish, *Annual Report of the American Historical Association for the Year 1899*, at 78 (Washington, D.C., 1900).

44. Senators were more upset over Taylor's removals than his recess appointments. For instance, Senator James Bradbury (D-Me.), who had sponsored the resolution requesting information from Taylor about the basis of his removals since he took office, complained on the Senate floor that "two thousand one hundred and three appointed in consequence of REMOVALS alone for the year ending June 30, 1849! That period embraces four months under the present Administration, and eight under that of the proceeding. I am informed that very few of the removals were made prior to the 4th of March" (the day of Taylor's inauguration). Cong. Globe, 31st Cong., 1st Sess. A47–A52 (Sen. Bradbury, D-Me.) (January 15, 1850). There are no recorded Senate speeches addressing Taylor's recess appointments.

45. See, e.g., 7 Op. Att. Gen. 186 (1855). See also 10 Op. Att. Gen. 356 (1862); 12 Op. Att. Gen. 449 (1868); 12 Op. Att. Gen. 455 (1868); 14 Op. Att. Gen. 562 (1875); 15 Op. Att. Gen. 207 (1877); 16 Op. Att. Gen. 522 (1880); 17 Op. Att. Gen. 521 (1883); 18 Op. Att. Gen. 29 (1884); 19 Op. Att. Gen. 261 (1889); 26 Op. Att. Gen. 234

(1907); 30 Op. Att. Gen. 314 (1914); 33 Op. Att. Gen. 20 (1921); 41 Op. Att. Gen. 463 (1960); 6 Op. Att. Gen. 585 (1982).

46. Whigs wanted Taylor to remove as many Democrats from federal offices as possible to open vacancies for Whigs. Holt, *Rise and Fall*, at 418.

47. Smith, *Presidencies of Taylor and Fillmore*, at 66.

48. See, e.g., Cong. Globe, 31st Cong., 1st Sess., at 500–501 (April 23, 1850) (statement of Sen. John Bell, W.-Tenn.); at 504 (statement of Senator Jesse Bright, D.-Ind.).

49. See 5 Op. Att. Gen. 227 (February 2, 1850).

50. Taylor's resolve to remove his entire cabinet was mentioned, or reported, by a number of contemporaneous observers. See, e.g., *The Life of Thurlow Weed including His Autobiography and a Memoir* 590–91 (Harriet A. Weed, ed., Boston: Houghton Mifflin, 1884); Bauer, *Zachary Taylor*, at 312.

51. See Andrew Jackson, Message to the Senate Protesting Censure Resolution (April 15, 1834).

52. See Cong. Globe, 31st Cong., 1st Sess. 90 (December 27 and 29, 1849) (approving House resolution); id. at 185 (approving Senate resolution).

53. Taylor, Inaugural Address, at 26–30.

54. Id. at 28–29.

55. See Cong. Globe, 31st Cong., 1st Sess. 405 (March 4, 1850). Initially, the House had considered addressing the resolution to the postmaster general, id. at 111 (January 7, 1850), which prompted a debate within the House on the constitutionality of its authority to make such a request to the postmaster general. The House resolved the matter by addressing the resolution directly to the president.

56. Cong. Globe, 31st Cong., 1st Sess. 1179 (June 11, 1850).

57. Richardson, *Compilation*, at 47–48. See also id. ("I think there is no reason for seriously apprehending that Texas will practically interfere with the possession of the United States").

58. Taylor complied unconditionally with over thirty resolutions requesting documents pertaining to various actions, including treaties, conventions, the boundary dispute between New Mexico and Texas, nominations, and his plan for statehood for California and New Mexico. Taylor did not claim, much less refuse to comply with any of these resolutions because of, executive privilege. He might not have asserted claims of executive privilege because many of the documents requested did not involve internal communications within the White House or between Taylor and other executive branch officials. Nevertheless, some requests were worded broadly, and Taylor responded to several with internal reports produced by cabinet members. In all likelihood, Taylor did not think in terms of executive privilege and believed that complying with the document requests showed proper deference to Congress or was the politically expedient thing to do.

59. See, e.g., Cong. Globe, 31st Cong., 1st Sess. 1344–54 (July 6, 1850).

60. Id. at 1353–54.

61. Some historians suggest that the House censured Taylor, while others do not. Both sides are right. It appears after considerable discussion that the House finally approved the three resolutions censuring three members of Taylor's cabinet for their conduct relating to the Galphin claim. Immediately after approving these resolutions, further efforts to amend them were made, which provoked the House to adjourn without acting on the proposed amendments. When the House reconvened on July 9, a motion was made to amend the resolutions to include explicit reference to Taylor. At this point, for the first time in the debate on the resolutions, concerns were expressed about whether formally censuring the president raised constitutional difficulties. Representative Isaac Holmes, a Democrat from South Carolina, suggested that "it was out of order in the proceedings of the committee . . . to embrace the President." Representative William Duer, a Whig from New York, expounded that Featherstone's proposed amendment required a consideration of the propriety of impeaching the president: "otherwise we are acting vainly and idly." Cong. Globe, 31st Cong., 1st Sess. 1359–60 (July 9, 1850). Duer elaborated further that "it is not proper for the House to examine into the conduct of any officer, and to put him on trial where no notice has been given, and no opportunity is afforded for [deference]." Id at 1360. Presumably, no one had expressed concerns similar to those of Duer in the deliberations on the resolutions up until then because the House had notified Taylor's secretary of war, treasury secretary, and attorney general that the House was considering their censure. Nevertheless, the news soon reached the House floor that Taylor was dying. Accordingly, the House, by a vote of 176–16, approved a resolution stating that "instead of discussing [Taylor's] cabinet, the House does now adjourn." Id. On Monday, July 15, 1850, the amendment to include a reference to Taylor in the censure resolution was formally withdrawn. Id. at 1371.

62. See Jean H. Baker, *James Buchanan* 115 (New York: Times Books, 2004); Elbert B. Smith, *The Presidency of James Buchanan* 104, 121, 177 (Lawrence: University Press of Kansas, 1975).

63. Besides Grant and Lee, Civil War commanders who served in the Mexican War included P. G. T. Beauregard (Confederacy), Simon Bolivar Buckner (Confederacy), Ambrose Burnside (Union), John C. Fremont (Union), Stonewall Jackson (Confederacy), Albert Sydney Johnston (Confederacy), Joseph Johnston (Confederacy), James Longstreet (Confederacy), George Meade (Union), George McClelland (Union), Fitz-John Porter (Union), Winfield Scott (Union), and William Tecumseh Sherman (Union).

64. 1 Ulysses Grant, *Personal Memoirs of U.S. Grant* 138–39 (New York: C. L. Webster, 1885–86).

65. The Black Hawk War, in May–July 1832, provided another opportunity for future Union and Confederate commanders to get firsthand combat experience. Shortly after becoming a colonel, Taylor was asked to lead a regiment and volunteer militia to assist with the army's efforts to stop a series of raids into white settlements in

a region north and northwest of Rock Island, Illinois, by a band of Indians led by a sixty-five-year-old Sauk chief known as Black Hawk. Though Taylor's men saw little combat, Taylor emerged from the experience with a deep-seated distrust of a volunteer army.

66. Davis fell in love with Taylor's daughter Sarah while he was serving under Taylor in the Black Hawk War. In 1835, Davis married her over Taylor's objection. Taylor opposed the marriage because he did not want his daughter to endure the hardships of being married to an army officer. When three months after her wedding Sarah died from malaria, Davis and Taylor were both devastated. Taylor blamed Davis for her death because he felt Davis should have known better than to take her with him on a trip into an area in which there was an outbreak of malaria. For the next decade, the two men did not talk to each other. In 1845, they met by chance and reconciled while they were both traveling on the same steamboat.

67. See, e.g., Letter from Zachary Taylor to Jefferson Davis, February 16, 1848 ("In all changes and operations which may take place and be carried out for the presidency, I must beg you, my dear General, that you will, without regard to what concerns me, look to your interest"). According to Davis's widow, Taylor's last words to Davis were, "Apply the Constitution to the measure, Sir, regardless of the consequences." Letter from Varina Davis to Her Mother, July 10, 1850, in Jefferson Davis, *Private Letters, 1823–1859* 63 (R. Strode, ed., New York: Harcourt, Brace & World, 1966).

68. See, e.g., Letter from Taylor to Jefferson Davis, August 16, 1847 (acknowledging that discussion of the slavery question "appears to have a contrary effect on the temper and passions of the masses, only adding fuel to the flames, and to widen instead of healing the breach between the parties concerned—I will not say interested, for those of the non slave-holding states have no interest in the matter. Let them go on to discuss the institutions of the South without notice as regards the matter in question, without its being noticed, but the moment they go beyond that point where resistance becomes right and proper, let the South act promptly, boldly and decisively, with arms in their hands if necessary, as that Union in that case will be blown to atoms, or will no longer be worth preserving").

69. For an example of Davis's strict constitutional construction, see Letter from Jefferson Davis to B. Pendleton, November 10, 1850 ("The framers of the Constitution were those who preferred revolution and separation from the mother country to submission—to taxation by others than their own representatives; they never would have consented to found a new government, in which the minority should be subject to the discretionary legislation of the majority. The Government they instituted was one of specific grants and enumerated subjects, all else reserved to the States and the people").

70. See Jefferson Davis, *Constitutionalist: His Letters, Papers and Speeches* 437–38 (Dumbar Rowland, ed., Jackson: Printed for the Mississippi Department of Archives and History, 1923) (quoting Davis in Senate debate on June 27, 1850).

71. See id. at 438–40 (quoting Davis in Senate debate on August 5, 1850).

72. See, e.g., Letter from Abraham Lincoln to Archibald Williams, April 30, 1848 ("Mr. Clay's chance for an election, is just no chance at all. . . . In my judgment, we can elect nobody but Gen. Taylor").

73. Cong. Globe, 30th Cong., 1st Sess. 184 (January 3, 1849). The House approved the resolution 82–81. Besides Lincoln, the representatives voting to approve the resolution included John Quincy Adams, Joshua Gidding, Alexander Stephens, and Amos Tuck.

74. See Letter from Abraham Lincoln to the Honorable John Clayton, Secretary of State, August 21, 1849.

75. See *Chicago Weekly Journal*, August 6, 1850; *Chicago Daily Journal*, July 27, 1850.

76. Abraham Lincoln, For Equalization of Foreign and Domestic Prices by a Protective Tariff, Remarks at Pittsburgh, Pennsylvania, February 15, 1861.

77. Id. at 201.

78. On Lincoln's appointments, see Michael J. Gerhardt, *The Federal Appointments Process: A Constitutional and Historical Analysis* 47, 49, 145 (rev. ed., Durham: Duke University Press, 2003).

79. See 10 Op. Att. Gen. 356 (1862).

CHAPTER 5

1. See, e.g., Letter from Henry Clay to James Clay, July 18, 1850.

2. See, e.g., Letter from Henry Clay to Thomas Hart Clay, August 6, 1850; Letter from Henry Clay to James Clay, July 18, 1850. Soon after Taylor died, Seward acknowledged the sharp decline in his influence over the White House and the corresponding rise in Clay's influence. See Elbert Smith, *The Presidencies of Zachary Taylor and Millard Fillmore* 167–69 (Lawrence: University Press of Kansas, 1988).

3. See Robert Rayback, *Millard Fillmore: Biography of a President* 214 (Buffalo, N.Y.: Published for the Buffalo Historical Society by H. Stewart, 1959).

4. Letter from Millard Fillmore to James Brooks, May 24, 1852, in 11 *Millard Fillmore Papers* 321–22 (Frank H. Severance, ed., Buffalo Historical Society, 1907).

5. Millard Fillmore, First Annual Message to Congress (December 2, 1850), in 5 *A Compilation of Messages and Papers of the Presidents, 1789–1897* 93 (James D. Richardson, ed., Washington, D.C.: U.S. Government Printing Office, 1900).

6. The law had no practical effect, since the slave trade was flourishing in northern Virginia.

7. See, e.g., New York v. United States, 505 U.S. 144 (1992).

8. See Cong. Globe, 31st Cong., 1st Sess., appendix, 1533 (August 12, 1850) (Sen. Jefferson Davis, D-Miss.) ("We are about permanently to destroy the balance of power between the sections of the Union, by securing a majority to one in both Houses of Congress").

9. See Smith, *Presidencies of Taylor and Fillmore*, at 185.

10. Many Southerners in Congress believed the Constitution required new states to go through territorial phases before admission into the Union. Congress followed this process for New Mexico and Utah but not for California. For an overview of the debates over this and other issues related to the Compromise of 1850, see, e.g., Fergus M. Bordewich, *America's Great Debate: Henry Clay, Stephen A. Douglas, and the Compromise That Preserved the Union* (New York: Simon & Schuster, 2012); Robert V. Remini, *Henry Clay: Statesman for the Union* 730–61 (New York: Norton, 1991); David M. Potter, *The Impending Crisis, 1841–1861* 112–20 (Don E. Fehrenbacher, ed., 1963); Holman Hamilton, *Prologue to Conflict: The Crisis and Compromise* 141–44 (Lexington: University of Kentucky Press, 1964).

11. See South Dakota v. Dole, 483 U.S. 203 (1987).

12. Prigg v. Pennsylvania, 41 U.S. (Pet.) 539 (1842).

13. See, e.g., Cong. Globe, 31st Cong., 2nd Sess. 1473–88 (July 31, 1850) (Statement of Sen. Jefferson Davis, D-Miss.).

14. See Letter from Daniel Webster to Haven Webster, July 21, 1850.

15. See Millard Fillmore, Special Message to the Congress (August 6, 1850).

16. See Letter from Millard Fillmore to Hamilton Fish, November 21, 1850. A month earlier, Fillmore had expressed the same point in a letter to his secretary of state. See Letter from Millard Fillmore to Daniel Webster, October 23, 1850.

17. Most of these laws were not enacted until after the Kansas-Nebraska Act of 1854. Indiana and Iowa in 1851 and Illinois in 1853 enacted laws barring the settlement of any African-Americans within their borders. Similarly, the legislatures of Connecticut, Delaware, Illinois, Iowa, New Hampshire, and New Jersey enacted resolutions approving *all* the measures enacted in 1850.

18. See U.S. Const., art. VI, sec. 1 ("This Constitution, and the Laws of the United States which shall be made in Pursuance thereof . . . shall be the supreme Law of the Land; and the Judges in every State shall be bound thereby, any Thing in the Constitution or Laws of any State to the Contrary notwithstanding").

19. Letter from Fillmore to Daniel Webster, October 28, 1850.

20. See Rayback, *Millard Fillmore*, 270–71 (citation omitted).

21. Letter from Fillmore to Hamilton Fish, November 21, 1850.

22. Fillmore, First Annual Message to Congress, at 79–93.

23. See Millard Fillmore, By the President of the United States A Proclamation (February 18, 1851), in 5 Richardson, *Compilation*, at 110.

24. See Millard Fillmore, Special Message to the United States Senate, February 19, 1851.

25. Letter from Daniel Webster to F. S. Lathrop and Others, October 28, 1850.

26. See Letter from Daniel Webster to Millard Fillmore, October 29, 1850; Letter from Daniel Webster to Millard Fillmore, April 13, 1851; Letter from Millard Fillmore to Daniel Webster, April 16, 1851.

27. See Letter from Daniel Webster to Millard Fillmore, April 13, 1851.

28. 11 *The Writings and Speeches of Daniel Webster* 408–21 (Boston: Little, Brown, 1903).

29. Id. at 242–62.
30. Id. at 267–90.
31. Id. at 237–41.
32. Cong. Globe, 31st Cong., 2nd Sess., appendix, 293–98.
33. See Henry S. Foote, *Casket of Reminiscences* 162–65 (Washington, D.C., 1880).
34. Cong. Globe, 31st Cong., 2nd Sess., 675–76, appendix, 320–23.
35. See Allan Nevins, *Ordeal of the Union*, vol. 1, *Fruits of Manifest Destiny, 1847–1852* 344 (New York: Scribner, 1947).
36. Letter from Daniel Webster to Harvey, October 2, 1851; Letter from Daniel Webster to Thomas Corwin, November 13, 1851.
37. See Robert V. Remini, *Daniel Webster: The Man and His Time* 689 (New York: Norton, 1997).
38. 60 U.S. 393, 19 (How.) 393 (1856).
39. After leaving the Supreme Court, Curtis argued fifty-four cases before the Court and successfully defended President Andrew Johnson in his Senate impeachment trial.
40. 53 U.S. (12 How.) 299 (1851).
41. See "Constitutionality of the Fugitive Slave Act," 5 Op. Att. Gen. 254 (September 18, 1850).
42. See "Pardoning Power of the President," 5 Op. Att. Gen. 532 (April 22, 1852). The incident prompting the pardon inspired Harriet Beecher Stowe to write her novel *Uncle Tom's Cabin* (1852).

CHAPTER 6

1. Though Pierce never finished his Senate term, his Democratic colleagues in the Senate recalled his fierce party loyalty. After Polk became president, he appointed Pierce as U.S. attorney for New Hampshire and later asked Pierce to be his attorney general. Pierce declined. Since Polk was adamant about appointing to his cabinet only people with no presidential ambitions, he most likely thought that Pierce had no presidential aspirations. Pierce explained that he was declining to return to Washington for personal reasons and had no intentions to reenter into full-time public service "except at the call of my country in time of war."
2. See Roy Franklin Nichols, *Franklin Pierce: Young Hickory of the Granite Hills* 203 (Philadelphia: University of Pennsylvania Press; London: H. Milford, Oxford University Press, 1931); Allan Nevins, *Ordeal of the Union*, vol. 2, *A House Divided, 1852–1857* 41 (New York: Scribner, 1947).
3. Inaugural Address, March 4, 1853, in 5 *A Compilation of Messages and Papers of the Presidents, 1789–1897* 197 (James D. Richardson, ed., Washington, D.C.: U.S. Government Printing Office, 1900).
4. Aware of Polk's dark-horse victory less than a decade before, Democrats hoped for the same result with Pierce and taunted Republicans, "We Polked you in 1844; we shall Pierce you in 1852."

5. William Rufus DeVane King served only a month as Pierce's vice president. After initially representing North Carolina in the House of Representatives, King served for nearly three decades as a senator from Alabama. Selected as vice president to appease his close friend and political ally James Buchanan, King moved to Cuba after the 1852 election for treatment of tuberculosis. Since he was too weak to return to the United States for the inauguration, he became the first (and thus far only) nationally elected official to take the oath of office on foreign soil. Although he regained enough strength to return to Alabama, he died there in April 1853.

6. Skowronek attributes Pierce's collapse as a president to political missteps including breaking his pledge in his inaugural address "not to reopen the slave question." Stephen Skowronek, *Presidential Leadership in Political Time: Reprise and Reappraisal* 68 (2nd ed., Lawrence: University Press of Kansas, 2011). This is probably true, though Pierce consistently adhered throughout his career to the same constitutional commitments with respect to the federal government's authority to interfere with slavery in the territories or the states.

7. Some historians maintain that "Democratic adherence to 'the school of the strictest construction of the constitution' was not indicative of any lack of faith in the wisdom or goodness of the people, but rather a skepticism about whether any government . . . could give adequate expression to the people's will. Such views arose from that profound skepticism and distrust of impersonal institutions which lay at the heart of Jacksonianism." Lawrence Frederick Kohl, *The Politics of Individualism: Parties and the American Character in the Jacksonian Era* 179 (New York: Oxford University Press, 1989).

8. Pierce, Inaugural Address, at 201–2.

9. Third Annual Message, December 31, 1855, in 5 Richardson, *Compilation*, at 202.

10. Fourth Annual Message, December 2, 1856, in 5 Richardson, *Compilation*, at 397.

11. See Franklin Pierce, Veto Message, May 3, 1834, in 5 Richardson, *Compilation*, at 249.

12. 60 U.S. (19 How.) 393 (1857).

13. See The Slaughter-House Cases, 83 U.S. 36 (1873).

14. For a full discussion of the criteria that Pierce and other antebellum presidents used in making lower court appointments, see my co-authored article with Michael A. Stein, "The Politics of Early Justice: Federal Judicial Selection, 1789–1861".

15. See generally Larry Gara, *The Presidency of Franklin Pierce* 129–33 (Lawrence: University Press of Kansas, 1991).

16. See generally id. at 149–55; Nevins, *A House Divided*, at 347–79.

17. At this critical juncture in his administration, Pierce, an ardent Democrat, opted to follow the Whig practice of allowing his cabinet to determine the administration's major policy initiatives. Although there are no contemporary records explaining why Pierce chose the practice that had largely died with Harrison, he may have done so because of the magnitude of the issue involved and his desire to identify the cabinet members on whom he could depend to represent him well in negotiating with congressional leaders.

18. The Ostend Manifesto, October 18, 1854.

19. Fallout from the Ostend Manifesto did not dissuade Pierce from ignoring two of Cushing's official opinions to approve a private band of proslavery soldiers led by William Walker to provoke rebellion in Nicaragua. See, e.g., "Illegal Military Expeditions," 8 Op. Att. Gen. 375 (1857); "Unlawful Military Expeditions," 8 Op. Att. Gen. 472 (1855). The revolution succeeded, Walker became Nicaraguan president, and Pierce recognized the new government.

20. See Nevins, *A House Divided*, at 58, 59.

21. For the details of Cushing's controversial political career, see John M. Belohlavek, *Broken Glass: Caleb Cushing and the Shattering of the Union* (Kent, Ohio: Kent State University Press, 2005); Claude Fuess, *The Life of Caleb Cushing*, 2 vols. (New York: Harcourt, Brace, 1923).

22. "Office and Duties of the Attorney General," 6 Op. Att. Gen. 326 (March 8, 1954).

23. See INS v. Chadha, 462 U.S. 919 (1983).

24. See "Resolutions of Congress," 6 Op. Att. Gen. 680 (August 23, 1854).

25. See "Relation of the President to the Executive Departments," 7 Op. Att. Gen. 453 (August 31, 1855). Cushing also supported Pierce's initiative, which Congress enacted in 1855, to create the Court of Claims to adjudicate the claims of Mexican War veterans against the United States. Today, the court is a specialized federal circuit court of appeals that hears patent claims and damage claims against the United States.

26. See United States v. Myers, 272 U.S. 52 (1926).

27. See, e.g., "Yazoo City Post Office Case," 8 Op. Att. Gen. 489 (1857) (upholding the power of southern postmasters not to deliver abolitionist publications in the mail).

28. See Gara, *Presidency of Franklin Pierce*, at 69–70.

29. See Nevins, *A House Divided*, at 73–74.

30. See "Extradition of Fugitives from Service," 6 Op. Att. Gen. 220 (1853); "Extradition of Fugitives from Service," 6 Op. Att. Gen. 229 (1853); "Reclamation of Fugitives from Service in Unorganized Territories," 6 Op. Att. Gen. 302 (1854); "Extradition of Fugitives from Service," 6 Op. Att. Gen. 466 (1854); "Constitutionality of the Law for the Extradition of Fugitives," 6 Op. Att. Gen. 713 (1854); "Extradition of Fugitives from Service," 7 Op. Att. Gen. 51 (1855); "Passmore Williamson's Case," 7 Op. Att. Gen. 482 (1855); "Defence of Marshals," 8 Op. Att. Gen. 444 (1853).

31. See "Relation of Indians to Citizenship," 7 Op. Att. Gen. 746, 749–53 (1856) (arguing that slaves are not citizens of the United States and analyzing the question of whether free slaves are citizens).

32. See William J. Cooper Jr., *Jefferson Davis, American* 265–66 (New York: Knopf, 2000) (citation omitted in original) (telling Davis on his last day in office, "I can scarcely bear the parting from you, who have been the strength and solace to me for four anxious years and never failed me").

33. Cooper, *Jefferson Davis, American*, at 283 (2000) (quoting Davis) (citation omitted in original).

34. For two historical overviews of the Kansas-Nebraska Act, see Nevins, *A House Divided*, at 78–121; Roy F. Nichols, "The Kansas-Nebraska Act: A Century of Historiography," 43 *Mississippi Valley Historical Review* 187–212 (1956).

35. On Bleeding Kansas, see, e.g., Gara, *Presidency of Franklin Pierce*, at 101–26; Nevins, *A House Divided*, at 301–46.

36. Franklin Pierce, Special Message, January 24, 1856.

37. Douglas conducted hearings to investigate the troubles in Kansas. At their end, he affirmed all of Pierce's findings and recommendations and agreed with Pierce that the emigrant aid societies from Massachusetts were responsible for Bleeding Kansas.

38. Franklin Pierce, Presidential Proclamation, February 11, 1856.

39. Nichols, *Franklin Pierce*, at 495 (quoting Pierce) (citation omitted in original).

40. Id. at 361 (quoting Pierce) (citations omitted in original).

41. Though few slaves were returned under the law and few rescuers prosecuted, there were enough incidents to intensify northern opposition to its enforcement. Earlier in Pierce's presidency, Sherman Booth and three others were arrested in Wisconsin for assisting in the rescue of Joshua Glover, a fugitive slave who had been working near a farm in Racine. After Booth's conviction in federal court his lawyer appealed to a state court, which issued a writ of habeas corpus and declared the Fugitive Slave Act void in Wisconsin. The Wisconsin Supreme Court affirmed the decision. A federal judge then ordered Booth's re-arrest. Legal issues in the case remained unresolved until the Supreme Court, in Abelman v. Booth, 62 U.S. 506 (1859), upheld the constitutionality of the Fugitive Slave Act of 1850 and the supremacy of federal courts over state courts on constitutional questions.

42. See "Suits against Marshals," 6 Op. Att. Gen. 500 (1854).

43. Michael F. Holt, *Franklin Pierce* 82 (New York: Times Books/Henry Holt 2012).

44. "Suits against Marshals," 6 Op. Att. Gen. 500 (1854).

45. "Reclamation of Fugitives from Service in Unorganized Territories," 6 Op. Att. Gen. 302 (1854).

46. "Extradition of Fugitives from Service," 6 Op. Att. Gen. 466 (1854).

47. "Constitutionality of the Law for the Extradition of Fugitives," 6 Op. Att. Gen. 713 (1854).

48. Caleb Cushing, "Yazoo City Post Office Case," 8 Op. Att. Gen. 489 (March 2, 1857).

CHAPTER 7

1. Shortly before accepting the nomination, Arthur met privately with Conkling. Conkling told Arthur not to take the job because he believed the ticket would lose and it would end Arthur's career. Arthur responded, "The office of the vice president is a greater honor than I ever dreamed of attaining." Kenneth D. Ackerman, *Dark Horse: The Surprising Election and Political Murder of President James A. Garfield* 128 (New York: Carroll & Graf, 2003) (citation omitted). The conversation

between the two men is known because when they were talking they did not notice a man sitting in the corner of the room. The man, who hid behind a newspaper that he pretended to be reading, was a reporter for the *Brooklyn Daily Eagle*. Id. at 127.

2. For the contest for control over patronage in New York and its consequences, see id. at 299–347.

3. Peter W. Schroth, "Constitutional and Administrative Law: Corruption and Accountability of the Civil Service of the United States," 54 *American Journal of Comparative Law* 553, 560 (2006).

4. Hayes placed John Jay's grandson in charge of the commission investigating the New York Customs House. After the Jay Commission's report, Hayes asked Arthur and Alonzo Cornell, the Customs House's naval officer, to resign. Both refused. Hayes then sent the names of their replacements to the Senate for confirmation, but the nominations were referred to the Commerce Committee, which Conkling chaired. The committee urged the Senate to reject the nominations, and it did. In the next session, Hayes again tried to secure the confirmation of Arthur's and Connell's replacements but failed. After Congress adjourned for the summer of 1878, Hayes fired Arthur and Cornell and named recess appointees to replace them. The Senate later confirmed his recess appointees.

5. See, e.g., 2 *The Works of James Abram Garfield* 499–519 (Burke A. Hinsdale, ed., Boston: J. R. Osgood, 1882).

6. Chester A. Arthur, First Annual Message to Congress, December 8, 1881.

7. The large number of abstentions reflected many Republicans' feelings that they were stuck between two, unattractive alternatives—approving the bill and dismantling the patronage system they had long supported *or* disapproving the bill at the likely cost of their seats in Congress.

8. For a description of the debates, see Justus D. Doenecke, *The Presidencies of James A. Garfield and Chester A. Arthur* 97–102 (Lawrence: University Press of Kansas, 1981).

9. U.S. Const., art. II, sec. 3.

10. These orders were issued pursuant to the authority given to the president by the Pendleton Act to extend the classified service. See Executive Order (May 7, 1883); Executive Order (December 5, 1883); Executive Order (January 18, 1884); Executive Order (April 23, 1884); Executive Order (June 12, 1884); Executive Order (July 18, 1884); Executive Order (July 22, 1884); Executive Order (November 10, 1884); Executive Order (December 5, 1884); Executive Order (January 24, 1885); Executive Order (February 11, 1885); and Executive Order (February 27, 1885).

11. See Doenecke, *Presidencies of Garfield and Arthur*, at 103.

12. 18 Op. Att. Gen. 29 (June 25, 1884).

13. 17 Op. Att. Gen. 530 (March 31, 1883).

14. 17 Op. Att. Gen. 554 (June 12, 1883).

15. 18 Op. Att. Gen. 58 (September 11, 1884).

16. See Zachary Karabell, *Chester Alan Arthur* 69 (New York: Times Books/Henry Holt 2004).

17. Although Arthur documented the removals in his Second Annual Message (December 4, 1882), he addressed the subject in his two other annual messages. Since the Pendleton Civil Service Act covered a small number of federal jobs and had not been fully implemented by the end of his presidency, it is unlikely to have been the primary reason for his reticence. It is possible that Arthur initially included the information about removals to burnish his image as someone committed to transcending the old patronage system. It is also possible that he excluded further information about removals because he did not want to do or say anything that would undermine that image.

18. Doenecke, *Presidencies of Garfield and Arthur*, at 93 (citation omitted).

19. Chester A. Arthur, First Annual Message (December 6, 1881).

20. Karabell, *Chester Alan Arthur*, at 71.

21. Roger Matuz, *The Presidents Fact Book* 195 (Bill Harris, ed., Black Dog and Levanthal Publishers, 2009) (citation omitted).

22. Hoar was the brother of Ebeneezer Hoar, who had been Grant's attorney general and whose Supreme Court nomination the Senate rejected in 1870. George was also a member of the special election commission that settled the disputed presidential election of 1876, and he drafted the Presidential Succession Act of 1886.

23. Gray was the first Supreme Court of Massachusetts justice to hire a law clerk. The clerk's name was Louis Brandeis.

24. Conkling had turned down Grant's offer to nominate him as chief justice. The opportunity was the last that Conkling had to return to public service. See generally Michael J. Gerhardt, *The Federal Appointments Process: A Constitutional and Historical Analysis* 151 (rev. ed., Durham: Duke University Press, 2003).

25. While the floor debate was intense because many senators disliked Conkling, the final vote to confirm his nomination was 39–12.

26. U.S. Const., art. I, sec. 6, cl. 2.

27. 17 Op. Att. Gen. 522 (February 21, 1883).

28. 17 Op. Att. Gen. 365 (May 26, 1882).

29. Jefferson Powell notes that President Washington had "notified the Senate that he considered his nomination of William Paterson to be an associate justice 'to have been null by the Constitution' because Paterson 'was a member of the Senate when the law creating that office was passed, and . . . the time for which he was elected has not expired.'" H. Jefferson Powell, *The Constitution and the Attorneys General* 214 (Durham, N.C.: Carolina Academic Press, 1999) (citation omitted in original).

30. See, e.g., Doenecke, *Presidencies of Garfield and Arthur*, at 81–84; Karabell, *Chester Alan Arthur*, at 84–86.

31. A pocket veto arises if Congress adjourns before the ten days are up that the Constitution allows a president to sign or veto a bill. President Madison cast the first two of them. For more on this subject, see "Calvin Coolidge," chapter 12.

32. Chinese Exclusion Bill, S. 71, 48th Congress (1882).

33. Chester A. Arthur, Veto Message of April 4, 1882.

34. Id.

35. Chinese Exclusion Act of 1882, Ch. 126, 22 Stat. 58, repealed by Ch. 344, Sec. 1, 57 Stat. 600 (1943). The new bill applied to "both skilled and unskilled laborers and Chinese employed in mining," and it prohibited federal courts from granting U.S. citizenship to any Chinese persons residing within the United States.

36. See Doenecke, *Presidencies of Garfield and Arthur*, at 81.

37. Chester A. Arthur, Veto Message of August 1, 1882.

38. Id.

39. Id.

40. See Override of Presidential Veto by Chester A. Arthur by the House and the Senate, 47 Cong., Ch. 375, 22 Stat. 213 (1882).

41. See 17 Op. Att. Gen. 297 (March 15, 1882).

42. 18 Op. Att. Gen. 18 (June 23, 1884).

43. Chester A. Arthur, Veto Message of July 2, 1884.

44. See Reynolds v. United States, 98 U.S. 145 (1879).

45. Inaugural Address of James A. Garfield, March 4, 1881.

46. Edmunds Anti-Polygamy Act of 1882, 47th Cong., Ch. 47, 22 Stat. 30 (1882).

47. Id.

48. 17 Op. Att. Gen. 314 (March 22, 1882).

49. See Doenecke, *Presidencies of Garfield and Arthur*, at 84–85.

50. Chester A. Arthur, First Annual Message to U.S. Congress, December 6, 1881.

51. See generally id. at 85–92.

52. Id. (citation omitted).

53. Id. at 91.

54. Id.

55. Id.

56. 106 U.S. 629 (1883).

57. Civil Rights Act of 1875, 43 Cong., Ch. 114, 18 Stat. 335 (1875).

58. See The Civil Rights Cases, 109 U.S. 3 (1883).

59. Id. at 26.

60. Chester A. Arthur, Third Annual Message to U.S. Congress, December 4, 1883.

61. Id.

62. 78 Stat. 241 (1964).

CHAPTER 8

1. See Henry Graff, *Grover Cleveland* (New York: Time Books, 2002) (back cover) (calling Cleveland "the best unknown president").

2. Id.

3. See 1 *The Papers of Woodrow Wilson* 112–13 (Arthur Link, ed., Princeton: Princeton University Press, 1966–94).

4. Grover Cleveland, First Inaugural Address, March 4, 1885.

5. John A. Garrity, "Grover Cleveland," in *The Presidents: A Reference History* 283, 286 (2nd ed., Henry Graff, ed., New York: Macmillan Reference Library, 1997) (citation omitted in original).

6. Message of Congress, reprinted in 11 *A Compilation of the Messages and Papers of the Presidents, 1789–1897* 4968 (March 1, 1886) (James D. Richardson, ed., Washington, D.C.: U.S. Government Printing Office, 1900).

7. Hendricks died November 25, 1885. For the twelve days from Hendricks's death until John Sherman's election as president pro tem of the Senate, no one stood in the line of presidential succession. The vice presidency remained unoccupied for the rest of Cleveland's first term.

8. Grover Cleveland, First Annual Message, December 8, 1885.

9. 24 Sta. 1 (1886). Superseding the Presidential Succession Act of 1792, the act provided that on the death, incapacity, or resignation of both the president and the vice president, the line of succession to the presidency was to fall to the cabinet in the chronological order of the creation of each department. This law remained in effect until the Presidential Succession Act of 1947, which the Twenty-fifth Amendment superseded in 1967.

10. "An Act to Fix the Day for the Meeting of Electors of President and Vice-President, and to Provide for and Regulate the Counting of Votes for President and Vice-President, and the Decision of Questions Arising Thereon," 49 Cong. Ch. 90, 24 Stat. 373 (1887).

11. 531 U.S. 98 (2000).

12. "An Act to Regulate Commerce," 49 Cong. Ch. 104, 24 Stat. 379 (1887).

13. Wabash, St. Louis & Pacific Railroad Company v. Illinois, 118 U.S. 557 (1886).

14. Robert E. Welch Jr., *The Presidencies of Grover Cleveland* 79 (Lawrence: University Press of Kansas, 1988).

15. One casualty of Cleveland's refusal to meddle with congressional lawmaking was his proposal for Congress to enact legislation "providing for the arbitration of disputes between laboring men and employers." See Grover Cleveland, Special Message, April 22, 1886; Grover Cleveland, Second Annual Message, December 6, 1886. He made the proposal in response to the Haymarket Square massacre, in which seven Chicago police officers had been killed and many others had been injured after they had broken up a labor rally and a bomb had exploded among their ranks.

16. Grover Cleveland, First Annual Message, December 8, 1885.

17. Alan Nevins, *Grover Cleveland: A Study in Courage* 372–73 (New York: Dodd, Mead, 1932).

18. Grover Cleveland, Third Annual Message, December 6, 1887.

19. Nevins, *Grover Cleveland*, at 381.

20. See Welch, *Presidencies of Grover Cleveland*, at 81–89.

21. For a good discussion of the debates over the tariff bill, see Nevins, *Grover Cleveland*, at 383–413.

22. Grover Cleveland, First Inaugural Address, March 4, 1885.

23. *New York Herald*, January 5, 6, 1886 (quoting President Cleveland).
24. Id.
25. Id.
26. Grover Cleveland, Veto Message, February 11, 1887. Newspaper editorials and public opinion sided with Cleveland's construction of the bill as a boondoggle for an "indiscriminate body of charity-seekers." Nevins, *Grover Cleveland*, at 331.
27. Grover Cleveland, Veto of the Texas Seed Bill, February 16, 1887.
28. Cleveland's principled objections to legislation favoring special interests foreshadow similar objections to earmarks.
29. According to the Justice Department's Office of Legal Counsel, the only nineteenth-century presidents to issue signing statements were Andrew Jackson, John Tyler, Abraham Lincoln, Andrew Johnson, and Ulysses Grant. See "The Legal Significance of Presidential Signing Statements," appendix, 17 Op. O.L.C. 131 (November 3, 1993).
30. Letter to the National Civil Service Reform League, December 25, 1885.
31. Id. (citation omitted).
32. Id. at 238.
33. Welch, *Presidencies of Grover Cleveland*, at 60.
34. Id. By waiting until the terms of Republicans expired, Cleveland's assistant postmaster general, Adlai Stevenson, replaced more than 40,000 fourth-class postmasterships. See Nevins, *Grover Cleveland*, at 251. In retaliation against the removals, the Republican-controlled Senate tabled Stevenson's nomination to the District of Columbia Supreme Court. In 1893, Stevenson returned to power as Cleveland's vice president.
35. See Leonard White, *The Republican Era: A Study in Administrative History, 1869–1901*, at 307 (New York: Macmillan, 1958).
36. See "An Act Regulating the Tenure of Certain Civil Officers," 39 Cong. Ch. 154, 14 Stat. 430 (1867).
37. See "An Act to Amend 'an Act Regulating the Tenure of Certain Civil Officers,'" 41 Cong. Ch. 10, 16 Stat. 6 (1869).
38. See generally Nevins, *Grover Cleveland*, at 255.
39. Id. at 254.
40. Id. at 257.
41. Id.
42. Id. at 258.
43. Id.
44. S. Res., 49th Cong., Cong. Rec. 2212 (1886).
45. See Nevins, *Grover Cleveland*, at 258.
46. Id. at 258–59.
47. See id. at 259.
48. The Senate debated the resolutions throughout the month of March 1886. Id. at 260.
49. See Cong. Rec. 2332 ff. (March 26, 1886).
50. Nevins, *Grover Cleveland*, at 260.

51. Grover Cleveland, Special Message to the Senate of the United States, March 1, 1886.

52. Nevins, *Grover Cleveland*, at 261.

53. Id. at 264.

54. See 17 Cong. Rec. 2783, 2784–2810 (March 26, 1886).

55. Cong. Rec. 2703 ff. (March 24, 1886).

56. Welch, *Presidencies of Grover Cleveland*, at 56.

57. See S. 512, 49th Cong. (1886).

58. "An Act to Repeal Certain Sections of the Revised Statutes of the United States Relating to the Appointment of Civil Officers," ch. 353, 24 Stat. 500 (1887). See also White, *The Republican Era*, at 31 (suggesting that the formal repeal of the Tenure in Office Act signified Congress's abrogation of its claim "to control presidential discretion in suspending or removing officials in the executive branch").

59. After leaving the presidency, Cleveland wrote that the fight he had with the Senate over the Tenure in Office Act "was an unpleasant controversy happily followed by an expurgation of the last pretense of statutory sanction to an encroachment upon constitutional Executive prerogatives, and thus was a time-honored interpretation of the Constitution restored to us. The President, freed from the Senate's tutelage, became again the independent agent of the people, representing a coordinate branch of their Government, charged with responsibilities which, under his oath, he ought not to avoid or divide with others, and invested with powers, not to be surrendered, but to be used under the guidance of patriotic intention and an unbounded conscience." Grover Cleveland, *Presidential Problems* (New York: Century Co., 1904).

60. Henry Abraham, *Justices and Presidents: A Political History of Appointments to the Supreme Court* 140 (2nd ed., New York: Oxford University Press, 1985).

61. Id.

62. Id. at 139 (emphasis in original).

63. See James Ely Jr., *The Chief Justiceship of Melville Fuller 1888–1910* 21 (Columbia: University of South Carolina Press, 1995).

64. Id. at 22.

65. Id. at 22 (citations omitted).

66. Fuller is one of four chief justices who were appointed by Democratic presidents. The others were Roger Taney (Andrew Jackson), Harlan Fiske Stone (Franklin D. Roosevelt), and Fred Vinson (Harry Truman). Republican presidents have appointed nine chief justices: Salmon Chase (Lincoln), Morrison Waite (Grant), Edward Douglass White (Taft), William Howard Taft (Harding), Charles Evans Hughes (Hoover), Earl Warren (Eisenhower), Warren Burger (Nixon), William Rehnquist (Reagan), and John Roberts (George W. Bush). Federalist presidents appointed the remaining chief justices: John Jay and Oliver Ellsworth (George Washington) and John Marshall (John Adams).

67. Ely, *Chief Justiceship of Melville Fuller*, at 24 (citation omitted).

68. See Pollock v. Farmers' Loan & Trust Company, 157 U.S. 429 (1895).

69. 198 U.S. 45 (1905).
70. Wilson appointed Louis Brandeis, John Clarke, and James McReynolds to the Supreme Court. Roosevelt's nine Supreme Court appointments were Hugo Black, Felix Frankfurter, Stanley Reed, William O. Douglas, Robert Jackson, Frank Murphy, James Byrnes, Harlan Fiske Stone (as chief justice), and Wiley Rutledge.

CHAPTER 9

1. Homer E. Socolofsky and Allan B. Spetter, *The Presidency of Benjamin Harrison* 16 (Lawrence: University Press of Kansas, 1987).
2. Harrison had trouble handling the tension between his need to use appointments to unify his administration and his campaign pledge to reform the civil service. He became frustrated because his appointments angered more people than they pleased and because he was unable to fulfill his campaign pledge to reform civil service and to temper the zeal of the most reform-minded people in his administration, including the young Theodore Roosevelt, whom he had appointed to the U.S. Civil Service Commission.
3. While Harrison has the distinction of being the only person from Indiana elected president, he was born in Ohio. Thus, he is sometimes counted as the fifth of eight Ohioans elected president.
4. See Henry Adams, *The Education of Henry Adams: An Autobiography* 320 (Boston: Houghton Mifflin, 1918) ("Mr. Harrison was an excellent President, a man of ability and force; perhaps the best President the Republican party put forward since Lincoln's death"). See also *The Autobiography of William Allen White* 358 (New York: Macmillan, 1946) ("Harrison ... brought to leadership in American politics the incarnate nobility of what his party would have been, were it not for its partisans"); Louis W. Koenig, Benjamin Harrison, in *The Presidents: A Reference History* 295 (2nd ed., Henry Graff, ed., New York: Macmillan Reference Library, 1997) (quoting journalist Henry Stoddard's comment, after ranking Cleveland, Theodore Roosevelt, and Woodrow Wilson as the three outstanding presidents between Lincoln and Coolidge, that "I feel as though I were doing an injustice to Benjamin Harrison not to crowd him into the three for, intellectually, he outranked them. He was the ablest of them all").
5. Windom left the Senate in 1883 when Garfield nominated him to serve as his treasury secretary. Blaine blocked the nomination, since the Minnesota delegation had nominated Windom for the Republican presidential nomination, which Blaine lost to Garfield. Shortly after Garfield died, Windom finished his Senate term. After failing to be reelected in 1883, he returned to law practice but subsequently joined the cabinet, though he died less than two years later.
6. Letter from Benjamin Harrison to Henry C. Greiner, Somerset, Ohio, October 9, 1888.
7. Benjamin Harrison, Inaugural Address, March 4, 1889.
8. E. W. Halford, "General Harrison's Attitude toward the Presidency," 84 *Century Magazine* 305 (June 1912).

9. Id. at 307.

10. Socolofsky and Spetter, *Presidency of Benjamin Harrison*, at 40 (citations omitted).

11. By the time the federal government attempted to enforce the antitrust laws against Standard Oil, it was no longer a trust.

12. The Sherman Anti-Trust Act ranks as "one of the most important laws passed by the 51st Congress. [It] established the United States as one of a handful of industrial countries that favored the regulation of business combinations. Although most of the early cases that were filed under this law brought adverse decisions for the government, the actions taken in 1890 shaped later antitrust policy. Also, there is evidence that business combinations tried to avoid appearances that would produce federal suits against them." Socolofsky and Spetter, *Presidency of Benjamin Harrison*, at 55.

13. 71 U.S. 2 (1866).

14. First Annual Message to Congress, December 3, 1889.

15. The act is called the Evarts Act to honor Senator William Evarts, who was a key sponsor and drafter of the bill that was enacted into law.

16. Richard H. Fallon Jr. et al., *Hart and Wechsler's The Federal Courts and the Federal Court System* 37 (5th ed., New York: Foundation Press and Thomson/West, 2003).

17. Id.

18. Lee Epstein and Jeffrey A. Segal, *Advice and Consent: The Politics of Judicial Appointments* 41 (New York: Oxford University Press, 2005).

19. Henry J. Abraham, *Justices and Presidents: A Political History of Appointments to the Supreme Court* 146 (2nd ed., New York: Oxford University Press, 1985).

20. Harrison to R. S. Taylor, July 23, 1889.

21. Although Quay had been chairman of the Republican National Committee for the first two years of Harrison's presidency, he resigned in 1891 after the party had suffered unexpectedly large losses in the midterm elections of 1890 and several newspapers charged him with various ethical improprieties.

22. Socolofsky and Setter, *Presidency of Benjamin Harrison*, at 189 (citation omitted).

23. In re Debs, 158 U.S. 564 (1894).

24. 156 U.S. 1 (1895).

25. 157 U.S. 429 (1895).

26. 163 U.S. 537 (1896).

27. See John Harrison, "The Story of In re Neagle: Sex, Money, Politics, Perjury, Homicide, Federalism, and Executive Power," in *Presidential Power Stories* 133 (C. Schroeder and C. Bradley, eds., New York: Foundation Press; [St. Paul:] Thomson/West, 2009).

28. Id. at 154 (citations omitted) ("The Court thus endorsed [that the] President can use resources available to him, including the United States Marshals, in order to secure federal interests from physical and legal threats. He does not have to leave that to the states").

29. Harrison agreed to do lectures in 1893, but Stanford had died by the time he delivered them.

CHAPTER 10

1. Robert E. Welch Jr., *The Presidencies of Grover Cleveland* 119 (Lawrence: University Press of Kansas, 1988) (citation omitted).

2. Grover Cleveland, Second Inaugural Address, March 4, 1893.

3. See U.S. Const., art. II, sec. 3 ("He shall from time to time give to the Congress Information of the State of the Union, and recommend to their Consideration such Measures as he shall judge necessary and expedient; he may, On Extraordinary Occasions, convene both Houses, or either of them").

4. Grover Cleveland, Proclamation 357—Convening an Extra Session of the Congress, June 30, 1893. In the interim, Cleveland had discovered a cancerous growth on his upper jaw and arranged to keep the operation secret. The operation was done on the steamer *Oenida* as it sailed the East River. Because Cleveland had no visible scars and used special packing in his mouth to simulate his upper jaw, he was able to keep the operation a secret. It did not become public knowledge until nine years after his death.

5. Grover Cleveland, Special Session Message, August 8, 1893.

6. "An Act Directing the Purchase of Silver Bullion and the Issue of Treasury Notes Thereon, and for Other Purposes," 51 Cong. Ch. 708, 26 Stat. 289 (1890).

7. In the House, there were 218 Democrats, 127 Republicans, and 11 Populists. The Senate had 44 Democrats, 38 Republicans, and 3 Populists.

8. Welch, *Presidencies of Grover Cleveland*, at 122. See also Alan Nevins, *Grover Cleveland: A Study in Courage* 541–42 (New York: Dodd, Mead, 1933).

9. Welch, *Presidencies of Grover Cleveland*, at 122.

10. John A. Garraty, "Grover Cleveland," in *The Presidents: A Reference History* 283, 288 (2nd ed., Henry Graff, ed., New York: Macmillan Reference Library, 1997).

11. See Welch, *Presidencies of Grover Cleveland*, at 122–23, Nevins, *Grover Cleveland*, at 540–47.

12. "An Act to Reduce the Revenue and Equalize Duties on Imports, and for Other Purposes," 51 Cong. Ch. 1244, 26 Stat. 567 (1890).

13. "The President to His Party; Democracy on Trial for Its Life in the Tariff Conference," *New York Times*, July 20, 1894.

14. See George Washington, Farewell Address, reprinted in 1 *A Compilation of the Messages and Papers of the Presidents* 212 (September 17, 1796) (James D. Richardson, ed., Washington, D.C.: U.S. Government Printing Office, 1900).

15. Quoted in "The Tariff Revised by Its Friends," *New York Times*, August 9, 1909.

16. Cong. Rec. 164 (1894) (Statement of Sen. William Stewart, R.-Nev.).

17. See Nevins, *Grover Cleveland*, at 547–48.

18. Woodrow Wilson, "Mr. Cleveland as President," *Atlantic Monthly*, March 1897, at 289–301 (describing Cleveland as a man "whom parties could not absorb").

19. Grover Cleveland, *Presidential Problems* 133, 134, 135 (New York: Century Co., 1904).

20. Id. at 146.

21. Cleveland, who called himself a "Jackson-man," never mentions Van Buren, who had been the only previous president who had dealt with an economic crisis of similar proportions.

22. "An Act to Reduce Taxation to Provide Revenue for the Government and for Other Purposes," 53 Cong. Ch. 349, 28 Stat. 570 (1894).

23. Grover Cleveland, First Annual Message (Second Term), December 4, 1893.

24. 157 U.S. 429 (1895).

25. Pollock v. Farmers' Loan & Trust Co., 157 U.S. 429, 607 (1895).

26. Welch, *Presidencies of Grover Cleveland*, at 153 (citations omitted).

27. See chapter 11, "William Howard Taft."

28. H. R. Exec. Doc. No. 130, 49 Cong. (1887).

29. Nevins, *Grover Cleveland*, at 551–52.

30. Grover Cleveland, Message to the Senate, February 15, 1893.

31. Grover Cleveland, Message to Congress on the Hawaiian Sovereignty, December 18, 1893.

32. Nevins, *Grover Cleveland*, at 558 (citation omitted).

33. James Blount, Report of the Commissioner to the Hawaiian Islands (Blount Report), Exec. Doc. No. 47, 53d Cong., 2nd Sess. (July 17, 1893).

34. Grover Cleveland, Message to Congress, December 18, 1893.

35. Id.

36. Id.

37. Welch, *Presidencies of Grover Cleveland*, at 174 (citations omitted).

38. Id.

39. See id.

40. In 1898, President McKinley persuaded Congress to approve a joint resolution favoring Hawaii's annexation. Newlands Resolution to Provide for Annexing the Hawaiian Islands to the United States, 2nd Sess., 55th Cong., July 7, 1898; 30 Stat. at L. 750; 2 Supp. R. S. 895.

41. Historians dispute the reasons for the United States' intervention in the affair. Possible explanations include (1) long-standing distrust of the British; (2) concerns that the British were using the dispute to extend their control over the region; (3) the belief that intervention was necessary to give meaning to the newly established Pan-American Union; and/or (4) the fact that many Americans wanted to plunder the gold in Guiana.

42. See Grover Cleveland, Second Annual Message (Second Term), December 3, 1894.

43. Walter Gresham, who had been the first secretary of state in Cleveland's second term, had advised Cleveland on the affair. After he died on May 28, 1894, Cleveland appointed Attorney General Olney to replace Gresham.

44. Richard Olney, On American Jurisdiction in the Western Hemisphere (Olney Doctrine), I U.S. Department of State, Papers Relating to Foreign Affairs (1895), at 545–62.

45. Id.

46. Id.

47. See Alfred Caste, "Richard Olney," in *American Statesmen: Secretaries of State from John Jay to Colin Powell* 393, 396 (Edward S. Milhalkanin, ed., Westport, Conn.: Greenwood Press, 2004).

48. Grover Cleveland, Special Message, December 17, 1895.

49. Id.

50. Id.

51. Id.

52. Nevins, *Grover Cleveland*, at 617 (citation omitted).

53. See U.S. v. Debs, 64 Fed. Rep. 724 (1894) (order granting writ of injunction).

54. Nevins, *Grover Cleveland*, at 616.

55. Cleveland maintained that sections 5298 and 5299 of the Revised Statutes authorized him to do so. Cleveland, *Presidential Problems*, at 94–95 (citation omitted).

56. Welch, *Presidencies of Grover Cleveland*, at 145.

57. Waldo R. Browne, *Altgeld of Illinois: A Record of His Life and Work* 154 (New York: B. W. Huebsch, 1924).

58. Id. at 168.

59. Id. at 626. Cleveland supposedly said, "If it takes every dollar in the Treasury and every soldier in the United States to deliver a postal card in Chicago, that postal card should be delivered." Id. at 628 (citation omitted in the original).

60. Welch, *Presidencies of Grover Cleveland*, at 145 (citation omitted).

61. See Michael Leff, "Grover Cleveland the Nonrhetorical Presidency," in *Beyond the Rhetorical Presidency* 289, 304 (Martin J. Medhurst, ed., College Station: Texas A&M University Press, 2008).

62. In re Debs, 158 U.S. 564 (1895).

63. Id. at 582.

64. Id. at 586.

65. Id. at 590.

66. James W. Ely, *The Chief Justiceship of Melville W. Fuller, 1888–1910* 136 (Columbia: University of South Carolina Press, 1995).

67. See Michael J. Gerhardt, *The Federal Appointments Process: A Constitutional and Historical Analysis* xxx–xxxi (rev. ed., Durham: Duke University Press, 2003).

68. Grover Cleveland, Executive Order, May 8, 1893.

69. See generally David E. Lewis, *The Politics of Presidential Appointments: Political Control and Bureaucratic Performance* 11–50 (Princeton: Princeton University Press, 2008).

70. See generally Gerhardt, *Federal Appointments Process*, at 142–46.

71. Nevins, *Grover Cleveland*, at 569–70.

72. See Henry B. Hogue, "Supreme Court Nominations Not Confirmed: 1789–2007," CRS Report, at 13 (2008).

73. Parsons v. United States, 167 U.S. 324, 325 (1897).

74. Id. at 344.

75. See Myers v. United States, 272 U.S. 52 (1926).

76. See Cleveland, *Presidential Problems; Fishing and Shooting Sketches* (New York: Outing Publishing, 1906); and *Good Citizenship* (Philadelphia: H. Altemus, 1908).

77. See W. Barksdale Maynard, *Woodrow Wilson: Princeton to the Presidency* 156–60 (New Haven: Yale University Press, 2008).

CHAPTER 11

1. Lewis L. Gould, *The William Howard Taft Presidency* 212 (Lawrence: University Press of Kansas, 2009).

2. See Paolo E. Coletta, *The Presidency of William Howard Taft* 201 (Lawrence: University Press of Kansas, 1973); Gould, *William Howard Taft Presidency*, at 45, 202.

3. Vermont and Utah were the only two states that Taft won in the 1912 election. Finishing second in the general election, Theodore Roosevelt had run as a third-party candidate. He received a majority of electoral votes in six states.

4. The other men during whose presidencies the Constitution was amended more than once were Washington, Andrew Johnson, and Wilson. Washington urged the ratification of the Bill of Rights, which was ratified in 1791, while the Thirteenth and Fourteenth Amendments were ratified in spite of Johnson's opposition. During Wilson's presidency, the Seventeenth, Eighteenth, and Nineteenth Amendments were ratified. Wilson supported the first and third of these, but most of the activity involved with respect to the ratification of the Seventeenth Amendment had occurred during Taft's presidency.

5. The other four were Madison (Jefferson's secretary of state), Monroe (Madison's secretary of state), John Quincy Adams (Monroe's secretary of state), and Hoover (Coolidge's secretary of commerce). James Buchanan was Pierce's minister to Great Britain when he was elected president. Although the latter office was regarded at the time as almost cabinet level, Pierce had not chosen Buchanan to be his successor, nor did he have the power to make the selection even if he had wanted to. Buchanan had served as Polk's secretary of state, but Polk disliked Buchanan and had little interest in who succeeded him.

6. The other four presidents are Madison, Monroe, Van Buren, and George H. W. Bush. In 1824, Monroe's secretary of state, John Quincy Adams, was a major candidate, but Monroe did not endorse Adams nor assist his campaign.

7. The other five were Washington, Taylor, Grant, Hoover, and Eisenhower.

8. Prior to his election as president, Taft had served in six different offices, to each of which he had been appointed—state court superior judge (1887–90), U.S. solicitor general (1890–92), federal appellate judge (1892–1900), and commissioner (1900–1901) and governor-general of the Philippines (1901–4), and secretary of war (1904–8). Taft served for eight years as a law professor at Yale prior to his appointment as chief justice of the United States in 1921. Subsequently, the only presidents with arguably as extensive, if not a more impressive, record, are Dwight Eisenhower, who had been a career army officer with numerous promotions and

distinctions, including supreme allied commander in the years 1943–45, followed by the presidency of Columbia University (1948–53) and supreme commander of NATO (1951–52); and George H. W. Bush, who had served in the House of Representatives (1967–71) and as ambassador to the United Nations (1971–73), chairman of the Republican National Committee (1974–75), director of the Central Intelligence Agency (1976–77), and vice president of the United States (1981–89).

9. Gould, *William Howard Taft Presidency*, at 46.

10. Coletta, *Presidency of William Howard Taft*, at 12.

11. William Howard Taft, *Our Chief Magistrate and His Powers* 147 (New York: Columbia University Press, 1925).

12. Id. at 157.

13. Id.

14. Coletta, *Presidency of William Howard Taft*, at 13.

15. Id. at 202.

16. 1 Henry F. Pringle, *The Life and Times of William Howard Taft: A Biography* 424–25 (New York: Farrar & Rinehart, 1939) (citation and emphasis in original omitted).

17. Id. at 425 (citation and emphasis in original omitted).

18. Gould, *William Howard Taft Presidency*, at 55.

19. Id. at 59.

20. See Coletta, *Presidency of William Howard Taft*, at 56–75.

21. Id. at 73–74.

22. Gould, *William Howard Taft Presidency*, at 80.

23. Id. at 83.

24. Id. at 99.

25. Id. at 46.

26. Id. at 99.

27. Id. at 46.

28. See id. at 65–78; Coletta, *Presidency of William Howard Taft*, at 77–100.

29. Gould, *William Howard Taft Presidency*, at 46.

30. See Pinchot to Dolliver, January 5, 1910, quoted in Gifford Pinchot, *Breaking New Ground* 448–49 (New York: Harcourt, Brace, 1947).

31. Letter from President William Howard Taft to Gifford Pinchot, January 7, 1910.

32. See Pringle, *Life and Times of Taft*, at 511.

33. William Howard Taft, Special Message of December 7, 1909.

34. Sundry Civil Appropriations Act for 1911, Pub. L. No. 61-266, Stat. 703 (1910).

35. See William Howard Taft, Message of the President of the United States transmitting the reports of the Commission on Economy and Efficiency, H.R. Doc. 62-1252 (1913); Message of the President of the United States transmitting reports of the Commission on Economy and Efficiency relative to the centralization of the Distribution of Government Reports and so forth, H.R. Doc. 62-428, H.R. Doc. 62-468, H.R. Doc. 62-670, S. Doc. 62-293 (1912).

36. The Need for a National Budget, Message from the President of the United States, H.R. Doc. 62-851 (1912).

37. Pub. L. No. 62-299, 37 Stat. 360 (1912).

38. Cong. Rec. 11744 (1912).

39. Message of the President of the United States Submitting for the Consideration of Congress a Budget, S. Doc. No. 62-1113 (February 26, 1913).

40. Ch. 6, 38 Stat. 251, 12 U.S.C. ch. 3 (December 23, 1913).

41. Pub. L. 67-13, 42 Stat. 20 (June 20, 1921).

42. Paolo E. Coletta, "William Howard Taft," *The Presidents: A Reference History* 347, 355 (2nd ed., Henry Graff, ed., New York: Macmillan Reference Library, 1997).

43. Id.

44. Gould, *William Howard Taft Presidency*, at 164–68.

45. William Howard Taft, Special Message of January 7, 1910; William Howard Taft, Third Annual Message, December 5, 1911.

46. As of when Taft left office (1913), the only presidents who had cast more vetoes than he had were Cleveland in each of his two terms, Theodore Roosevelt (eighty-two), and William McKinley (forty-two).

47. Taft noted in his veto message that this provision was especially problematic because it gave the majority the power to "remove arbitrarily, and without delay, any judge who may have courage to render an unpopular decision." He demanded the withdrawal of this provision in light of "the necessity for an independent and untrammeled judiciary." 17 *A Compilation of the Messages and Papers of the Presidents* 7637 (James D. Richardson, ed., New York: Bureau of National Literature, 1918).

48. On the same day that Taft submitted his veto along with an opinion from the attorney general on the constitutionality of the bill, the Senate overrode the veto 63–21. On March 1, 1913, the House overrode Taft's veto by a vote of 246–95.

49. William Howard Taft, Veto Message of February 28, 1913.

50. It appears as if William McKinley had considered Taft but appointed Joseph McKenna to the Court in 1897.

51. Roosevelt's third appointee was William Moody in 1906.

52. Gould, *William Howard Taft Presidency*, at 128 (quoting Taft).

53. Id. (quoting Taft).

54. Merlo J. Pusey, *Charles Evans Hughes* 272 (New York: Macmillan, 1951) (citation omitted in original).

55. Pringle, *Life and Times of Taft*, at 534 (citation omitted in original).

56. Id. at 535 (citation omitted in original).

57. Id. at 536 (citation omitted).

58. Id. (citation omitted in original).

59. Henry J. Abraham, *Justices, Presidents, and Senators: A History of U.S. Supreme Court Appointments from Washington to Bush II* 132 (4th ed., Lanham, Md.: Rowman and Littlefield, 2008) (citation omitted).

60. Id. (citation omitted).

61. Id. at 137–38 (citation omitted).
62. Gerald Gunther, *Learned Hand: The Man and the Judge* 275 (New York: Knopf, 1994) (citation omitted).
63. "Knox Seems Barred from the Cabinet," *New York Times*, February 10, 1909, 1.
64. U.S. Const., art. I, sec. 6.
65. See Knox-Taft Telegrams, *New York Times*, February 13, 1909, 6.
66. "Knox Relief Passes Senate," *New York Times*, February 12, 1909, 3.
67. "Way Clear for Knox to Enter Cabinet," *New York Times*, February 16, 1909, at 1.
68. See Michael Stokes Paulsen, "Is Lloyd Bentsen Unconstitutional?" 46 *Stanford Law Review* 907 (1994).
69. 198 U.S. 45 (1905).
70. Ch. 309, 36 Stat. 539 (June 18, 1910).
71. Pub. L. No. 62-116, 37 Stat. 79, Ch. 73 (April 9, 1912).
72. Gould, *William Howard Taft Presidency*, at 134.
73. 2 U.S.C. sec. 241 (June 25, 1910).
74. Theodore Roosevelt signed into law the first campaign finance bill, the Tillman Act of 1907, 34 Stat. 864 (January 26, 1907), which restricted corporate contributions for political purposes.
75. See Newberry v. United States, 256 U.S. 232 (1921).
76. See Burroughs v. United States, 290 U.S. 534 (1934); United States v. Classic, 313 U.S. 299 (1941).
77. The Federal Election Campaign Act of 1971, Pub. L. No. 92-225, 86 Stat. 3 (February 7, 1972). This statute was hardly the last word on the subject. In 1976, the Supreme Court in Buckley v. Valeo, 424 U.S. 1 (1976), struck down portions of the law, including its limitations on campaign expenditures. Over the next several decades Congress struggled to fix the law within the framework of the First Amendment, as construed by the Court, to regulate the impact that people or corporations of enormous wealth have had on elections.
78. See, e.g., McConnell v. FEC, 540 U.S. 93, 116 (2003); Federal Election Commission v. National Right to Work Commission, 459 U.S. 197, 209 (1982); United States v. International Union United Auto, 352 U.S. 567 (1957).
79. Ch. 395, 36 Stat. 825; codified as amended at 18 U.S.C. sec. 2421 et seq.
80. Hoke v. United States, 227 U.S. 308 (1913).
81. Stafford v. Wallace (1922); Board of Trade of the City of Chicago (1923).
82. Taft dissented in the famous case of Adkins v. Children's Hospital of the District of Columbia, in which the Supreme Court struck down a minimum-wage law for women in the District of Columbia.
83. William Howard Taft, Special Message, June 16, 1909.
84. Gould, *William Howard Taft Presidency*, at 56.
85. Three states voted against ratification—Connecticut, Rhode Island, and Utah. Three other states—Pennsylvania, Florida, and Virginia—did not vote on the amendment.
86. Coletta, *Presidency of William Howard Taft*, at 133.

CHAPTER 12

1. See David Greenberg, *Calvin Coolidge* 1–3 (New York: Times Books, 2006).

2. Id. at 2 (citations omitted).

3. Id. (citations omitted).

4. See, e.g., Senator Tom Coburn, R.-Oklahoma, Floor Statement, August 4, 2010; Senator Richard Burr, R.-N.C., Press Release, November 10, 2009 (quoting Coolidge's statement that "the nation that forgets its defenders will itself be forgotten").

5. Calvin Coolidge, Fourth Annual Address, December 7, 1926.

6. *New York Times*, December 8, 1926, at 14.

7. Greenberg, *Calvin Coolidge*, at 3.

8. Calvin Coolidge, "The Press under a Free Government," Speech to the American Society of Newspaper Editors, January 17, 1925.

9. Calvin Coolidge, Inaugural Address, March 4, 1925.

10. Id.

11. Id.

12. Calvin Coolidge, First Annual Message, December 6, 1923.

13. Donald McCoy, *Calvin Coolidge: The Quiet President* 14 (Lawrence: University Press of Kansas, 1988) (citation omitted in original).

14. Id. at 156 (citation omitted).

15. Calvin Coolidge, Third Annual Message, December 8, 1925.

16. Id.

17. Id.

18. Calvin Coolidge, Fourth Annual Message, December 7, 1926.

19. Id.

20. Cong. Rec., 69th Cong., 1st Sess., part 11, p. 13069 (1926).

21. Robert Cowley, "Calvin Coolidge," in *To the Best of My Ability: The American Presidents* 212 (James M. McPherson, gen. ed., New York: Dorling Kindersley, 2000).

22. See McCoy, *Calvin Coolidge*, at 289 (suggesting that Coolidge was reticent "because he was naturally shy and frugal in speech with people he [did not] know well").

23. Greenberg, *Calvin Coolidge*, at 61–65.

24. See generally McCoy, *Calvin Coolidge*, at 167.

25. C. Bascom Slemp, *The Mind of the President: As Revealed by Himself in His Own Words* 10 (Garden City, N.Y.: Doubleday, Page, 1926).

26. McCoy, *Calvin Coolidge*, at 286.

27. Robert H. Ferrell, *The Presidency of Calvin Coolidge* 67–72 (Lawrence: University Press of Kansas, 1998).

28. Id. at 72.

29. Coolidge underenforced prohibition laws. He authorized his Justice Department to use wiretapping and Congress agreed to appropriate more money for the Coast

Guard to combat bootlegging, but these and other tactics did little to prevent people from evading the law. See Daniel Okrent, *Last Call: The Rise and Fall of Prohibition* 266, 278–79 (New York: Scribner, 2010).

30. See Ferrell, *Presidency of Calvin Coolidge*, at 43–44.

31. Id. at 44.

32. U.S. Const., art. I, sec. 3, cl. 7.

33. Cong. Rec. 18 1536–2452 (1922).

34. See, e.g., Laton McCartney, *The Teapot Dome Scandal: How Big Oil Bought the Harding White House and Tried to Steal the Country* (New York: Random House, 2009).

35. 43 Stat. Chapter 16 (February 8, 1924).

36. See David A. Logan, "Historical Uses of a Special Prosecutor: The Administrations of Presidents Grant, Coolidge, and Truman," CRS Report, at 12 (November 23, 1973).

37. See Leslie E. Bennett, "One Lesson from History: Appointment of Special Counsel and the Investigation of the Teapot Dome Scandal," Brookings Institution, November 25, 1999.

38. See United States v. Sinclair, 279 U.S. 749 (1929).

39. Cong. Rec. 1728–29 (1924).

40. See McCoy, *Calvin Coolidge*, at 210–12.

41. Senate Res. 282, 67th Congress (1922).

42. Cong. Rec. 3410 (1924).

43. Slemp, *Mind of the President*, at 215 (quoting Coolidge).

44. Id. at 216.

45. McCoy, *Calvin Coolidge*, at 218 (citation omitted).

46. See id. at 217.

47. See Ferrell, *Presidency of Calvin Coolidge*, at 150.

48. Calvin Coolidge to Harry M. Daugherty, March 27, 1924.

49. See generally David O. Stewart, *Impeached: The Trial of Andrew Johnson and the Fight for Lincoln's Legacy* (New York: Simon & Schuster, 2009).

50. Francis Russell, *The Shadow of Blooming Grove: Warren Harding in His Times* 87 (New York: McGraw-Hill, 1968) (citation omitted).

51. 272 U.S. 52 (1926).

52. Chief Justice Taft wrote the majority opinion in the case. The dissenters were Justices Brandeis, Holmes, and McReynolds.

53. A state grand jury had indicted Daugherty and Harding's Alien Property Custodian (prompting the Senate to investigate this office as well). Russell, *Shadow of Blooming Grove*, at 630.

54. McGrain v. Daugherty, 273 U.S. 135 (1927).

55. U.S. Const., art. I, sec. 5.

56. See "Congress: The Legislative Week February 7, 1927," *Time*, February 7, 1927.

57. Ferrell, *Presidency of Calvin Coolidge*, at 128 (citation omitted).

58. See David Cannadine, *Mellon: An American Life* 345–48 (New York: Knopf, 2006).

59. Cong. Rec., 68th Cong., 1st Sess., Part VI, p. 6087.

60. Ferrell, *Presidency of Calvin Coolidge*, at 173 (quoting Coolidge) (citation omitted).

61. Id (citation omitted).

62. McCoy, *Calvin Coolidge*, at 246.

63. See generally Alpheus Mason, *Harlan Fiske Stone: Pillar of the Law* 181–200 (New York: Viking Press, 1956).

64. McCoy, *Calvin Coolidge*, at 173.

65. For the definitive biography of Hand, see Gerald Gunther, *Learned Hand: The Man and the Judge* (New York: Knopf, 1994).

66. McCoy, *Calvin Coolidge*, at 277 (quoting Coolidge) (citation omitted).

67. Mason, *Harlan Fiske Stone*, at 199.

68. See Michael J. Gerhardt, *The Federal Appointments Process: A Constitutional and Historical Analysis* 165 (rev. ed., Durham: Duke University Press, 2003).

69. For the remainder of his vice presidency, Dawes was chided for sleeping on the job. Nor was this his first misstep with the Senate. In his first speech to the Senate as vice president, he urged senators to abandon certain practices, including seniority and the filibuster. The Senate overwhelmingly rejected the invitation. See Michael J. Gerhardt, *The Power of Precedent* 121 (New York: Oxford University Press, 2009).

70. McCoy, *Calvin Coolidge*, at 280 (citation omitted).

71. U.S. Const., art. II, sec. 2, cl. 1 (the President "shall have Power to Grant Reprieves and Pardons for Offences against the United States, except in Cases of Impeachment").

72. The two presidents who made no pardon decisions were William Henry Harrison and James Garfield.

73. Greenberg, *Calvin Coolidge*, at 82.

74. See McCoy, *Calvin Coolidge*, at 197.

75. Cong. Rec. 8660 (May 15, 1924).

76. Greenberg, *Calvin Coolidge*, at 79.

77. U.S. Const., art. I, sec. 7.

78. Okanogan Indians, et al. v. US., 279 U.S. 655 (1929).

79. Id. at 690, referencing H.R. Doc. No. 493, 70th Cong, 2nd Sess.

80. 68 Cong. Rec. 4771.

81. Opinion of Attorney General Sargent, May 22, 1928.

82. Calvin Coolidge, Veto Message, Cong. Rec. 9524–26 (May 23, 1928).

83. See, e.g., Charles A. Beard, *An Economic Interpretation of the Constitution of the United States* (New York: Macmillan, 1913); Charles A. Beard, *Economic Origins of Jeffersonian Democracy* (New York: Macmillan, 1915); Henry W. Bikle, "The

Silence of Congress," 41 *Harvard Law Review* 200 (1927); Frederick H. Cooke, "The Pseudo-Doctrine of the Exclusiveness of the Power of Congress to Regulate Commerce," 20 *Yale Law Journal* 297 (1911); John W. Davis, "The Growth of the Commerce Clause," 15 *American Lawyer* 213 (1907).

84. Calvin Coolidge, Fourth Annual Message, December 7, 1926.

85. Calvin Coolidge, First Annual Message to Congress (quoted in McCoy, *Calvin Coolidge*, at 304).

86. Id. at 305.

87. 44 Stat. 568 (May 20, 1926).

88. Commercial airlines were deregulated decades later pursuant to legislation signed into law by President Carter. See The Airlines Deregulation Act of 1978, Pub. L. No. 95-504 (October 24, 1978).

89. Greenberg, *Calvin Coolidge*, at 131.

90. See Pub. L. No. 632 (February 23, 1927), 69th Cong.

91. See Calvin Coolidge, Fourth Annual Message (1927) ("The Government is not the insurer of its citizens against the hazards of the elements. . . . The Government does not undertake to reimburse citizens for loss and damage incurred under such circumstances. It is chargeable, however, with the rebuilding of public works and the humanitarian duty of relieving its citizens of distress").

92. Id. at 135 (citation omitted).

93. An Act for the Control of Floods on the Mississippi River and Its Tributaries, and for Other Purposes, Pub. L. No. 70-391, 45 Stat. 534 (1928); An Act for the Purpose of Rehabilitating Farm Lands in the Flood Areas, Pub. L. No. 70-77, 45 Stat. 53 (1928). One biographer suggests the 1927 bill to have been a significant step in the direction of "big government." David Greenberg, "Help! Call the White House! How the 1927 Mississippi Flood Created Big Government," Slate, September 5, 2006.

94. Theodore Roosevelt Jr., Diary, October 2, 1923.

95. Cong. Rec., 68th Cong., 1st Sess., Part I, p. 459.

96. 66 Cong. Rec. 5413 (March 3, 1925).

97. Report of Committee on Foreign Relations Favoring Membership of the United States in the Permanent Court of International Justice, 68th Cong., 2nd Sess., February 24, 1925, at 10, 16.

98. Cong. Rec. 6825 (January 27, 1926).

99. Michael Dunne, *The United States and the World Court, 1920–1935* 69 (New York: St. Martin's Press, 1988) (citation omitted).

100. Calvin Coolidge, Sixth Annual Message to Congress, December 4, 1928.

101. 46 Stat. 243, T.S. No. 796, 94 L.N.T.S. 57.

102. Coolidge's son died from an infection arising from a blister he developed from playing barefoot on the White House tennis court. Other presidents who lost children were John Adams, Jefferson, Lincoln, and Kennedy.

103. McCoy, *Calvin Coolidge*, at 251.

CHAPTER 13

1. In 1980, Carter received ten fewer electoral votes than Hoover received in his reelection campaign and eleven less than Van Buren got in his.

2. U.S. Const., amend. XX.

3. Burton I. Kaufman and Scott Kaufman, *The Presidency of Jimmy Carter* 29 (2nd ed., Lawrence: University Press of Kansas, 2006).

4. See Julian Zelizer, *Jimmy Carter* 58 (New York: Times Books / Henry Holt, 2010).

5. Id. at 31.

6. See Kaufman and Kaufman, *Presidency of Jimmy Carter*, at 31.

7. Id. at 33. Carter explained, "I kept on my desk 'The buck stops here' that I inherited from Harry Truman. [I alone had to decide] should I go to Camp David, should I launch a military strike against Iran, should I normalize relations with China, should I permit the Panama Canal to be given to the Panamanians to operate. Those decisions can only be made by one person and so there is loneliness there." Interview by Cokie Roberts, Presidential Conversations on the Constitution: Jimmy Carter, WHYY Television Broadcast, October 8, 2004.

8. Zelizer, *Jimmy Carter*, at 55.

9. See Stephen Skowronek, *Presidential Leadership in Political Time: Reprise and Reappraisal* 70 (2nd ed., Lawrence: University Press of Kansas, 2011).

10. Kaufman and Kaufman, *Presidency of Jimmy Carter*, at 98–99.

11. Jimmy Carter, "The Malaise Speech," July 15, 1979.

12. Kaufman and Kaufman, *Presidency of Jimmy Carter*, at 179.

13. The cabinet members were James Schlesinger (Defense), Michael Blumenthal (Treasury), Joseph Califano (Health and Human Services), Griffin Bell (Justice), and Brock Adams (Transportation). After leaving office, Carter acknowledged that firing these cabinet members "was a mistake on my part. [I] should have handled the individual cabinet officers on a private and individual basis [and] over a period of time [rather than all at once] because it was too dramatic." Carter, interview by Cokie Roberts.

14. Kaufman and Kaufman, *Presidency of Jimmy Carter*, at 180.

15. See Alonzo McDonald, Carter Presidency Project, Interview with Alonzo McDonald, Miller Center of Public Affairs at the University of Virginia, ar. 13–14, 1981.

16. 92 Stat. 2445 (1978).

17. Harold C. Relyea, "Paperwork Reduction Act Reauthorization and Government Information Management Issues," CRS Report, at 5–6 (July 4, 2007) (citations omitted).

18. The Paperwork Reduction Act of 1980, Pub. L. No. 96-511, 94 Stat. 2812 (December 11, 1980).

19. "House Narrowly Approves Increase in Debt Ceiling," *New York Times*, September 29, 1977.

20. See generally "U.S. Debt Ceiling: How Big Is It, and How Has It Changed?" *The Guardian*, July 15, 2011.

21. 410 U.S. 113 (1973).

22. See generally Michael J. Gerhardt, *The Federal Appointments Process: A Constitutional and Historical Analysis* 146–47 (rev. ed., Durham: Duke University Press, 2003).

23. Id. at 119.

24. Exec. Order No. 11972, 42 Fed. Reg. 9,659 (February 14, 1977).

25. For example, Carter's judicial appointments were 14.3 percent African-American, 6.2 percent Hispanic, and 15.4 percent women. In contrast, Reagan's judicial appointments were 1.9 percent African-American, 3.7 percent Hispanic, and 8.2 percent women. George H. W. Bush's judicial appointments were 6.8 percent African-American, 4.2 percent Hispanic, and 18.8 percent women. While Clinton's were 16.4 percent African-American, 6.7 percent Hispanic, and 29.3 percent women, George W. Bush's judicial appointments were 7.1 percent African-American, 9 percent Hispanic, and 22 percent women. By the middle of his third year in office, Obama's judicial appointments were 27.5 percent African-American, 2.5 percent Hispanic, and 47.5 percent women.

26. See, e.g., Steven G. Calabresi, "The Congressional Roots of Judicial Activism," 20 *Journal of Law and Politics* 557, 584 (2004); Donald W. Fyr, "Judicial Selection: New Players, Same Game," 38 *Emory Law Journal* 771, 775 (1989).

27. See Russell Wheeler, "White Paper on Judicial Nominations and Confirmations, for the April 21, 2011, ACS Panel on Judicial Nominations, at the University of Georgia Law School, Athens, Georgia," Brookings Institution.

28. See Carter, interview by Cokie Roberts ("I used the pardon authority very liberally[.] Some Presidents since then have pardoned practically no one because of the controversies involved").

29. Exec. Order No. 11967, 42 Fed. Reg. 4,393 (January 24, 1977).

30. Zelizer, *Jimmy Carter*, at 55.

31. Kaufman and Kaufman, *Presidency of Jimmy Carter*, at 35.

32. 92 Stat. 1304 (October 17, 1978).

33. Kaufman and Kaufman, *Presidency of Jimmy Carter*, at 200.

34. Id. at 199–200.

35. See Taiwan Relations Act, 93 Stat. 14 (1979). See also Jimmy Carter, Address to the Nation on Diplomatic Relations between the United States and the People's Republic of China, 2 Pub. Papers 2264 (December 15, 1978) ("The United States of America and the People's Republic of China have agreed to recognize each other and to establish diplomatic relations as of January 1, 1979").

36. Sino-American Mutual Defense Treaty, December 2, 1954, 6 U.S.T. 433.

37. For an earlier Supreme Court decision supporting this position, see United States v. Curtiss-Wright Export Corp., 299 U.S. 304, 319 (1936) (holding that in "this vast external realm [of foreign affairs,] with its important, complicated, delicate and manifold problems, the President alone has the power to speak or listen as a representative of the nation. He makes treaties with the advice and consent of the

Senate; but he alone negotiates. Into the field of negotiation the Senate cannot intrude; and Congress [is] powerless to invade it").

38. See Goldwater v. Carter, 444 U.S. 996 (1979).

39. Taiwan Relations Act, 22 U.S.C. sec. 3301 (1979).

40. Brief for the Respondents in Opposition, Goldwater v. Carter, 444 U.S. 996 (No. 79-856).

41. See Goldwater v. Carter, 444 U.S. 996 (1979).

42. Zelizer, *Jimmy Carter*, at 76.

43. See e.g., Kathryn S. Olmstead, *Challenging the Secret Government: The Post-Watergate Investigations of the CIA and FBI* 177 (Chapel Hill: University of North Carolina Press, 1996) ("Jimmy Carter imposed stricter controls on the secret agencies through an executive order").

44. Executive Order 12036 (January 24, 1978) (strengthening Executive Order 11905, February 18, 1976).

45. Loch K. Johnson, *America's Secret Power: The CIA in a Democratic Society*, 109 (New York: Oxford University Press, 1989).

46. Gerald F. Reimers, "Foreign Intelligence Surveillance Act," 4 *Journal of National Security Law* 55, 67 (2000).

47. Id.

48. Carter's acknowledgment of his role in negotiating the Camp David Accord unwittingly reflects his penchant to assume all the responsibility for doing something, a recurrent problem with his administration. See Carter, interview by Cokie Roberts ("[T]here's no doubt that I negotiated at Camp David with Begin and Sadat very well aware that anything I said at Camp David as a contribution of the US would [be] upheld by the Congress and the President did have that authority to negotiate. So yes the President's right to conduct foreign affairs, to recognize any government in the world that he chooses, to appoint diplomats and to withdraw them from office on the spur of the moment—those kinds of things are extremely important to the ability of a President to negotiate a peace agreement").

49. For an overview of the history of deregulation of the airline industry, see Andrew Downer Crain, "Ford, Carter, and Deregulation in the 1970s," 5 *Journal of Telecommunications and High Tech Law* 413 (2007).

50. Airline Deregulation Act, 92 Stat. 1705 (1978).

51. CERCLA, 42 U.S.C. secs. 9601–75 (1980).

52. U.S. Const., art. I.

53. CERCLA, 42 U.S.C. sec. 9606(a) (1980).

54. Alaska National Interest Lands Conservation Act, 94 Stat. sec. 2371 (1980).

55. American Antiquities Act, 16 U.S.C. sec. 431 (1906).

56. See Proclamations No. 4611-4627, Fed. Reg. 57,009; 57, 013; 57, 019; 57, 025; 57, 031; 57, 035; 57, 043; 57, 053; 57, 059; 57, 067; 57, 073; 57, 079; 57, 087; 57, 091; 57, 101; 57, 113; 57, 119 (December 1, 1978).

57. Alaska National Lands Conservation Act, Pub. L. No. 96-487 (December 2, 1980).

58. 92 Stat. 1783, 50 U.S.C. secs. 1801–29 (1978). See also Executive Order 12036, sec. 2-2.

59. Crain, "Ford, Carter, and Deregulation," at 434–35.

60. See State of the Union Address, 1 Pub. Papers 90 (January 19, 1978).

61. Jimmy Carter, Ethics in Government Message to Congress, 1 Pub. Papers 786, 786 (May 3, 1977) ("This bill will establish far-reaching safeguards against conflicts of interest and abuse of public trust by government officials"); Remarks on Signing S. 555 into Law, 14 Weekly Comp. Pres. Doc. 1854, 1854 (October 26, 1978).

62. Government in Ethics Act, 92 Stat. 1824 (1978).

63. Morrison v. Olsen, 487 U.S. 654, 696–97 (1988).

64. Id. at 727 (Scalia, J., dissenting).

65. See generally Ken Gormley, *The Death of American Virtue: Clinton v. Starr* (New York: Crown, 2011).

66. 28 U.S.C. sec. 351 (1980).

67. See Harry T. Edwards, "Regulating Judicial Misconduct and Dividing Good Behavior for Federal Judges," 87 *Michigan Law Review* 765 (1989).

68. See, e.g., Statement of President Carter on Signing Judicial Councils Reform and Judicial Conduct and Disability Act of 1980 into Law, 16 Weekly Comp. Pres. Doc. 2239, 2240 (October 15, 1980) ("Experience has shown that if only the massive machinery of impeachment is available, some valid complaints will not be remedied"); Cong. Rec. 25,371 (1980) (Statement of Rep. Robert Kastenmeier) ("[A]rticle III, section 1, of the Constitution of the United States . . . was designed to give judges maximum freedom from possible coercion or influence by the other two branches of Government").

69. See, e.g., Hastings v. Judicial Conference of U.S., 829 F.2d 91 (D.C. Cir.), cert. denied, 485 U.S. 1014 (1987); Matter of Certain Complaints under Investigation by an Investigating Committee of Judicial Council of the Eleventh Circuit, 783 F.2d 1388, motion to vacate denied 476 U.S. 1112, cert. denied 477 U.S. 904 (1986); McBryde v. Committee to Review Circuit Council Conduct and Disability Orders of Judicial Conference of the U.S., 83 F.Supp.2d 135, affirmed in part, vacated in part 264 F.3d 52, rehearing en banc denied 278 F.3d 29, cert. denied 537 U.S. 821 (1999).

70. Since the inception of the Judicial Conduct and Disability Act, four subjects of referrals have been impeached and removed from office (Harry Claiborne, Alcee Hastings, Walter Nixon, and Thomas Porteous). The House impeached another judge who resigned before the Senate began his impeachment trial (Samuel Kent). Another judge (Robert Collins) resigned before the House commenced impeachment proceedings against him.

71. Since Carter left office, the most significant expansions of the cabinet have been Clinton's elevation of the Environmental Protection Agency to cabinet status and the establishment of the Department of Homeland Security under George W. Bush.

72. See, e.g., Cong. Rec. 32,872 (statement of Rep. Eldon Rudd).

73. 438 U.S. 265 (1978).

74. U.S. Const., amend. XIV, sec. 1.

75. 347 U.S. 483 (1954).

76. See Bolling v. Sharpe, 347 U.S. 497 (1954).

77. See, e.g., Interview and Question-and-Answer Session with Representatives of Black Media Associations, 14 Weekly Comp. Pres. Doc. 318, 322 (February 16, 1978) ("[We] filed a brief that was prepared by the Solicitor General, [Wade] McCree. . . . This is the White House position, because I personally approved the brief"); Interview and Question-and-Answer Session with Group of Editors and News Directors, 2 Pub. Papers 1225, 1230 (June 30, 1978) ("We consulted with the Black Caucus members and others before the Attorney General presented the brief from the Justice Department. And I read the brief and approved it personally").

78. See Carter, interview by Cokie Roberts ("I agreed with the *Bakke* case . . . I think that affirmative action in some form without rigid quotas is still badly needed in this country and I hope it will continue for the next decade or more").

79. Jimmy Carter, Memorandum on Affirmative Action, 2 Pub. Papers 1320 (July 20, 1978) ("I want to make certain that, in the aftermath of *Bakke*, you continue to develop, implement and enforce vigorously affirmative action programs. I also want to make certain that the Administration's strong commitment to equal opportunity and affirmative action is recognized and understood by all Americans").

80. 60 U.S. 397 (1857).

81. Lincoln Caplan, *The Tenth Justice: The Solicitor General and the Rule of Law* 31 (New York: Knopf, 1987).

82. Metro Broadcasting, Inc. v. FCC, 497 U.S. 547 (1990).

83. Adarand Constructors v. Pena, 515 U.S. 220, 227 (1997).

84. See, e.g., President's News Conference, 2 Pub. Papers 1231, 1236 (July 12, 1977); Maine Remarks and a Question-and-Answer Session at a Town Hall Meeting, 1 Pub. Papers 344, 356 (February 17, 1978).

85. Congress added thirty-nine months to the initial deadline of 1978. H.J. Res. 638, 95 Cong. 2nd Sess. (1978).

86. The ERA died on June 30, 1982, more than ten years after Congress had ratified it in 1972. Gilbert Y. Steiner, *Constitutional Inequality: The Political Fortunes of the Equal Rights Amendment* 1–4 (Washington, D.C.: Brookings Institution, 1985).

87. See, e.g., Address to the Nation on the Panama Canal Treaties, 1 Pub. Papers 258 (February 1, 1978); Address to the Nation on the Diplomatic Relations between the United States and the People's Republic of China, 2 Pub. Papers 2264, 2265 (December 15, 1978); Anti-Inflation Program Address to the Nation, at 1839 (October 24, 1978).

88. Address to the Nation on Energy and National Goals, at 1235 (July 15, 1979).

89. Farewell Address to the Nation, at 2889, 2890 (January 14, 1981).

90. See Carter, interview by Cokie Roberts ("I would like to declassify all my records from the White House. . . . I think the concealment of facts is almost invariably a mistake in the long run and sometimes has immediate consequences adversely for those who concealed the facts").

91. Conversation with the President, Interview by Tom Brokaw of NBC News, Bob Schieffer of CBS News, Robert MacNeil of the Public Broadcasting Service, and Barbara Walters of ABC News, December 28, 1977, in II Administration of Jimmy Carter, Public Papers 2200 (1977).

92. Shoon Kathleen Murray and Peter Howard, "Variation in White House Polling Operations: Carter to Clinton," 66 *Public Opinion Quarterly* 527 (2002).

93. Carter, interview by Cokie Roberts.

94. John F. Kennedy, Speech to the Greater Houston Ministerial Association, September 12, 1960.

95. See, e.g., Jimmy Carter on March 29, 1976, in Howard Melton Norton and Bob Slosser, *The Miracle of Jimmy Carter* 83 (Plainfield, N.J.: Logos International, 1976) (quoting candidate Carter's telling a Sunday school class, "We should live our lives as though Christ were coming this afternoon").

96. Kaufman and Kaufman, *Presidency of Jimmy Carter*, at 45.

97. See, e.g., Remarks and a Question-and-Answer Session at a Town Hall Meeting in Pittsburgh, Pa., at 2503, 2506 (October 29, 1980) ("I don't think there ought to be any religious test for political acceptability, and I don't think there ought to be any political test for religious fellowship. [The American] people will make a sound judgment, recognizing the necessity for the separation of church and state. I have never found any incompatibility between my religious convictions and my duties as President").

98. Reagan believed his election reaffirmed the propriety of public acknowledgments of religious values. He acknowledged a divinity in public addresses nearly five times as often as Carter did.

99. See Carl Sferazza Anthony, *First Ladies: The Saga of the Presidents' Wives and Their Power* 60–63, 371–73, 460, 463 (New York: William Morrow, 1990).

100. Mrs. Carter was the second First Lady to testify before Congress.

Index